# Menus from History

# MENUS FROM HISTORY

## Historic Meals and Recipes for Every Day of the Year

## Volume 2

Janet Clarkson

**GREENWOOD PRESS**

*An Imprint of ABC-CLIO, LLC*

A B C  CLIO

Santa Barbara, California • Denver, Colorado • Oxford, England

**Library of Congress Cataloging-in-Publication Data**

Clarkson, Janet, 1947–
   Menus from history : historic meals and recipes for every day of the year /
Janet Clarkson.
     p. cm.
   Includes bibliographical references and index.
    ISBN 978–0–313–34930–0 (hard copy : alk. paper) — ISBN 978–0–313–34931–7 (ebook)
1. Cookery—History. 2. Dinners and dining—History. 3. Food habits—History. 4. Menus. 5.
Cookery, International. I. Title.
TX645.C534   2009
641.3—dc22        2009011351

13 12 11 10 9    1 2 3 4 5

This book is also available on the World Wide Web as an eBook.
Visit www.abc-clio.com for details.

ABC-CLIO, LLC
130 Cremona Drive, P.O. Box 1911
Santa Barbara, California 93116-1911

This book is printed on acid-free paper ∞

Manufactured in the United States of America

The publisher has done its best to make sure the instructions and/or recipes in this book are
correct. However, users should apply judgment and experience when preparing recipes, especially
parents and teachers working with young people. The publisher accepts no responsibility for the
outcome of any recipe included in this volume.

# Contents

## Volume 1

# Volume 2

# List of Menus Chronologically

| | | |
|---|---|---|
| August 22, 70 BCE | Italy | An Ancient Roman Dinner, Rome |
| May 28, 1368 | Italy | Wedding Feast, Milan |
| September 23, 1387 | England | Feast for King Richard II, Durham House, London |
| October 13, 1399 | England | Coronation Feast of King Henry IV, Great Hall of Westminster, London |
| August 2, 1413 | England | Harvest Meals in an English Medieval Manorial Household, Acton Hall, Acton, Suffolk |
| February 23, 1421, | England | Coronation Feast of Queen Catherine, Westminster Hall, London |
| December 4, 1424 | England | Funeral Feast of the Bishop of Bath and Wells, Bishop's Palace, Wells, Somerset |
| September 16, 1425 | England | Induction Feast of the Bishop of Bath and Wells, The Bishop's Palace, Wells, Somerset |
| November 6, 1429 | England | Coronation Feast of King Henry VI, Great Hall of Westminster, London |
| September 22, 1465 | England | Installation Feast of the Archbishop of York, Cawood Castle, York |
| September 22, 1465 | England | Installation Feast of the Archbishop of York, Cawood Castle, York |
| June 4, 1469 | Italy | Medici Wedding Feast, Palazzo Medici, Florence |
| October 28, 1478 | England | Dinner of the Worshipful Company of Wax Chandlers, Newcastle-upon-Tyne |
| July 6, 1483 | England | Coronation Feast of King Richard III, Westminster Hall, London |
| March 9, 1504 | England | Inthronization Feast of the Archbishop of Canterbury, The Archbishop's Palace, Canterbury |
| August 16, 1522 | England | Dinner of the Wardens of the Drapers' Company, Home of the Master of the Company, London |
| June 19, 1549 | France | Banquet for Queen Catherine, Bishop's Palace, Paris |

# List of Menus
# by Country

| America | Luxurious Dinner for the King's Officers, Boston, Massachusetts | January 3, 1774 |
|---|---|---|
| Antarctica | Midwinter Dinner, Winter Quarters, Commonwealth Bay, Adelie Land | June 22, 1912 |
| Argentina | Dinner to Honor President Juan Perón, Alvear Palace Hotel, Buenos Aires, Argentina | December 18, 1948 |
| Australia | Centennial Banquet, Sydney, Australia, Town Hall | January 26, 1888 |
| | Dinner for Fox Films, Hotel Australia, Sydney | February 4, 1916 |
| | Dinner for the Bushmen's Corps, Adelaide | March 5, 1900 |
| | Luncheon to Celebrate Opening of Sydney Harbour Bridge RMS *Maloja*, Sydney Harbour | March 19, 1932 |
| Austria | Last Meal of the Crown Prince of Austria, Royal Hunting Lodge, Mayerling | January 29, 1889 |
| | Hotel Dinner, Hôtel Hochschneeberg, Schneeberg | September 25, 1907 |
| Canada | Second Annual Dinner of the Toronto Board of Trade, Horticultural Gardens, Toronto, Ontario | January 4, 1899 |
| | English Royals Dine in Canada, Chateau Frontenac, Quebec | May 17, 1939 |
| | Women's Institute Luncheon, Hotel Windsor, Alliston, Ontario | June 8, 1923 |
| | Dinner in a Wigwam, Burnt Church Point, Miramichi Bay, New Brunswick | August 7, 1853 |
| | Hotel Dinner, Grand Hotel, Yarmouth, Nova Scotia | August 25, 1911 |
| | Dinner for the Governor-General, The Arlington, Cobourg, Ontario | September 4, 1874 |
| | Dinner for Princess Elizabeth, Ottowa | October 11, 1951 |
| | Tribute Dinner for a Cow, Red Deer, Alberta | October 16, 1912 |
| | Queen Victoria Diamond Jubilee Ball, Toronto City Armouries, Toronto | December 28, 1919 |

# List of Menus
# by Occasion

## Club/Society/Institute/Company Meal

| | | |
|---|---|---|
| October 28, 1478 | England | Dinner of the Worshipful Company of Wax Chandlers, Newcastle-upon-Tyne |
| August 16, 1522 | England | Dinner of the Wardens of the Drapers' Company, Home of the Master of the Company, London |
| March 11, 1687 | England | Ironmongers' Company Dinner, Ironmongers Hall, Fenchurch Street, London |
| January 30, 1710 | England | Calves Head Club Annual Feast, London |
| October 29, 1742 | England | Dinner for the Worshipful Company of Barbers and Surgeons, The Barber-Surgeons Hall, Monkwell Square, London |
| September 30, 1847 | England | Sheriff's Dinner, Hall of the Fishmongers' Company, London |
| July 28, 1848 | England | First Annual Dinner of the First Vegetarian Society of England, Manchester |
| September 8, 1853 | United States | Temperance Banquet, Metropolitan Hall, New York |
| October 1, 1854 | United States | Dinner in Utopia, Red Bank, Monmouth County, New Jersey |
| July 5, 1856 | United States | Firemen's Dinner, American Exchange Hotel, San Francisco, California |
| January 23, 1862 | Germany | Dinner of Exotic Animals, Hamburg |
| December 1, 1869 | England | Australian Meat Banquet, Lambeth Baths, London |
| December 16, 1870 | United States | Chicago Press Club's First Annual Banquet, Briggs House, Chicago, Illinois |
| November 30, 1871 | England | Patriotic Dinner, The Freemasons' Tavern, London |
| April 21, 1881 | France | Banquet of the French Vegetarian Society, Rue St. Honoré, Paris |
| September 15, 1883 | New Zealand | Masons' Banquet to Celebrate Their New Lodge, Criterion Hotel, Taranaki |
| August 30, 1885 | Norway | Medical Conference Dinner, Bergen |

| April 14, 1886 | France | Stanley Club Dinner in Honor of Louis Pasteur, Continental Hotel |
|---|---|---|
| January 10, 1888 | United States | Holland Society Annual Dinner, Hotel Brunswick, New York |
| December 11, 1888 | England | Encyclopædia Britannica Dinner, Hall of Christ's College, Cambridge |
| January 4, 1889 | Canada | Second Annual Dinner of the Toronto Board of Trade, Horticultural Gardens, Toronto, Ontario |
| June 5, 1889 | United States | Journalists' Dinner, Bohemian Club, San Francisco, California |
| September 7, 1889 | Sweden | Dinner for the Congress of Orientalists, Stockholm |
| March 8, 1891 | United States | Dinner Given by the "Chinese Delmonico," Lenox Lyceum, New York |
| May 13, 1891 | England | Dinner for Nobody's Friends, Hôtel Metropole, London |
| September 10, 1891 | United States | Fat Men's Club Clambake, Power's Hotel, Dorlon's Point, South Norwalk, Connecticut |
| October 24, 1891 | Norway | Medical Dinner, Bergen |
| June 12, 1893 | England | After-Concert Dinner, King's College, Cambridge University, Cambridge |
| September 20, 1894 | United States | Library-Themed Dinner for the American Library Association, Annual Conference, Grand View House, Lake Placid, New York |
| October 5, 1894 | United States | Druggists' Luncheon, Steamboat *Sandy Hook*, New York |
| January 17, 1895 | United States | Benjamin Franklin Honored by *Typothetæ*, Hotel Brunswick, New York, 1895 |
| February 5, 1895 | United States | Debut Dinner at the New York Vegetarian Society's Vegetarian Restaurant No. 1, New York |
| October 4, 1896 | Denmark | Insurance Company Dinner, Copenhagen |
| February 2, 1897 | United States | First Annual Banquet of the Founders and Patriots of America, Hotel Manhattan, New York |
| February 22, 1897 | England | George Washington's Birthday Celebration, Hotel Cecil, London |
| December 15, 1897 | Italy | Piemontese Society Banquet, All Hotel Campidoglio |
| February 19, 1898 | United States | Creole Dinner for the New Orleans Press Club, The Atheneum, New Orleans, Louisiana |
| March 1, 1898 | United States | 63rd Annual Dinner of the St. David's Society, Hotel Savoy, New York |

| | | |
|---|---|---|
| December 20, 1919 | United States | Heinz Company 50th Anniversary Dinner, Pittsburgh, Pennsylvania |
| June 8, 1923 | Canada | Women's Institute Luncheon, Hotel Windsor, Alliston, Ontario |
| February 1, 1928 | United States | Broadway Association Dinner to Celebrate the Dodge Brothers' Sign, Hotel Astor, New York |
| December 9, 1928 | France | Firefighters Banquet, Hôtel de la Madeleine, Barberaz |
| May 16, 1929 | United States | First Academy Awards Banquet, Blossom Room, Roosevelt Hotel, Hollywood, California |
| May 5, 1932 | England | "May Dinner," Simpson's on the Strand, London |
| August 17, 1934 | United States | Henry Ford's "All Soy" Dinner, Century of Progress International Exposition, Chicago, Illinois |
| November 22, 1934 | United States | German Society 150th Anniversary Dinner, Hotel Astor, New York |
| January 15, 1935 | England | Portuguese Luncheon, Café Royal, London |
| January 24, 1937 | United States | Gourmet Society Eat "Eskimo Fare," Cavanagh's, New York |
| November 17, 1937 | England | Humble Meal, Café Royal, London |
| February 21, 1947 | France | Business Dinner, Hotel Lutetia, Boulevarde Rapail, Paris |
| April 10, 1948 | United States | Dinner for President Harry S. Truman, The Gridiron Club, Hotel Statler, Washington, DC |
| January 31, 1952 | England | Luncheon at the Variety Club, 35 Dover Street, London |

**Commemorative Event**

| | | |
|---|---|---|
| August 22, 70 BCE | Rome | An Ancient Roman Dinner |
| September 16, 1425 | England | Induction Feast of the Bishop of Bath and Wells, The Bishop's Palace, Wells, Somerset |
| September 22, 1465 | England | Installation Feast of the Archbishop of York, Cawood Castle, York |
| September 13, 1619 | England | Dinner Celebrating the Founding of Dulwich College, Camberwell, Surrey |
| December 22, 1769 | America | First Celebration of Forefathers' Day Dinner, Old Colony Club of Plymouth, Massachusetts |
| September 17, 1830 | United States | Centennial Dinner, Exchange Coffee House, Boston, Massachusetts |
| January 25, 1882 | United States | Burns Night Supper, Sutherland's, New York |

## Daily Meal

**Dinner Party**

| February 6, 1802 | United States | Dinner with President Thomas Jefferson, The White House, Washington, DC |
| January 22, 1848 | United States | Dinner for Six Gentlemen, Revere House, Bowdoin Square, Boston, Massachusetts |
| April 29, 1851 | England | Dinner for Ottoman Visitors, Mayor's Residence, Winchester, England |
| August 27, 1855 | Crimea | "Great Martial Banquet Alfresco," Scutari |
| January 19, 1864 | France | Dinner for 36, Home of Alexandre Dumas, Paris |
| October 30, 1865 | United States | Dinner with Sir Morton Peto, Delmonico's, New York |
| November 16, 1875 | United State | Dining with James McNeill Whistler, Chelsea, London |
| June 22, 1912 | Antarctica | Midwinter Dinner, Winter Quarters, Commonwealth Bay, Adelie Land |
| October 27, 1936 | Tibet | Dinner with a Tibetan Monk, Gyantsé, Tibet |
| November 9, 1975 | France | Quiet Dinner for Two in Paris, *Chez Denis*, Paris |
| December 31, 1995 | France | Final Dinner Party Given by François Mitterand, Souston, Landes |

## Diplomatic/Political Meal

| May 9, 1676 | Syria | Dinner at the English Embassy, Aleppo |
| May 25, 1816 | England | Parliamentary Dinner, Carlton House, London |
| July 19, 1821 | England | Coronation Banquet of King George IV, Westminster Hall, London |
| July 3, 1846 | England | Dinner for Ottoman Visitors, Reform Club, London |
| July 9, 1851 | England | Midnight Supper with Queen Victoria, Guildhall, London |
| April 29, 1851 | England | Dinner for Ottoman Visitors, Mayor's Residence, Winchester, England |
| August 21, 1863 | Germany | Frankfurt Congress of Princes Banquet, Römer, Frankfurt |
| March 6, 1865 | United States | Abraham Lincoln's Inauguration Ball, Patent Office, Washington, DC |
| June 7, 1867 | France | Dinner of the Three Emperors, Café Anglais, Paris |
| July 1, 1868 | Turkey | Ottoman Sultan Entertains the French Prince, Constantinople (Istanbul) |
| July 25, 1873 | Italy | Dinner for the Shah of Persia, Royal Palace, Turin |

## Holiday/Feast Day Meal

## Hotel and Restaurant Fare

| | | |
|---|---|---|
| April 1, 1931 | Mexico | One-Dollar Lunch, Hotel Agua Caliente, Tijuana |
| December 6, 1933 | United States | Repeal Dinner, Waldorf-Astoria Hotel, New York |
| June 21, 1937 | Indonesia | Dinner with Amelia Earhart, Hotel Grand Preanger, Bandung (Bandoeng), Batavia |
| February 20, 1943 | United States | Wartime Luncheon, Stork Club, New York |
| December 13, 1943 | India | Catering Menu, Calcutta |
| May 8, 1945 | England | VE Day Dinner, Simpson's-in-the-Strand, London |
| July 20, 1952 | Japan | International Meal, Imperial Hotel, Tokyo |
| August 23, 1956 | United States | Luncheon Specials of the Day, MGM Studios, Culver City, California |
| October 18, 1959 | United States | Snacking at the Siesta Drive-In Movie Theater, Sarasota, Florida |

## In-Flight Meal

| | | |
|---|---|---|
| September 11, 1919 | Airship *R.33* | Day's Meals aboard an Airship, *R.33*, En Route from Norfolk, England, to Amsterdam |
| October 3, 1953 | *KLM* Flight | Dinner on the Inaugural Flight, Super Constellation, KLM Airlines |
| April 12, 1961 | Space | First Meal in Space, Vostok 1 |
| July 21, 1969 | Moon | Dining in Space |
| January 21, 1976 | Concorde | Luncheon En Route from London to Bahrain during the Inaugural Flight of the Concorde |

## Military Meal

| | | |
|---|---|---|
| March 23, 1855 | England | Queen's Guard Dinner, St. James' Palace, London |
| April 18, 1861 | United States | Confederate Soldier's Dinner, Army Camp, near Pensacola, Florida |
| March 21, 1871 | New Zealand | Dinner for the Rifle Volunteers, Auckland |
| October 25, 1882 | England | Dinner for the Royal Horse Guards, Town Hall, Holborn, London |
| March 4, 1894 | United States | Irish Revolutionary Veterans Dinner, Central Opera House, East Sixty-Seventh Street, New York |
| March 7, 1895 | United States | Dinner for the New York Association of Union Prisoners, Murray Hill Lyceum, New York City |
| March 5, 1900 | Australia | Dinner for the Bushmen's Corps, Adelaide |

| | | |
|---|---|---|
| January 20, 1919 | France | Luncheon in Honor of U.S. President Woodrow Wilson, Luxembourg Palace, Paris |
| July 18, 1921 | Mexico | Picnic for the Mexican President, San Luis Potosi, Mexico |
| May 14, 1933 | United States | President Franklin D. Roosevelt's Daily Fare, The White House, Washington, DC |
| January 8, 1936 | United States | Jackson Day Dinner, Mayflower Hotel, Washington, DC |
| June 11, 1939 | United States | Picnic for the English Royals, "Springwood," Hyde Park, New York |
| October 9, 1947 | United States | Eggless, Poultryless Meals for President Harry S. Truman, The White House, Washington, DC |
| April 10, 1948 | United States | Dinner for President Harry S. Truman, The Gridiron Club, Hotel Statler, Washington, DC |
| December 18, 1948 | Argentina | Dinner to Honor President Juan Perón, Alvear Palace Hotel, Buenos Aires, Argentina |
| April 27, 1956 | England | Soviet Leaders Luncheon aboard the Train to Portsmouth |
| March 17, 1959 | United States | St. Patrick's Day Banquet, The White House, Washington, DC |
| April 5, 1960 | United States | State Dinner, The White House, Washington, DC |
| November 13, 1961 | United States | Dinner with Pablo Casals, The White House, Washington, DC |
| August 3, 1969 | Romania | Luncheon Given by President Richard M. Nixon, Romanian State Guest House, Bucharest |
| October 14, 1971 | Iran | Banquet to Celebrate the Persian Empire, Persepolis |
| April 15, 1973 | United States | Week's Menu for the First Family, The White House, Washington, DC |
| July 7, 1976 | United States | Bicentennial Dinner, The White House, Washington, DC |
| February 25, 1983 | England | Dinner with the British Prime Minister, No. 10, Downing St., London |
| February 24, 1999 | United States | State Dinner, The White House, Washington, DC |

**Railway Meal**

| | | |
|---|---|---|
| September 18, 1901 | United States | Meals in the Pullman Dining Car, in the Funeral Train of President William McKinley |
| May 31, 1925 | France | French President Lunches aboard a Luxury Train |
| March 15, 1933 | United States | Breakfast on the "42nd Street Special," Chicago to Los Angeles by Rail |

## Religious Occasion

| February 23, 1421 | England | Coronation Feast of Queen Catherine, Westminster Hall, London |
| December 4, 1424 | England | Funeral Feast of the Bishop of Bath and Wells, Bishop's Palace, Wells, Somerset |
| September 16, 1425 | England | Induction Feast of the Bishop of Bath and Wells, The Bishop's Palace, Wells, Somerset |
| September 22, 1465 | England | Installation Feast of the Archbishop of York, Cawood Castle, York |
| March 9, 1504 | England | Inthronization Feast of the Archbishop of Canterbury, The Archbishop's Palace, Canterbury |
| April 4, 1828 | France | Good Friday Dinner, Tuileries, Paris |
| September 3, 1858 | Ireland | Cardinal's "Fast," Dundalk |
| July 11, 1883 | United States | Trefa Banquet, Highland House, Cincinnati, Ohio |
| May 4, 1907 | England | Kosher Banquet, London |
| September 28, 1929 | SS *Majestic* | "Menu for Jews" aboard the SS *Majestic* |
| April 11, 1941 | England | Good Friday Wartime Lunch, Barrow-in-Furness, Cumbria |

## Royal Meal

| September 23, 1387 | England | Feast for King Richard II, Durham House, London |
| October 13, 1399 | England | Coronation Feast of King Henry IV, Great Hall of Westminster, London |
| February 23, 1421 | England | Coronation Feast of Queen Catherine, Westminster Hall, London |
| November 6, 1429 | England | Coronation Feast of King Henry VI, Great Hall of Westminster, London |
| February 16, 1476 | Italy | Banquet to Honor Neopolitan Princes, Florence |
| July 6, 1483 | England | Coronation Feast of King Richard III, Westminster Hall, London |
| June 19, 1549 | France | Banquet for Queen Catherine, Bishop's Palace, Paris |
| November 20, 1576 | England | Dining with Queen Elizabeth I |
| August 18, 1617 | England | King James I's Breakfast, Hoghton Tower, Preston, Lancashire |
| August 9, 1652 | France | Dinner to Honor the Prince de Conde |

| July 29, 1981 | England | Royal Wedding Breakfast for Prince Charles and Lady Diana, Buckingham Palace, London, England |
| March 3, 1997 | HMY *Britannia* | Final Voyage of the HMY *Britannia*, Karachi |

## School/Hospital/Prison Meal

| September 13, 1619 | England | Dinner Celebrating the Founding of Dulwich College, Camberwell, Surrey |
| November 4, 1829 | England | Common Hospital Diet, Devon and Exeter Hospital |
| August 12, 1835 | England | Daily Meals in the Poorhouse, Fishlake, Yorkshire |
| November 2, 1847 | United States | Dinner with Emily Dickinson, Mount Holyoke Female Seminary, South Hadley, Massachusetts |
| May 2, 1900 | United States | Dinner at the Sanitarium, Battle Creek, Michigan |
| January 14, 1901 | England | Mallard Night Feast, All Souls' College, Oxford |
| May 19, 1911 | United States | Prison Menu for a Week, Indiana State Prison |
| December 14, 1920 | United States | Hospital Fare, St. Luke's Hospital, Chicago, Illinois |
| September 24, 1928 | United States | Prison Dinner, Leavenworth State Penitentiary, Kansas |

## Shipboard Meal

| July 10, 1675 | HMS *Assistance* | Officers' Dinner at Sea, HMS *Assistance*, near Gibraltar |
| March 25, 1842 | United States | Charles Dickens Eats aboard an American Canal Boat |
| August 29, 1844 | SS *Great Western* | Daily Bill of Fare aboard the SS *Great Western* |
| November 24, 1847 | Steamer *Clyde* | Dining aboard a West India Steamer, SS *Clyde*, Barbados |
| March 12, 1853 | *Robert F. Ward* | Antebellum Riverboat Menu, *Robert F. Ward*, Mississippi River |
| November 5, 1855 | Clipper *Ringleader* | Dinner aboard a Clipper Ship *Ringleader* |
| June 3, 1856 | *Champion of the Seas* | Meal aboard a Clipper Ship En Route to Melbourne, Australia |
| January 7, 1866 | SS *New York* | Dinner aboard Steamship SS *New York* |
| May 6, 1875 | SS *Prussian* | Breakfast at Sea, SS *Prussian* |

| July 8, 1936 | SS *Hamburg* | Breakfast at Sea, SS *Hamburg* |
| March 29, 1937 | RMS *Orontes* | Luncheon Crossing the Equator, SS *Orontes* |
| June 10, 1939 | SS *Lurline* | Luncheon at Sea, SS *Lurline* |
| May 7, 1940 | HT *Queen Mary* | Officers' Luncheon, HT *Queen Mary* |
| August 15, 1945 | SS *Matsonia* | Victory Dinner aboard the SS *Matsonia* |
| September 2, 1947 | TSS *Kedmah* | Dinner aboard the First "Hebrew" Ship, TSS *Kedmah* |
| March 24, 1953 | RMS *Queen Elizabeth* | Breakfast at Sea RMS *Queen Elizabeth* |
| September 12, 1957 | SS *Strathaird* | Children's Meals aboard the SS *Strathaird* |
| October 12, 1962 | SS *America* | Columbus Day Dinner aboard the SS *America* |
| May 12, 1982 | QE II | Lunch En Route to the Falkland Islands, RMS *Queen Elizabeth 2* |
| March 3, 1997 | HMY *Britannia* | Final Voyage of the HMY *Britannia*, Karachi |

**Social Event**

| June 4, 1469 | Italy | Medici Wedding Feast, Palazzo Medici, Florence |
| November 1, 1624 | England | All Hallow's Day Dinner, New College, Oxford |
| August 9, 1652 | France | Dinner to Honor the Prince de Conde |
| September 6, 1663 | Morocco | Dinner with the Moors |
| April 19, 1770 | Wales | Coming-of-Age Party, Wynnstay Hall, Denbighshire |
| December 3, 1782 | England | Tithe-Audit Dinner, Weston Longville, Norfolk |
| October 21, 1787 | France | All-Potato Dinner Les Invalides, Paris |
| November 28, 1809 | France | Gourmet's Dinner, *Rocher de Cancale*, Rue Montorgeuil, Paris |
| November 10, 1828 | England | Lord Mayor's Dinner, Guildhall |
| June 28, 1838 | England | Coronation Dinner for the Poor, St. Martin-in-the-Fields, London |
| May 22, 1901 | United States | Seafood Feast, Squantum Club, East Providence, Rhode Island |

**Vegetarian Meal**

# July

## July 1

Prince Napoléon-Jerome Bonaparte (1822–1891) was close adviser to his cousin Napoleon III and in 1852 was named heir-presumptive of the Second Empire. In 1868 he traveled to Turkey and was entertained at a sumptuous dinner by the Sultan of the Ottoman Empire, Abdülaziz (1830–1876). Banquets held by the royal and imperial courts of many Eastern and Asian countries at this time appeared to look to European cuisine as the gold standard of diplomatic dining—at least when a European dignitary was the honored guest. On this occasion the dinner was a real mix of French and Turkish dishes (or at least dishes named that way), although the order of service was quite European.

---

Potage à la Reine
*

BEUREQ
Poissons à la Turque
Filet de boeuf Godard
Poulets nouveaux à l'Orientale
Côtelettes d'Agneau aux petits—pois
*

HIAR DOMASSY
*

Homard en Belle Vue
Asperges Bouillies, sauce au beurre
*

PUNCH A LA ROMAINE
*

Dindonneaux rôtis au jus
*

PILAW
*

Visnali ekmek
Gelée macédoine de fruits
Faouk-gheuksu

---

Several of the classic French dishes with their classic garnishes are here, such as *Potage à la Reine*, fillet of beef *à la Godard*, lobster *en Bellevue*, and the ubiquitous punch Romaine. Two more are given French-styled names that are a nod to the host country—the fish "à la Turque" and the chicken "à l'Orientale." Interspersed with these are the *börek* or *bùrèk* (savory pastries), *pilaf* (pilau), and *vişneli-ekmek* (a sweet bread with cherries). The Sultan perhaps wanted to show his sophistication and knowledge of European cuisine as well as demonstrate his own culture to his guest.

Pilau (see March 30) is a rice-based staple dish common in the East. Rice is the basis of Eastern cuisine as bread is in the West, and—like the other rice-based dishes of risotto, paella, and biryani—it is capable of infinite variation from peasant staple to aristocratic art form, depending on the circumstances.

The *fromage glacé* (iced cheese) sounds odd but is essentially ice cream. In the words of a *Sporting Magazine* correspondent in 1812 "*fromage* at Paris is a lax term for any substance compressed. Thus a *fromage d'Italie* is a Bologna sausage and a *fromage glacé* is a kind of ice" (see April 4)

---

### Stewarding for the Sultan

The food for the Sultan is cooked by one man and his aids, and none others touch it. It is cooked in silver vessels, and when done each kettle is sealed by a slip of paper and a stamp, and this is broken in the presence by the High Chamberlain, who takes one spoonful of each separate kettle before the Sultan tastes it. This is to prevent the Sultan's being poisoned. The food is almost always served up to the Sultan in the same vessels in which it was cooked, and these are often of gold, but when of baser metal the kettle is set into a rich golden bell-shaped holder, the handle of which is held by a slave while the Sultan eats. Each kettle is a course, and is served with bread and a kind of pancake, which is held on a golden tray by another slave. It requires just twice as many slaves as there are courses to serve a dinner to him.

. . . The Sultan never uses a plate. He takes all his food direct from the little kettles, and never uses a table and rarely a knife or fork. A spoon, his bread or pancake or fingers are far handier. The whole household is at liberty to take meals where it suits him or her best, and thus everyone is served with a small tray, with a spoon, with a great chunk of bread, and the higher ones only get the pancakes.

*The New York Herald*, quoted in*The Steward's Handbook* by Jessup Whitehead (1903).

---

### Recipes

~~~

The first two recipes are taken from the first book of Turkish recipes to be published in English—the *Turkish Cookery Book: A Collection of Receipts, Cmpiled by Turabi Efendi, from the Bst Turkish Authorities*—in 1862.

## Tùrk Bùrèghi (Boureq)

Put on the dresser a pound of flour, make a hole in the centre, in which put a tea-spoonful of salt, break in two eggs, mix all together; then add sufficient water, and form it a softish flexible paste, divide it in two, and roll them out the size of the baking tin you intend to use; then sprinkle some melted fresh butter over, and fold over the edges of the paste so as to hide the butter; throw a little flour both under and over, and roll them out again as before, repeat the same five or six times more; then butter the baking tin, in which lay the two pieces of paste; then lay any preparation you choose all over it, half an inch thick, an cover it with the other paste; then make about fifteen deep holes in the paste here and there with the point of a knife, and bake it a nice brown on both sides. When done, cut it in diamonds, dish up tastefully, and serve hot.

## Vishnà Ekmèghi (Visnali ekmek)

Put a pound of loaf sugar into a stewpan with a pint of water, put it on the fire. When boiling, skim it, then add two pounds of morella cherries with the stalks taken off and the stones taken out, stir with a wooden spoon, and boil them down until getting tender; then cut two French penny rolls lengthwise in eight slices, put the yolks of two eggs in a basin, with eight tablespoonfuls of milk, and beat it up well; dip quickly each slice in it, and fry till a nice colour on both sides in hot fresh butter. When all done, lay them in a convenient pie dish, then put the cherries over with the syrup; if you find the syrup too thick, add a little water, set it on a moderate charcoal fire, and let it simmer until the syrup is absorbed, then serve.

## Roman Punch, No. 1

Grate the yellow rind of four lemons and two oranges upon two pounds of loaf sugar. Squeeze the juice of the lemons and oranges; cover it and let it stand until next day. Strain it through a sieve, mix with the sugar; add a bottle of cham-pagne and the whites of eight eggs beaten to a froth. It may be frozen or not, as desired. For winter use snow instead of ice.

## Roman Punch, No. 2

Make two quarts of lemonade, rich with pure juice lemon fruit; add one table-spoon of extract of lemon. Work well and freeze; just before serving, add for each quart of ice half a pint of brandy and half a pint of Jamaica rum. Mix well and serve in high glasses, as this makes what is called a semi or half ice. It is usually served at dinners as a *coup de milieu.*
 Mrs. F. L. Gillette and Hugo Zieman, *The White House Cook Book* (1903).

Pilau: see March 30.
Potage à la Reine: see February 17.
Gelée macédoine de fruits: see May 13.

# July 2

Peruvian Presidential Dinner
Lima, Peru, 1906

The President of Peru, José Pardo y Barreda (1864–1947) was honored at a dinner in Lima in 1906. The occasion is not specified on the menu, but the dinner demonstrates the generic nature of diplomatic cuisine. There are no Peruvian, or any other South American specialties here. Both the language and the style of dishes are French—the international standard of banquet cuisine at this time.

---

Frivolites Assorties
Galantine de Dindoneau a la Gelee
Alouettes Lucullus
Filet de Boeuf Sauce Madeire
Aspic de Foie Gras
Dindoneau Rotis Truffe
Petites Salade a la Russe
Dessert Assortis
Fruits de Saison
*

Xeres
Rhin
Champagne Frappé

---

There are two dishes worth highlighting at this dinner. *Alouettes* are larks —tiny songbirds common in European gardens. They are now protected, but until recent times were much prized by gourmets for their delicate flesh. Small birds seem to be eaten in two situations. The resourceful poor have always eaten whatever they can pick or snare, including "pests" such as the sparrow and the rook. The palate-jaded wealthy, on the other hand have always gone to extraordinary lengths to secure supplies of the rare, the fat, and the tasty such as the ortolan (see December 31) and the lark. The dish of larks as it was presented at this dinner was prepared in a particularly extravagant manner because it was styled "Lucullus" after the ancient Roman gourmet of that name (see November 17).

The other interesting dish is the *Salade à la Russe*. "Russian" style dishes became fashionable in the second half of the nineteenth century, and *borsch* (see December 26) and Russian salad appear on many banquet menus. Russian salad has many variations, but most commonly it consists of chopped vegetables, with or without meat or fish, with a mayonnaise-style dressing. As with the history of many dishes, the popular theory of the origin of Russian Salad does not always fit the facts. The details of the story vary, but Russian Salad is usually said to have been invented in the 1860's by a French Chef in Russia, by the name of Olivier—which accounts for its alternative name of Salade Olivier. The dish however appeared on the menu at the

Inauguration ball of President James Buchanan in Washington in 1857. A recipe for it appears in a cookbook written in 1863 in England (see below), which would be an astonishingly short time for it to be formalised in this way if it was a new invention.

## Recipes
~~~

---

### Russian Salad

This is composed of cooked carrots, beetroot, parsnips, either punched or scooped in shapes, or merely cut in neatly-formed squares or oblongs; to these add common gherkins also cut, a few capers, some scraped horseradish, lobster or prawns, or ham, or any kind of meat cut up in small squares; season with mayonaise, vinegaret, or Tartar sauce; and when dished up either in a bowl or in an aspic, or cold vegetable border, garnish the surface of the salad with very small round balls of Russian caviare, to be obtained at Crosse and Blackwells, Soho-square.

*The Cook's Guide and Housekeepers and Butler's Assistant*, Charles Elmé, Francatelli. 1863

---

Many dishes styled "Lucullan" contain quantities of truffles, as does the following recipe.

---

### Larks with Truffle

Prepare four dozen of larks and take off the fillets; melt some butter in a *sauté-pan*; put in the fillets like scollops, and put over them truffles cut like farthings; put into a stewpan four spoonfuls of *espagnole* and two of *consommé*, and add the carcases or *débris* of the larks from which the gizzards have been taken, with a glass of *champagne*; let it stew half an hour; skim and rub it through a tammy; reduce it to half glaze; the fillets and truffles being cooked, drain off the butter, preserving the juice; put the fillets, truffles, and juice into the *fumet,* without allowing it to boil; toss it well, and finish with half a pat of butter.

Antoine Beauvilliers, *The Art of French Cookery* (1827).

---

Sauce Madeira: see February 28.

## July 3

### Dinner for Ottoman Visitors
### Reform Club, London, England, 1846

The famous Victorian chef, Alexis Soyer (1810–1858), was an expert at mass catering. He was instrumental in developing the soup kitchens of Ireland during the potato famine and improving the feeding of the ordinary soldier in the Crimea (see August 17). On July 3, 1846, however, in his role as chef to the elite Reform Club on Pall Mall, he had a mere 200 to feed. The guests of honor who were to receive the full benefits of his creative genius were Ibrahim Pasha (1789–1848), the Viceroy of Ottoman-ruled Egypt and his retinue. It appears that money was no object on this occasion, and Soyer's inventive powers were given free reign.

---

### FIRST SERVICE:

*Seize Potages*: Quatre à la Victoria, quatre à la Louis Phillipe, quatre à la Colbert, quatre à la Comte de Paris, aux legumes printaniers.

*Seize Poissons*: Quartre de turbots, sauce à la Mazarine, quatre de saumons de Severne à la crême, quatre de buissons de filets de merlans à l'Egyptienne, quatre de truites saumonée en matelotte marinière.

*Seize Relevés*: Quatre de chapons a Nelson, quatre de saddleback of Southdown mouton rôti à la Soyer, quatre de poulardes en diadême, quatre de saddleback d'agneau rôti à la Sévigné.
     Baron of Beef à l'Anglaise.
     Entrée pagodatique de ris de Luxor.

### SECOND SERVICE:

*Cinquante-Quatre Entrées*: Six de poussins printaniers à l'ambassadrice, six de cotelettes de mouton à la réform, quatre de ris de veau piqués en Macédoine de légumes, quatre de petits vol-au-vents aux laitances de maquereaux, quatre de timballes de riz qux queues d'agneau, quatre de jambonneau braisées au vin de Madère, quatre de volailles farcies à la Russe aux légumes vertes, quatre de pâtés chaudes de cailles à la banquière, quatre de rissolettes à la Pompadour, quatre de grenadines de bœuf à la Beyrout, six de cotolettes d'agneau à la Vicomtesse, et quatre de turbans epigramme de levereau au fumé.

*Seize Rôts*: Quatre de turkey poult piqués et bardés, quatre de cannetons au jus de bigarades, quatre de levereaux au jus de groseilles, et quatre de gros chapons au cresson.

*Cinquante-quatre Entremets*: Six de gelées de Macédoine de fruits au Dantsie, quatre de turbans de meringues demi-glacée, quatre de Charlotte Prussienne, six de croquantes d'amandes aux cérises, quatre de galantines à la voliére, quatre de mirotons de homard à l'Indienne, quatre de salades de volaille à la Soyer, quatre de haricots verts au beurre noisette, six de tartelettes pralinées aux abricots, quatre de pain de pêches au noyeau, quatre de petits pois à l'Anglo-Francaise, et quatre de gelées cristalisés à l'Ananas.

*Relevés de Rôts*: La crême d'Egypte à l'Ibrahim Pasha, le gâteau Britannique à l'amiral, quatre de jambons glacées en surprise, quatre de manivaux de champignons au curaçao en surprise, quatre de cotelettes en surprise à la réform, deux de meringues Chinoise pagoda aux fraises.

Soyer performed as expected and produced a meal that was *"recherché* and excellent in all its departments.'' Two particularly novel and original dishes were singled out for exhaustive description by the press. They were *pièces montées*—large ornamental edible constructions reminiscent of medieval subtleties (see September 23), and Soyer's special skill and passion.

The *Gateau Britannique a l'amiral* was the representation of an old man-of-war, filled with frozen peach mousse and fruits, and complete with English and Egyptian flags made of edible rice paper. As the meal progressed, the melting ice caused the sponge cake hull to slump into a wreck, to the amusement of many of the guests. The *Cream of Egypt l'Ibrahim Pacha* consisted of a pyramid of meringue "stones" and sheets of "waved sugar" two-and-a-half-feet high, surrounded by fruit and surmounted by an elegant pineapple cream on the top of which there appeared a portrait of the Pasha's father Mehemet Ali. The illustrious guest carefully picked up the portrait, and "after showing it to several of his suite, placed it in his bosom. What was his Highness's astonishment however, on again looking at the spot, to observe in the cream, as under a glass, a highly-finished portrait of himself, surrounded by a very carefully-executed frame" (Soyer 1847). The chef was prevailed upon to share the secret of the portraits via an interpreter. In the end, "though everything was eatable in it, this magnificent dish was respected, and remained untouched until the end of the banquet, though everybody tried to partake of the fruit which surrounded it.''

Recipes

<div align="center">~~~</div>

Soyer's signature dish was featured on this menu, as it still is at the Reform Club today.

---

Reform Club Mutton-Cutlets

For ten nicely trimmed cutlets, seasoned with salt and white pepper, mince very finely a quarter-pound of lean dressed ham; and with it mix a quarter-pound of fine bread-crumbs. Brush the cutlets with egg, and dip them into the ham and crumbs, and fry them for ten minutes in a saute-pan, in which oil to fry them has been made quite hot (if the pan will not hold the whole, keep hot those already done till the whole are finished). They should be full of gravy; serve on a border of mashed potatoes, with the bones pointing outwards, and pour plenty of "Reform Sauce" over the cutlets.

Christian Isobel Johnstone, *The Cook and Housewife's Manual* (1847).

---

Sauce à la Réform

Cut up two middling-sized onions into thin slices and put them into a stewpan with two sprigs of parsley, two of thyme, two bay-leaves, two ounces of lean uncooked ham, half a clove of garlic, half a blade of mace, and an ounce of fresh butter; stir them ten minutes over a sharp fire, then add two tablespoonfuls of Tarragon vinegar, and one of Chili vinegar, boil it one minute; then add a pint

of brown sauce, or sauce Espagnole [see January 18], three tablespoonfuls of preserved tomatoes, and eight of Consomme; place it over the fire until boiling, then put it at the corner, let it simmer ten minutes, skim it well, then place it again over the fire, keeping it stirred, and reduce until it adheres to the back of the spoon; then add a good tablespoonful of red currant jelly, and half do. of chopped mushrooms; season a little more if required with pepper and salt; stir it until the jelly is melted, then pass it through a tammie into another stewpan. When ready to serve, make it hot, and add the white of a hard-boiled egg cut into strips half an inch long, and thick in proportion, four white blanched mushrooms, one gherkin, two green Indian pickles, and half an ounce of cooked ham, or tongue, all cut in strips like the white of egg; do not let it boil afterwards. This sauce must be poured over whatever it is served with.
Alexis Soyer, *The Gastronomic Regenerator* (1847).

Macedoine de Fruits: see May 13.

## July 4

Independence Day Dinner
Park House, Mt. Clemens, Michigan, 1899

Commodore George Dewey (1837–1917), the man called "The Hero of Manila" was honored at a dinner in Michigan on the fourth of July 1899. Dewey was not present himself—he did not return from his tour of duty in the Phillipines until September of 1899—but his image, captioned with "The Hero of Manila," was on the cover of the menu. Dewey had a thoroughly distinguished naval career. He destroyed the Spanish naval forces in Manila Bay during the brief Spanish-American War (April--December 1898), without losing any of his own men in combat. According to the Navy Department Library, he is the only person in the history of the U.S. Navy to have attained the rank of Admiral of the Navy, an honor awarded to him in 1899 in recognition of his victory.

LITTLE NECK CLAMS.

CONSOMME, Royal, with Rice.          MOCK TURTLE.

Lettuce.     Young Onions.     Gherkins.     Tomatoes.
Pickled Beets.     Olives.     Cucumbers.

BAKED BLUEFISH, Fine Herbs.
Potato Croquettes.

BOILED OX TONGUE, with Spinach.

PRIME ROAST BEEF, au Jus.

ROAST TAME DUCK, Apple Sauce.

SPRING LAMB, Mint Sauce.

ICE, a l'Orange.

SOFT SHELL CRABS, Fried, Tartar Sauce.

TURKEY WINGS, Fricasseed, with Peas.

CHARLOTTE OF APPLES, Wine Sauce.

Green Peas.     Fried Eggplant.     Wax Beans.

Mashed Potatoes.     Boiled Potatoes.

WATERCRESS SALAD.      MAYONNAISE OF CHICKEN.

Tomato Catsup.     Worcestershire Sauce.     Gherkins.

Chow-Chow.     Salad Dressing.

CHERRY PIE.     FIG MINCE PIE.     CUSTARD PIE.

STRAWBERRY SHORTCAKE.

CRÈME DE MENTHE JELLY.

CARAMEL ICE CREAM.     WATERMELON.

HOME-MADE BREAD.     ASSORTED CAKES.

Assorted Fruit.     Mixed Nuts.     Layer Raisins.

American, Edam, Roquefort, and Swiss Cheese.

Water Crackers.

TEA.     COFFEE.     BUTTERMILK.     MILK.

---

The dinner was typical for the time, starting with oysters, offering an iced punch after the heavy meat dishes, and ending with pies, jellies, and ice cream. It was not over-fussy, however—the menu was in English, there were no *pièces montées* (large decorative pastry constructions), and a range of everyday relishes were offered. The organizers also made no attempt to name menu dishes after the hero they were honoring, nor is there any other reference to the Navy or the seafaring life.

## Recipes

~~~

<div style="border:1px solid">

### Soft Shell Crabs

Use them only when freshly caught, as the shells harden after twenty-four hours. Pull off the sand bags, and the shaggy substance from the side; then wash, and wipe dry; sprinkle with *salt* and *pepper*; roll in *crumbs*, then in *egg*, again in *crumbs*; and fry in *smoking hot lard*.

Mary Johnson Bailey Lincoln, *Mrs. Lincoln's Boston Cook Book* (Boston, 1884).

</div>

Mock turtle soup was usually made from a calf's head, because the large amount of cartilage produced the same desirable "texture" (what would now be called "mouthfeel") of turtle. It was initially used as a substitute when real turtle became more scarce and expensive, but eventually became popular in its own right, so that it is not unusual to see both turtle soup and mock turtle soup on the same menu.

---

### Mock Turtle Soup

The calf's head should be soaked in cold water, and washed very clean. To a large head, take six quarts of water; boil it four hours; [The head may be dressed for dinner ...] strain the liquor into a stone jar, and set it away to cool over night, or until the fat cools; then skim off the fat; take two quarts of the liquor, one dozen cloves, one dozen pepper-corns, salt, two onions, two carrots, and two turnips cut fine; boil this two hours cut into small pieces what you have left of the head, or as much as is required, put it into a soupot, with the rest of the stock, and boil it one hour; strain the liquor in which the vegetables were boiled into this, and let it boil an hour and a half; then add three spoonfuls of browned flour, braided into half a pound of butter, and a pint of red wine; give it one boil. Have ready some forcemeat balls, made of some of the head and brains, chopped fine and seasoned with pepper, salt, cloves, and sweet herbs, mixed very hard with two eggs, and fried in hot butter; also six eggs boiled hard, and two lemons sliced; put the forcemeat balls, lemon, the yolk of the eggs, and three table-spoonfuls of soy, into the bottom of the tureen; then turn the soup on this, and send it to the table very hot. All this will make about five quarts of soup.

E. Putnam, *Mrs. Putnam's Receipt Book* (New York, 1867).

---

### Watercress Salad

Carefully wash a pint of fresh watercresses, free them from all decayed leaves, break them in lengths of about two inches, and shake them dry in a clean towel; arrange them neatly on a cold dish, and dress them with three tablespoonfuls of oil, one of vinegar, and a dust of salt and pepper. Dandelion, oyster-plant, chicory, escarole, and nasturtium may be served in the same way.

*Miss Corson's Practical American Cookery and Household Management* (1886).

---

Potato Croquettes: see December 7.
Chow-Chow: see July 27.
Strawberry Shortcake: see May 14.

## July 5

Firemen's Dinner
American Exchange Hotel, San Francisco, California, 1856

The first hotel to open in San Francisco was in 1846, two years before gold was discovered. It was the City Hotel, a rough public house where guests shared rooms, and often a bed. Within a decade the town was booming, and many new hotels had opened including the American Exchange Hotel—a decent family hotel with a separate ladies' entrance. It was at this venue that

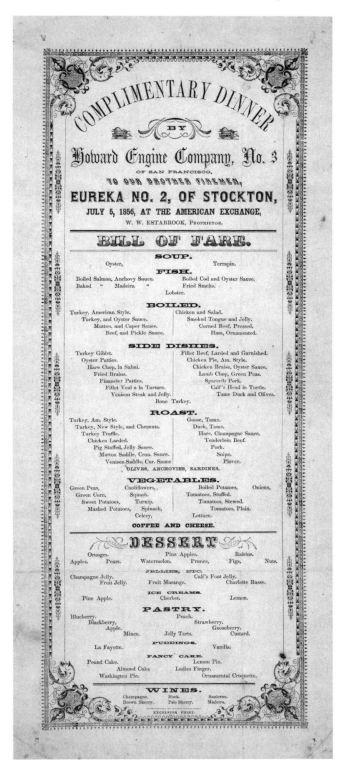

Fire Engine Co. menu. Courtesy of Library of Congress.

the Howard Engine Company No. 3 of San Francisco gave a complimentary dinner for "our brother firemen Eureka No. 2 of Stockton" on July 5, 1856.

### SOUP
Oyster,          Terrapin

### FISH
Boiled Salmon, Anchovy Sauce     Boiled Cod and Oyster Sauce.
Baked    "   ,   Madeira    "              Fried Smelts.
Lobster

### BOILED
Turkey, American Style.          Chicken and Salad.
Turkey, and Oyster Sauce.        Smoked Tongue and Jelly.
Mutton, and Caper Sauce.         Corned Beef, Pressed.
Beef, and Pickle Sauce.          Ham, Ornamented.

### SIDE DISHES
Turkey Giblet.         Fillet Beef, Larded and Garnished.
Oyster Patties.         Chicken Pie, Am. Style.
Hare Chop, in Salmi.        Chicken Braise, Oyster Sauce.
Fried Brains.         Lamb Chop, Green Peas.
Financier Patties.        Sparerib Pork.
Fillet Veal a la Tartare.        Calf's Head in Turtle.
Venison Steak and Jelly.        Tame Duck and Olives.
Bone Turkey.

### ROAST
Turkey, Am. Style.          Goose, Tame.
Turkey, New Style, and Chestnuts Duck, Tame.
Turkey, Truffle.          Hare, Champagne Sauce.
Chicken Larded.          Tenderloin Beef.
Pig Stuffed, Jelly Sauce.          Pork.
Mutton Saddle, Cran. Sauce.          Snipe.
Venison Saddle, Cur. Sauce.          Plover.
OLIVES, ANCHOVIES, SARDINES.

### VEGETABLES
Green Peas, Cauliflowers, Boiled Potatoes, Onions,
Green Corn Squash.          Tomatoes,
Stuffed. Sweet Potatoes,          Turnip.          Tomatoes, Stewed.
Mashed Potatoes,          Spinach,          Tomatoes, Plain.
Celery,          Lettuce.

### COFFEE AND CHEESE

---

### DESSERT
Oranges.          Pine Apples.          Raisins.
Apples.          Pears.          Watermelon.          Prunes, Figs, Nuts.

JELLIES, ETC.
Champagne Jelly.          Calf's Foot Jelly.
Fruit Jelly.          Fruit Marange.          Charlotte Russe.

ICE CREAMS
Pine Apple.          Cherbet.          Lemon.

PASTRY
Blueberry,          Peach,
Blackberry,          Strawberry,
Apple,          Gooseberry,
Mince.          Jelly Tarts.          Custard.

PUDDINGS
Lafayette.          Vanilla.

FANCY CAKES
Pound Cake.          Lemon Pie.
Almond Cake.          Ladies Fingers.
Washington Pie.          Ornamental Croquette.

WINES
Champagne.          Hock. Sauterne.
Brown Sherry.          Pale Sherry.          Madeira.

French—however badly spelled or misused—was still the usual menu language in America, Europe, and Britain at this time, so it is interesting that apart from the single *"a la Tartare"* there are no French terms on this extraordinarily comprehensive Gold Rush era menu.

America had clearly already established its love of sweet dishes by this time, as the dessert choices show. The ices and jellies would have required significant quantities of ice for the churns, presumably cut and brought down from the mountains and stored in well-insulated cellars as far into summer as possible.

"Jelly" is a quick, easy dessert treat today, made in moments from a packet of flavored gelatin and hot water, the only time element to be taken into consideration being the cooling and setting time. Once upon a time it was the opposite—an incredibly laborious process because the gelatin had to be made first. Gelatin is a protein produced by the breakdown of collagen in animal tissue. It is extracted by the long, slow simmering of bones, and the long, tedious process of concentrating and clarifying the resulting broth which then becomes the jelly when flavoring is added. Ox-heels and calves feet were particularly useful, and this menu includes "calf's foot jelly," although it does not tell us what flavor it was. An earlier method of obtaining gelatin was to use hartshorn, which is exactly what is says—the horns of a deer. Another gelling agent was isinglass (used in the recipe here) made from the swim bladder of fish such as the cod and sturgeon. In more recent times plant gels have become available that are acceptable to vegetarians or those with religious reasons for avoiding some forms of gelatin, such as pectin, agar, and carrageenan (Irish moss).

## Recipes

~~~

The recipe for jelly below is taken from *Modern Household Cookery* published in 1854 by Sarah Josepha Hale. She was the influential editor of *Godey's Lady's Book*, one of America's very successful nineteenth-century women's magazines, as well as a number of cookbooks.

---

### Calf's Foot Jelly

The stock for this must be made the day before. Cut up six neat's [calves] feet in shreds, wash them and put them in a pot; cover with water, and boil six hours; strain into a flat dish; when cold, remove the oil from the surface, and wash with warm water. Beat ten eggs into a basin, add the rind and juice of ten lemons, four sticks of cassia, four blades of mace, and a few cloves; beat all together; put the stock to melt in a large stewpan, and when melted add the other articles; stir constantly till boiling; then add as much sugar as will sweeten it (about a pound and a quarter will be enough), and half a bottle of sherry; pour into a flannel bag and pour back till clear; fill into moulds or glasses.

---

Washington pie is actually made from a sponge cake mixture, like the famous Boston cream pie. It is probably called pie because it was cooked in shallow pans or pie dishes.

---

### Washington Pie

Three quarters of a pound of sugar; half a pound of butter beat to a cream; add a cup of cream, half a teaspoonful of saleratus, six eggs beat up well; flavor it with lemon; add a pound of flour; bake it in round tin pans, or a wooden box-cover, about fifteen or twenty minutes; when cold, lay one on a plate, and spread over it marmalade, or any other jelly, as thick as the cake; then cover it with another cake. Frost it, or not, as you please.

*Filling:* Two ounces of butter, quarter of a pound of sugar, two eggs, and one lemon; beat all together without boiling.

E. Putnam, *Mrs. Putnam's Receipt Book: And Young Housekeeper's Assistant* (New York, 1867).

---

Caper Sauce: see December 8.
Charlotte Russe: see September 4.
Ladies Fingers: see March 12.
Lemon Pie: see June 8.
Pound Cake: see April 19.
Oyster Sauce: see August 7.
Sauce Madeira: see February 28.

## July 6

Coronation Feast of King Richard III
Westminster Hall, London, England, 1483

There was a mere ten days between the declaration of Richard III (1452–1485) as king of England and his coronation—an impossibly short time, it would seem, to prepare a sufficiently magnificent feast. The organization for the planned coronation of his nephew, Edward V was, however, already well underway, and no doubt the catering continued without much regard to the intense political machinations going on outside the kitchens. By the time of Richard III's coronation, Edward and his younger brother had disappeared to become remembered in history as "The Princes in the Tower," their uncle indelibly, but controversially, associated with their murder.

| FIRST COURSE. | SECOND COURSE. | THIRD COURSE. |
|---|---|---|
| Frumentie with veneson and bruett Tuskayne | Gely partied with a devise | Blaundsorr |
| Viand comford riall | Viand blanc in barre | Nosewis in compost |
| Mamory riall | Pecokes in his hakell and trapper | Venyson rost |
| Bief and moton | Roo reversed in purpill | Telle in barre |
| Fesaunt in trayne | Runers rost | Langettes de lyre |
| Cignett rost | Betorr rost | Pety chek in bolyen |
| Crane rost | Peiene rost | Egrettes rost |
| Capons of hault grece in lymony | partriche rost | Rabettes souker rost |
| Heronshewe rost | Pomes birt | Quailes rost |
| Gret carpe of venyson rost | Scotwhelpes rost | Briddes brauncher rost |
| Grett luce in eger doulce | Rollettes of veneson farced | Freshe sturgion with fenell |
| Leche solace | Gret carpe and breme in foile | Creves de ew doulce |
| Fretor Robert riall | Leche frument riall planted | Leche fiole and canell |
| Gret flampayne riall | Frettour rosett and jasmine | Frittour crispe |
| Custard Edward planted | Tart burbonet bake | Rosettes florished |
| A sotiltie | Venyson bake | Oranges bake |
|  | A sotiltie | Quynces bake |
|  |  | A sotilty |

A fine three-course meal was prepared for the king and the most noble guests, although the third course was never served due to the lateness of the hour. It was preceded by "an' harold [herald] of arms proclaymyng the feast" throughout the hall.

Perhaps as many as 3,000 guests were fed on this day, and as at all great medieval feasts, there were separate bills of fare for different social ranks. The "lordes and ladyes" received two courses of ten dishes each, the "comons," a single course of six dishes. The lesser folk would have enjoyed, and been suitably impressed by, the *soltities* (subtelties, see September 23) but were not offered the finest dishes—the fine birds such as the peacock, cygnet, crane, egret, and partridge, nor the most finely decorated jellies, custards, and other pastries.

Some of the dishes on this bill of fare remain mysterious. There are many obstacles in the study of very old manuscripts: deciphering the handwriting, scribal errors, sometimes a mix of languages, and inconsistent spelling. The English are not known for eating dog—but what else could "scotwhelps" be (see also September 22)? The third-course dish "Nosewis in compost" is a puzzle. "Composts" (February 23) were common dishes at feasts, but "nosewis" remains a mystery. Does it reference "nose," which also meant the blossom end of a fruit, and therefore mean a fragrant dish? It does not seem likely that it references "nosewort" which is garden cress.

This feast clearly demonstrates the great medieval love of spices and flavorings. There is a persisting myth that spices were used very heavily in the middle ages to disguise the taste of rotting meat. The wealthy could afford to have meat killed as they needed it and could afford to buy exotic imported spices: neither of these were available to the poor. People in the middle ages enjoyed well-flavored food, just as today. The range of spices and flavorings used at this feast includes some ingredients rarely used today. The purchase list included long pepper (*Piper longum*, or Javanese long pepper), graynes (grains) of paradise (or Guinea pepper), and quantities of rosewater, damask water, and saunders (sandalwood, used for its fragrance and also to give a red coloring) as well as cloves, liquorice, galingal, annes (aniseed), mustard (over a barrel full), saffron (11 ¼ lb.), pepper (28 lb.), cinnamon (39 lb.), and ginger (26 lb.) plus "26 lb. and one firkin" of green ginger in syrup, and a considerable quantity of pure gold leaf.

A considerable range of sauces were made in the medieval period. Many would have been included in this meal as traditional accompaniments to some of the dishes; two are specifically mentioned—"Robert" with the fritters, and *eger doulce* (aigre-douce, or sweet and sour sauce) with the *luce* (pike).

## Recipes

~~~

Sauce Robert is an onion sauce that was still popular many centuries later. The following recipe is taken from a late-fourteenth-century French manuscript called *Le Viander de Taillevent*.

---

### Barbe Robert (Sauce Robert)

Take small onions fried in lard (or butter according to the day), verjuice, vinegar, mustard, Small Spices and salt. Boil everything together.

---

The following recipe is from *The Forme of Cury* by the master cooks of King Richard II, written about 1390 . An *egurdouce* was a "sweet and sour" dish (from the French *aigre* meaning sour and *douce* meaning sweet). Recipes of the time almost never gave any quantities, and the instructions were very minimalist. At the time very few people were literate, and cooks learned by doing. The books were meant as *aides-memoire* for the master cooks, not as detailed sets of instructions for anyone to follow. The language is difficult to understand today, and this means that the recipes are open to wide interpretation. One translation is given here.

---

### Egurdouce of Fysshe

Take Loches oþer Tenches oþer Solys smyte hem on pecys. fry hem in oyle. take half wyne half vynegur and sugur & make a siryp. do þerto oynouns icorue raisouns coraunce. and grete raysouns. do þerto hole spices. gode powdours and salt. messe þe fyssh & lay þe sewe aboue and serue forth.

*Translation*: Take loaches or tenches or soles, chop them in pieces, fry them in oil. Take half wine half vinegar and sugar, and make a syrup. Add cut onions, currants and raisins. Add whole spices, good powders (spices) and salt. Serve the fish with the sauce about it and serve it forth.

---

Frumenty: see February 23.

## July 7

### Bicentennial Dinner
### The White House, Washington, DC, 1976

During the Bicentennial of the American Revolution, President Gerald Ford (1913–2006) invited Queen Elizabeth and Prince Phillip of England to visit the United States. The royal visitors arrived on July 6, and in the usual tradition, they were welcomed at a state dinner at the White House the next evening.

---

| | |
|---|---|
| *Sterling* | New England Lobster en Bellevue |
| *Chenin* | Sauce Rémoulade |
| *Blanc* | |
| *1972* | |

*Beaulieu*                                 Saddle of Veal
*Vineyard*                                 Rice Croquettes
*Cabernet Sauvignon*                       Broccoli Mornay
*1968*
                                           Garden Salad
                                           Trappist Cheese

*Schramsberg*
*Blanc de Blancs*
*1973*

                                       Peach Ice Cream Bombe
                                        with Fresh Raspberries

                                           Petits Fours

                                           Demitasse

---

The 224 guests included Telly Savalas, Bob Hope, and Captain and Tenille, who were also to provide entertainment. The dinner was held in a massive tent complete with carpeted floor, red velvet walls, crystal chandeliers, and air conditioning. Guests were seated at tables of eight to ten. The tables were laid with cloths of mist grey cotton printed with sprigs of daisies and bands of

President Gerald Ford and Queen Elizabeth. Courtesy of the Ford Library.

pink ribbon, and the centerpieces were mixed summer flowers—adding, said *The New York Times*, "an impressionstic touch."

State dinners must be organized with military precision. The time frame is often very tight, and on this evening the dinner had to be completed in one hour and fifteen minutes—without any appearance of hurrying. With over 200 guests to serve, this meant that a substantial amount of the preparation had to be done in advance. It was "an all-purpose international menu," as official dinners usually are. The dishes were described in detail in *The New York Times*, and Chef Henry Haller provided several of his recipes for the paper.

## Recipes

~~~

---

### Broccoli Mornay

| | |
|---|---|
| 1 1/2 cups veal or chicken stock | 1 1/2 cups milk |
| 1 head of broccoli | 6 tablespoons butter |
| 7 tablespoons flour | 1/2 cup grated Parmesan cheese |
| 3 large egg yolks, beaten until thin. | 2 tablespoons butter |
| 2 to 3 tablespoons lemon juice | salt and white pepper to taste |
| 1 cup whipped cream | butter and grated Parmesan cheese for topping. |

Cut broccoli into small flowerets, reserving leaves and stems for later use in soup. Wash flowerets well and cook for about eight minutes in rapidly boiling well-salted water until tender but still firmly al dente. Drain in a colander and blanch under cold running water. Drain on absorbent paper towel. Arrange in a single layer in one or two lightly buttered gratin dishes.

Melt butter in a large saucepan and when it is hot, stir in flour. Let bubble very gently over very low heat for 3 or 4 minutes. Bring veal stock and milk to a boil together and pour all at once into bubbling roux, stirring constantly. Simmer uncovered for about five minutes, stirring frequently until sauce is thick and smooth. Stir in cheese and butter over low heat, until cheese and butter are completely melted. Remove from heat.

Slowly pour some of the hot sauce into beaten egg yolks, beating constantly as you do so. When half the sauce has been added, slowly pour egg mixture back into sauce remaining in the saucepan, beating constantly. Heat for 2 or 3 minutes, stirring, being careful not to let sauce boil. Remove from heat and adjust seasonings, adding lemon juice, salt, and pepper. Fold in whipped cream. Cool to lukewarm.

Pour sauce over cooked broccoli in 12 inch long oval gratin dish. Broccoli should be well covered with sauce. Dot liberally with butter and sprinkle with a thin layer of grated cheese. Place under hot broiler for about 7–8 minutes, or until sauce is bubbling and golden brown on top.

Serve immediately.

## July 8

Breakfast at Sea
SS *Hamburg*, 1936

The SS *Hamburg* was built for the Hamburg-Amerika Line for the transatlantic route and launched in 1926. She regularly carried passengers between
Hamburg and New York until she was converted for wartime use by the
Nazis. The passengers who were presented with this substantial menu on
the morning of July 8, 1936, could be forgiven for thinking that it was brunch
rather than simply breakfast.

---

FRUIT
Oranges, Grapefruit, Apples, Cantaloupe, Honey Dew Melon
Stewed Prunes          Baked Apples
Raspberries, Huckleberries and Cream.

FRUIT AND VEGETABLE JUICE
Orange, Grapefruit, Tomato, and Sauerkraut Juice.

PRESERVES
Four Fruit, Black Currant and Apricot Marmalade,
Quince and Strawberry Jelly      Honey

BEVERAGES
Coffee Hamburg Mixture Coffee New York Mixture
(*extra strong if desired*) Coffee HAG and . . . Coffee
Engl. Breakfast Tea, Orange Pekoe, Ceylon, Oolong, Marco Polo,
Linden Blossom, Peppermint, Camomile, Elder Blossom Tea
Cocoa      Chocolate Milk      Malted Milk

TOAST, PASTRY, BRAN MUFFINS AND GINGER BREAD
CEREALS
Oatmeal, Hominy, Buckwheat-Porridge, Rice and Milk
Puffed Rice      Grape Nuts      Kellogg's All Bran
Cream of Wheat      Corn Flakes      Shredded Wheat
Fleischmann's Yeast

EGGS, OMELETTES AND CAKES.
Fried Eggs with Chicken Liver      Scrambled Eggs. . .
Poached Eggs      Turkish Omelet with Artichoke Bottoms
German, Apple, of Cherry Pancake
Buckwheat, Wheat, Hominy, or Rice Cake with
Sausage, Bacon, Maple Syrup or Honey

FISH
Fried Sea Bass
Salted Mackerel, Melted Butter

MEAT
Veal Chops with Spaghetti Steak à la Minute
Mutton Tenderloin with Bacon      Steak Tartare

FROM THE GRILL
Kippered Herring      Smoked Haddock
Sweetbread with Beechnut Bacon Tenderloin Steak
Lamb Chops      Deerfoot Sausage
Breakfast Ham      Beechnut Bacon
POTATOES
Prepared in any style

COLD DISHES
Roast Veal      Roast Beef
Rolled Ham      Boiled Ham
Home-made Sausage      Tea Sausage

CHEESE
Gervais      Swiss

There are two interesting facets to this menu. The first is the number of choices mentioned by brand name, which may represent passenger demand or clever product placement and incentives on the part of the companies concerned. Aside from the coffee and cereal, two American small-goods manufactures are featured alongside the traditional experts in that business—the Germans. Deerfoot Sausage was made by a Masachussets company started in 1847. The company managed every point of the process, from rearing the pigs to packaging, and made a virtue of their higher price with their motto, "they cost more—try them and see why." The success of Beechnut Bacon was a similar marketing triumph. The company pioneered the packaging of its bacon in clear glass jars, proudly displaying its fat and the fact that it was sliced to "micrometer thinness to insure a crisp fry."

The other feature is the number of "health foods." Sauerkraut juice has a reputation for its health giving properties—in particular its benefits to the bowel—and no doubt was included for the benefit of the German passengers. It is high in vitamin C, which certainly made it valuable in the past on long sea voyages to prevent the dreaded scurvy. Sauerkraut has been made along the same lines since ancient times, by the process of lacto-fermentation of cabbage. Several species of bacteria (for example, *leuconostoc*, *lactobacillus*, *pediococcus*) are able to cause fermentation of sugars in the cabbage, and a by-product of the process is the production of lactic acid. It is the high acidity which allows the sauerkraut to keep for long periods of time, in the same way that vinegar is used in pickling. Bowel function is a preoccupation of a significant proportion of people—particularly travelers, and the All-Bran, bran muffins, and prunes were there for the benefit of the American passengers, as was the Fleischmann's Yeast, which was advertised on the basis that three cakes a day would cure constipation.

Recipes

~~~

---

### The True German Way
### of Making Sour Crout, or Sour Cabbage

Take white cabbages, and clean them well from all the green and superfluous leaves; cut through the middle, and take the hearts out; cut and slice the cabbages as small as possible, but cut them no longer than they are perfectly nice and fine. Rub the inside of the cask well with yeast, it will help to sour the cabbage, and prevent the salt liquor from running out. When there is a quantity cut (not all which is to be done), spread it upon a dry table, salt it moderately, and roll it well. Do not pull too much at a time, as it cannot be worked thro' sufficiently; strew a little coriander-seed over it, if agreeable. Put it into the cask, and press it down very hard; repeat this till the cask is quite full; cover it with vine-leaves, put a dry cloth over them, and leave it till next morning, then put on the head of the cask over the leaves and cloth, and put a very heavy weight upon it, to keep it quite close. October is the proper time to do it; it will be fit to eat in two months.

When the cabbage is taken out to dress, be careful to take off all that looks whitish; it is not good till it begins to grow yellow; the deeper the cabbage lies, the finer and better it will be. When what is wanted is taken out for one dressing, cover the cabbage with vine-leaves, as long as they can be got, and when they fail, with a dry cloth. Take great care the salt liquor does not run out, if it does, the cabbage will infallibly spoil. Boil the cabbage with a good deal of butter in a well-tinn'd vessel; put no more water than just enough to cover it, with a sheet of paper over it, and let it boil till sufficiently done.

Charlotte Mason, *The Ladies' Assistant* (London, 1787).

---

Buckwheat Cakes: see March 24.
Cream of Whea: seet December 14.
Hominy: see May 19.
Oatmeal Porridge: see June 27.
Poached Eggs: see June 20.


## July 9

### Midnight Supper with Queen Victoria
### Guildhall, London, England, 1851

The Corporation of the City of London held a grand entertainment on July 9, 1851, to celebrate the successful collection of the objects of the Great Exhibition of the Industry of All Nations that was to open in October of the same year.

Queen Victoria (1819–1901) honored the company with her attendance—the Great Exhibition was, after all, the special project of her husband Prince Albert (1819–1861). The Queen observed the quadrilles, then took a turn around the hall herself, to the gratification of the other guests, and then

returned to her throne. The company slowly filed past and made their obei-
sance (which took some considerable time), and at midnight Her Majesty
and the Royal Party were conducted by the mayor to a crypt under the hall,
where supper was waiting.

---

THE ROYAL TABLE.

Purée de Volaille à la Reine.        Potage à l'Aurore.
Cailles à la Macédoine.        Bordure de Legumes à la Russe.
Noix de Veau à la Gelée.        Cotelettes d'Agneau aux Petits Pois.
Aspic de Levrauts à la Belle-Vue.        Saumon au Beurre de Montpellier.
Mayonnaise de Volaille à la Ravigote.        Boudin de Foies Gras aux Trufles.
Pâté de Canetons à la Rouennaise.        Jambon de Mayence au Vin de Madère.
Chapons à la Pompadour.        Cochon de lait à la Chinoise.
Pâté Monstre à la Cité de Londres.
Hure de Sanglier de la Forêt des Ardennes.
Galantine Impériale de Chapons àl'Amazone.
Pyramide de Volaille à l'Albion.

Buisson de Trufles de Périgord.        Buisson de Crevettes.
Suédoise de Fraises.        Compote de Pêches aux Amandes.
Pain de Cérises.        Gateaux à la d'Artois.
Bavaroise de Groseilles.        Macédoine de Fruits à la Gelée.
Compote d'Ananas.        Feuilletage à l'Orange.
Croque-en-Bouche à la Crème.        Baba en Surprise.

---

Some rare and special wines accompanied the dinner, including an amontillado "of curious antiquity" and a sherry that was 125 years old which
had been bottled for the Emperor Napoleon. The food was also of "the most
*recherché* character"—a great nineteenth-century compliment meaning that
it was rare, or particularly choice, and had been especially sourced at great
effort for the occasion.

The *Pâté Monstre à la Cité de Londres*, or City of London pie, is an almost
legendary dish. There is a recipe by this name in the curiously titled *Archimagirus Anglo-Gallicus* by Theodore Mayerne, "Physician to the late King
Charles," published in 1658. It appears as the first entry in the book, suggesting its importance, then it disappears from culinary history for nearly
two centuries. In 1864, the author of *Chambers Book of Days* gives a brief
biography of Mayerne in which he mentions the pie, then rather mysteri-
ously says that "some half-a-dozen years ago, with very slight alterations—
only adopted after deep consultation, to suit the palates of the present day
—a pie was made from the above recipe, which gave complete satisfaction to
the party of connoisseurs in culinary matters, who heartily and merrily
par-took of it." It may be that this midnight supper (the slight incongruity
of the dates notwithstanding) was the very event at which the pie was
recreated.

Recipes

~~~

---

### The London Pye

Take of Marrow-bons, eight, cock-Sparrowes, or Larks, eighteen, Potato-roots, one pound, Eringo-roots, a quarter of a pound, Lattice-stalks two ounces, Chestnuts forty, Dates half a pound, Oysters, a peck, Citron-rindes preserved, a quarter of a pound, Hartichokes, two or three, Yelks of hard Egs, twelve, Lemmons sliced, two, Barberries picled, one handfull, Gross Pepper, a quarter of an ounce, Large mace half an ounce, Corrents a quarter of a pound. Liquor it when it is baked with white-wine, butter and sugar.

---

### General Observations on Pies

You must generally observe that no kind of flesh whatsoever may be put in paste before it be mortified, therefore you must let that flesh which you do intend to put in paste to be sufficiently mortified, which may be done by hanging it in the Aire, or by burying of it under ground, for the space of twenty and four houres, after which you must beat the said flesh-meat more or less with a wooden rowlett or Pestell according to the said fleshes thickness and hardness, which is a third way to mortifie it: so likewise must you observe that beef and mutton must be more beaten and mortified, than any other flesh whatsoever.
   Theodore Mayerne, *Archimagirus Anglo-Gallicus* (London, 1658).

---

Suédoise (of apples): see December 26.

## July 10

### Officers' Dinner at Sea
### HMS *Assistance*, near Gibraltar, 1675

Henry Teonge (1621–1690), an English parson, joined a small squadron of His Majesty's ships in 1675 as a Navy chaplain. The frigates were to reinforce an earlier squadron which had been sent on an expedition against the "Barbary States" of North African (of Morocco, Algiers, Tunis, and Tripoli) who had menaced shipping in the area for centuries. By May the following year Teonge was enjoying his visit to Aleppo (see May 9), but on July 10, 1675 the squadron was only a few weeks into its voyage and was nearing the Rock of Lisbon, on the coast of Portugal. Captain William Houlding decided to give a fine dinner to his officers aboard his flagship, HMS *Assistance*. Teonge wrote

> We are past the Cape Roca [Rock of Lisbon], but could not discover it by reason of the fog. This day our noble Captain feasted the officers of his small squadron with four dishes of meat: viz. four excellent hens and a piece of pork boiled in a dish; a gigget of excellent mutton and turnips; a piece of beef of eight ribs, well

seasoned and roasted; and a couple of very fat green geese; last of all, a great Cheshire cheese; a rare feast at shore. His liquors were answerable, viz. Canary, sherry, Rhenish, claret, white wine, cider, ale, beer, all of the best sort; and punch like ditchwater; with which we conclude the day and week in drinking to the King and all that we love; while the wind blows fair.

The Diary of Henry Teonge, edited by Sir E. Denison Ross and
Eileen Power (New York: Harper & Brothers, 1927).

At this early stage of the voyage there was plenty of fresh food still. Animals were kept aboard and killed as needed, but there was a finite supply and once they were all gone, the crew were reliant on salted meat (often referred to as "salt horse") until land was reached again. This salted meat was sometimes so old and hard that a day's ration would be towed behind the ship on a rope to try to soften it and make it *less* salty.

A couple of Teonge's comments seem strange and need some explaining. They show how words change in meaning over time. "Green" geese were not discolored because the flesh was decomposing. "Green" in this context means young, as in "green cheese." Teonge also seems to be suggesting that the punch was unpleasant, but he means as common as ditchwater—in other words, very plentiful.

Cheshire cheese is Britain's oldest named cheese, and references to it date to the eleventh century. Originally it simply meant any cheese made in the region of Cheshire, rather than a particular style. It was the cheese favored by the Royal Navy, which purchased vast quantities of it for victualling its ships for long voyages, and in fact in the nineteenth century it was the only cheese purchased by the Navy.

## Recipes

~~~

William Rabisha wrote a popular cookbook called *The Whole Body of Cookery Dissected* in 1661. The following recipes are from this book. His recipe for "baked" goose is what would be called a pie today—the pastry shell acting like a casserole dish, and also—if the crust did not become damp or cracked —like a can, allowing the contents to be kept for quite some time. Pies were often prepared especially to take aboard ship for this reason. Rabisha suggested that a rabbit could be included along with the goose, but it is fairly certain that no live rabbits were aboard the *Assistance* as there has been a long-standing belief amongst sailors that they bring bad luck on board ship.

---

### How to Bake a Goose

Break the bones of your Goose, and parboil him, then season him with Pepper and Salt, a little Cloves and Mace; if you please, you may bake a Rabbet or two with it, because your stubble-Geese are very fat, and your Rabbets dry, you need not lard either: Bake it in good hot butter paste. Tis the Goodwifes pye upon the season, or against a good time; by the Rules aforesaid, you may bake any other gross flesh or fowl, according to its nature or quality.

---

---

### How to Roast a Jigget of Mutton

Your Jigget of Mutton is the leg and half the loyn cut to it, draw it with Lemmon-pill and Time, roast it soberly, save the gravie in a dish under it, put therin Claret-wine, two or three Onions cut in halves, two Anchovies, a spoonful or two of Elder-Vinegar, let this boyl up together; then put in a few minced Capers and Sampier, with a Nutmeg sliced; this is sauce for your Jigget of Mutton; you may add what gravie you have to it; and Oyster-liquor.

---

## July 11

### Trefa Banquet
### Highland House, Cincinnati, Ohio, 1883

The dinner held by the Hebrew Union College on the evening of July 11 for 200 guests (both Jew and Gentile) should have been one of great pride and celebration. The first class of four American-trained rabbis had just graduated. The larger picture was the hope, at least in the eyes of the college founder Rabbi Isaac Mayer Wise, that a new era of religious unity was approaching in which the various factions within Judaism—from strict Orthodox to liberal Reformists—would be reconciled.

Not even in the worst nightmare of those present could the evening have turned into a greater disaster. It was not just a ruined evening. Irreparable damage was done to the hope of religious unity, and the ruin was all on account of the food.

---

MENU

Little Neck Clams (Half Shell)
*Amontillado*
*Sherry*
POTAGES

Consomme Royal
"Sauternes"
POISSONS

Fillet de Boef, aux Champignons
Soft Shell Crabs,

RELEVEE

Poulets, a la Viennoise
Asparges Sauce, Vinaigrette Pommes
"Punch Romaine"        [Pate]
Grenouilles a la Crème and Cauliflower
ROTI

Vol au Vents de Pigeons, a la Tyrolienne
Salade de Saitue [Laitue]
"G. H. Mumm Extra Dry"

HORS-D'OEVERS
Bouchies de Volaille, a la Regeurs
Olives Caviv, Sardelles de Hollands
Brissotine au Supreme Tomatoe,

| | |
|---|---|
| A l'Amarique, Pommes Duchesse | Mayonnaise |
| Salade of Shrimp, | SUCRES |
| "St. Julien" | Ice Cream. |
| ENTRÉE. | Assorted and Ornamental Cakes |
| Sweet Breads, a la Monglas | ENTREMENTS |
| Petits Pois, a la Francaise | Fromages Varies     Fruits Varies |
| "Deidesheimer" | "Martell Cognac"     Café Noir |

To say that this was an unacceptable meal to many if not most of those present would be an understatement of gargantuan proportions. All religions have rules (or at least strong traditions) in relation to food. The body of Jewish law that deals with what food can and cannot be eaten is called *Kashrut*. As with all law, religious or otherwise, interpretations vary and are the subject of constant debate, even amongst the most devout. The rules are extensive, but amongst other things they determine which animals may be eaten (and which parts), how the animals must be killed, how the meat must be handled before it is eaten, and what may not be eaten with it (specifically, milk and milk products). Food that meets this standard is *kosher* (allowed); food that does not is *trefa* (forbidden).

The first dish to appear was clams, which are completely forbidden (*treif*) as are all shellfish. Several rabbis left the dining hall immediately. Others refused to eat anything at all but stayed to listen to the speeches. Worse (or more) was to come. Crab and shrimp turned up later in the meal. Dairy produce—forbidden at the same meal as meat—appeared in several guises, in the cream sauce for the frog and cauliflower dish (frogs being *treif* in any case), the mayonnaise, the ice cream, and the cheese course. The blaming, scapegoating, and denials began immediately, but whether the debacle was due to error, ignorance, stupidity, or sabotage, the damage was done.

## Recipes

~~~

All vegetables are kosher, but as insects are treif, all vegetables must be carefully inspected for them.

*Petits Pois à la Française* and *Potatoes Duchesse* are classic ways of preparing these vegetables.

---

### Petits Pois, à la Française

Put one pint of fresh-shelled green peas into a saucepan with a little cold water, stirring in a piece of butter; add salt and a bunch of parsley; cook with the lid on. When sufficiently done and the liquid reduced add a small piece of kneaded butter; then take from the fire and finish by incorporating a large piece of butter

---

divided in small bits. The peas should be well buttered and thickened so that the liquid be entirely absorbed.

*Kneaded butter* is frequently used at the last moment to thicken sauces and cook small vegetables. In order to prepare this auxiliary, it is necessary to lay a piece of butter on a plate or in a small vessel, and incorporate into it slowly with a wooden spoon, a sufficient quantity of flour to form a smooth paste, but not too consistent, so that it can easily be dissolved by the heat.

---

### Potatoes, Duchess

Peel and cut up some raw potatoes; boil them in salted water, drain it off as soon as they are done and cover over with a clean cloth; let steam for a few moments in a slack oven, then remove and rub a few at a time through a sieve; put this puree into a saucepan, and for each pound stir in quickly one ounce of butter, live raw egg-yolks, salt, nutmeg, a pinch of sugar and two tablespoonfuls of good raw cream, and a handful of grated parmesan. Pour the preparation on a floured table and roll in one and three-quarter inch diameter balls, lengthen these and roll them in bread-crumbs to have them assume an oblong form two and five-eighths inches by one and three-quarter inches; flatten to the thickness of half an inch, cut off the four corners, dip them in melted butter, then in breadcrumbs and lay them on a liberally buttered baking sheet, pouring more butter over; push into a very hot oven and when of a fine color remove from the oven and serve.

Charles Ranhofer, *The Epicurean* (1894).

---

"Sweet Breads" (Sweetbreads): Kosher recipe for, see May 5.
Punch à la Romaine (Roman punch): see July 1.

## July 12

### Reform Democrats Hold a Crow Banquet
### Detroit Opera House, Detroit, Michigan, 1876

The presidential election in America's centennial year was the closest and most controversial in history. Neither candidate won the required majority of the Electoral College vote, and the issue was not resolved until the eve of the inauguration of Rutherford B. Hayes in March 1877.

At the Democratic National Convention in June 1876, the political reformer Samuel J. Tilden (1814–1886) was chosen as the presidential candidate, and the party believed it had its best chance of winning in 20 years. In July the Reform Democrats held a banquet in Detroit with the following bill of fare.

---

SOUPS.
Mack Crow Ni.

FISH
Crowfish.    Crowabs.

SIDE DISHES.
Crow de Pullette      Tilden Crow.      Jonkelly Sauce
Crow tracks from St.Louis.

ROAST.
Crow rib.      Fillet de Crow with greens.
Crow mo to every subscriber.

MADE DISHES.
Scalloped crow.      Crow tarts.      Crow a la St. Louis.
Hendricks crow on toast.
Onistguvment crow.

BOILED.
Crow.      Crow.      Crow.      Crow.      Crow.      Crow.      Crow.

DESSERT AND DRINKS.
Croweem cakes.      Brandy and crowton.      Crowman punch.
Crow whisky.      Thurman whine.
Mumm.

The *Detroit Tribune* summed up the evening by saying "on the whole it was a funny gathering, and many funny things were said." The dinner was nominally held by the "Onist Men Onistguvment Club" (honest men, honest government club) and the guests were "the starving wretches who, for sixteen years have been obliged to keep their noses out of the public crib."

The newspaper made no specific comment about the menu, obviously assuming that it could speak for itself. But what was it saying? This was a menu full of metaphorical crow. The English language is rich with food metaphors: people talk turkey, tell fishy stories, have half-baked ideas, and face raw facts. Sometimes people are forced to eat their words, eat humble pie, or eat crow.

There has been a long-standing prejudice about eating crows, although their close relatives the rooks are considered quite palatable. There is a general tendency for humans to avoid choosing carrion-eaters as food, and crows are also seen as harbingers of death in many cultures. The phrase was originally "to eat boiled crow," meaning to be forced to eat something distasteful. It first appeared in the 1850s, and in the election of 1872 became inextricably linked with the American political scene when Horace Greeley became the "boiled crow"—perhaps unappetizing to both parties when he switched allegiance from the Liberal Republican Party to the Democrats.

There can be many shades of meaning to "eating crow." It came to mean the same as eating one's words, or eating humble pie—that is, admitting error, being humiliated, and recanting. At this banquet, the "crow" (particularly "boiled crow") seems to be a metaphor for the Republican Party, which the reformists were going to eat up. The banqueters were also clearly "crowing about" their plans.

The menu extends the joke by including some other examples of word play —*mack crow ni* is presumably macaroni and *crowabs* are presumably crabs.

The political propaganda message was also emphasized by the honoring of several key players and locations in the names of dishes.

## Recipes

~~~

---

### Macaroni Soup

Boil a pound of the best macaroni in a pound of good stock; when it becomes tender, take out half of it. To the remainder add some more stock, and boil it till the macaroni will pulp through a fine sieve. Add a pint of boiling cream, the macaroni that was first taken out, and half a pound of grated Parmesan cheese; make it hot again, but do not let it boil. Serve with a French roll.

T. Webster and Mrs. Parkes, *An Encyclopaedia of Domestic Economy* (New York, 1855).

---

## July 13

### Dinner of the Thirteen Club
### Central Restaurant, New York, 1900

The fear of anything associated with the number 13 (*triskaidekaphobia*) occurs in several cultures around the world. The phobia appears to have very ancient and obscure origins, which has led to it having a great variety of modern explanations. For many, the fear determines many daily acts. For others it is a ridiculous and primitive superstition needing serious debunking. A group of the latter individuals formed the *Thirteen Club* in New York in 1881. Their particular goal was to debunk the superstitious belief that if thirteen dined together at the same table, one of them would die within the year. By the end of the decade there were 400 members, and in the lifetime of the club they included five U.S. presidents. They held regular dinners on the thirteenth of every month.

Club members tempted fate in as many ways as they could. It was particularly relished when the 13th fell on a Friday (as it did in 1900) as this was

### 189th Regular Dinner—Menu

| | |
|---|---|
| I | Little Necks |
| II | Consommé anglaise |
| III | Celery |
| IV | Filet of bluefish, bordelaise, potatoes julienne |
| V | Sweetbreads in cases à la reine |
| VI | French peas |
| VII | Domestic duck, apple sauce |
| VIII | Lettuce and tomato salad |
| IX | Ice cream |
| X | Cake |
| XI | Fruit |
| XII | Roquefort cheese |
| XIII | Coffee |

held in particular horror by those suffering from *paraskavedekatriaphobia*. No opportunity was lost to invoke the number 13. Dinner began at 13 past the hour and finished at 13 o'clock (i.e., 1 A.M.), 13 sat to a table, and there were 13 dishes, 13 toasts and 13 responses, and the club had 13 officials.

The club motto was "We who are about to die, salute you." The décor frequently featured such things as opened umbrellas, coffins, and skeletons; there was much funereal black, or unlucky green. Diners might have to pass under a ladder to enter, and salt was deliberately spilled. On one momentous occasion the guests were 13 undertakers who had escaped injury in car number 13 in a rail accident the previous week.

The idea would have been anathema in France, where the fear of thirteen at table was sufficient that an independent gentleman could make a career of becoming a professional *quatorizième* or fourteenth guest. This gentleman would be an agreeable, cultured individual and a good conversationalist, and he would dress each evening in the correct attire—ready at a moment's notice should a footman be sent for him. He was dismissed at a moment's notice if the invited guest turned up, even if he had not yet eaten (although he would still be paid).

Recipes
~~~
Bordelaise sauce is one of the basic sauces from the French classic repertoire.

---

### Bordelaise sauce

Simmer four shallots, chopped very fine, in two ounces of butter. When thoroughly warmed through add one-half glass of Bordeaux claret and reduce until nearly dry. Then add one pint of brown gravy and boil for five minutes. Then add one-quarter of a pound of sliced parboiled beef marrow, and a little chopped garlic, if that flavor is desired. Sprinkle with chopped parsley, and before serving stir in slowly two ounces of fresh butter. Serve poured over meats, or separate.
Victor Hirtzler, *The Hotel St. Francis Cook Book* (1919).

---

### Consommé Anglaise (Plain Consommé)

[Is] made with plenty of veal bones to give it a gelatinous taste; served with green peas and small squares of white chicken meat in each plate.
Charles Fellows, *The Culinary Handbook* (Chicago, ca. 1904).

---

## July 14

### Dinner for the American Ambulance
### Lycée Pasteur, Neuilly-sur-Seine, France, 1916

Long before the United States entered World War I the country gave a huge amount of assistance to its old revolutionary friend, France. The United

Souvenir de l'Ambulance Américaine
14 JUILLET 1916

American Ambulance menu cover.

States had founded an american hospital at Neuilly in 1906, and within weeks of the outbreak of World War I in 1914 the *Lycée Pasteur* (Pasteur School) building was converted by the American team into "a large Hospital for the wounded of every nation." It was referred to as the "Ambulance Section" or even just "the American Ambulance." The word *ambulance* in French does not simply refer to a vehicle as it does in English-speaking countries. Originally it referred to an entire mobile military hospital such as used to be used at the front line. It was only later that it came to mean any military hospital, as well as the emergency transport vehicle.

The American Ambulance Field Service grew out of this hospital, and many young American men became volunteer drivers. Some of them became famous later in life for their literary work, including Ernest Hemingway, E. E. Cummings, John Dos Passos, and Dashiell Hammett.

On "Bastille Day," France's national day, a dinner was held at the Lycée building, to thank those involved in the American Ambulance.

---

DÉJEUNER

~~~

Jambon d'York à la Gelèe
Œufs pochés Mornay
Poulet sauté Marengo
Paté en croute de l'Ambulance
Salade de Saison
Glaces Panachées
Gâteaux secs
Coupe de fruits refraichis
Café
Graves Premières :-: Medoc
Cigares.

The chicken Marengo on this menu was probably chosen deliberately. The dish is named after the famous battle in which Napoleon soundly defeated the Austrians on June 14, 1800. Aside from the fact that it was the anniversary of the event, it would have been very appropriate to draw attention to a French victory as the nation geared up to war again. The greatest myth about the dish is that it was created by Napoleon's Chef Dunan immediately after the battle, with the only ingredients he could scrounge up. In reality, Napoleon was notoriously disinterested in food, Dunan was not in his employ at the time, and—most tellingly—the first written mention of it does not appear for nearly two decades. The truth is, nineteenth-century chefs loved naming recipes after famous people and events.

## Recipes
~~~

Ingredients for many so-called classic dishes are often quite varied, and chicken Marengo is no exception. Different recipes include tomatoes, crayfish, mushrooms (or truffles), garlic, parsley, ham, and lemon juice, with a garnish of croutons and/or fried eggs. The following recipe is from a French cookbook, *The 366 Menus and 1200 Recipes of the Baron Brisse*, published in 1868.

---

### Chicken à la Marengo

Cut up a chicken into joints, and cook in olive oil and a little salt, put in the legs before the other pieces, as they take longer to cook. When a good colour and nearly done, add a bouquet of mixed herbs, pepper, mushrooms, and some slices of truffles; place the chicken on a dish, and add the oil drip by drop to some *Italian sauce*; stir the whole time. When warm, pour over the chicken, and garnish with fried eggs and sippets of fried bread. If preferred, clarified butter may be used instead of oil.

---

### Italian Sauce

Simmer a lump of butter as big as two eggs in a saucepan, with two tablespoonsful of chopped parsley, one tablespoonful of chopped eschalots, and the same quantity of minced mushrooms, add a bottle of white wine; reduce the sauce, and moisten with a tumblerful of velouté sauce and half a tumblerful of stock; boil over a quick fire, skim off all grease, and as soon as the sauce is thick enough, take off the fire, and keep warm in a bain-marie.

---

## July 15

### Dinner aboard a U.S. Mail Ship
### USMS *Philadelphia*, 1913

The men aboard the United States Mail Ship *Philadelphia* sat down to the following dinner on July 15, 1913. It is unclear from the menu whether this was an officers' meal, but the range of choices seems rather generous for ordinary seamen of the time.

---

Ox Tail Soup

—

Codfish, Parsley Sauce

—

Corned Beef and Cabbage

—

Boiled Fowl & Bacon

—

Roast Lamb and Mint Sauce

—

Green Peas     Baked and Boiled Potatoes

—

Cold Meats:
Roast Beef     Boiled Ham

—

Cabinet Pudding     Assorted Cakes
Ice Cream

—

Edam Cheese

—

Dessert     Coffee

---

The ship regularly traveled the transatlantic route and apparently also carried very valuable cargo at times. In January 1909 it is said she had $343,470 in silver ingots aboard when she left New York.

Cooks aboard ships have unique problems to cope with. There is no provisioning between ports, so stores must be very accurately gauged and planned. Fresh food is a particular problem, especially the sort of fruit and vegetables that cannot be frozen such as salad vegetables and other perishables such as milk, butter, and eggs. In the past the great lengths of time a vessel was at sea presented huge problems. Today it is rare for a ship to be more than a week away from land, although in practice there may be all sorts of reasons why going ashore is impossible—during times of international conflict and severe weather for example.

## Recipes

~~~

Whether or not a vessel belongs to the Navy, a cruise line, or another commercial interest, there are always large numbers of men to be fed. The following recipes are taken from the *General Mess Manual and Cookbook for Use on Board Vessels of the United States Navy*, published in 1904. Each recipe provides 100 servings.

---

### Boiled Fish (and Parsley Sauce)

Place 75 pounds of fish in cold water, adding plenty of salt and 1 pint of vinegar. Place on the fire in pans or fish kettles and allow to simmer until tender. Take out fish when cooked. Make sauce with 2 quarts of water and 1 quart of milk. Put on Fire until it boils. Thicken with cornstarch or flour; chop a bunch of parsley with pepper and stir into the sauce. Pour over fish and serve.
   (NOTE. This sauce is suitable for all boiled and baked fish.)

---

### Roast Lamb

Use 90 pounds of lamb. Wipe thoroughly with towel soaked in salt water and place in dry pans, adding three sliced onions and three sliced carrots. Dredge with pepper, salt, and flour, using the latter liberally. Roast in closed oven for thirty minutes, then baste with boiling water, and cook for one hour and a half, watching the meat carefully and seeing that there is plenty of water in the pan with which to baste it. Upon removing the meat when done, stir into the gravy a little more flour, add 2 quarts of boiling water, and let it simmer for five minutes in the oven or on top of the galley.

---

### Boiled Potatoes

Sixty pounds of potatoes will be required. Wash thoroughly; place in copper in cold water and boil for thirty-five minutes.

---

Cabinet Pudding: see June 30.

## July 16

### Dinner at Sea
### SS *Lahn*, 1900

The SS *Lahn* was a ship of the Norddeutscher Lloyd Bremen Line. She was launched in 1887, and until October 1901 she regularly sailed the Bremen-Southampton-New York route. There was accommodation aboard for 1,030 passengers, including 700 in third class—a large proportion of whom (on the outward journey) were German migrants who entered their new country through the control point at Ellis Island.

The *Lahn* left Bremen for New York on July 10 and must have been somewhere in the Atlantic after its routine stops at Cherbourg and Southampton when the passengers (the class is not stated) sat down to the following dinner.

---

Consomme aux pates d'Italie
Fondue au parmesan
Roast beef au jus      Potatoes a la poulette
Fried chicken a la viennoisse
Mock turtle ragout

Roast capon
Plums Lettuce salad
Pudding a l'Italienne
Strawberry ice-cream      Pastry
Fruit
Coffee

Menus aboard the ships of this shipping line were always written in both German and English. The "English" was culinary English, which means it was Anglo-French. The menu language becomes even more convoluted on account of the Italian contribution to the dishes. On the German side of the menu the soup contains *nudeln* (noodles), which becomes *pâté d'Italie* ("paste" from Italy—i.e., pasta) on the English side. Noodles and pasta are the same thing of course, both being small pieces of dough boiled, but to the English and French, it was "pasta" that was put into clear soup, not noodles.

The most intriguing dish on this menu is the fondue. The word comes from the French word *fondre* (to melt) and generally means a dish composed of melted cheese. The dish is claimed by the Swiss as their own speciality, but in reality melted cheese dishes have been popular for millennia—there is mention in Homer's *Iliad* of a mixture of Pramian wine, goat's cheese and barley flour—because they are a useful way of using up leftover ends of cheese. Recipes by the name of *fondue* only really start to appear in English cookbooks in the last few decades of the nineteenth century. Most of them have very little resemblance to the obligatory 1970s party favorite of a bowl of cheesy sauce sitting over a small flame, with long-handled forks with which to spear then dip a variety of tidbits. Depending on the additional ingredients and variety of cooking methods, a fondue can resemble Welsh rabbit (see March 14, a soufflé, or even an omelette, so it is pointless then to argue about an "authentic" fondue.

## Recipes

~~~

Given that there are a number of types of fondue, this one would be appropriate for its position in this menu. It is really more like a soufflé.

### Fondue of Cheese

Take three ounces of flour, moisten with half a pint of cream and half a pint of milk, and a quarter of a pound of butter; stir all these ingredients over a brisk fire till they become paste; remove it from the fire, and mix in eight yolks of eggs, a quarter a of a pound of grated Parmesan cheese, and a quarter of a pound of fine Gruyere cheese, cut into dice. When the dinner is called, whip the whites; mix them in also, and bake the fondue in a tolerably quick oven. This same mixture answers for small fondues in paper cases.
*The Thorough Good Cook*. George Augustus Sala. 1896.

---

### Potatoes a la Poulette

These are potatoes cooked, sliced, then reheated gently in Poulette Sauce (see below).

---

### Poulette Sauce

Melt an ounce of butter and stir in ½ ounce of flour, cook for a few minutes without browning the flour, then stir in 1 pint of white stock, stir till it boils, and cook for at least 15 minutes, thicken with 2 yolks of eggs, season with salt and pepper, and finish with half an ounce of fresh butter.

*The Book of Sauces*. Charles Herman Senn. Chicago. 1915

---

## July 17

### Dinner on the Mountain
### The Aletschhorn, Switzerland, 1859

The English mountaineer Francis Fox Tuckett (1834–1913) and his three companions made the first ascent of the Aletshorn on June 18, 1859. He had put forth the idea some days before with the landlord of the hotel where he was staying on one of his "pedestrian tours" of Switzerland, but local opinion was that it was too early in the season and likely to be dangerous. Tuckett "throws out a hint" to several walking companions, and the hint rapidly becomes a *bonne idée* (good idea), and then a firm commitment to attempt the "doubtless difficult, but yet possible" climb.

The preparations got under way immediately, according to *Peaks, Passes, and Glaciers* written by the Alpine Club in 1862:

> . . . numerous solemn consultations in the kitchen, at which everybody assisted . . . the great tin can, carried like a knapsack, and holding an indefinite number of bottles, was produced and nearly filled with good, sound *vin du pays*—not for want of anything better, but because there is much truth in Bennen's remark "its all one up aloft." A bottle or two of champagne was added, by way of enabling me to study the expansion of gaseous bodies under diminished atmospheric pressure—of course, for no other purpose. As for solids, it need not be here told how poulet and ham, sausage and mutton, bread, cheese, butter and honey, with other good things galore, were duly consigned to a roomy "*Hutte*" or basket, nor how "*noch ein stück*" ["a little"] of this, that, and the other, was added to fill up any crannies, till all were satisfied that there was no danger of a deficiency.

By the night of July 17, they had found an ideal resting place for the night in a narrow cave with a spring which "proved a very convenient source of supply for our subsequent culinary operation."

> . . . our arrangements for the night being at length completed, we began to think about dinner: so, lighting my Russian furnace [a camp stove], a "*casserole*" of water was boiling merrily in less than five minutes, and a cake of Chollet's

*"Julienne au gras"* being sliced into it, we were soon busily engaged upon a couple of quarts of really excellent soup and vegetables, as a first course, followed by *pièces de résistance* and *entremets* in the shape of mutton, veal, ham, and sausage. The soup, both from the manner of its production and intrinsic excellence, seemed to make a profound impression on my companions, who had, I suspect, previously imagined the brown-looking cakes out of which vegetables seemed to spring into existence flowers from a conjuror's hat, to be *"der Herr's"* supply of cavendish. . . . Bohren especially could not get the *"vortreffliche Suppe"* ["excellent soup" ] out of his head

After a short sleep and an early breakfast they set off for the peak, after "a moderate but sufficient supply of provisions and a bottle of champagne were consigned to a knapsack, the wine-can strapped on the porter's shoulders." The "champagne experiment" was, unfortunately for science, a failure as the bottle was forgotten en route to the top.

The cakes of "portable soup" (the forerunner of stock-cubes) which were so well received on the cold mountainside were made by the famous French firm of Chollet and Co. They were by far the world's major producer of dried vegetables to armies and expeditions. Soyer used them in the Crimea (see August 27) as did the great wagon trains on the westward migration routes in America.

## Recipes

~~~

A *"julienne"* is a mix of thinly sliced vegetables. The *"maigre"* soup is meatless, for fast days, the *gras* ("fat") version contained meat stock.

---

### Julienne au gras

Cut in small pieces or thin slices, carrots, turnips, parsnips, leeks, celery, potatoes, onions, each equal parts; chop some lettuce, sorrel and chervil; fry them all in fresh butter and then add enough rich (fat) broth; place on a low heat until everything is thoroughly cooked, then pour in a soup bowl, in which, if you wish, you have already added bread, or vermicelli or any other pulp, or better yet, a small quantity of potatoes: you can add asparagus and peas, in the season, making an even better julienne.

*Manuel Du Cuisinier et de La Cuisinière À L'usage De La Ville Et De La Campagne* (1829).

---

## July 18

### Picnic for the Mexican President
### San Luis Potosi, Mexico, 1921

The National Chamber of Commerce and Trade in San Luis Potosi, Mexico, chose an unusual form of entertainment to honor Mexican President Alvaro Obregón (1880–1928). They took him on a picnic on July 18, 1921. Obregón was President of Mexico between 1921–1924. He maintained a good relationship with the United States and instigated reforms at many levels in postrevolutionary Mexico but was assassinated in 1928 by a religious fanatic.

---

COMIDA CAMPESTRE

Arroz a la valenciana.
*(Rice, Valencia style)*

Cabrito en barbacoa.
*(Barbequed goat)*

Lechon con salsa ranchera.
*(Suckling pig with ranch dressing)*

Frijoles
*(Beans)*

Dulce
*(Sweets)*

Café
*(Coffee)*

Cerveza
*(Beer)*

---

The word *barbecue* is derived from the Arawak *barbacòa*, meaning a framework of sticks supported by posts. The word had two uses—it applied to a sleeping frame and also a frame over which meat or fish could be dried and smoked. The Arawak are the indigenous people of the West Indies, and *barbecue* comes down through the Spanish word *baracoa*. The word first appeared in English in the late-seventeenth century under a wide variety of spellings.

Experts and enthusiasts debate the supposed differences between salsa and sauce—how thick or smooth it should be and whether cooked or not—but both words are derived from *sal*, the Latin for salt—as does the word salad. Salt, salsa, sauce, and salad were all originally intended as "seasoning" for a meal.

## Recipes

~~~

Goat is cooked in the same way as sheep and can be substituted in this recipe.

---

### Barbecued Sheep

Dig a hole in ground, in it build a wood fire, and drive four stakes or posts just far enough away so they will not burn; on these build a rack of poles to support the carcass. These should be of a kind of wood that will not flavor the meat. When the wood in the pit has burned to coals, lay sheep on rack, have a bent stick with a large sponge tied on one end, and the other fastened on one corner of the rack, and turn so that it will hang over the mutton; make a mixture of ground mustard and vinegar, salt and pepper, add sufficient water to fill the sponge the necessary number of times, and let it drip over the meat until done; have another fire burning near from which to add coals as they are needed.

Estelle Woods Wilcox, *Buckeye Cookery* (Minneapolis, 1877).

Dulce can mean any form of sweet dish.

### Dulce (Baked Raisins)

Pick the stems from each raisin and wash in boiling red wine; then put them in an infusion of cognac, Marsala wine and slices of fresh lemon for three days. Remove and heap them in bunches about the size of large goose-eggs and wrap each bunch in large fig leaves, layer upon layer, and bake for a half-hour in a light oven. When serving turn the leaves back and send to the table hot.

May. E. Southwood, *One Hundred & One Mexican Dishes* (1906).

### Frijoles (Beans)

In the bottom of a bean-jar put a whole onion with a clove stuck in it, three whole cloves of garlic, four pieces of mustard pickle and three tablespoonfuls of the mustard vinegar. Over this put a layer of uncooked red beans and a piece of salt pork, then more beans; over all a tablespoonful of sugar. Fill with hot water and bake slowly all day. Renew with hot water from time to time.

May. E. Southwood, *One Hundred & One Mexican Dishes* (1906).

## July 19

### Coronation Banquet of King George IV
### Westminster Hall, London, England, 1821

George IV (1762–1830) was a gluttonous, spendthrift womanizer—the complete antithesis of his father, the much loved but intermittently "mad" George III. The new king started as he meant to continue, by spending £240,000 (equivalent to over £16 million today) on his coronation—making it the most expensive ever held in Britain. The ceremony was followed, as was traditional, by a magnificent feast.

HOT DISHES.—160 tureens of soup, 80 of turtle, 40 of rice, and 40 vermicelli; 160 dishes of fish, comprising 80 of turbot, 40 of trout, 40 of salmon; 160 hot joints, including 80 of venison, 40 of roast beef, with three barons, 40 of mutton and veal; 160 dishes of vegetables, including potatoes, peas, and cauliflowers; 480 sauce-boats, 240 of lobsters, 120 butter, 120 mint.

COLD DISHES.—80 dishes of braized ham; 80 savory pies; 80 dishes of daubed geese, two in each; 80 dishes of savory cakes; 80 pieces of beef braized; 80 dishes of capons braized, two in each; 1,190 side-dishes of various sorts; 320 dishes of mounted pastry; 320 dishes of small pastry; 400 dishes of jellies and creams; 160 dishes of shell-fish, 80 of lobster, and 80 of crayfish; 161 dishes of cold roast fowls; 80 dishes of cold house-lamb.

Three hundred guests sat down to this banquet. There was one notable absence—the King's wife, Caroline of Brunswick (1768–1821), whom he had hated since meeting her the day before their wedding and had prevented from attending the proceedings.

Galleries had been specially constructed for the occasion in Westminster Hall so that the less important visitors could have the honor of watching the feast. The gallery guests were hungry—it had been a long day coronation-watching—and at least one peer of the realm managed to throw a capon in a handkerchief to his hungry relatives.

The most interesting dish served at the feast was not listed on the formal bill of fare. It was *dillegrout,* a symbolic dish that had been served to the monarch at coronations ever since 1066. This was the last occasion on which it was served. The story is that William the Conqueror crowned himself King of England on Christmas Day in 1066 but postponed the festivities until he was joined by his wife, Matilda of Flanders. At the subsequent feast he was so taken with a simple white soup that he presented the cook with a manor and lands in Addington. The dish became the symbolic rent "paid" at the coronation of every subsequent monarch. The exact nature of the soup is not certain. Initially it appears to have been made from almond milk, chicken, and spices, but at George IV's coronation it may have been more in the nature of a savory white "pudding" of herbs and pork boiled in a pig's caul.

Coronation of George IV. Courtesy of Library of Congress.

> Quantities of Food and Wine for the Coronation Banquet.
>
> 7,442 lbs. of beef; 7,133 lbs. of veal; 2,474 lbs. of mutton;
> 20 quarters of house-lamb; 20 legs of house-lamb; 5 saddles of lamb;
> 55 quarters of grass-lamb; 160 lambs' sweetbreads; 389 cow-heels;
> 400 calves' feet; 250 lbs. of suet; 160 geese; 720 pullets and capons;
> 1,610 chickens; 520 hens for stock; 1,730 lbs. of bacon;
> 550 lbs. of lard; 912 lbs. of butter; 84 hundred of eggs.
>
> Champagne, 100 dozen; Burgundy, 20 dozen; claret, upwards of 200 dozen;
> hock, 50 dozen; Moselle, 50 dozen; Madeira, 50 dozen;
> sherry and port, about 350 dozen; iced punch, 100 gallons.

The feast was also the last time that the traditional ceremony of the challenge by the King's champion (see October 13) was held. Various noblemen performed traditional honorary roles. Lord Denbigh (1796–1865) had the honor of serving the King, which required him at one point to cut up an 11-pound pineapple—a rare and exotic hothouse treat at the time.

## Recipes

~~~

### Vermicelli Soup, White or Brown

Blanch as much vermicelli as is wanted, by putting it on the fire in cold water; let it boil up, then strain it off, and put it into cold water; let the vermicelli stay in the water until it is cold (if it is left on a sieve to drain while hot, it becomes lumpy, and will not dissolve again), strain it quite dry from the cold water, put as much best stock as you want soup. If it is for white, make a liaison of six eggs.

### A Fowl a la Daube

Bone a large fowl without cutting the skin, and singe it; put in it a small piece of the prime of Westphalia ham (about the size of the breast of the fowl), then fill it with a good force-meat, and braise it in a white braise; when done, take it up and dry it; then glaze it, and put mushrooms on the dish, and the fowl at the top: garnish either with croutons, or paste baked for that purpose.

Braised Ham: see April 2.

## July 20

### International Meal
### Imperial Hotel, Tokyo, Japan, 1952

The Imperial Hotel in Tokyo was designed by the famous architect Frank Lloyd Wright to replace the old timber hotel that had stood on the site since 1890. The new hotel had only just opened in 1923 when a devastating earthquake hit Tokyo and Yokohama, killing thousands. The hotel was slightly damaged, but functional, and instantly became a refuge for embassy officials and the homeless.

The hotel provided a comprehensive *á la carte* menu, but for those guests who wanted their luncheon choices simplified, they offered a "Tiffin" menu.

---

TIFFIN
Potage Purée Crécy
~~

Fried Halibut, Tartar Sauce Y 470
Brochette of Chicken with Pilaff Y 500
Minute Steak with Fried Potatoes Y 600
Coleslaw
~~
Roll      Butter
Coffee

---

This appears to be a three-course menu, with the choice of main course determining the cost of the meal. The only classic "tiffin " (see different interpretations March 31 and April 25) feature of this meal is that it was offered at lunchtime, not at dinner. The food itself, the progression of courses, and the type of food served were entirely European. Only the name remains to give an "Asian" cast to the meal, perhaps to remind the guests that they were in fact away from home.

The three main choices would have been familiar and unthreatening to the guests. There is the traditional fish with Tartare sauce and the ubiquitous steak and chips, and even the apparently Eastern concept of skewered meat and pilaff had been well known in America and Europe since the seventeenth century (see March 30). The single vegetable or salad side offered with all of these main meals is coleslaw, a dish with a very interesting linguistic history.

The word comes from two Dutch words—*kool* meaning cabbage and the word for salad, pronounced *sla*, and together they have given rise to a huge number of spellings of "coleslaw." Folk etymology (see March 14) has engendered some strange interpretations of the basic cabbage salad idea, and the changed language in its turn triggered a change in the whole concept. At some time, the word "cole" was heard as "cold," which also fitted the dish, so it stuck. There were two results of this. One, that the "cold" now referring to the temperature, the "slaw" is left to represent the cabbage. It was then only one small step for someone to make a dramatic change to the basic (but now completely hidden) concept, and come up with "hot slaw."

### Recipes
~~~

Tartar(e) sauce is a common accompaniment to seafood. The recipe has evolved somewhat since it became popular in the first half of the nineteenth century. It was made with mustard and vinegar with chopped shalots and herbs; now it is more common to use mayonnaise and usually includes capers and gherkins.

---

### Tartare Sauce

| | |
|---|---|
| 2 yolks of eggs, | cayenne, |
| mustard, | 1 pint salad oil, |
| 1/4 gill tarragon vinegar, | [1 tablespoon] Bechamel or |
| | Veloutée sauce, |
| 2 tablespoonfuls chopped gherkins, | 1 tablespoonful of chopped capers, |
| 1 tablespoonful of chopped parsley, | 1/4 teaspoonful of mixed tarragon and |
| | chervil finely chopped. |

Put the yolks of eggs in a basin, place it in a shallow pan containing some crushed ice, add a teaspoonful of salt, a good pinch of white pepper, a pinch of cayenne, and a teaspoonful of mustard; stir well together, and add, gradually, the salad oil and tarragon vinegar. When the sauce is smooth and creamy stir in a good tablespoonful of cold Bechamel or veloutee sauce, add the gherkins, capers, parsley, tarragon, and chervil. Do not mix the gherkins, capers, etc., until the sauce is finished, as it is likely to cause the sauce to turn if put in too soon. A few drops of lemon juice may be added if the sauce is found too thick.

Charles Herman Senn, *The Book of Sauces* (1915).

---

Soup à la Crecy: see March 23.

## July 21

### Dining in Space
### The Moon, 1969

The Apollo 11 space flight was the first mission to land men on the moon. There were three men on board—Commander Neil Armstrong, Command Module Pilot Michael Collins, and Lunar Module Pilot "Buzz" Aldrin. The spaceship was launched on July 16 at 13:32 UTC (Coordinated Universal Time). At 02:56 UTC on July 21, Armstrong stepped out of the lunar module onto the moon's surface, closely followed by Aldrin—Collins remaining behind in the command module.

Space food had improved a great deal in the eight years since Yuri Gagarin became the first man in orbit (see April 12). The Apollo 11 astronauts had a range of food choices in individual meal packs, and they were much more recognizable as real food than the early aluminium tubes of paste. The food was presented in various forms indicated by the legends R (rehydratable), DB (dry bite), WP (wet pack), IMB (intermediate moisture bite), and SBP (spoon bowl packet).

Armstrong and Aldrin ate two meals during their excursion to the moon and back in the lunar module.

There were additional items aboard the lunar module, and these included extra beverages, dried fruit, candy bars, bread, ham salad (tube), and two wet packs of turkey and gravy.

## Lunar Module

| MEAL A | MEAL B |
|---|---|
| Bacon squares (8) (IMB) | Beef Stew (R) |
| Peaches (R) | Cream of chicken soup (R) |
| Sugar cookie cubs (6) (DB) | Date fruit cake (4) (IMB) |
| Coffee (R) | Grape Punch (R) |
| Pineapple-grapefruit drink (R) | Orange drink (R) |

## Meals aboard the Command Module

| DAY 1 AND DAY 5 (21st) | DAY 2 (18th) | DAY 3 (19th) | DAY 4 (20th) |
|---|---|---|---|
| MEAL A (breakfast) | | | |
| Peaches (R) | Fruit cocktail (R) | Peaches (R) | Canadian bacon and applesauce (R) |
| Bacon Squares (8) (IMB) | Sausage Patties (SBP) | Bacon squares (8) (IMB) | Sugar coated corn flakes (R) |
| Strawberry Cubes (4) (DB) | Cinnamon toasted bread cubes (4) (DB) | Apricot cereal (4) (db) | Cocoa (R) |
| Grape Drink (R) | Cocoa (R) | Grape Drink (R) | Orange-grapefruit drink (R) |
| Orange Drink (R) | Grapefruit Drink (R) | Orange Drink (R) | |
| MEAL B | | | |
| Beef and potatoes (WP) | Frankfurters (WP) | Cream of Chicken soup (R) | Shrimp cocktail (R) |
| Butterscotch pudding (R) | Applesauce (R) | Turkey and Gravy (WP) | Ham and potatoes (WP) |
| Brownies (4) (IMB) | Chocolate Pudding (R) | Chocolate Pudding (R) | Fruit Cocktail (R) |
| Grape punch (R) | Orange-grapefruit drink (R) | Orange-grapefruit drink (R) | Date fruit cake (4) (IMB) |
| | | | Grapefruit drink (R) |
| MEAL C | | | |
| Salmon salad (R) | Spaghetti with meat sauce (SBP) | Tuna sala (R) | Beef Stew (WP) |
| Chicken and rice (SBP) | Pork and scalloped potatoes (SBP) | Chicken stew (SBP) | Coconut cubes (4) (DB) |
| Sugar cookie cubes (6) (DB) | Pineapple fruit cake (IMB) | Butterscotch pudding (R) | Banana pudding (R) |
| Cocoa (R) | Grape punch (R) | Cocoa (R) | Grape punch (R) |
| Pineapple-grapefruit drink (R) | | Grapefruit drink (R) | |

There are special problems associated with eating in space. There is no refrigeration, so food must be preserved in other ways. Fuel must be conserved as much as possible. The zero gravity situation means that droplets of water and food crumbs can float around and cause all sorts of problems with equipment. The confined space and great risks mean an increased risk of tension—and food being one way of reducing stress, the psychological benefits of having a range of familiar food is very important. All meals must also fulfil calorie and nutritional requirements.

The entire meal plan for the command module indicates how these problems were addressed during the Apollo 11 flight. The dining plan began with Meal B on day 1 (the astronauts having had breakfast before takeoff.)

## July 22

Royal Wedding Breakfast
Buckingham Palace, London, England, 1896

Princess Maud of Wales (1869–1938), the granddaughter of Queen Victoria, married her first cousin, Prince Carl of Denmark (1872–1957), the future King Haakon VII of Norway, on July 22, 1896. The public celebrations surrounding the wedding were, as would be expected, at a lower key than that of her older brother and heir to the throne (the future George V) three years earlier, but in spite of the minimal street decorations, the newspapers had much to report. Princess Maud was popular and beautiful and looked ''collected and self-possessed,'' and her groom was handsome in his military uniform, and the sun shone all day. Queen Victoria had managed to marry off yet another of her descendants into another royal house of Europe, and the diplomatic alliance was unquestionably sensible and useful.

The ceremony was carried out in the chapel at Buckingham Palace, and the wedding breakfast followed.

---

POTAGES.
A la Princess.
Vermicelle à la Windsor.

ENTRÉES (CHAUDES).
Côtelettes d'Agneau à l'Italienne.
Aiguillettes de Canetons aux pois.

RELEVÉS.
Filets de Bœuf à la Napolitaine.
Poulets gras au Cressons.

ENTRÉES (FROIDES)
Chaudfroids de Volaille sur Croûtes.
Salades d'Homard.
Jambons decoupés à l'Aspic.
Langues decoupés à l'Aspic.
Mayonnaises de Volaille.
Roulades de Veau à la Gelée.

---

—

Haricots verts.     Epinards.

—

Gelées et Crêmes.

It is always interesting to see what is chosen for important feasts when money is no object. This menu was fine and classic, without any vulgar novelties or surprises. There were no dishes especially created for the day—the *Potage à la Princess* had been created in honor of the bride's mother, Princess Alexandra of Denmark, before her own wedding in 1863, and the *Vermicelle à la Windsor* was one version of the classic Windsor soup invented by Queen Victoria's chef Charles Elmé Francatelli (see April 9).

Even though this was a royal wedding breakfast, it was held at lunchtime and would have been a little less formal than at dinner. The number of cold dishes also suggests a summer lunchtime meal.

## Recipes

~~~

*Aiguillettes* are thin strips or slices. Using this preparation of duck would have made for easier serving than using whole duck, which would then have needed carving.

### Braized Ducks, with Stewed Peas

Braize the ducks as directed in the foregoing case [see below], and when done, dish them up with stewed peas round them; sauce with a brown sauce in which some of the broth from the ducks has been reduced. They may also be prepared as follows: Put two ounces of butter in a stewpan on the fire when melted, add two tablespoonfuls of flour, and stir this over the fire until the roux becomes of a fawn-colour; then add a quart of good broth or gravy, carefully working the whole while mixing. Stir this sauce on the fire, and when it boils, put the ducks trussed for boiling into it, and also a quart of young peas, and a faggot of parsley and green onions. Allow these to stew very gently by the side of the stove for about an hour; when the ducks are done, take them out of the sauce, skim off all the grease, remove the faggot of parsley; and if there is too much sauce, boil it down to its proper consistency, pour the peas and sauce over the ducks, previously dished up, and serve.

### Braized Ducks

They should be trussed in the usual way, and placed in an oval stewpan with a carrot, an onion stuck with two cloves, and a garnished faggot of parsley; moisten with sufficient white stock to cover the ducks, put a buttered paper over them and set them to boil gently on a slow fire for about an hour.

Charles Elmé Francatelli, *The Modern Cook* (1846).

Chaud-froid: see July 25.
Poulets Gras au Cressons: see February 21.

## July 23

Luncheon after the Fire
Hotel St. Francis, San Francisco, California, 1906

The Hotel St. Francis opened on March 21, 1904, and was immediately recognized as one of the finest hotels in the world. Two years later, early in the morning of April 18, 1906, San Francisco suffered a devastating earthquake that was quickly followed by an even more devastating fire. It is said that the Hotel St. Francis was the last building to catch fire, and it was one of the few to survive—severely damaged but with its structure intact.

Repair and restoration of the hotel began immediately. In the amazingly short time of a little over four months, it was open again for business on July 23 in the form of the St. Francis Annex—a temporary structure, "fitted with all modern conveniences," built in the center of Union Square park. The first meal in the new hotel was a luncheon held on this day by the Californian Promotion Committee.

---

Grapefruit

Essence of Chicken, in cups

Celery    Salted Almonds    Olives

Fillet of Striped Bass, Meuniere
Cleo Potatoes

Broiled Squab on Toast
Lettuce and Tomato Salad

Fancy Ice Cream

Assorted Cakes

Coffee

St. Francis Cocktail
St. Francis White Seal
Baron R. De Luze Dry Comet
Apollinaris

---

The chef of the Hotel St. Francis from 1904–1926 was Victor Hirtzler (ca. 1875–1935), a gifted and theatrical man who had worked for Tsar Nicholas II and King Don Carlos of Portugal. San Francisco was already noted for its food, but Hirtzler almost single-handedly elevated its culinary reputation to one of the finest food cities in the world. He prided himself on offering a vast array of dishes to the hotel guests: there were 203 different choices amongst the egg dishes for example. Like celebrity chefs before and since, Hirtzler also published a cookbook, which he named in honor of the hotel, as he explained in the preface:

I have named my book *The Hotel St. Francis Cook Book* in compliment to the house which has given me in so generous measure the opportunity to produce and reproduce, always with the object of reflecting a cuisine that is the best possible.

## Recipes

~~~

---

### Essence of chicken

Put in a casserole one chopped raw fowl, or plenty of carcasses, necks, etc., of raw chickens. Add the whites of three eggs, stir well, and add slowly two quarts of strong chicken broth. Bring to a boil, strain through a napkin, and serve in cups.

---

### Sauce Meunière

This is a butter sauce and is principally used for fish.

Place the fish or meat on a platter and sprinkle with a little salt and pepper, chopped parsley and the juice of a lemon. Heat in frying pan four ounces of butter to a hazelnut color and pour over the dish.

---

### Cléo Potatoes

Cut raw potatoes in pear shapes the size of an egg, parboil in salt water, then put in a well-buttered pan pointed end up, sprinkle with melted butter and roast in oven, basting all the time till brown. When done, salt and serve on napkin, garnished with parsley.

---

### Broiled Squab

Split the squab, season well, roll in oil and broil. Serve on a piece of freshly-made toast, cover with maitre d'hotel sauce, and garnish with half a lemon and watercress.

*Maitre d'hôtel sauce.* One-quarter pound of fresh butter, juice of one lemon, and chopped parsley. Mix well. This sauce is not to be used hot.

Victor Hirtzler, *The Hotel St. Francis Cook Book* (1919 edition).

---

Salted Almonds: see April 3.

## July 24

### Dining with Marie-Antoinette
### Le Petit Trianon, Versailles, France, 1788

Marie-Antoinette (1755–1793) was an Austrian Archduchess who became Queen of France only a few years after she had married the future Louis

XVI of France in 1770, at the age of 14. Marie-Antoinette has probably been unfairly treated by history, which has judged her guilty of a lifetime of lavish expenditure, frivolous lifestyle, and a lack of concern about her subjects. She has certainly been cleared of uttering the infamous phrase ''let them eat cake'' when she heard of the hungry at the gates, asking for bread—the story was part of the postrevolutionary anti-royalist propaganda.

The young king gave his wife the small château known as the Petit Trianon in the grounds of the Palace of Versailles for her personal use and pleasure. It had been built originally for Mme. de Pompadour, the mistress of his grandfather, Louis XV. Marie-Antoinette certainly made the Petit Trianon her place of escape. No one could enter without her express permission (even, it is said, her own husband), and it was here that she could play at being a country shepherdess. The meals, of course, were anything but in the rural peasant style, as this menu for July 24, 1788, shows.

QUATRE POTAGES
Le riz
Le Scheiber
Les croutons aux laitues
Les croutons unis pour Madame.

DEUX GRANDES ENTRÉES
La pièce de bœuf aux choux
La longe de veau à la broche.

SEIZE ENTRÉES
Les pâtés à l'espagnol
Les côtelettes de mouton grillées
Les hatelets de lapereaux
Les ailes de poulardes à la maréchale
Les abatis de dindon au consommé
Les carrés de mouton piqués à la chicorée
Le dindon poele à la ravigote
Le ris de veau au papillote
La tête de veau sauce pointue
Les poulets à la tartare
Le cochon de lait à la broche
La poule de Caux au consommé
Le caneton de Rouen à l'orange
Les filets de poularde en casserole au riz
Le poulet froid
La blanquette de poularde aux concombres

QUATRE HORS-D'ŒUVRE
Les filets de lapereaux
Le carré de veau à la broche
Le jarret de veau au consommé
Le dindonneau froid

---

DIX PLATS DE ROTS
Les poulets
Le chapon pané
Le levraut
Le dindonneau
Les perdreaux
Les lapreaux

SEIZE PETITS ENTREMETS [not detailed]

---

This was the typical meal structure in aristocratic France at the time, with a strictly even number of dishes in each course, with great symmetry in the overall numbers.

## Recipes

~~~

*Hatelets* or *Atelets* are ornamental silver skewers. Meat for hatelets was usually coated with egg and breadcrumbs before grilling or frying, and eventually the word also came to apply to this sauce or coating.

*Levereaux* are hares. The following recipe specifies rabbit, but hare (or any other meat) can be substituted.

---

### Rabbits, en Hatelet

Cut up your rabbits, and stew them with half a glass of white wine, some broth, a bunch of herbs, salt and whole pepper. When they are done, and the sauce reduced so as to hang about the meat, let them cool, and put them upon small skewers; wet them with an egg beat up, and grate bread over them; then, dip them in their fat, and grate bread over them a second time, and grill them; serve them dry upon the skewers.

François Menon, *The French Family Cook (Cuisine Bourgeoise)* (1793).

---

*Ravigote sauce*, here served with the turkey (*dindon*), is a bright green sauce that has been popular for centuries. The name comes from the French verb *ravigoter,* meaning to cheer or revive. This quality supposedly comes from the four herbs it traditionally contained—tarragon, chervil, chives, and burnet, all of which are considered restorative. There are several versions, depending on whether it is to be served warm (as here) or cold (a vinaigrette style).

---

### Sauce Ravigote

Chop a Clove of Garlick, Charvil [Chervil], Burnet, Taragon, Garden Cresses, Civet, all in proportion to their Flavour; when well washed and squeezed, infuse it with a little Cullis without boiling; sift it with Expression; then add a Bit of

> Butter, Flour, Pepper, and Salt, boil it to a good Consistence and add a Lemon Squeeze sufficient to make it relishing or tart tasted.
> François Menon, *The Professed Cook* (1769).

Le caneton de Rouen à l'orange (Duck with orange): see January 21.

## July 25

### Dinner for the Shah of Persia
### Royal Palace, Turin, Italy, 1873

In 1873, the longest-reigning royal ruler in the history of Persia (Iran), Nasser al-Din Shah Qajar (1831–1896) became the first Persian monarch to visit Europe. Naturally, while in Italy he was the guest of King Victor Emmanuel (1820–1878) and his family. The visit caused great excitement, not least amongst the press who avidly reported every detail of the tour. *The Times* correspondent in Italy included the menu of one of the state dinners at the royal palace in Turin.

---

Potage.—Sagon à l'Impériale.
(Maigre.) Princess aux écroûtons.
Petits patés à la Russe et aguilletes de soles.
Truites à la Jean Bart; sauce Américaine.
Filet de bœuf à l'Anglaise; sauce Madère.
Crepinettes d'estourgeon; sauce Genoise.
Suprême de poulard à la Rohan.
Chaudfroid de cailles à la Parisienne.
Fonds d'artichauts garnis, haricots à l'Allemande.
Vins.—Xeres, 1824; Château Margau.

HORS D'ŒUVRES.
Canapés de caviar à la Russe et jambonneau de pintades.
(Maigre)—Mayonnaise de bar en Bellevue.
Vins.—Johannisberger de la cave de Metternich.
Punch à la Romaine.
(Rôt.) Faisans piqués et ortolans; bouquetin; salade.
Savarin au noyau.
Suedoise garnie de fruit.
Croquembouche de pastilles d'abricot.

DESSERT.
(Glacés.) Ecume de chocolat à l'Espagnole; Framboise;
Cedrat.
(Tokay, 1670)

---

Journalists do not of course simply confine themselves to reporting facts. The event was an irresistible opportunity for English and European newspapers to make patriotic and jingoistic comments. *The Times* reporter noted that "The Italian papers amuse themselves with long particulars respecting the habits of the Shah and his numerous suite the justice they continue to do to Christian meals, notwithstanding their alleged preference for the messes of their private orthodox cookery." ("Messes" in this case not being pejorative, but referring to "servings"—see January 6.)

The European newspapers could also not be expected to resist noting that the roasted *"bouquetin"* (*stambecco*, or *chamois*) appearing on the menu was killed by King Victor Emmanuel himself at Valdieri (in the Piedmont region), adding "It is thus that those who can dine in Italy."

Other than the special royal contribution, this menu was typical of a high-class dinner in Europe at the time. The most expensive ingredients were sturgeon, caviar, and ortolans, the most visually pleasing presentations— the *suedoise*, *chaud-froid* (see recipe here) and *croque-en-bouche*, and the classic garnishes and sauces, with punch and the finest wines served at the exactly correct moments. The day being a Friday, there were also several *"maigre"* (meatless) options for those adhering strictly to the rules of the Catholic Church.

## Recipes

~~~

Chaud-froid literally means warm-cold. There are various meanings in cooking.

The classic chaud-froid is made from boneless poultry cooled then coated in a jellied white, pink, or brown sauce. Chauds-froid were very popular at nineteenth-century dinners partly because they could be prepared well in advance, but also because they were highly decorative, the glazed and garnished meat often being arranged in a spectacular pyramid on an elevated dish.

The *366 Menus and 1200 Recipes of the Baron Brisse* (1868; English translation 1905) gives the method of making a chaud-froid of partridge. The method is exactly the same for a chaud-froid of quail.

---

### Chaud-Froid de Perdreaux

Roast your partridges, fillet them; pound all the meat off the carcasses in a mortar with truffles and mushrooms; simmer the bones in a tumblerful of white wine, season with truffle trimmings, eschalots, and a laurel leaf; leave on the fire until reduced to about three quarters the quantity; squeeze through a cloth, add two tablespoons of clear stock to it, stir half of this sauce into the pounded meat, mix it thoroughly with a wooden spoon in a saucepan until it boils, pass through a tammy, and leave till cold. Place the fillets round an entrée dish with slices of truffle, cut the same shape, between each one; fill the centre with the purée, cover the whole with the remainder of the sauce, and garnish round with clear meat jelly.

---

Croque-en-bouche means, literally, "crisp in the mouth." It refers to a pyramid of sweets decorated with a spun sugar coating that provides the crunch. Today they are made (often for weddings) with *profiteroles*—small buns made of choux paste (see November 7), but in the nineteenth century they were often made from caramelized fruits, such as the apricots in this case.

Punch à la Romaine (Roman punch): see July 1.
Sauce Madeira: see February 28.
Suedoise: see December 26.

## July 26

Lunch aboard the Royal Yacht
*Maha-Chakri*, Copenhagen, Denmark, 1897

His Majesty the King of Siam Chulalongkorn (1853–1910), also known as Rama V and "The Great Beloved King," was the first Siamese (Thai) king to visit Europe (and Russia) when he made a nine-month tour in 1897. On July 26 he and his retinue were aboard the royal yacht in Copenhagen harbor.

---

DEJEUNER
*

Hors d'oeuvres
Consomme double en tasse
Homard a la Parisienne
Gigot de Pres-sale a la Danoise
Chaud-Froid de volaille a la Siamoise
Sarcelles sur canape
Coeur do laitue
Bombe Royale
Palmier
Deserts and Fruits

---

At first glance this would seem to be a very European menu for a nineteenth-century king of Thailand. The "gold standard" for those diplomatic dinners attended by Europeans even in Asia had been European style for a long time. Chulalongkorn's father, King Mongkut, was determined to bring the technological advances of the West to his country and to that end had hired English tutors for his 80-odd children by his 39 wives. Once he became king himself, Chulalongkorn sent many of his sons, brothers, and nephews to school in England.

The menu does contain dishes *à la Danoise* and *à la Siamoise*, suggesting that this was indeed a diplomatic dinner, and both host and guest countries were to be acknowledged. This produces an intriguing scenario at this dinner—the king of Siam sitting down to a European dish styled *à la Siamoise*.

Classic French cuisine has many dishes named for particular countries or regions. They represent what the adapting country saw as the quintessential features of the local cuisine they were acknowledging. Sometimes this is obvious—such as dishes *à la Perigeux* or Perigord style, which always contains truffles, which the region is famous for, but often it is less obvious, and there is little consistency across recipes with the same name.

## Recipes

~~~

*Sarcelles* are teals. Small birds (grouse, snipe, squab, woodcock, etc.) were often served on a *canapé*, which originally meant a piece of toast (see January 21). The following recipe specifies grouse, but the method is the same for any small bird.

---

### Grouse, Roasted Plain

Singe, draw, wipe, and truss two fine fat grouse. Place them in a roasting-pan with half a cupful of water, spread a little butter over each, and season with a pinch of salt. Put them into a brisk oven, and let cook for eighteen minutes, taking care to baste frequently with their own gravy; then untruss. Have a hot serving-dish ready; place two bread canapes [below] on it; arrange the grouse over, and decorate the dish with a little watercress. Strain the gravy into a sauce-bowl, and serve it separately.

---

### Canapes for Game

Cut out the desired number of canapes from a loaf of American bread (a stale one is preferable) one and a half inches thick. Trim neatly, pare off the crusts; then cut out a piece in the centre of each, from end to end, so that the cavity will hold the bird easily when sending to the table. Spread a little butter over them, place on a tin plate; then brown in the hot oven until they obtain a good golden color. Remove from out the oven, arrange them on a hot dish, and they will be ready to serve.

  Alexander Filippini, *The Delmonico Cook Book : How to Buy Food, How to Cook It, and How to Serve It* (ca. 1890).

---

Alexis Soyer gave a recipe for Pork Cutlets à la Siamoise in his book *The Gastronomic Regenerator*, published in 1847. This is the sauce recipe.

---

### Sauce ``à la Siamoise''

Peel forty button onions, then put half a teaspoonful of sugar in a stewpan, and place it over the fire; when melted and beginning to brown, add two ounces of butter and the onions keep tossing them over the fire until they get rather brown, add a pint of brown sauce, and half the quantity of consomme; let boil on the corner of the stove till the onions are done, keeping it well skimmed, the onions must be tender but not broke. Take them out carefully with a colander spoon and place them in a clean stewpan; reduce the sauce till it adheres to the back of the spoon, add a tablespoonful of French mustard, and pass it through a tammie over the onions; have also twenty little balls the size of marbles, cut from some gherkins, which put in the sauce, warm altogether, but do not boil, dress the onions and gherkins in the centre, sauce over and serve.

Chaud-froid: see July 25.

## July 27

### Lunch En Route to the Canal Zone
### aboard the SS *Colon,* 1908

Until the completion of the Panama Canal in 1914, the only way to sail between the Atlantic and Pacific Oceans and avoid the treacherous Cape Horn (and more than halve the distance) was to cross the narrow Isthmus of Panama by train. The Panama Railroad Steamship Line owned five steam ships, one of which was the SS *Colon,* to carry its passengers to its rail links. The SS *Colon* traveled between New York and the railroad company's Atlantic terminus of Colón (Aspinwall). On July 27, passengers sat down to the following luncheon.

White Onions    Bean Soup    Chow Chow
Baked Pork and Beans
Mutton Stew    Currrant Fritters
Baked Potatoes
Stewed Prunes    Baked Apples
Tea, Cake, Coffee
Cold Cuts to Order
Roast Beef    Roast Mutton
Boiled Veal    Corned Beef
Ham    Tongue    Sardines
Corned Pork    Bologna    Smoked Salmon
Cold Slaw
American, Edam, Roquefort Cheese
Assorted Crackers.

This was a substantial but simple meal, and it is likely that it did not vary a great deal each day. There are no fancy dishes and the menu is written in English. There are no delicate or fragile fresh ingredients. The apples, potatoes, onions, and the cabbage for the coleslaw—or "cold slaw" as it is called on this menu (see July 20) are all capable of prolonged storage without spoiling. Guests who so desired had the choice of enlivening their abundant plain meats with chow-chow, a very popular mixed vegetable pickle.

## Recipes

~~~

---

### Chow-Chow (Superior English Recipe)

This excellent pickle is seldom made at home, as we can get the imported article so much better than it can be made from the usual recipes. This we vouch for as being as near the genuine article as can be made: One quart of young, tiny cucumbers, not over two inches long, two quarts of very small white onions, two quarts of tender string beans, each one cut in halves, three quarts of green tomatoes, sliced and chopped very coarsely, two fresh heads of cauliflower, cut into small pieces, or two heads of white, hard cabbage.

After preparing these articles, put them in a stone jar, mix them together, sprinkling salt between them sparingly. Let them stand twenty-four hours, then drain off all the brine that has accumulated. Now put these vegetables in a preserving kettle over the fire, sprinkling through them an ounce of turmeric for coloring, six red peppers, chopped coarsely, four tablespoonfuls of mustard seed, two of celery seed, two of whole allspice, two of whole cloves, a coffee cup of sugar, and two-thirds of a teacup of best ground mixed mustard. Pour on enough of the best cider vinegar to cover the whole well; cover tightly and simmer all well until it is cooked all through and seems tender, watching and stirring it often. Put in bottles or glass jars. It grows better as it grows older, especially if sealed when hot.

---

### Currant Fritters

Two cupfuls dry, fine, bread-crumbs, two tablespoonfuls of prepared flour, two cups of milk, one-half pound currants, washed and well-dried, five eggs whipped very light, one-half cup powdered sugar, one tablespoonful butter, one half teaspoonful mixed cinnamon and nutmeg. Boil the milk and pour over the bread. Mix and put in the butter. Let it get cold. Beat in next the yolks and sugar, the seasoning, flour, and stiff whites; finally, the currants dredged whitely with flour. The batter should be thick. Drop in great spoonfuls into the hot lard and fry. Drain them and send hot to table. Eat with a mixture of wine and powdered sugar.

---

### Bologna Sausage

Two pounds of lean pork, two pounds of lean veal, two pounds of fresh lean beef, two pounds of fat salt pork, one pound beef suet, ten tablespoonfuls of powdered sage, one ounce each of parsley, savory, marjoram and thyme, mixed. Two teaspoonfuls of cayenne pepper, the same of black, one grated nutmeg, one teaspoonful of cloves, one minced onion, salt to taste. Chop or grind the meat and suet; season, and stuff into beef skins; tie these up, prick each in several places to allow the escape of steam; put into hot, not boiling water, and heat gradually to the boiling point. Cook slowly for one hour; take out the skins and lay them to dry in the sun, upon clean, sweet straw or hay. Rub the outside of the skins with oil or melted butter, and place in a cool, dry cellar. If you wish to keep them more

> than a week, rub ginger or pepper on the outside, then wash it off before using. This is eaten without further cooking. Cut in round slices and lay sliced lemon around the edge of the dish, as many like to squeeze a few drops upon the sausage before eating. These are very nice smoked like hams.
>   F. L. Gillette, *White House Cookbook* (1887).

Baked Apples: see December 14.

## July 28

### First Annual Dinner of the First Vegetarian Society of England
### Manchester, England, 1848

The Vegetarian Society of the United Kingdom was formed in September 1847, at a meeting held at a vegetarian hospital in Ramsgate, Kent. The first annual meeting was held the following year in Manchester, and 232 attendees (almost half the membership) sat down to a dinner devoid of both animal flesh and "intoxicating beverages." *The Globe* newspaper recorded the feast with great interest.

> FIRST COURSE: Large savoury omelet, vegetables, rice fritters, vegetables, beetroot; onion and sage fritters, vegetables, savoury pie; mushroom pie, vegetables, bread and parsley fritters; beetroot, vegetables, force-meat fritters, vegetables, large macaroni omelet; water the only beverage.
>
> SECOND COURSE: Plum pudding, moulded rice, almonds and raisins, cheesecakes, figs; custards, grapes, flummery; sponge cakes, red and white currants, moulded sago, fruit tarts; water the only beverage.

The word "vegetarian" had been in use for about a decade (the more common term had been "Pythagoreans," after the famous Greek philosopher and mathematician who espoused such a diet), but the formation of the new society consolidated "vegetarian" as the name of choice for those who elected to abstain from eating the flesh of animals.

Throughout history individuals and small groups have avoided animal flesh for a variety of reasons, but it was an uncommon choice (amongst those with the economic freedom to choose) until the nineteenth century. The early movement was driven by Christian religious groups and was underpinned by the philosophy that it was spiritually bankrupt to kill animals for food. It was associated with the high moral ground in other, less obvious ways too. Vegetarians of the time (as at this dinner) almost always abstained from alcohol, and many also from all condiments including salt. The rationale for the avoidance of condiments is not clear, but it does appear that they were considered too stimulating. The argument is reminiscent of the ancient humoral theory (see February 23) that explained the medieval prohibition of meat on days of particular religious observance, that it was "heating" and therefore stimulated the passions (and especially lust).

## Recipes

~~~

---

### Root, Herb, and Other Savoury Pies

Potatoes two pounds onions two ounces; butter one ounce; water half a pint. Pare and cut the potatoes; put a layer of onions cut small between the layers of potatoes; season with pepper and salt; lay the butter at the top in small pieces pour in the water cover the whole with paste and bake.

The onions may be replaced by mushrooms cut small. Hard boiled eggs cut in slices or small pieces may be distributed between the layers. Half an ounce of tapioca or sago is an improvement; these should be well washed and steeped in cold water before they are added; or they may be reduced to a jelly and added to the pie when baked. When mushrooms are not used, the flavour may be improved by the addition of a little ketchup which may either be added when the pie is made, or poured in with a little melted butter, etc., after the pie has been baked. Some add a little celery or powdered sage, sliced turnips, carrots, asparagus or other vegetables.

---

### Fritters (``Other Kinds'')

Bread crumbs four ounces boiling water or milk half pint; eggs two to four; butter half an ounce. Pour the boiling fluid upon the bread crumbs, and let them soak one hour; beat the mixture with a fork removing all hard pieces add the beaten eggs and butter; and if intended to be sweet, add from two to four ounces of sugar, and a little lemon rind and juice; also if preferred three ounces of currants or four of chopped apples or other fruit, and fry. If intended to be savoury, substitute for the sugar etc., onions previously boiled in two or three waters and chopped small, two to four ounces; oatmeal one ounce; sage one tea spoonful; lemon thyme and sweet marjoram half a tea spoonful of each; a little pepper and salt. Mix the whole well, adding more fluid when necessary; fry and serve up with brown sauce.

This mixture may also be baked whole as an omelet, in a buttered dish.

John Smith, *The Principles and Practice of Vegetarian Cookery* (1860).

---

Sponge Cake: see May 14.

## July 29

### Royal Wedding Breakfast for Prince Charles and Lady Diana
### Buckingham Palace, London, England, 1981

When Prince Charles (b. 1948), the heir to the throne of England, married Lady Diana Spencer (1961–1997) in Westminster Abbey on July 29, 1981, the event was watched around the world. The ceremony finished at 12:10 P.M., and the royal party returned to Buckingham Palace, where, after their public appearance on the balcony, they sat down to the traditional wedding breakfast. Visiting heads of state (hereditary monarchs and elected presidents) and important political figures were entertained by the prime minister at in informal lunch at the Bank of England—the wedding breakfast itself was a private affair for 120 guests made up of family members and close friends.

The menu, prepared by the palace staff, was elegant and light as was appropriate for a summer lunch after an exhausting and no doubt stressful morning. Only one dish was specially created—a chicken dish named in honor of the new Princess of Wales.

---

Quenelles de Barbue Cardinal,
(*Brill in Lobster Sauce*)

Suprême de Volaille Princesse de Galles,
(*Chicken Breasts stuffed with Lamb Mousse,
coated in brioche crumbs and fried in butter*)

Fève au Beurre, Maïs à la Crème, Pommes Nouvelles,
(*Buttered Beans, Creamed Corn, New Potatoes*)

Salade
(*Salad*)

Fraises et Crème Caillée
(*Strawberries with Cornish Cream*)

Wine
Brauneberger Juffer Spatlese 1976
Chateau Latour 1959
Krug 1969
Taylor's Port 1955

---

The total cost of this simple luncheon for 120 guests was $40,000—but that did include the five-tier wedding cake.

---

### Facts about The Royal Wedding Cake

The cooks were Chief Petty Officer David Avery who was assisted by Training Officer Lieutenant Motley at the Royal Navy Cookery School.

Every single nut and piece of dried fruit was hand picked, a process that took two days and was code-named "Operation Sultana."

Navy Rum was included in the recipe.

It was made nearly three months before the event, to allow it to mature.

The cake had five tiers; the largest layer took 8 1/2 hours to cook and measured 4 1/2 feet in diameter.

The cake weighed 224 lbs. (49 lbs. of which were in the marzipan and icing).

It was decorated with the interwoven initials "C" and "D," sugar flowers, sugar doves, and Naval insignia.

Prince Charles cut the cake with his ceremonial sword.

## Recipes

~~~

Lobster sauce has been a traditional accompaniment to fish such as brill for a long time.

### Lobster Sauce,
### to Serve with Turbot, Salmon, Brill, &c.

(Very Good.)
1 middling-sized hen lobster,
3/4 pint of melted butter,
1 tablespoonful of anchovy sauce,
1/2 oz. of butter,
salt and cayenne to taste,
a little pounded mace when liked,
2 or 3 tablespoonfuls of cream.

Choose a hen lobster, as this is indispensable, in order to render this sauce as good as it ought to be. Pick the meat from the shells, and cut it into small square pieces; put the spawn, which will be found under the tail of the lobster, into a mortar with 1/2 oz. of butter, and pound it quite smooth; rub it through a hair-sieve, and cover up till wanted. Make 3/4 pint of melted butter [see next recipe]; put in all the ingredients except the lobster-meat, and well mix the sauce before the lobster is added to it, as it should retain its square form, and not come to table shredded and ragged. Put in the meat, let it get thoroughly hot, but do not allow it to boil, as the colour would immediately be spoiled; for it should be remembered that this sauce should always have a bright red appearance. If it is intended to be served with turbot or brill, a little of the spawn (dried and rubbed through a sieve without butter) should be saved to garnish with; but as the goodness, flavour, and appearance of the sauce so much depend on having a proper quantity of spawn, the less used for garnishing the better.

### Melted Butter (Sauce)

1/4 lb. of butter,
a dessertspoonful of flour,
1 wineglassful of water,
salt to taste.

Cut the butter up into small pieces, put it in a saucepan, dredge over the flour, and add the water and a seasoning of salt; stir it one way constantly till the whole of the ingredients are melted and thoroughly blended. Let it just boil, when it is ready to serve. If the butter is to be melted with cream, use the same quantity as of water, but omit the flour; keep stirring it, but do not allow it to boil.
*Beeton's Household Manual* (1861).

## July 30

### Banquet Honoring Howard Hughes
### Rice Hotel, Houston, Texas, 1938

Howard Hughes (1905–1976) was an American engineer, industrialists, film producer, philanthropist, and passionate aviator, and one of the world's wealthiest men. An eccentric billionaire can, by definition, indulge any of his whims, but Hughes in spite of his wealth was a tortured soul. He was phobic about germs all his life, and as a result avoided a great deal of normal, everyday social contact such as shaking hands, and he had to pick everything up with paper towels. The severity of his symptoms fluctuated but he may well have suffered from obsessive-compulsive disorder. Many of his anxieties and obsessive behaviors centered around food; he would eat the same foods for months on end, then change his preferences without any warning; he gave his staff elaborate rituals about opening cans of food; at times he would sort the peas on his plate according to size; his food was cooked with a stop-watch and if there was the shortest delay between cooking and serving the staff would have to throw out the meal and start over.

Hughes was often invited to banquets and dinners by groups wishing to honor him for his achievements, or prevail upon him for donations or investment. Presumably when he was in the grip of his social anxiety and food phobia he refused those invitations. On July 30, 1938, he (and his "intrepid crew") did attend a dinner given "in celebration of his just completed Round-The-World air flight publicizing the World's Fair to be held in New York City" and in recognition of "Their RemarkableFlight Around the World, and in Appreciation of Their Invaluable Contribution to the Scientific Development of Commercial Aviation." The dinner was given by "his Fellow Townsmen of Houston, Texas," and sponsored by the Houston Chamber of Commerce.

---

MENU

Cantaloupe and Watermelon, Parisienne.
Hearts of Colorado Celery. Ripe and Green Jumbo Olives.
Smothered Chicken on Toast.
Potatoes au Gratin. New Butter Beans.
Lettuce, Tomato, Asparagus Tips Salad, French Dressing.
Ice Cream à la Howard.
Cakes.
Coffee and Cream.

---

Hughes's tastes were known to be for plain food, and this menu certainly is not fancy or fussy. The ice cream is named in his honor, although the flavor is not mentioned. He was very fond of ice cream and remained faithful to one flavor for a long time before suddenly changing it. There is a famous story about his developing a passion for Baskin-Robbins' banana nut ice cream just as the company discontinued it. His staff made a special order for the minimum amount of 350 gallons, but by the time it was delivered, Hughes had changed his preference to French vanilla.

## Recipes
~~~

---

### Smothered Chicken

1 broiler chicken about 2 1/2 pounds
4 tablespoons butter
2 tablespoons flour
1–2 teaspoon salt
1 pint milk

Put chicken in greased shallow pan, skin side down, and sprinkle lightly with salt. Prepare a sauce of butter, flour, salt and milk. Pour sauce over chicken and cook in moderate oven 1 hour. Turn chicken and continue cooking 1–2 hour longer or until tender and lightly browned
*Chillicothe Constitution-Tribune*, June 12, 1936.

---

### Potatoes au Gratin

Grease a baking dish. Arrange slices of cold boiled potatoes on bottom. Sprinkle with grated cheese, salt and pepper. Dot with butter. Repeat process until all materials needed are used. Add enough milk to almost cover the top later. Bake in hot oven (400° F.) 20 to 25 minutes. Allow one medium sized potato per serving.
*The Lily Wallace New American Cookbook* (1946).

---

One of Hughes's long-term favorite ice cream flavors was cherry.

---

### Cherry Ice Cream

One cup cherry juice, drained from can of sour, pitted, very red cherries;
2–3 cups sweetened condensed milk;
one teaspoon lemon juice;
1–2 cup cherry pulp measured after being put through food chopper,
1 cup whipping cream.

Blend sweetened condensed milk, cherry juice, and lemon juice thoroughly. Add measured cherry pulp. Chill. Whip cream to custard-like consistency and fold into chilled mixture. Pour into freezing pan of automatic refrigerator. Place in freezing unit. After mixture is about half frozen, remove from refrigerator. Scrape mixture from sides and bottom of pan. Beat until smooth but not until melted. Smooth out and replace in freezing tray until frozen for servings.
*Chillicothe Constitution-Tribune*, July 2, 1936.

**July 31**

King's Dinner
France, 1826

A correspondent to the *Dublin Literary Gazette* in 1830 included in his letter an extract from the French journal *Voleur*. The article contained details of the French royal family dinners, and the correspondent commented:

> A man of letters has pretended that we might judge the manners of a nation by the luxury or frugality of the great. If this opinion is well founded, the following document is precious for the history of its old monarchy, of the republic, and the restoration. We merely guarantee the facts, and leave it to moralists to appreciated the consequences.

The monarch in question was Charles X, and another of the menus from the article is featured on April 4. The royal family dinner on July 31 was according to the following bill of fare:

---

Croûtons aux racines.
Pâté de cailles.
Ailes de canetons aux navets.
Marinade de poulets aux epinards.
Côtelette de mouton panée.
Filet de poularde aux olives.
Brioche.
Haricots blancs.
Poule de Caux.
Œufs brouillés.
Artichokes en feuillage.
Culs blancs.
Faisans.
Tourte d'abricots.

---

What does this menu reveal about the French nation at that the time? Is the meal any more or less grand than it would have been served at dinner on an ordinary day in an English royal household? The individual dishes are not much of a clue. Menus in England were written in French, and the only word that really gives this away as being French is the *brioche*, a bread enriched with butter and eggs (see February 24) which rarely appeared on English menus by that name. Duck is common on English menus, although the particular combination with turnips is very French. One unusual note is the presence of the boiled eggs. Eggs in any form have always been considered a lunchtime dish, so it is possible that this was in fact lunch.

Recipes

~~~

*Caneton aux navets* (duck with turnips) is one of the classic and popular French dishes. There are many variations of the basic idea. In today's menu, the wings (*ailes*) alone were used, but the basic recipe is the same.

## Canard aux Navets

Roast a duck; let it be rather underdone; then separate the legs and wings from the body, thus making five pieces. Next fry a few slices of turnips in butter, with a little powdered sugar to colour them; then throw in a pinch of flour, and moisten with stock and a little gravy, seasoning to your taste, and adding some parsley and green onions; skim, and when the turnips are done, put them into a stewpan separately, with a very little of their sauce. Boil the duck in the remaining sauce; then skim, and serve altogether.

*French Domestic Cookery, by an English Physician* (1825).

## Haricots Blancs

Put some new white haricot beans into boiling water with salt; let them stew till half done; strain them through a sieve when you take them off the fire, and put them on again to finish in stock, with a carrot, a bunch of sweet herbs, and an onion stuck with a clove; serve with what meat you choose, or soup.

E. Crawford, *French Cookery Adapted for English Families* (1853).

Artichokes were served two ways at this dinner—with the leaves, and as *culs blancs* (the bottoms, in white sauce).

## Artichauts En Feuillage
## (Artichokes with the Leaves)

Scald them first in boiling Water a few minutes; then boil them in Broth, with a faggot of sweet Herbs, a few slices of Lard under them, and two or three Cloves; drain, and take the Choaks out as the first; pour a Cullis therein, mixed with Butter, Pepper, Salt, and a Lemon Squeeze.

B. Clermont, *The Professed Cook; or, The Modern Art of Cookery, Pastry, and Confectionary* (1778).

Brioche: see February 24.
Tourte d'Abricots: see August 24.

# August

## August 1

### Banquet for the Official Opening of London Bridge
### London, England, 1831

The citizens of London celebrated with great pride in 1831 when the "new" London Bridge was completed. The previous bridge had stood for 600 years: this "new" bridge was to last only 136 years, its construction proving to be inadequate for modern traffic. It was sold in 1968 and reassembled at Lake Havasu in Arizona, as a tourist attraction.

The official opening was held on August 1, which was also the anniversary of the accession of the German House of Hanover to the throne of England in 1714. The date was no doubt chosen to honor King William (1765–1837), who, with Queen Adelaide (1792–1849), were the guests of honor at the spectacular opening ceremony. Fifteen hundred guests attended the banquet which was held on the bridge itself, under a magnificent canopy formed of the flags of all nations. Below are the quantities needed for the celebration.

---

370 dishes of chickens
150 hams and tongues
75 raised French pies, etc.
75 pigeon pies
40 sirloins of beef
50 quarters of lamb
250 dishes of shellfish, etc.
200 ditto salads, cucumbers, etc.
200 fruit tarts
200 jellies, creams, & strawberries
350 lb. weight pine apples
100 dishes hothouse grapes
100 dishes nectarines, peaches, apricots, etc.
100 dishes greengages, Orlean plums, etc.
100 dishes currant, gooseberry, raisin, etc.
150 ornamented Savoy cakes
300 dishes ice cream etc.
300 turtles, roast chickens, etc.
840 dozen of the choicest wines

True to ancient tradition, the royal table was the most beautifully decorated. At its center was an ornate three-piece *plateau* of "exquisite workmanship" over six-feet long with pillars, figures of the three Graces, and 48 candles, "the effect, when lighted . . . may be conceived but not adequately described." Also in keeping with tradition, the royal table was served the finest of the dishes prepared by the caterer, Mr. Leech of the famous London Coffee House in Ludgate-hill.

Refrigeration science was still in its infancy at this time, and there were certainly no commercial applications. How then, did the caterer prepare sufficient food for 1,500 people—a task that would have taken many days of preparation? One of caterers' best friends for centuries had been the pie. A pastry shell, if not cracked or damp, would remain airtight and preserve food for a long time (although it would not meet food safety requirements today).

The French pies and pigeon pies on this menu could have been prepared well in advance and set aside, perhaps for extra security remaining in their metal "molds" until serving time. The folk of the nineteenth century had a prolonged love affair with decorative molded dishes of all sorts, thanks to the technological developments of the Industrial Revolution. Sprung metal molds in a huge variety of complex, ornate designs were made which removed the necessity to "raise" pies by hand—the standard method since the medieval era. "French pies" were particularly highly decorated raised pies and were standard items at fine banquets. Pigeon pies were also associated with the well-to-do. Birds were considered delicate food suitable for finer folk,

THE NEW LONDON BRIDGE,
As it appeared on Monday August 1st 1831 at the Ceremony of opening by their Majesties.

London Bridge, opening day. Courtesy of Library of Congress.

and in any case only the wealthy were able to maintain pigeon-cotes. The pies were often made with the pigeons' feet sticking up out of the top of the pie to identify the contents.

Molds were also used for cold "set" dishes such as jellies and custards, *chartreuses* (see November 9) of meat and vegetables, as well as puddings and cakes—including the Savoy cakes which appear on this and almost every other civic menu of the time.

## Recipes

~~~

---

### Savoy Cake, or Sponge Cake in a Mould

Take nine Eggs, their weight of Sugar, and six of Flour, some grated Lemon, or a few drops of Essence of Lemon, and half a gill of Orange-flower Water, work them as in the last receipt [see below]; put in the orange-flower water when you take it from the fire; be very careful the mould is quite dry: rub it all over the inside with Butter, put some pounded Sugar round the mould upon the butter, and shake it well to get it out of the crevices: tie a slip of paper round the mould, fill it three parts full with the mixture, and bake it one hour in a slack oven; when done, let it stand for a few minutes, and take it from the mould, which may be done by shaking it a little.

["previous receipt"] Break into a round-bottomed Preserving Pan, nine good sized Eggs, with one pound of sifted Loaf Sugar, and some grated Lemon Peel;— set the pan over a very slow fire, and whisk it till it is quite warm (but not too hot to set the Eggs) remove the pan from the fire, and whisk it till cold, which may be a quarter of an hour, then stir in the flour lightly with a spattle.

William Kitchiner, *The Cook's Oracle* (1836).

---

### Pigeon Pie

Do not put any beefsteak in the bottom of the pie, as it soaks up the juice in which the pigeons ought to be done, and leaves them dry; therefore, if it is put in, let it be at the top; put butter, thyme, pepper, and salt into each; boil the giz-zards first; put in the pigeons, wrapping each in a vine-leaf, and over it a thin slice of bacon. If there is any salmi of game or pigeons, put in a little; if not, put in water, with hard yolks: farce-balls may be added, and a clove of garlic; stick some of the pigeons' feet in the middle of the crust. For a nice pie, use puff paste; but any other will do for a family pie.

*Domestic Economy, and Cookery, for Rich and Poor* (London, 1827).

---

## August 2

### Harvest Meals in an English Medieval Manorial Household
### Acton Hall, Acton, Suffolk, 1413

Dame Alice de Breyene was a wealthy English gentlewoman when she was widowed in 1386. She left her marital home in Gloucestershire and returned with her two daughters to Suffolk to be close to her family, and set up home at Acton Hall. The manor house was set in an estate of 900 acres of farm and woodland and had its own brew house, bakehouse, and chapel. The household book kept by her steward for the period September 29, 1412, to September 28, 1413, contains a meticulous record of the expenses, purchases, and management of supplies for the household, including the number of people provided for at each meal (family, servants, farm workers, visitors, and visitors' servants), and the food and drink consumed.

The entry for August 2, 1413, is brief but reveals a great deal.

> Meals: Breakfast 20, dinner 40, supper 40. Sum 100
>
> Wed. 2. Guests—John Scoyl with 27 boon workers, the bailiff of the manor with the harvest-reeve, William Cowpere, the whole day. Pantry: 50 white, and 6 black loaves, and 32 loaves for the boon-workers; wine from supply, ale from stock. Kitchen: 80 white herrings, 1 1/2 salt fish, one stockfish. Purchases: 3 thornbacks, 7 soles and 5 plaice 17d. milk and cream 5d. eggs 6d. Provender: hay from stock for 5 horses, fodder for same, 3pk oats.

From this Wednesday entry it is obvious that it was one of the frequent fast (i.e., fish) days required by the Church at that time. It was also the

Harvesting grain woodcut.

beginning of the harvest: the provision for the harvest workers is noted, and there is a sharp increase in the number of meals from 52 the previous day, building to a total of 2,200 for the month (the busiest in the year, with almost double the number of meals prepared in March).

The absolute primacy of bread in the diet at that time is also abundantly clear from this record. All social classes consumed bread in huge quantities by today's standards— each person consuming between 2 and 3 pounds a day. The difference was in the type of bread eaten: the higher the social position, the finer and whiter the bread. Black bread was made from coarse wholemeal or rye or a mixture and was food for peasants and servants.

The amount of ale used each day was not noted, but from the brewing records it can be calculated that the average consumption was of the order of 1 gallon per person, per day. Ale was the drink of choice, even for children. It was low in alcohol, and on the whole probably safer than the water supply. Ale does not keep well, and it was brewed every 2–6 days for immediate consumption. The difference between beer and ale is that hops are used in the production of beer and account for its better keeping qualities. It is not certain when hops were introduced to England from Europe—various sources claim dates between the seventh and the sixteenth centuries, but ale remained the standard home brew for centuries.

## Recipes
~~~

Fish preserved by drying or salting was a staple in households such as this, to supplement the supplies of fresh fish for the many non-meat days a year decreed by the Church. Stockfish was usually made from cod hung on "stocks" (sticks) and air-dried in the cold northern climate of Scandinavia.

---

### To Boile Stockfish

Take Stock fish when it is well watered, and picke out all the baste cleane from the fish, then put it into a pipkin, and put in no more water than shall cover it, and set it on the fire, and as soone as it beginneth to boyle on the one side, then turne the other side to the fire, and assoone as it beginneth to boile on the other side, take it off, and put it into a Colender, and let the water runne out from it, but put in salt in the boyling of it, then take a little faire water and sweete butter, and let it boyle in a dish untill it bee something thick, then powre it on the stockfish and serve it.

*The Good Housewife's Jewell* (England, 1596).

---

## August 3

### Luncheon Given by President Richard M. Nixon
### Romanian State Guest House, Bucharest, Romania, 1969

The visit of President Richard M. Nixon (1913–1994) to Romania in 1969 caused a great deal of interest and controversy. The visit was at the invitation of the communist leader of Romania, Nicolae Ceauşescu (1918–1989) and was to be not only Nixon's first overseas trip as president of the United States, but also the first of any American president to any communist country.

The visit was to be symbolic. Although there was no official discussion agenda and no decisions were expected to be made, every visit has political or diplomatic implications, and as soon as the invitation was accepted, the spin-doctors went to work to stress that this was not an anti-Soviet move. The visit caused other problems at a more mundane level. The Romanian

Army Band had to learn to play the "Star Spangled Banner," and accommodation had to be found for the 600 or so media people and peripheral officials in Bucharest, which had only three high-class hotels.

There was very little time for official talks in any case. The entire round trip was a long weekend. The Nixons left the United States on Friday, August 1, visited Lahore, Pakistan, Romania, and England and were home again on Sunday, August 3. They arrived in Bucharest on Saturday afternoon, and as is normal diplomatic tradition on the first evening of a visit, were entertained that evening at a state dinner at the Council of Ministers building. Diplomatic tradition also requires that the visitors return the compliment the following day, which the Nixons did at a luncheon on Sunday at the Romanian State Guest House.

---

Florida Crab Mousse

Roast Sirloin of Beef Colorado
Bouquetière of Vegetables California

New Mexico Tomato Salad
New Jersey Blueberries
Petits Fours

Demi-Tasse

---

This was no leisurely Sunday luncheon. The meal began at 1 P.M., and at 3:30 P.M. the Nixons left for Mildenhall Air Force Base in England. The basic ingredients for this meal obviously traveled with the party, and it is clear that the menu was an opportunity for a final nationalistic statement.

## Recipes

~~~

### Crab Mousse

Pound a cup of crab meat (in a generous cup by the way) and the unbeaten whites of two eggs in a mortar until the whole is reduced to a pulp. Add gradually, pounding the whole time, a half cup of cold bechamel. After the sauce has all been added and the combination has been thoroughly soothed, press through a fine sieve and set aside to cool. Now beat stiff and dry two egg whites and also a cup of thick whipping cream until firm through. Add half a teaspoonful of salt, and a pinch or more of pepper, if liked, to the crab. Now fold in the beaten egg and whipped cream. Turn the mixture into a buttered mold, set the mold in a pan with a number of folds of paper beneath, and pour in boiling water to half the height of the mold. Do not allow the water to boil, but cook gently until the mixture is firm on a low fire. Unmold and serve with Hollandaise or other fish sauces.

*The New York Times*, August 27, 1911.

Petits Fours: see November 14.

## August 4

### Dinner aboard the Pride of the Fleet
### RMS *Imperator*, 1920

When the *Imperator* made her maiden voyage in June 1913, she was the pride of the Hamburg-Amerika Line fleet. She was the largest passenger ship in the world—the "Colossus of the Ocean"—capable of carrying over 4,500 passengers and designed as a floating hotel. One of the first-class restaurants aboard was named the Ritz-Carlton, after the luxurious London hotel of that name, and the famous French chef Auguste Escoffier (1846–1935) from the hotel was prevailed upon to ensure that the *Imperator*'s eight kitchens could turn out fine hotel-quality food.

The pride of the fleet became part of the war reparations when Germany was defeated in World War I. The Reparations Commission awarded the *Imperator* to Great Britain (over the objections of the United States, which thought it had greater claim), and she was transferred to the Cunard Line in late 1919. After refitting she became once again a luxury transatlantic cruise ship. On July 31, 1920, she left Southampton, England, with a list of notable and titled visitors aboard, arriving on July 6 in New York. Two days out from their arrival, some of the passengers (the class is not stated) sat down to the following dinner.

---

MENU.

Hors d'œuvres (variés)

—

Pot au Feu.      Cream of Barley.

—

River Trout—Shrimp Sauce.
Aiguillette d'Aigrefin—Sauce Tartare.

—

Noisettes de Pré Salé—Reforme.
Kromeskis—Polonaise.

—

Sirloin and Ribs of Beef—Horseradish Sauce.
French Beans.      Boiled Rice.
Boiled New, and Roasted Potatoes.

—

Roast Turkey—Sausage—Cranberry Sauce.

—

Salade de Saison.

—

Pouding Marie-Louise.
Parisienne Fancies.
Bavarois Chocolat

—

French Ice Cream.

—

Dessert.      Coffee.

---

Recipes

~~~

</div>

Kromeskies are similar to croquettes (see May 4) and can be made from any cold meat such as chicken or sweetbreads (see March 3), as well as fish and oysters.

---

<div align="center">

Kromeskies

1 lb. cold meat
1 oz. butter
Onion, flour, and seasoning
1/4 lb. lard
Materials for batter
1 egg

</div>

(1) Chop one onion and fry it pale yellow in one ounce of butter (2) Cut the cold meat in small dice (3) When the onion is yellow, add to it an ounce of flour; stir until smooth, then add half a pint of boiling water, or cold gravy, and stir until the sauce is ready to boil. (4) Put in the cold meat, a tablespoon of chopped parsley, a teaspoonful of salt, and the yolk of one raw egg, and stir till the mixture is scalding hot. (5) Turn it out on an oiled platter, spreading it an inch thick, and let it cool. (6) When it is cold, cut it in strips an inch wide and two inches long; pat them into even shapes with a knife blade dipped in cold water; drop them into the Plain Frying Batter [see below], lift them out with a fork and drop them into smoking hot fat to fry golden brown. (7) When they are done, lay them on brown paper for a moment to free them from grease, pile them nicely on a clean napkin, garnish them with sprigs of parsley, and serve them hot.

---

<div align="center">

Plain Frying Batter

</div>

Mix a quarter of a pound of flour with the yolks of two raw eggs, a level saltspoonful of salt, half a saltspoonful of pepper, quarter of a saltspoonful of grated nutmeg, one tablespoonful of salad oil (which is needed to make the batter crisp) and one cup of water, more or less, as the flour will take it up; the batter should be stiff enough to hold the drops from the spoon in shape when they are let fall upon it; now beat the whites of two eggs to a stiff froth, beginning slowly, and increasing the speed until you are beating as fast as you can; the froth will surely come; then stir it lightly into the batter.

Juliet Corson, *Cooking School Text Book and Housekeepers' Guide to Cookery and Kitchen Management* (New York, 1879).

---

<div align="center">

Marie-Louise Pudding

</div>

Wash a small cupful of Carolina rice and simmer it very slowly in a pint of milk, adding a little cream at the end. To be extra well cooked.

Sweeten and flavour to taste, mixing in a little finely-chopped candied peel. When cool, add the well-beaten yolks of 4 eggs. Whip the whites to a froth and add them lightly in just before you steam the pudding.

Ornament a mould as if for a cabinet pudding with candied peel cut in circles, size of threepenny bits, cherries, &c., Serve with Frothed Sauce round the pudding and hand some also with it in a boat.

This pudding would be good buried in ice, then the sauce should be cold custard, flavoured with 1/2 teaspoonful of maraschino and a whole one of brandy.

*The Cookery Book of Lady Clark of Tillypronie* (1909).

Horseradish Sauce: see February 10.
Pot au Feu: see April 7.
Reform Sauce: see July 3.
Shrimp Sauce: see April 20.
Tartare Sauce: see July 20.

## August 5

### Frederick the Great's Dinner
*Sans Souci*, Potsdam, Germany, 1786

It was the habit of King Frederick II (1712–1786) of Prussia to inspect his dinner menu in advance, add his comments to it, and mark his choices of the dishes he wished to be served with an "x." Twelve days before his death, this is the menu as it was returned to the kitchen.

Soupe aux choux à la Fonque (x)
Du boeuf aux panais et carottes (x)
Des poulets en cannelons aux concombres faris au blanc a l'Anglaise
[struck out by His Majesty and replaced by "des cotelettes dans du papier"]
Petits potes à la Romaine
Roast young Couleussen
Du saumon à la Dessau (x)
Des filets de volaille a la Pompadour, avec des langues de boeuf et des croquettes
Portuguese cake [struck out by His Majesty, with the annotation "des gauffres"
instead]
Green peas (x)
Fresh herrings (x)
Pickled cucumbers

There is very little that is obviously Prussian in this dinner. Royalty and the wealthy ate in a similar fashion no matter where they ruled in Europe. Classic dishes in classic order appeared on menus traditionally written in French (which did not change in Prussia until 1889 when Wilhelm II threw out the French chefs and ordered that menus were to be written in German).

Frederick II ruled Prussia from 1740–1786. He had the common touch and was popular with his people in spite of his belief in absolute rule. One of his edicts was however most unpopular, causing his loyal subjects to become quite creative in their resistance. He tried to restrict the sale of coffee.

Coffee originated in Abyssinia (Ethiopia). It became established in the Arab empire in the sixteenth century and was taken up with increasing enthusiasm in Europe in the seventeenth century. From the beginning, coffee caused concern to despotic rulers because people gathered at coffee houses to drink it—facilitating subversive talk and action. As early as 1511 the governor of Mecca tried to ban it for that reason, as did Charles II of England in 1675 when he issued *A Proclamation for the Suppression of Coffee Houses* (which he withdrew less than a week later under pressure from his own ministers).

Frederick, who was passionately fond of coffee himself, had a more pressing reason for controlling it—an economic one. A royal monopoly was imposed on coffee in 1766 for a number of reasons: the belief that the importation of coffee would cause money to flow out of the country and contribute to economic ruin (rather than filling the royal coffers), a prevailing medical opinion that considered coffee to be harmful (especially in respect to damaging potency and fertility), and the reluctance on the part of the wealthy to see their favorite beverage become cheap enough for ordinary folk (with the justification that the poorer folk would surely be ruined by it). By 1777, aware that he was far from winning the battle, Frederick dressed up his command in military and patriotic sentiment.

> It is disgusting to notice the increase in the quantity of coffee used by my subjects, and the amount of money that goes out of the country as a consequence. Everybody is using coffee; this must be prevented. His Majesty was brought up on beer, and so were both his ancestors and officers. Many battles have been fought and won by soldiers nourished on beer, and the King does not believe that coffee-drinking soldiers can be relied upon to endure hardships in case of another war.

Ultimately, of course, Frederick was unsuccessful, and a thriving coffee (and cake) culture developed in Germany. In this meal, Frederick ordered *gauffres*—plain wafers—instead of cake. Wafers are made in the same way as waffles but are thinner and can be shaped while hot.

## Recipes

~~~

---

### Sauce à la Pompadour

Fry or sweat white a few chopped mushrooms and shalots in a little butter. When well melted, add to them six spoonsful of sauce tournee (see below) and two spoonsful of consomme. Stew them for three-quarters of an hour on the corner of the stove, and skim off the fat: you must keep your sauce rather thin; then throw in a thickening made of the yolks of three eggs. Moisten with a spoonful or two of cream; add a little pepper and salt, and work the sauce well. When it is done, have a little parsley chopped very fine, blanch it, drain it, and let it cool, that it may look quite green; mix it with the sauce, and serve up. A little lemon-juice may not be amiss, but remember that acids will always alter the taste of good sauces to their disadvantage, except when highly seasoned.

---

---

### Sauce Tournee

Take some white thickening [see next recipe], dilute it with some consomme or broth of fowl; neither too thin nor too thick. I must repeat what I have already said, that a sauce when too thick will never admit of the fat being removed. Let it boil on the corner of the stove. Throw in a few mushrooms, with a bunch of parsley and green onions. Skim it well, and when there is no grease left, strain it through a tammy, to use when wanted.

---

### White Roux (White Thickening)

Put a good lump of butter into a stewpan, let it melt over a slow fire, and, when melted, drain the butter and squeeze out the buttermilk; then powder it over with flour, enough to make a thin paste; keep it on the fire for a quarter of an hour, and take care not to let it colour; pour it into an earthen pan to use when wanted.
   Louis Eustache Ude, *The French Cook* (1815).

---

Cabbage Soup: see August 28.
Wafers, Waffles: see January 26.

## August 6

### King's Lunch
### Royal Palace, Milan, Italy, 1898

On May 7, 1898, the workers in Milan, Italy, organized a strike to protest against the rising price of bread and consequent widespread hunger. General Fiorenzo Bava-Beccaris placed the city under military rule and quelled the demonstration with cannon fire. Over a hundred people were killed and a thousand injured—for which Bava-Beccaris was rewarded by King Umberto I (1844–1900) with personal congratulations and a medal. Less than twelve months later the king was assassinated by one of the angry anarchists. A few months after the infamous "Bava-Beccaris massacre," the king sat down to the following lunch at his palace in Milan.

---

MENU

Risotto au jus.     Consommé
Omelette naturelle.
Cotelettes de poulets panée
Ris de Veau à la milanaise
Salade
Profiteroles au chocolat
Dessert

---

   This menu demonstrates a common misconception about Italian food as it is seen by the rest of the world. It shows that it is possible to have an Italian meal without pasta. In fact, pasta is a southern Italian dish, and that it has become synonymous with "Italian" food is because most Italian migrants came from the poorer south and established their local cuisine wherever they settled. In the richer north, around Milan, rice is grown, and *risotto* is a starchy staple, along with maize which is used to make *polenta*. Risotto is made from special varieties of rice (such as arborio and carnaroli) which give the overall creamy texture but with each grain retaining some "bite." There are an almost infinite number of variations on the basic recipe and a great deal of debate as to the correct and authentic method of cooking it. The king clearly had a very basic version, cooked *au jus* (with stock) at the beginning of his meal.

## Recipes
~~~

*Ris de Veau* causes confusion because it seems to translate as "the smile of a calf." They are actually sweetbreads, which are not made from sweet bread dough but are the thymus or pancreas glands (see February 12) of a young animal.

---

### Sweet-Breads à la Milanaise

Sweet-breads fried as in preceding receipt [see next recipe] are placed in the centre of a hot platter. Small piped macaroni broken into two or three inch lengths is cooked with tomatoes and neatly arranged in a circle around them.

Veal sweet-breads are best. They spoil very soon. The moment they come from market, they should be put into cold water, to soak for about an hour; lard them, or rather draw a lardoon of pork through the centre of each sweet-bread, and put them into salted boiling water, or, better, stock, and let them boil about twenty minutes, or until they are thoroughly done; throw them then into cold water for only a few moments. They will now be firm and white. Remove carefully the skin and little pipes, and put them in the coolest place until ready to cook again.

Parboil them as just explained. Cut them in even-sized pieces, sprinkle over pepper and salt, egg and bread-crumb them, and fry them in hot lard.

Mary Newton Foote Henderson, *Practical Cooking and Dinner Giving* (New York, 1877).

---

The following is a simple, classic risotto. There are many versions of *risotto à la Milanaise*, many of them containing saffron, or peas. This particular recipe is very simple, and is perhaps similar to the *risotto au jus* at the king's lunch.

---

### Risotto à la Milanaise

Melt a small piece of butter in a saucepan. Brown in the butter a medium sized onion, cut in thin slices. When the onion is browned, take it away from the saucepan and add little by little the rice, stirring it with a wooden spoon. Every time that the rice becomes dry, add some hot broth (or hot water) until the rice is completely cooked. Add salt and pepper and a little saffron, if you like it.

When the rice is almost cooked, add to it some brown stock. Dress with parmesan cheese and some butter. Mix well and serve hot. This dish must not be allowed to be overcooked or cooled before eating.

Maria Gentile, *The Italian Cook Book: The Art of Eating Well* (New York, ca. 1919).

Profiteroles, choux paste for: see November 7.

## August 7

### Dinner in a Wigwam
### Burnt Church Point, Miramichi Bay, New Brunswick, Canada, 1853

Moses Henry Perley (1804–1862) was a prominent nineteenth-century Canadian naturalist. He had two great passions—the Indian cause and fishing—and he played official roles in both areas, becoming commissioner of Indian Affairs for Canada in 1841, and fishery commissioner in 1855. For all that he was self-taught, Perley was recognized as a leading ichthyologist, and fishing was not merely an academic and occupational pursuit for him, it was also his hobby. He must have been a reasonable cook, too, to judge from a letter he wrote to a friend while on one of his recreational fishing expeditions.

---

August 7

Sunday, August 7. In the cool of the evening, Coley and I caught thirty-seven trout, and at sunset I received a party of visitors from Miramichi. Such a night as we put in! Such songs, speeches, toasts and uproar, I never heard. They all slept in camp on the fir boughs, and a more comfortable set of gentlemen you never saw anywhere. We have had an excellent breakfast, and now they are out fishing in a boat belonging to the Indians. Whilst I stay in camp and look after dinner.

*Bill of Fare settled thus:*
Boiled salmon—oyster sauce.
Fried bass.
Lobster, cold.
Fried trout.
Pork chips.
Cold ham.
Boiled shoulder of pork.
New potatoes, string beans, Windsor beans, carrots, beets.
Snipe and plover.
Blueberries and raspberries.

Neither the Astor nor the National ever turned out a better breakfast than we had this morning, and I have no fears for the dinner. The wigwam is a perfect picture to-day, the most stylish and sporting thing I ever saw.

---

It is ironic that Perley's great enthusiasm for fish and fishing, and his prolific writings on them enhanced awareness of the great natural resource that was the waters and wilderness of New Brunswick—thereby contributing to the damage done to them by hordes of campers and sportsmen.

## Recipes
~~~

---

### Salmon, to Boil

This fish cannot be too soon cooked after being caught; it should be put into the kettle with plenty of cold water and a handful of salt—the addition of a small quantity of vinegar will add to the firmness of the fish—let it boil gently; if four pounds of salmon, fifty minutes will suffice; if thick, a few minutes more may be allowed.

The best criterion for ascertaining whether it be done, is to pass a knife between the bone and the fish—if it separates readily, it is done, this should be tried in the thickest part; when cooked, lay on the fish-strainer transversely across the kettle, so that the fish, while draining, may be kept hot. Place a fish-plate upon the dish on which the salmon is to be served, fold a clean white napkin, lay it upon the fish-plate, and place the salmon upon the napkin. Garnish with parsley.

---

### Lobsters to Be Eaten Cold

Procure the lobsters alive. Hen lobsters are the best, as they have spawn in and about them. Put them in boiling water, along with some salt, and boil from half an hour to three-quarters of an hour, or more, according to the size. When done, take them out of the water and wipe the shells. Before they are quite cold, rub the shells carefully, so as not to bruze the meat. Split the body and tail lengthwise, in two pieces. This may be done with a knife. Place the whole of the pieces ornamentally on a dish and garnish with parsley.

---

### Oyster Sauce

Save the liquor in opening the oyster, and boil it with the beards, a bit of mace, and lemon peel. In the meantime throw the oysters into cold water and drain it off. Strain the liquor and put it into a stewpan and as much butter, mixed with a little milk, as will make sauce enough, but first rub a little flour with it. Set them over the fire, and stir all the time, and when the butter has boiled once or twice, take them off, and keep the sauce near the fire but not on it, for if done too much, the oysters will be hard. Squeeze a little lemon-juice and serve.

*The Dominion Home Cookbook, by A Thorough Housewife* (Toronto, 1868).

## August 8

Breakfast aboard a Japanese Ship
MS *Chojo Maru,* 1932

National tastes are perhaps most strongly expressed through breakfast choices. People may be very adventurous at lunch and dinner, but most prefer traditional favorites to start the day. The Japanese O.S.K. Line ships such as the *Chojo Maru* were designed with American and European travelers in mind, and the necessity of interpreting Western breakfast dishes, and translating those concepts on the menu, makes for some strange reading.

---

BREAKFAST

Summer Orange.    Plum
Garden Radish.    Green Lettuce.
Rolled Oats with Milk.
Cornflakes — Puffed Rice.
Fish Ball, Tomato Sauce.
Toad in the Hole.
Meat Curry and Rice.
Potatoes, Boiled and Straw.

(TO ORDER) From the Grill 5 to 10 minutes.
Aitchbone Steak, Saute Onion.
Broiled Ham.    Breakfast Bacon.
EGGS—Boiled. Fried. Poached. Scramble Cocotts.
OMELET—Plain, Parsley, Onion, Savoury, Meat.
Waffle Cake.
Hot-roll.    Buttered and Dried Toast.
Crackers.
Maple Syrup, Honey.
Strawberry Jam and Marmalade.
TEA—Ceylon, Oolong, Green, Coffee & Cocoa.

---

The catering department obviously knew that their guests did not want a Japanese breakfast. The only concessions to Japanese cuisine are the fish balls, the green tea, and perhaps the meat curry. All of the basics of a Western breakfast are on the menu—cereal, bacon or ham, several types of eggs, and bread or toast with honey and preserves. It is impossible to know what the guest who ordered "scramble cocotts" would get—scrambled eggs are well enough known (see August 19), and eggs *en cocotte* are baked in small individual dishes.

The strangest breakfast item is the Toad in the Hole. It has been a favorite dish in England, particularly in the North, since at least the early-eighteenth century, and it is one variation of the concept of stretching a quantity of meat by cooking it or serving it with a large amount of a starchy filler—the same concept as *furmenty* with venison (see February 23) or dumplings with stew. It is a variation of Yorkshire pudding (see December 24), in which pieces of

M.S. "Chojo Maru," Dining Room and Cabin De Luxe.

*Chojo Maru* dining room.

meat (especially sausages) are actually cooked *in* the batter, making a one-dish meal—but in its country of origin it is unequivocally a dinner, not a breakfast dish.

## Recipes

~~~

---

### Japanese Fish Balls

Take any boiled fish, cold, and mix with rice, boiled to a paste. Roll in flour to balls the size of large marbles; toss into boiling goma-seed oil, and fry a golden brown.

---

### Sumomo Sui and Amai

(Plums, Sour and Sweet)

Have a sirup made of half a cupful of water, two cupfuls of sugar, a quarter cupful of vinegar, and half a teaspoonful of mixed spices, ground. When it is boiling drop in the plums, and let boil slowly for twenty minutes. Add half a cupful of mirin sauce, or any other desired spirits, and let all come to a boil once. Remove, and serve.

---

### Scrambled Eggs, Japanese Style

Eggs; green pepper; cold boiled rice; mushrooms.

Break into frying pan half a dozen eggs, stirring lightly with knife. Add quickly, before egg begins to cook, a tablespoonful of chopped green pepper, the juice of an onion, half a cupful of chopped mushrooms, and half a cupful of boiled rice. Toss all quickly together. Cook over a very slow fire, and serve hot.

Sara Bosse, *Chinese-Japanese Cook Book* (1914).

## August 9

Dinner to Honor the Prince de Conde
France, 1652

France was in turmoil in the middle of the seventeenth century. Louis XIV (1638–1715) was still a minor, and between 1648–1653 the country was in the grip of a series of power struggles that became known as *la Fronde* (named for a sling used in children's games, or as a weapon in the streets). One of the chief players was Louis II de Bourbon, the Prince de Condé (1621–1686). During his own lifetime he was known as "The Great Condé" on account of his prowess, and he is still considered one of the greatest military men of all time. On July 2, Condé led the *Frondeurs* to the gates of Paris and met with the royal troops under the Vicomte de Turenne (1611–1675) and engaged in what was to be called the battle of Faubourg Saint Antoine. He would have been defeated but for the action of the 24-year-old Duchesse de Montpensier (1627–1693) who ordered that the gates under her jurisdiction be opened and the Bastille cannon be fired at the royalists.

A few weeks after the battle, the statesman Mathieu Molé (1584–1656) gave a dinner in his honor which cost 1,965 livres. It was a fish day (see February 23).

---

*Fourteen potages maigres*, one of Rhine crayfish and Spanish wine, one of oysters from Angouleme and eggs of red partridges;

*Fourteen kinds of fish*, a salmon; a jack; carp with eggs Champlostreuz; Swiss trout; turbot from Havre; matelotte de lamproyes d'Angers; hoche-pot de gibier de riviere; gibelotte de poissons meles; eel a la broche; pate de barbottes du Rhone; fricasee de lottes aux asperges; fresh cod with green gooseberries; d'aloses de Rouen grillees; d'esperlant farinas au cedrat.

*Fourteen different roasts*. Six of boiled fish, six of fish a la poisle; four of river game a la broche.

*Fourteen salads*: three different kinds of boiled vegetables; three of herbs; six of differently dressed eggs; two of citrons musques.

*Fourteen assiettes gaufrees*: seven of pastry with cream, seven of pastry with fruits.

*Twenty-eight plates of fruit and dessert*, desquels six agnanats (pine-apples) toute entiers; twelve packets of fleurs de jonquilles a confire.

---

The French tradition was for great symmetry in meal service. There was always an even and balanced number of dishes—spectacularly so in this meal, with 14 dishes of each type. There is a great range of dishes from cod with green gooseberries to a homely sounding *hoche-pot de gibier de riviere* ("hot-pot of river game") to candied jonquils. The fruits were very exotic and expensive—the pineapples were very rare in Europe at that time.

A *hoche poche* (*hotchpotch, hochepot, hodge-podge, hus-pot*: see March 29) is a one-pot dish that can be made as simply or as extravagantly as circumstances will allow. The name simply means a mixture or jumble of things. In this case, it being a "maigre" day, it was made entirely of fish, so it would have been something like a chowder.

## Recipes

~~~

---

### Candied Jonquils

Fill the moulds with Sugar *a la grand Plume*, (ninth degree) when it [is] half cold, press Jonquil Flowers in it, with a little Skewer, and dry it in the Stove as the preceding [orange flowers, see below].

Boil some Sugar to the seventh Degree, (viz. *soufflé*) put some Orange-flowers to it, and take it off the Fire for about a quarter of an hour, or till the Flowers discharge their Juice, as it refreshes the Sugar; put it upon the Fire again to bring it to the fame Degree; let it cool to half, put it into moulds, and dry it in a Stove of a moderate heat, kept as equal as possible. It is known to be candied, by thrusting a small skewer into the corner of each mould to the bottom, and the top must be sparkling like a diamond ; put the moulds upon one side, to drain a good while before you take out the Candy, turn it over upon white Paper, and keep it always in a dry place.

B. Clermont, *The Professed Cook* (1776).

---

## August 10

### Dinner aboard an Immigrant Ship
### SS *Zeeland*, 1907

The small country of Belgium provided many of the world's immigrants in the nineteenth century. The political situation was unstable, there was a severe land shortage, and in the 1840s the potato blight caused widespread hardship as it did in Ireland. Belgians were encouraged to immigrate by their own government, and they were welcomed in the United States, which was actively recruiting labor. Second and third waves of Belgian migrants followed after each of the world wars. Many of the estimated three million Belgians who traveled to America and Canada between 1875–1935 did so aboard ships of the Red Star Line, such as the SS *Zeeland*, which regularly traveled the route between Antwerp and New York.

The *Zeeland* left Antwerp on August 3, 1907, on one of her outward voyages. On August 10, two days out from New York, her passengers sat down to the following dinner.

---

RADISHES SARDINES OLIVES
BLOATER TOAST

Crème Du Barry      Consommé Monte Carlo
Carp, Sauce Genevoise
Pommes Anglaise

Calf's Head à la Rachel

Prime Ribs of Beef
Princess Beans Egg     Plant Fritters

Médallion de Veau
Young carrots fines herbes     Pommes Parisienne

Roast Squab, Compôte of Peaches
Escarole Salad

Almond Pudding     Apple Hedgehog
Strawberry Ice Cream     Méringues

CHEESE: Camembert Roquefort American
Fruit Dessert
Coffee

Passengers are politely requested to order their wine etc., beforehand.

There are no specifically Belgian dishes on this menu. Shipping lines on the whole tended to provide generic "European" dishes with no strong national identity so that all passengers would find something vaguely familiar to eat.

The only cause for surprise for some passengers might have been the escarole salad, depending on what they were expecting. There is a great deal of confusion between escarole, endive, and chicory. The names are used loosely and often interchangeably by growers and in markets, although there are regional preferences. The scientific classification is the only certain one. Chicory is *Cichorium intybus*, and it is called common chicory, Belgian endive, or witlof. The small tightly packed leaves have a slightly bitter taste and can be used raw in salads or cooked as any other green vegetable. It is a popular vegetable in Europe, but it is the root of the plant that is most important commercially, as it can be roasted and used as a coffee substitute. Endive is *Cichorium endivia*—but it is called chicory in the United States and England. It is grown specifically for its leaves, which again can be used raw or cooked. There are two main types of escarole—the flat leaf (called the Batavian endive, or escarole) and the curly leaf type.

## Recipes
~~~

Dishes styled "*du Barry*" feature cauliflower (see January 10), and *Crème Du Barry* is nothing more than cauliflower soup enriched with cream. The following recipe is a very plain version, taken from a book of recipes contributed by World War I Belgian refugees to Britain.

### Cauliflower Soup

After you have boiled a cauliflower, it is a great extravagance to throw away the liquor; it is delicately flavored and forms the basis of a good soup. Wash well your cauliflower, taking great care to remove all grit and insects. Place it to simmer with its head downwards, in salted water; and, when it is tender, remove it. Now for the soup. Let all the outer leaves and odd bits simmer well, then pass them through a sieve. Fry some chopped onions, add the liquor of the cauliflower and the pieces that have been rubbed through the sieve, add a little white pepper and a slice of brown bread. Let all cook gently for half-an-hour, then, just before serving it, take out the slice of bread and sprinkle in two teaspoonfuls of grated Gruyere cheese.

Mrs. Brian Luck, editor, *The Belgian Cook-book* (1915).

---

### Apple Hedgehog (Iced Apples)

About 3 dozen good boiling apples,
1/2 lb. of sugar,
1/2 pint of water,
the rind of 1/2 lemon minced very fine,
the whites of 2 eggs,
3 tablespoonfuls of pounded sugar,
a few sweet almonds.

Peel and core a dozen of the apples without dividing them, and stew them very gently in a lined saucepan with 1/2 lb. of sugar and 1/2 pint of water, and when tender, lift them carefully on to a dish. Have ready the remainder of the apples pared, cored, and cut into thin slices; put them into the same syrup with the lemon-peel, and boil gently until they are reduced to a marmalade: they must be kept stirred, to prevent them from burning. Cover the bottom of a dish with some of the marmalade, and over that a layer of the stewed apples, in the insides of which, and between each, place some of the marmalade; then place another layer of apples, and fill up the cavities with marmalade as before, forming the whole into a raised oval shape. Whip the whites of the eggs to a stiff froth, mix with them the pounded sugar, and cover the apples very smoothly all over with the icing; blanch and cut each almond into 4 or 5 strips; place these strips at equal distances over the icing sticking up; strew over a little rough pounded sugar, and place the dish in a very slow oven, to colour the almonds, and for the apples to get warm through. This entremets may also be served cold, and makes a pretty supper-dish.

*Beeton's Book of Household Management* (1861).

---

Calf's Head: see January 30.
Meringues: see February 18.

## August 11

Luncheon aboard a World War I Troop Ship
SS *Megantic*, En Route from Alexandria, Egypt, to Marseilles, France, 1916

During wartime, governments have special powers to appropriate any and every ship to war service. Magnificent luxury cruise ships were employed during both world wars as troop ships. The SS *Megantic* of the White Star

Line—sister ship to the *Titanic* (see April 2)—was converted to a troop ship when World War I broke out and regularly carried Canadian and Australian soldiers too and from the front.

She was carrying soldiers of the 1st AIF (Australian Imperial Force) from the battlefield of Gallipoli in Turkey when the following lunch was served on August 11, 1916. According to the handwritten note on the menu, the ship was somewhere between Alexandria and Marseilles.

---

HOT
Puree of Split Peas

—

Chicken Pot Pie
Boiled Mutton, Caper Sauce
Spaghetti a la Napolitaine
Baked Jacket and Puree Potatoes

—

BUFFET
Roast Sirloin of Beef
House-Made Brawn     Luncheon Sausage

—

SALADS
Beetroot     Cucumber

—

Compote of Prunes and Custard     Assorted Pastry

Cheese     Biscuits

---

For soldiers who had been living in trenches, eating rations, this meal must have been luxurious indeed. Perhaps even the "luncheon sausage" seemed like a treat. Luncheon meat or luncheon sausage is a pale pink amorphous cylinder made from precooked meat and preservatives and has two virtues—it keeps well, and even more importantly, it is cheap. There are many variations on the theme—and many of the names are based on the very distant association with European sausages, such as boloney (from Bologna), stras (from Strasbourg), German sausage or Fritz, but, inexplicably in some parts of Australia—"Devon." Wartime was a great factor in the popularization of luncheon meats as it was exempt from rationing. A generation of wartime children grew up with it, and it is uncommon to completely reject the food of one's childhood, however different one's adult palate turns out to be. It becomes a comfort food, usually high in carbohydrates and easy to eat. Strangely, "spaghetti" makes the comfort food list for many who have no Italian heritage at all, and in this case it usually refers to a version with meat, tomatoes, and cheese, such as the ubiquitous Bolognaise or Napolitane sauce of thousands of "Italian" restaurants outside of Italy. Authenticity is irrelevant when it comes to adopted dishes which have become comfort food favorites.

The other ubiquitous comfort food dish that appears on this menu—for those of British birth—is custard. No Englishman would think his "pudding" complete without custard. It is so absolutely associated with England that even the French call it *Crème Anglais*.

A "compote" is a very old term. It used to be compôte, the accent symbol indicating an omitted "s". In other words, originally it was "compost," meaning a random mixture, and this is how it appears on many medieval menus (see February 23).

Recipes

~~~

---

### Spaghetti alla Napolitana

| | |
|---|---|
| 1/2 pound spaghetti | 2 sprigs of parsley |
| 1/2 pound round steak | 2 cups canned tomatoes |
| 1/4 pound salt pork or bacon | 6 dried mushrooms |
| 1 small onion | 1/2 cup grated cheese |
| 1 clove of garlic | |

Grind the salt pork and try out in a saucepan. When it begins to brown, add the onion, ground; parsley, chopped; shredded garlic and the mushrooms, previously soaked. When the vegetables are brown, add the meat, coarsely ground; and when that is brown, add the tomatoes. Simmer slowly till of a creamy consistency.

Cook spaghetti, without breaking it, and drain carefully. Put into a hot serving dishe, sprinkle one half-cup grated cheese over it, then pour hot sauce over it. Lift with two forks till thoroughly mixed.

Bertha M. Wood, *Foods of the Foreign Born* (Boston, 1922).

---

### Compote of Prunes

Wash 1 lb. of prunes and put them in a pan with three-quarters of a pint of water and six lumps of sugar, the rind of half a lemon cut in strips, six cloves and an inch of cinnamon stick; simmer gently for twenty minutes. Then remove the lemon, cloves, and cinnamon, add quarter of a pint of claret, and cook very slowly till tender. Serve nicely piled in the centre of a round dish.

M. Jebb Scott, *Menus for Every Day of the Year* (London, 1912).

---

Brawn: see April 28.
Caper Sauce: see December 8.
Jacket Potatoes: see March 4.
Puree of Split Peas (soup): see March 7.

## August 12

Daily Meals in the Poorhouse
Fishlake, Yorkshire, England, 1835

The inmates of the poorhouse in the English village of Fishlake were probably more concerned with quantity than variety in their daily diet. The quantity was always grossly inadequate, and there was certainly very little variety. The days were distinguished only by the main meal, and this day in 1835 being a Wednesday, they had a dinner of potato and meat pie to look forward to.

---

BREAKFAST
Boiled Milk and Bread

DINNER:

| | |
|---|---|
| Sunday: | Beef and Bacon and Broth. |
| Monday: | Pudding and Broth. |
| Tuesday: | Cold Meat or Dumplings. |
| Wednesday: | Potato and Meat Pie. |
| Thursday: | Buttermilk and Sweetened Milk and Bread. |
| Friday: | Potato and Meat Pie. |
| Saturday: | Beer or Milk Porridge. |

SUPPER.
Boiled Milk and Bread.

---

The daily dietary given above was recorded by an investigator assigned to report on the conditions of the community poorhouses as changes to the Poor Law gradually instituted across the country. He noted that at Fishlake there were nine inhabitants (six men and three women) under the supervision of the master and his wife, and that the house was whitewashed three times a year, but infested with vermin. He ordered that henceforth baking (bread) be done once a week in line with the other parishes, suggesting that the normal practice was to bake less frequently. No wonder the bread (which would have been of the coarsest kind) was served boiled in milk.

As bad as it was, the poor folk who tucked into their dinner on this day would probably have been blissfully aware that it was about to get a whole lot worse. According to the Poor Law Act of 1601, it was the responsibility of local parish communities to care for their own poor. Relief could be provided to the poor in their own homes, and such poorhouses as existed—like Fishlake for example—had only a small number of inhabitants and retained their connection with the community. By the early-nineteenth century the attitude to the poor had changed, however. There had developed a concept of deserving and undeserving poor. The latter were believed to be poor because they were lazy and choosing not to work. The amendments to the Act which went into law in 1834 were a direct result of the belief by some that this overgenerous relief encouraged the "indolent poor" to deliberately avoid working for a living.

The tone of the Act was clearly punitive. Workhouse conditions were intended as a deterrent to admission. Small parish poorhouses were combined into large institutions, and no relief was to be supplied to poor people in their homes. Wives were separated from husbands and children from parents. Drab uniforms were worn, the working day was very long, the work tedious and gruelling, and the food ration barely adequate for survival. There were many opportunities for unscrupulous masters to make a profit: reducing the meagre ration further and buying cheap and often adulterated flour and milk or rotting vegetables and meat.

Families already destitute and starving would try desperately to stay out of the workhouse, and anecdotes abounded of workhouse inmates offending so as to be sent to enjoy the better conditions in prison. The dreadful situation received widespread publicity in 1845–46 with the scandal of the Andover workhouse. The master was infamous for his cruelty, and the paupers at Andover were so hungry that they fought over the rotting bones that they were supposed to be crushing for fertilizer.

## Recipes

~~~

The meat and potato pie at the poorhouse would not have had fine buttery pastry, a great proportion of chunky meat, and rich gravy. It would have probably been a much lesser version of the one below, taken from a nineteenth-century cookbook. It might have been simply meat with a mashed potato topping. It was expected that the nineteenth-century housewife be charitable towards poorer neighbors (the "deserving" ones, at any rate), and many books of the time had chapters on cookery for the poor.

---

### Cheap Pastry of Potato in Which Cheap Mince or Stew May Be Neatly Served

Mash the potatoes with a little milk, and a bit of butter, with salt, and a point of finely-shred onion if you like. Border a flat dish thickly with this, and mark it, and place a layer of mash over the dish; brown it in the oven or before the fire, and scoop out the centre, or leave it as a crust, and serve in it hashed beef-heart, kidney-collop, salt or other fish warmed up.

Christian Isobel Johnstone, *The Cook and Housewife's Manual* (1828).

---

## August 13

### Dinner for Admiral Togo Heihachiro
### Knickerbocker Hotel, New York, 1911

Admiral Togo Heihachiro (1848–1934) of the Japanese Imperial Navy, the son of a samurai, and a great naval hero, made a 16-day visit to the United States in 1911. He arrived on August 3 aboard the magnificent Cunard liner *Lusitania* (see September 9), and by August 13 there was still no slackening in the pace of dinners and meetings. Togo had lunch with ex-president Roosevelt on that day and in the evening attended a private dinner given in his honor by the Third Assistant Secretary of State Chandler Hale. A private dinner meant there were no speeches but also not a lack of glamour. It was exclusive. It was held at the Knickerbocker Hotel, for only 20 guests, at $100 a plate, and was said to be one of the most elaborate dinner parties ever held in New York. The guests ate from the hotel's famous solid gold service in a dining room that had been transformed into a flower garden.

Frivolities Japonaise
Supreme of Cantaloup Cocktail
Consomme Ox Tail, Amontillado
Salted Almonds
Filet of English Sole, Veronique
Noix de Ris de Veau Pique
Haricots de Lima Nouveaux
Pommes Tour d'Argent
Punch a la Togo
Poussin de "Bruyere" en Cocotte, Perigourdine
Caneton Souffle, Vendome.     Salade Huguenots
Rocher de Glace, Voile a l'Orientale.
Friandises.     Café Noir

Royal Sherry, Sandringham Palace, 1870.
Johanissberger Schoss Austlese (Fuest Metternich's Cabinet ), 1893
Magnums Pol Roger, Cuvee de Reserve, 1898
Pommery Nature, 1900
Heideck Monopole Brut, 182
G. H. Mumm's Cordon Rouge, 1900.
Chartreuse Grand Jeune, 1869
Grande Fine Champagne, 1830.

Admiral Togo had been educated in England and was very familiar with Western food. It seems that he did not need to take up the Knickerbocker's offer that "he will be provided with any Japanese dishes he may desire, and they will be provided by the Knickerbocker's own kitchen staff."

There was a common tradition of naming the punch for an honored guest, as happened at this dinner, and the *Frivolities Japonaise* were obviously also intended as a compliment, but the real treat was the table centerpiece of spun sugar. It was a model of Togo's flagship, the battleship Mikasa, complete with every turret and gun, and working searchlights and wireless outfit. *The New York Times* reported with obvious pride "Nothing has pleased Togo more since he has been in America than that wonderful ship of sugar."

## Recipes

~~~

Sole Véronique is a classic dish of poached sole garnished with grapes, invented by famous French chef Auguste Escoffier about 1903. This version of the recipe comes from *The Times* (of London) in December 1922.

### Sole Véronique

The fillets are poached in an earthenware dish, and are generally served in the same dish, but experience shows that they can be very satisfactorily transferred

> each to a tiny earthenware casserole, in which they keep very hot, often a problem in serving dinners to advantage in the cold weather.
>
>     The fillets should be slightly beaten, seasoned, folded, and laid in the well-buttered dish, and poached gently with a sauce made of the fish trimmings, a few drops of lemon, a little white wine and water, a little chopped onion, and some parsley stalks, carefully strained. The fish must then be drained and the sauce considerably reduced and thickened and *reinforced* by 1 1/2 oz. of butter and added to the fish. If the fillets are served in the large dish, they should be quickly glazed after the sauce has been poured over them, but this is not necessary if the small casseroles are used. But in either case skinned and iced muscat grapes must be added at the last moment.

Salted Almonds: see April 3.

## August 14

Ministerial Fish Dinner
The Ship Tavern, Greenwich, London, England, 1878

It was a tradition for a large part of the nineteenth century for the Members of Parliament to celebrate the close of the Parliamentary Session with a fish dinner at a tavern on the Thames. Specifically, it was the "Whitebait Dinner" because it happened to be the season for that particular delicacy. In 1878 the organizers decided to add interest by putting a historic spin on the menu (as in the menu of February 2). Forty men enjoyed the following repast:

> Ye annuale whytebait dinner of Hyr Majestye's Ministers on Wednesdaie, ye 14th August, 1878, atte ye Hostelrie 'ye ept ye Shippe, atte Greenwiche. This bill of ye fare is drawn in playne Englysh, without any cloake of Frenche or other foreygne tongue, for the sadde and sobere comforte of friends, and that ye may know what ye are asked to accept. Ye Bille of ye Fare. Ye Soupe.—Soupe made from ye turtle and alsoe soupe made from ye greene fatte of ye same. Ye Fyshe. —Ye flounders curyously cooked, and salmonne served in lyke mannere; ryssoles of ye lobstere; ye lyttel soles, fryed; ye pudynges of ye whyting; ye eles skynned and stewed inne ye riche wyne of Oporto; ye omelette of crabbe in ye style as servyd to ye Guards of ye Blue Seale; ye troute from ye River Spey, grylled with ye sauce of Tartar; salmonne inne collopes, with ye sauce in Cyprus fashionne. Ye whytebaite be-frizzled and also be-devylled. Fleshe and Fowle.- Sweetbreades with ye mushrooms added thereunto; ye haunche of ye royale bucke, with haricotte beanes servyd therewith; ye antient hamme, from ye citye of Yorke, grylled in wyne of Champagne; ye grouse from ye Northe Countree; hogge bacon and young beanes. Ye Sweetes &c.—Apprycottes flavoured with noyau; pudynges iced after ye Nesselrode mannere; lyttel cakes made with ye cheese from Parma, inne Italie; ye ices flavoured with oranges and strauberres; dives fruytes which are your desertes, and ye wynes of Champagne and manie outlandysh countrees. Ye diner will be servyd after ye manner of ye Russian people. Ye guests are bydden to eate after ye Hungarie manner.

Whitebait are very young, very tiny fish—usually herring, but the name is applied to different species in different parts of the world. It was always served in two ways at the dinner—fried and devilled

The tradition began with the member for Dagenham, Sir Robert Preston (1740–1834). He had a small fishing cottage at Dagenham Reach, and got into the habit of inviting his old friend George Rose (1744–1818), the secretary of the treasury, who then suggested Mr. William Pitt (1759–1806) might also enjoy the respite. When Pitt became prime minister in 1804, it was decided that the distance was too far from his responsibilities for such an important man, and a venue close to the city was chosen for a regular fish dinner. Over the years the tradition grew until by 1878 there were 40 worthy members in attendance.

## Recipes

~~~

Whitebait is a great favorite with all who visit London during the months of May, June, and July, when this delicacy is at its most sweet perfection.

---

### Fried White-Bait

To fry white-bait, drain it on a sieve, and then sprinkle it out of your hand lightly upon plenty of flour strewn thickly over a cloth; and, with the fingers of both hands spread apart, quickly and lightly handle the white-bait; and as in a few seconds it will by these means have become well covered with flour, having put it by handfuls into a wire frying basket, shake away all the superfluous flour, and dip the basket containing the prepared white-bait into some very hot clean lard.

A few minutes will suffice to fry the white-bait of a silvery tinge, yet perfectly crisp; pile it up on a napkin, garnish with fried parsley, and. serve it quite hot and crisp, with cayenne, quarters of lemons, and brown bread and butter, separately.

---

### Devilled White-Bait

To devil white-bait, it must be fried a first time in the usual way; and then after being sprinkled over with ground black pepper and salt, is to be fried a second time in very hot frying fat: this being done, season it again with cayenne pepper and salt, and serve quite hot.

Charles Elmé Francatelli, *Cook's Guide and Housekeeper's and Butler's Assistant* (1863).

---

Nesselrode Pudding: see June 30.
Tartar Sauce: see July 20.
Turtle Soup: see November 10.

# August 15

Victory Dinner
aboard the SS *Matsonia,* 1945

When "Victory over Japan Day" or "Victory in the Pacific Day," or simply VJ Day, was declared on August 15, 1945, the *Matsonia* was at sea on the return journey to San Francisco from Hawaii. The ship's cooks immediately set to work to produce a menu that screamed patriotism. The dishes no doubt were simply renamed to emphasize the joy and relief that the war was over.

---

Celery Vassilevsky        Marinated Herring Attlee

Green and Ripe Olives

Potage United States

Filet of Sole Mountbatten

Boiled Corned Brisket of Beef with Cabbage a la Halsey

Special Vegetable Platter with Egg au Stalin

Chicken Giblets Saute a la Nimitz

Chop Suey a la Chiang Kai Shek

Roast Loin of Pork with Apple Sauce a la Truman

Prime Ribs of Beef a la MacArthur

Stewed Tomatoes        Steamed Rice        Broccoli au Beurre

Roast Potatoes        Mashed Potatoes

Assorted Cold Cuts au Blamey

Fruit Salad with Central Pacific Dressing

Cake USO        Jello AWVS

Cheese with Crackers

Fresh Fruit

Coffee

---

The menu is a dictionary of the leaders of the main protagonists of the war. They were the Soviet military leader Aleksandr Vasilevsky (1895–1977), the Supreme Allied Commander of Southeast Asia, Lord Louis Mountbatten (1900–1979), the Commander of the U.S. Third Fleet in the Pacific, William Halsey (1882–1959), the Soviet leader Joseph Stalin (1878–1953), the Commander in Chief of the U.S. Pacific Fleet, Chester Nimitz (1885–1966), the Chinese leader Chiang Kai Shek (1887–1975), the U.S. President Harry S. Truman (1884–1972), U.S. General Douglas MacArthur (1880–1964), Australian Field Marshall Sir Thomas Blamey (1884–1951), and the new Prime Minister of England Clement Attlee (1883–1867) who had been Winston Churchill's deputy during most of the war.

It is ironic that the dish named for Chiang Kai Shek is not Chinese at all. Chop suey is an entirely American invention. The phrase chop suey is apparently derived from the Cantonese *shap sui,* meaning "mixed bits." The classic story of its invention occurs at the time of the visit of the Viceroy of China, Li Hung Chang to America in 1896. He stayed at the Waldorf Hotel in New York, and he brought his own cooks with him, and a popular version of the story is that the dish was an attempt by Chang's cooks to make a dish acceptable to both American and Chinese palates. In reality, the dish had already been noted in print in America in 1888 with the definition of "A staple dish for the Chinese gourmand is chow chop svey [sic], a mixture of chickens' livers and gizzards, fungi, bamboo buds, pigs' tripe, and bean sprouts stewed with spices." In 1904 the American origin was clearly confirmed in another publication, the *Rochester Post-Express*: "One of the Chinese merchants of New York . . . explained that chop suey is really an American dish, not known in China, but believed by Americans to be the one great national dish of the Celestials." Chang's visit probably only served to popularize a dish that was already being made by Chinese immigrants.

## Recipes

~~~

---

Gai Yuk Chee Yuk
(Chicken and Pork Chop Suey).

One half pound of breast of chicken;
one half pound of lean pork;
three tablespoonfuls of sweet lard;
one half pound of mushrooms;
one half bunch of celery;
one dozen lotus seeds;
one half can of bamboo shoots;
two pounds of bean sprouts;
one and one half tablespoonfuls of syou
a dash of cayenne pepper,
and salt,

Take half a pound of chicken cut from the breast and half a pound of lean pork, and cut both into small pieces. Heat three tablespoonfuls of sweet lard; when it is well melted, put the above meat in the fat and fry until brown, stirring to keep it from burning. Have ready the following ingredients: One half pound of fresh or dried mushrooms which have been washed in lukewarm water (if dried mushrooms are used, soak them for ten minutes and pull off the stalks), half a bunch of celery chopped small, a dozen lotus seeds or water chestnuts peeled and cut into thin slices. Cut up one onion, also half a can of bamboo shoots and two pounds of bean sprouts. Wash all well and drain in colander. Put all these, except the bean sprouts, with the meat, and cook for ten minutes; now add the bean sprouts, one and one half tablespoonfuls of syou, a dash of cayenne pepper, and salt, and cook for five minutes. Serve with rice.
Sara Bosse and Onoto Watanna, *Chinese-Japanese Cook Book* (ca. 1914).

---

# August 16

### Dinner of the Wardens of the Drapers' Company
### Home of the Master of the Company, London, England, 1522

The Worshipful Company of Drapers was founded in 1361, and it is ranked third in order of precedence of the livery companies of England (see October 28). In common with the other livery companies, the drapers held an annual Election Dinner. The selection of new wardens and office-bearers did not take place at these dinners; they were always chosen beforehand but were sworn to secrecy until the big day when they were "openly chosen." The nomination of the new ward of the Drapers' Company traditionally took place after evensong on the Feast of Assumption (August 15), and was followed "according to the old custom" with a "potation" (a drink). In 1522 the election dinner took place on August 17, but the chosen ones attended a small private dinner on the sixteenth. John Milborn was Lord Mayor of London in 1521 and acted several times as the master of the Drapers' Company. The "parlour" referred to in this record is presumably in his home.

> On the Sunday after the solemne mass of our Lady, here dined in the parlour, at the sideboard, the master [Milborn], the four wardens and their wives, our two chaplains, and Richardson and his wife [the whole 3 large messes]. The fare for Sunday dinner, besides a cold sirloin of beef that had served for breakfast, consisted of "4 pr. Capons, 2 swans, 2 geese, 2 pikes, half a buck, bak'd, and 5 pasties; and, for a reward, 5 conies, 18 pigeons, 2 tarts, and afterwards, pears and filberds.
>
> William Herbert, *The History of the Twelve Great Livery Companies of London*, Vol. I (1837).

This menu highlights a number of words that are used in quite a different way today. Today the word "mess" is only used in a military context, but at the time of this meal a "mess" referred to a group of people (usually four) eating together from the same dish. Banquet menus and guest lists were planned according to the number of messes. Forks were not introduced into England until the early-seventeenth century, so all the food on the table would have been prepared so as to be able to be eaten with the fingers, a spoon, or from the point of a knife—either directly from the dish, or after being transferred to the guest's individual "trencher" made of bread or wood.

The word "reward" is also used in an unfamiliar manner in this description. At this time it meant an extra supply or allowance of food or an extra dish, although it seems to refer to the second course at this particular meal.

Five pasties would not seem to be sufficient for 13 people today, but a pasty then often meant a single large piece of meat wrapped in dough—sometimes a whole haunch of venison that might take up to 24 hours to cook. Enclosing food in a dough "coffin" was a common method of cooking, transporting, and storing food in the days before shaped metal baking dishes, plastic storage containers, and refrigeration. Thick hard crusts made with rye flour, provided they stayed dry and did not crack, would exclude air and preserve the food for considerable periods of time. The term ''baking'' in fact meant just this—cooking something wrapped in pastry, in an oven, and a ''bake-mete'' was a pie or pasty of any ''meat,'' with meat referring to any food.

## Recipes
~~~

Birds such as capons and geese were often ''farced'' (stuffed) before roasting, and it is likely, given the significance of the occasion, that this was done at this meal. Roasting was done on a spit before the fire and was quite distinct from baking, which was done in the oven after enclosing the meat in dough of some sort.

---

### To Fasse Capon or Goose

To fasse goos or capon tak parsly saige and isope suet and parboile it in freche brothe then tak it up and put ther to herd yolks of eggs hewene then tak grapes mynced onyons and pouder of ginger canelle peppur and salt and fers the goos or capon with it and rost them and serue them.

---

### Cony (Rabbit) Rost

A conye tak and drawe hym and parboile hym rost hym and lard hym then raise his leggs and hys winges and Sauce hym with venegar and pouder of guinger and serue it.
  *A Noble Boke off Cookry ffor a Prynce Houssolde or Eny Other Estately Houssolde* (ca. 1500).

---

Roast Venison: see January 6.

## August 17

Henry Ford's ''All Soy'' Dinner
Century of Progress International Exposition, Chicago, Illinois, 1934

The automobile pioneer Henry Ford (1863–1947) invited 30 journalists to dinner in the executive lounge of the Ford exhibit at the Chicago World Fair in 1934. They were apparently very wary when they learned what they were to be served—a meal made almost entirely from soy beans.

---

Tomato Juice Seasoned With Soy Bean Sauce
Salted Soy Beans
Celery Stuffed with Soy Bean Cheese
Puree of Soy Bean
Soy Bean Cracker

Soy Bean Croquettes with Tomato Sauce
Buttered Green Soy Beans
Pineapple Ring with Soy Bean Cheese
and
Soy Bean Dressing
Soy Bean Bread with Soy Bean Relish
Soy Bean Macaroons
Apple Pie (Soy Bean Crust)
Cocoa With Soy Bean Milk
Soy Bean Coffee
Assorted Soy Bean Cookies
Assorted Soy Bean Candy

The theme of the Century of Progress Fair was technological change and the dependence of industry on scientific research and a perfect theme for Ford. He believed passionately in the interdependence of agriculture and industry, and particularly in agricultural crops as a source of industrial products. It was this belief that led to his interest in soybeans, and initially their application to industry. He was once photographed wearing a suit made from soybean fabric, and he developed a prototype car made from soybean plastic, but he soon became equally passionate about their use as food for humans.

Once piqued, Ford's interest in the culinary uses of soybeans became almost evangelical. He supported the development of recipes in the laboratory run by his childhood friend Edsel Ruddiman, and in his own home by his personal chef Jan Willemse, who was instructed to find ways to serve them at every meal. Not everyone was as enamored as he was in the results

Ford's soy plastic car, 1941. (AP Photo)

of these recipe experiments—one staff member was reported to have said of his soybean biscuit that it was "the vilest thing ever put into human mouths." Nevertheless, the campaign was enormously successful, and although the Ford Company discontinued its research into the soybean after Henry's death, the interest of nutritionists, cookbook writers, and the general public was established.

The soybean (*Glycine max.*) is much higher in protein than any other plant food (and it is high-quality protein for humans) and is also rich in oil (20 percent). It is justifiably the most widely consumed plant food in the world. The advent of World War II was a huge boost to the production of soybeans. Soybean oil was useful in the manufacture of explosives, and its nutritional features meant that it could be used as a substitute on both the meat and wheat-free days. Interest in the soybean finally took off in the 1960s when, with increasing interest in the cultures of the East and the technological development of meat analogues, the West realized what the East had known for millennia—that soy beans are best eaten when processed in some way, such as in soy milk, tofu, tempe, miso, natto, and soy sauce.

---

I believe that industry and Agriculture are natural partners. Agriculture suffers from lack of a market for its product. Industry suffers from a lack of employment for its Surplus men, Bringing them together heals the ailments of both. I see the time coming when a farmer not only will raise raw materials for industry, but will do the initial processing on his farm. He will stand on both his feet—one foot on soil for his livelihood; the other in industry for the cash he needs. Thus he will have a double security. That is what I'm working for!

Henry Ford

---

## Recipes

~~~

---

### Puree of Soybeans Soup

One cup soybean pulp
1 tablespoon finely chopped celery leaves
2 tablespoons chopped onion
3–4 cups meat stock
1 tablespoon flour
2 1/2 cups milk
1 tablespoon butter
1 teaspoon salt
1/8 teaspoon pepper

Cook the soybean pulp which has been put through a coarse sieve, with the celery, onion, and meat stock. Add to a sauce which has been made of the other ingredients. Serve hot with crackers or toast.
*Chilicothe Constitution Tribune*, April 19, 1940.

---

### Soybean Facts

Two pounds of soybean oil will make enough glycerine to fire five anti-tank shells.

One lb. of soy flour = 3 lbs. of roast beef or 42 eggs in protein content.

*Wartime display advertisement* (1944).

---

### Soybean Sugar Cookies

Sift together 1 1/2 cups flour, 1 tablespoon salt, 4 tablespoons baking powder. Cream 2/3 cup soybean oil and 1 2/3 cups sugar. Add 2 beaten eggs and 2 3/4 cups soybean bran. Add milk and sifted dry ingredients, alternately. Drop by spoonfuls on greased baking sheet and bake 15 mins in moderately hot oven.
*Ada Weekly News*, May 14, 1936.

---

### First Mention of Tofu by a Westerner

I will here briefly mention the most usual, common and cheap sort of food all China abounds in, and which all men in that empire eat, from the emperor to the meanest Chinese, the emperor and great men as a dainty, the common sort as necessary sustenance. It is call'd teu fu, that is, paste of kidney-beans. I did not see how they made it. They draw the milk out of the kidney-beans, and turning it, make great cakes of it like cheeses, as big as a large sieve, and five or six fingers thick. All the mass is as white as the very snow, to look to nothing can be finer. It is eaten raw, but generally boil'd and dressed with herbs, fish, and other things. Alone it is insipid, but very good so dressed and excellent fry'd in butter. They have it also dry'd and smok'd, and mix'd with caraway-seeds, which is best of all. It is incredible what vast quantities of it are consum'd in China, and very hard to conceive there should be such abundance of kidney-beans. That Chinese who has teu fu, herbs and rice, needs no other sustenance to work . . . .

Domingo Fernández de Navarrete, *A Collection of Voyages and Travels* (1665).

---

## August 18

### King James I's Breakfast
### Hoghton Tower, Preston, Lancashire, England, 1617

King James VI of Scotland (1566–1625) became King James I of England on the death of his cousin, Queen Elizabeth I (1533–1603), uniting both countries under one crown for the first time. He did not return to Scotland until 1617, and when he did so it was at considerable expense on the part of his subjects. It was expected during royal progresses (tours) of the time that towns and individuals along the way would provide accommodation, supplies, and entertainment to the honored guests and their huge retinues for no other reward than the honor of doing so. The desire to make a favorable impression on his king literally bankrupted Sir Richard Hoghton (d. 1630) who ended up in the debtor's prison after the King stayed at his ancestral home of Hoghton Tower for several days in August 1617, en route to Scotland.

On the morning of August 18, the bill of fare for the King's breakfast was as follows:

| | | |
|---|---|---|
| Sallettes | pigges roste | wild boare pye |
| boyld capon | venison roste | jiggites of mutton boyld |
| could mutton | Duckes boyld | soucd . . . [missing word] |
| veale roste | sallet | gamon [of b]acon |
| boyld chickinges | Redd Deare pye cold | chicking pye |
| Rabbettes roste | capons roste | soucd capon |
| shoulder of mutton roste | Poultes roste | dried hogges cheeke |
| chyne of beefe roste | phesant | humble pie |
| pastie of venison | hearons | tarte |
| turkie roste | muttons boyld | made dishes |

This seems like a strange morning meal, accustomed as most Westerners are to cooked breakfast only at weekends, with the weekday staple being cereal or perhaps toast. For much of history the norm has been two main meals a day, with the timing of these meals being influenced by the hours of devotion determined by the Church and seasonal and agricultural factors. The main meal of the day in medieval times took place between 10 A.M. and noon, with "supper" being taken in late afternoon or early evening. Those who wished would break their overnight fast with a little bread and ale, or perhaps something left over from the night before, but breakfast was not a distinct meal. Over the centuries, the hour for "dinner" (the main meal) slowly advanced, and it became necessary to have a more substantial repast early in the day.

"Traditional" breakfasts are a modern phenomenon. The full British breakfast of bacon and eggs and perhaps other items is essentially a nineteenth-century development. Cold breakfast cereals on the other hand are the work of American health gurus such as the Kellogg brothers and did not come about until the second half of the nineteenth century.

## Recipes

~~~

### An Excellent Way to Boil Chickens

If you will boile Chickens, young Turkies, Pea-Hens or nay house Fowle daintily, you shall after you have trimmed them drawne them, trust [trussed] them, and washt them, fill their bellies as full of Parsley as they can hold, then boile them

Engraving of King James and Queen Anne.

with salt and water only till they be enough: then take a dish and put into it veriuice [verjus], and butter and salt and when the butter is melted, take the Parsley out of the Chickens bellies and mince it very small, and put it to the veriuice
and butter and stirre it well together, then lay in the Chickens and trim the dish
with sippets, and so serve it forth.
   Markham, Gervase, *The English Huswife: Containing the Inward and Outward Vertues Which Ought to Be in a Compleate Woman* (London, 1615).

"Humble Pie" might sound like a strange dish to serve the king, but in fact
it was very popular. The name comes from the "nombles" or "umbles" of the
deer, meaning the entrails or offal, which were the traditional perquisites of
the gamekeeper. The following recipe demonstrates its popularity by suggesting the substitute ingredients of a lamb's head and "purtenances" (the
specific name for lamb offal), should the real thing not be available.

## To Make an Umble-pye

Or, For Want of Umbles to Doe It with a Lambes Head and Purtenance
   Boyle your meate reasonable tender, take the flesh from the bone, and mince
it small with Beefe-suet and Marrow, with the Liver, Lights, and Heart, a few

sweet Hearbs and Currans. Season it with Pepper, Salt, and Nutmeg: bake it in a Coffin raised like an Umble pye, and it will eate like unto Umbles, that you shall hardly by taste discerne it from right Umbles.
John Murrell, *A New Booke of Cookerie* (London, 1617).

Venison Pasty: see January 2.

## August 19

### Hotel Breakfast
### Exchange Station Hotel, Liverpool, England, 1912

Railway companies commonly run hotels at their major intersections to retain the other profit to be made from supplying travelers' other needs. It is interesting to compare this menu with that of the Glasgow Station Hotel of June 27, 1908. This breakfast menu is for the *table d'hote* (see October 10), and cost three shillings.

Tea     Coffee     Chocolate
Pure China Tea (to order)
Fruit     Stewed Fruits

Porridge

Fried Whiting
Grilled Halibut
Haddock     Kippers

Boiled and Poached Eggs
Scrambled Eggs (to order)

Ham Omelette (5 minutes)
Sugar Corn (to order 5 minutes)

Minced Veal and Poached Eggs
Liver and Bacon
Sausages and Bacon

or Cold Meats
Chops and Steaks (to order 20 mins)
Cutlets (to order 10–12 mins)
Grilled Kidneys (to order 10 mins)

Cantaloup Melon 9d.

The most ordinary foods sometimes have interesting histories, or at least lead to other interesting ideas. Almost the only time the verb or adjective "scramble" and "scrambled" is used now is in relation to eggs, but this is a relatively recent usage. The phrase "scrambled eggs" appeared in a *Times* article of 1853, and there was a recipe for them in the American *Mrs. Hale's*

*New Cook Book*, by Sarah Josepha Hale, published in 1857. Isabella Beeton, however, in her incredibly comprehensive *Household Manual* (1861) did not have a recipe for scrambled eggs, so it cannot have been a common usage at that time. Perhaps they were called something else.

A "scramble" used to mean an unseemly rabble, such as the one for the royal leftovers that occurred on the occasion of King James' visit to Oxford in 1687 (see September 5). Before they were scrambled, eggs were "mumbled" or "rumble-tumble." In a culinary sense, "to mumble" is "to cook to a soft pulp." "Mumbling" did not just apply to egg dishes. There are instructions for how "To mumble Rabbets and Chickens" in *The Compleat Housewife: Or, Accomplished Gentlewoman's Companion*, by E. Smith, published in 1728.

## Recipes

~~~

---

### Scrambled Eggs

Put a tablespoonful of butter into a hot frying pan; tip around so that it will touch all sides of the pan. Having ready half a dozen eggs broken in a dish, salted and peppered, turn them (without beating) into the hot butter; stir them one way briskly for five or six minutes or until they are mixed. Be careful that they do not get too hard. Turn over toast or dish up without.

  Mrs. F. L. Gillette and Hugo Ziermann, *White House Cook Book* (1093).

---

### Calf's Liver and Bacon

2 or 3 lbs. of liver,
bacon,
pepper and salt to taste,
a small piece of butter,
flour,
2 tablespoonfuls of lemon-juice,
1/4 pint of water.

Cut the liver in thin slices, and cut as many slices of bacon as there are of liver; fry the bacon first, and put that on a hot dish before the fire. Fry the liver in the fat which comes from the bacon, after seasoning it with pepper and salt and dredging over it a very little flour. Turn the liver occasionally to prevent its burning, and when done, lay it round the dish with a piece of bacon between each. Pour away the bacon fat, put in a small piece of butter, dredge in a little flour, add the lemon-juice and water, give one boil, and pour it in the middle of the dish. It may be garnished with slices of cut lemon, or forcemeat balls.

  *Beeton's Household Manual* (1861).

---

Porridge: see June 27.

## August 20

Mining Company Dinner
Calaveras Hotel, Angel's Camp, California, 1914

When the mining company executive W. J. Loring returned home from England "to renew his memories of the old Mother Lode of California" his friends and colleagues entertained him at a special dinner. The menu was planned around a mining theme—the intention clearly being to honor the man himself as well as the industry that had brought great prosperity to the region. Almost a hundred years later, the same menu functions as a fine summary of the history of the California Gold Rush.

The venue itself—the Calaveras Hotel—was one of the first family hotels to open in the region. It was started in 1877 by Olivia Rolleri, one of the many Italian immigrants who flocked to the area during the Gold Rush. The hotel was famous for its Sunday dinners and "Grandma" Rolleri's famous takeout

---

MENU
—

COCKTAIL
The Will Loring Welcome
—

SOUP
Consomme, Utica Mine
—

HORS-D'OEVRES

*Zinfandel*          Salted Almonds—Olives—Radishes
—

ENTREES

*Welch's*            Oyster Patties, Demarest Style
*Grape Juice*        Ravioli a la Mother Lode
—

ENTREMENTS
Fruit Salad, Melones

*Mineral*            —

*Waters*             ROASTS
Chicken, Lightner Style—Asparagus Tips Venison a la Chasseur
—Sauce Bret Harte—Bell Peppers a la Plymouth Gold
—

DESSERT
Ice Cream, Martin (of Angels, Not New York)
Fancy Cakes
Fruits, Cheese, Coffee & Cognac

---

ravioli. It is presumably this ravioli, or a special version of it, that is on the menu for this dinner.

It is interesting that a fruit juice was featured as one of the beverages on this fine hotel menu. Although Prohibition did not become law across the whole nation until 1920 (see December 6), the temperance movement was increasingly powerful, and nonalcoholic drinks were offered at many events. Welch's grape juice was a phenomenally successful product. It was developed by a dentist, Thomas Bramwell Welch, a very religious man and staunch prohibitionist. He and his family mastered the skill of pasteurizing grape juice (thus preventing its fermentation) to be used as sacramental "wine." It was promoted at the Chicago World Fair in 1893, but was spectacularly boosted to fame when it was served by Secretary of State William Jennings Bryan (himself a prohibitionist) at a diplomatic dinner in 1913. A diplomatic dinner without wine was startling enough, but in 1914 the Secretary of the Navy Josephus Daniels banned alcohol aboard naval ships and substituted Welch's grape juice. There was no significant competition, and it only remained for Prohibition to be enacted for it to become a household name.

---

### KEY TO THE MENU NAMES

*Utica Mine*: the major source of gold in the Angel's Camp area. Four million dollars worth of gold was taken out in just two years in the 1890s.

*Demarest Mine*: named after the mining engineer D. C Demarest who built mining equipment in the 1880s.

*Mother Lode*: a major vein of gold. The vein discovered in California in the 1840s was 120-miles long and up to four-miles wide.

*Melones*: a mining town near some of the richest deposits.

*Lightner*: Abia T. Lightner constructed the first gold stamp mill in the area.

*Bret Harte*: a miner who became an author and wrote about the Gold Rush era.

*Plymouth Gold*: a mining company.

*Martin of Angels*: Angel's presumably refers to the Gold Rush town of Angel's Camp, founded by the brothers George and Henry Angel, gold prospectors who opened the trading post from which the town grew. "Martin" may be the aviation pioneer Glenn L. Martin who had a company in Santa Ana.

---

### Recipes

~~~

---

### Ravioli

Put on the bread board about two pounds of flour in a heap; make a hollow in the middle and put in it a piece of butter, three egg-yolks, salt and three or four tablespoonfuls of lukewarm water. Make a paste and knead it well, then let it stand for an hour, wrapped or covered with a linen cloth. Then spread the paste to a thin sheet, as thin as a ten-cent piece.

Chop and grind pieces of roast or boiled chicken meat: add to it an equal part of marrow from the bones of beef and pieces of brains, three yolks, some crumbs of bread soaked in milk or broth and some grated cheese (Parmesan or Swiss). Rub through a sieve and make little balls as big as a hazel-nut, which are to be placed at equal distances (a little more than an inch) in a line over the sheet of paste.

Beat a whole egg and pass it over the paste with a brush all around the little balls. Cover these with another sheet of paste, press down the intervals between each ball, and then separate each section from the other with a knife. Moisten the edges of each section with the finger dipped in cold water, to make them stick together, and press them down with the fingers or the prongs of a fork. Then put to boil in water seasoned with salt or, better still, in broth. The ravioli are then to be served hot seasoned with cheese and butter or with brown stock or tomato sauce.

Maria Gentile, *The Italian Cook Book: The Art of Eating Well* (New York, ca. 1919).

Salted Almonds: see April 3.

## August 21

Frankfurt Congress of Princes Banquet
Römer, Frankfurt, Germany, 1863

The Austrian Emperor Franz Joseph I (1830–1916) invited the sovereigns of the Central European states that made up the German Confederation to a congress in the Imperial free city of Frankfurt in 1863. The central event was naturally a banquet, and the bill of fare was "a curiosity in its way," according to the English *Globe* newspaper, which reported it in detail.

*Erbach et St. Julien en carafons.*
Le potage chevalière,
Le consommé de volaille;

*Gold Sherry, Exhibition prize wine.*
Les croquettes de Cailles,
Les canapés de Caviar,

*Champagne des Souverains [Cliquot].*
Les truites (sauce crevettes),
Les filets de turbot en Bellevue.

*1837 Hockheim, domaine de la ville libre de Francfort.*
Le quartier de boeuf historique,
Les dindes truffées perigueux.

*1859 Chateau Lafitte Monopole.*
Les supremes de perdreaux au congrès des princes,

Les côtelettes de poulets a l'impériale,
Les baldons de gelinottes l'Irlandaise (sur socle),
Les tranches de homards galdées (sur socle),

*1862 Assmannhausen, domaine ducal*
Les asperges en branches (sauce au beurre),
Les fonds d'artichauds à la Lyonnaise,
Les haricots verts à l'Anglaise,
Les petits pois à la Francaise,

*1858 Rauenthal, Exhibition medal winner.*
Les chapons du mans à la broche,
Le cimier du chevreuil à l'Infante
Les Faisans de Bohême à la Saint-Remi,
Les daubes de bécasses (sur socle),

*Port-à-port vieux*
Les ananas à la ville de Francfort,
Les timbales d'abricots mousseux,
Les canons royaux,
Les cascades diplomates,
Les glaces d'échange,

*Ausbeer wein.*
Le dessert,
Les fruits variées.

The German Confederation had been formed from 39 member states at the Congress of Vienna in 1815, in the wake of the defeat of Napoleon. From its inception there was intense rivalry between Austria and Prussia for supremacy. In an attempt to avert the Prussian Chancellor Otto von Bismarck's (1815–1898) plans for a "little Germany" which would exclude Austria, Franz-Joseph arranged "the Congress of Princes" to discuss reform of the Federation. The banquet itself appeared to be a success as the *Globe* reported that "the fathers of that city, in their banquet to the sovereigns, had put their whole strength into the vinous bill of fare" and "the Sovereigns, it is no breach of confidence to mention, did full justice to the qualities and quantities of the excellent wines set before them. " The Congress itself, however, was ultimately worse than a failure, serving to escalate the hostility between the two nations and resulting in outright war in 1866.

The aspects of the bill of fare that were "curious" to the newspaper correspondent were those that reinforced that this was not merely a social event, but that there was a powerful political agenda at work. The coronation symbolism was clear. The dinner was held in the Hall of the Emperors in the Römer (City Hall), the place of coronations for centuries. The *quartier de boeuf historique* was representative of the whole ox roasted in the town square for the emperor's loyal subjects on coronation day since ancient times. The first slice was traditionally cut by the Arch-Steward, who presented it to the Emperor to symbolize the abundance of the empire. Many of the other dishes have regal names and imperial allusions: the breast of partridge *au congress des princes* was obviously invented for the occasion; the chicken *a l'imperiale* is self-explanatory; the saddle of deer *à l'Infante* was named for one of the Spanish princesses.

Some of the other menu items are more puzzling—the *canons royaux* (royal cannons) and *cascades diplomates* (diplomat waterfalls), for example. These were presumably sweet dishes invented or adapted for the occasion by the imperial chefs. Overall, however, this was classic European cuisine, with almost no concession to "Germany," apart from the pheasants from the forests of Bohemia (considered the finest pheasants in Europe), and the rather more exotic *ananas* (pineapples) from Frankfort, which surely was a way of boasting of the hothouse facilities of the town.

## Recipes

~~~

### Artichokes à la Lyonnaise

Take three large artichokes, and divide each into eight pieces, remove the hard parts, the choke, and nearly all the leaves; trim what remains, and throw them into cold water as you do them; wash and drain them well, spread half a pound of butter on the bottom of a stewpan, and lay your artichokes on it, sprinkling them with salt and pepper: half an hour before they are wanted, put them over a brisk fire, cover the stewpan and put fire on that also, taking care that they do not burn. When they are of a nice light colour, serve them, pouring butter over them.

Richard Dolby, *The Cook's Dictionary and Housekeeper's Director* (1833).

The following recipe, which uses "any poultry" can be adapted to make the *Les Croquettes de Cailles* [Quails].

### Poultry Croquettes (Using any Poultry)

Melt a bit of butter in a stewpan; put into it chopped parsley and mushrooms, two spoonfuls of flour, salt, pepper, and nutmeg. Fry it, and pour in stock and a little cream. This sauce ought to have the consistence of thick milk. Cut up any poultry, which has been cooked the day before, into dice. Put them into the sauce and let it get cold. Form it into balls, and cover them with breadcrumbs. Wash these in eggs which have been beaten up, and roll them in bread crumbs a second time. Fry to a good colour, and serve with a garnish of fried parsley.

Harriet Toogood, *The Treasury of French Cookery* (1866).

Canapes de Caviar: see May 13.
Petits Pois a' la Francaise: see July 11.
Sauce Perigeux: see April 14.

## August 22

### An Ancient Roman Dinner
### Rome, 70 BCE

There are not many detailed descriptions of the food served at specific meals in ancient Rome, and very few that can be dated reasonably accurately. One of the most detailed is that of the feast given at the inauguration of Lucius Cornelius Lentulus Niger (d. about 56 BCE) to the honored role of Flamen Martialis (the priest dedicated to the service of Mars, the Roman god of war). It has been suggested that this took place on August 22 (the Romans used a different calendar, though), in the year 70 BCE.

The feast was given by the Pontifex Maximus (High Priest) Quintus Caecilius Metellus Pius (ca. 130 or 127 BCE—63 BCE), and amongst the important guests was Julius Caesar (100 BCE– 44 BCE). The only women present were the Vestal virgins (virginal female priests dedicated to Vesta, the goddess of the hearth).

---

The *gusto*.

Before the dinner proper came sea hedgehogs; fresh oysters, as many as the guests wished; large mussels; sphondyli; field fares with asparagus; fattened fowls; oyster and mussel pasties; black and white sea acorns; sphondyli again; glycimarides; sea nettles; becaficoes; roe ribs; boar's ribs; fowls dressed with flour; becaficoes; purple shellfish of two sorts.

The *cena*.

The dinner itself consisted of sows' udder; boar's head; fish-pasties; boar-pasties; ducks; boiled teals; hares; roasted fowls; starch pastry; Pontic pastry.

---

There are a number of difficulties in working out what was actually eaten in Roman times. Latin essentially died as a spoken language with the Roman Empire. Its survival in religious and scientific fields did not extend to the culinary sphere, and many terms can only be translated by educated guesswork. In addition, the only surviving Roman cookbook is *De re Coquinaria* (On Cookery) by "Apicius"—but not only are there three contenders for the name, the actual compilation that survives comes from the late-fourth or early-fifth century and is presumably based on earlier copies.

One great difficulty in interpreting—and especially in attempting to re-create Roman meals, is that two essential ingredients of the time are uncertain. A plant called *laser* (or silphium) which was much used by the Romans is now extinct. The reasons are unclear, and it appears to have happened very suddenly. The plant was harvested from the wild in North Africa; it was not cultivated. One year it simply did not come up again—perhaps due to over-harvesting in combination with a bad season—a devastating blow to the communities which were economically dependent on it as a crop. Most authorities believe *laser* was similar to *asafoetida* (*Ferula assafoetida*), which is used in Indian cooking today.

The other difficulty is that a sauce called *garum* or *liquamen* was absolutely fundamental to Roman cookery, but no recipe has survived. It was the universal salty condiment and was made from fermenting some species of fish intestines, as Asian fish sauce is made today. It was a very smelly process, so the manufacture was done outside of the cities. The liquid resulting from the fermentation process was mixed with other ingredients—wine, vinegar, pepper, etc., the exact recipe no doubt varying from one cook to another.

The *sphondyli* that appeared at the inauguration feast appears to have two meanings in Apicius. Sometimes it means a vegetable (parsnip or artichokes) and sometimes a type of mussel—the most likely at this meal is that it referred to the latter. The *glycimarides* are also shellfish, "sea hedgehogs" are sea urchins, and *becaficoes* are fig-peckers (small birds). Finally, the pastry would not have been the fine, "short" pastry of today because the Romans used oil, not butter in cooking—they despised animal fat—and oil does not make good pastry.

## Recipes

~~~

---

### Sow's Udder or Belly (Sumen)

Sow's udder or belly with the paps on it is prepared in this manner: the belly boil, tie it together with reeds, sprinkle with salt and place it in the oven, or, start roasting on the gridiron. Crush pepper, lovage, with broth, pure wine, adding raisin wine to taste, thicken the sauce with roux and pour it over the roast.

---

### A Dish of Sea-Nettles
### (Patina de Urtica)

A dish of sea-nettles, either hot or cold, is made thus: take sea-nettles, wash and drain them on the colander, dry on the table and chop fine. Crush 10 scruples of pepper, moisten with broth, add 2 small glasses of broth and 6 ounces of oil. Heat this in a sauce pan and when cooked take it out and allow to cool off. Next oil a clean pan, break 8 eggs and beat them; combine these with the above preparations, place the pan on hot ashes to give it heat from below, when done [congealed] sprinkle with pepper and serve.

Joseph Dommers Vehling, *Cookery and Dining in Imperial Rome* (1936).

---

## August 23

### Luncheon Specials of the Day
### MGM Studios, Culver City, California, 1956

Metro Goldwyn Mayer (MGM) was the most powerful movie studio in Hollywood (Culver City) for many decades. At its peak, one movie a week was turned out from its studios and included some of the best-loved and most successful ever made—films like *Gone with the Wind*, *The Wizard of Oz*, and *Ben Hur*.

A huge organization had to ensure that its staff was fed, and MGM had a restaurant at Culver City. The luncheon menu on August 23, 1956, provided plenty of choice.

---

*Specials of the Day*

### LUNCHEON

French Market Soup with Cheese Croutons:      Cup   15;   Bowl   20

CLUB LUNCHEONS
| | |
|---|---|
| Fresh Shrimps with Curry, a l'Indienne, Steamed Rice | 1.00 |
| Fluffy Omelett Filled with Creamed Chicken | 95 |
| Grilled Knackwurst and Boston Baked Beans en Casserole, Pickled Beets | 1.05 |
| Veal Cutlet Holstein with Tomato Sauce and Spaghetti, Milanaise | 1.15 |
| Baked Sugar-Cured Virginia Ham with Cider Sauce | 1.15 |

Julienne of Celery and Carrots Steamed Parsley Potatoes
        Bread and Butter      Coffee, Tea, Milk

FEATURED SALADS
| | |
|---|---|
| Ripe Elberta Peach, Fresh Prunes with Cottage Cheese and Sour Cream | 1.00 |
| Diced Turkey Salad, Deviled Eggs and Asparagus Tips | 1.25 |
| Watermelon Wedge | |
| Large Fruit Compote, Supreme, Assorted Finger Sandwiches on | 1.10 |
| Raisin Nut Bread | |

CHEF'S SUGGESTIONS
| | |
|---|---|
| Braised Turkey Leg with Vegetables and Potatoes du jour, Cole Slaw | 75 |

        Bread and Butter      Coffee, Tea, Milk 5c Extra

SANDWICHES
| | |
|---|---|
| Open Face Sandwich of Crisp Bacon, Tomatoes, Chives and Sour Cream | 65 |
| on Toast | |
| Imported Sardines, Sliced Egg, Onion and Lettuce on Rye | 75 |
| Denver Sandwich, Pancake Style | 65 |

DESSERTS
Custard Pie   25           Brown Betty Pudding, Wine Sauce   15
Raspberry Layer Cake   25        Green Apple Pie   15
Chilled Canteloupe   35
Ice Cream   20          Sherbet   20          Jell-O   15
Iced Watermelon   35

---

To give some perspective on the cost of the menu items, the minimum wage in 1956 was $1.00 per hour, and the average weekly wage was about $62.

Recipes

~~~

---

### Brown Betty

| | |
|---|---|
| 6 cooking apples | Apple corer |
| 1/2 cup molasses | Measuring cup |
| 1/2 cup cold water | Baking dish |
| 4 tablespoonfuls | brown sugar |
| Butter | Breadcrumbs |

Take 6 large, tart apples, core them and peel them and cut them into small slices.

Take a baking dish, butter the inside and cover the bottom with one layer of apple slices. Sprinkle a layer of breadcrumbs over the apple, then lay more apple over the crumbs, and so on until you have used all the apple. There must be a layer of crumbs on top.

Measure 1/2 cupful of black molasses and 1/2 cupful of cold water.

Add to this 4 tablespoonfuls of brown sugar and stir till the sugar is dissolved.

Pour the mixture over the apple and crumbs and drop four little bits of butter on top of all.

Put the dish in a moderate oven for about 3/4 of an hour, or until it is nicely browned on top, and the apples are soft. Try them with a fork.

Serve hot with cream or hard sauce.

*When Mother Lets us Cook* (1908).

---

The Denver sandwich is also called the Western sandwich. As with so many "classics," there are disputes as to the authentic ingredients and the claimed inventor. The only common feature seems to be that all recipes include egg.

---

### Denver Sandwich

1 egg
3 slices toast
mayonnaise
sliced tomatoes
Chopped onion and green pepper (optional)
Snappy cheese which melts smoothly

Scramble egg in butter and place between slices of toast. Spread the top of the second slice with mayonnaise and cover it with sliced tomatoes and a sprinkling of chopped onion and green pepper (pickle relish would be a good substitute and it is ready to spread on). Cover with the third slice of toast spread with mayonnaise. Cut in half, place on serving plate and cover with the cheese which has been melted in a double boiler. Serve immediately.

*Oakland Tribune*, December 30, 1941.

---

## August 24

King George IV's Visit to Scotland
Great Hall of Parliament House, Edinburgh, 1821

When King George IV (1762–1830) of England visited Scotland in 1821, it was the first visit of a reigning monarch to that country since 1650. The King had been encouraged by his advisors to take a tour in an attempt to improve his image which had suffered on account of his treatment of his wife at his coronation (see July 19). He was welcomed at an elaborate civic banquet in Edinburgh. The service of a grand meal was still in the same style as it had been since medieval times—two great courses each with a vast number of dishes arranged to give the maximum visual impact.

---

FIRST COURSE.

(1) Cotelettes d'Agneau sauce au Concombres.

(2) Vol au Vent au Blanquette de Truffes.

(3) Filets de Soles, Sauce Hollandaise.

(4) Potage de Tortue Relevee par,

1. Poisson; 2. Venaison;

3. Grouse et Dindonneaux

(5) Grenade farce, sauce aux Champignons.

(6) Filets de Grouse aux Choux Sauce Piquante

(7) Tendrons de Vea aux Poie

(8) Potage a la Reine. Releve par,

1. Poisson; 2. Venaison;

3. Grouse et Dindonneaux.

(9) Filets de Pigeons a l'Italien.

(10) Escalopes de Poulets a l'Essence

(11) Saute Grouse aux Truffes

(12) Boudins a la Reine.

CENTRE DISHES.

(21) Nougat.

(22) Gold Frame.

(23) Vase.

(24) Silver Ice Pail.

(25) Couronne.

(26) Gold Frame.

(27) Piece Monte.

(28) Large Silver Branch, with Lights.

(29) Caramel de Fruit

(30) Gold Frame.

(31) Gold Frame.

(32) Silver Ice Pail

(33) Piece Monte.

(34) Piece Monte.

(35) Silver Ice Pail

(36) Vase

(47) Pate de Pigeons Garni.

(48) Chartreuse de Legumes.

(49) Un oie dobe aux truffes et Champignons

(50) Jambon Braise aux Legumes.

(51) Poulets au Gros Sel.

(52) Petits Pates d'une Emincee

(53) Chartreuse de Legumes.

(54) Quartier d'Agneau sauce au Chevreuil.

(55) Poularde au Riz, garni au Croquettes

(56) Canards aux Filets de Lapreaux.

(57) Chartreuse de Legumes garnie.

(58) Peties Pates d'Arioles aux Cervelles de Veau.

(59) Poulets aux Truffes.

(60) Jambon Braise aux Legumes.

(13) Tranches de Saumon a la Maitre d'hotel

(14) Potage de Grouse

Relevee par,

1. Poisson; 2. Venaison;

3. Grouse et Dindonneaux.

(15) Fricandeau sauce aux Tomates

(16) Saute de filets de Poulet.

(17) Vol au Vent aux Truffes

(18) Potage a la Tortue

Releve par,

1. Poisson; 2. Venaison;

3. Grouse et Dindonneaux.

(37) Gold Frame.

(38) Caramel de Fruit

(39) Large Silver Branch, with Lights

(40) Piece Monte

(41) Gold Frame

(42) Couronne

(43) Silver Ice Pail

(44) Vase

(45) Gold Frame

(46) Nougat.

(61) Casserole de Pieds d'Agneau au Riz.

(62) Chartreuse aux Choux-Fleurs

(63) Pate Chaud de Pigeons.

## SECOND COURSE.

(1) Cailles Roties

(2) Gelee d'Ananas

(3) Petits Pois a la Francaise.

(4) Vol au Vent d'Abricots Caramel

(5) Salade en Aspic.

(6) Dindonneaux Roti.

(7) Crème au Maraschino.

(8) Beignets d'Artichaux a la Sauce.

(9) Patisserie

(10) Homard en Aspic.

(11) Gelee de Vin

(12) Chartreuse d'Abricots.

(13) Champignons Grille3.

(14) Patisserie.

(15) Salade en Aspic.

(16) Crème a l'Italien.

(17) Grouse Roti.

(18) Homard Garnie.

(19) Vol au Vent de Fruit.

(20) Petits Pois a la Francaise

(21) Gelee de Noyau.

(22) Cailles Roti.

(23) Piece Monte

(24) Haricot Vert

(25) Dindonneaux Rotis

(26) Un Aspic

(27) Gelee d'Ananas.

(28) Pate Froid

(29) Choux-Fleurs a la Bechamelle

(30) Tourte d'Abricots

(31) Crème a l'Italienne

(32) Cailles Rotis

(33) Piece Monte

(34) Dindonneaux Rotis

(35) Crème de Marasquin

(36) Tourte de Fruit

(37) Hariots Verts

(38) Pate Froid

(39) Gelee de Vin

(40) Un Aspic

(41) Grouse Rotie

(42) Choux-fleurs a la Crème

(43) Patisserie

The manager of the whole event was Sir Walter Scott (1771–1832), 1st Baronet, and author of *Ivanhoe*, *Rob Roy*, and a number of other historical novels. The occasion was a grand opportunity for the Scots to demonstrate their national pride, and at this event the tartan became the national dress of Scotland.

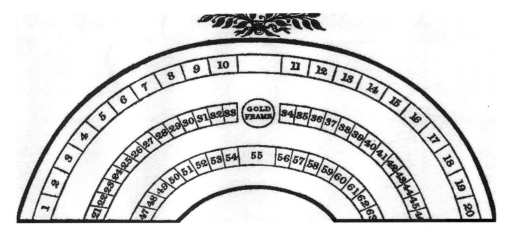

Table layout for King's visit to Scotland.

The author of *Domestic Economy, and Cookery, for Rich and Poor, by a Lady,* who included the bill of fare in her book, noted that "His majesty ate of the first course, turtle and grouse soups, stewed carp, and venison; of the second, grouse, and apricot tart. At dinner he drank Moselle and a little Champagne: at the dessert, he drank Claret."

Recipes

~~~

The following recipes are for dishes similar to those chosen by the King at this dinner.

---

### Carp

When you kill your carp, save all the blood, and have ready some nice gravy, made of beef and mutton, seasoned with pepper, salt, mace, and onion. Before you put in your fish, strain it off, and boil your carp before you put it into the gravy. Set it on a slow fire about a quarter of an hour, and thicken the sauce with a large piece of butter rolled in flour; or you may make your sauce thus: take the liver of the carp clean from the guts, three anchovies, a little parsley, thyme, and an onion. Chop these small together, and take half a pint of Rhenish wine, four spoonsful of vinegar, and the blood of the carp. When all these are stewed gently together, put it to the carp, which must first be boiled in water with a little salt and a pint of wine; but take care not to do it too much after the carp is put into the sauce.

William Augustus Henderson, *Modern Domestic Cookery* (1828).

---

### Toarte d'Abricots

Cut each in two, and break the stones to get at the kernels; if the fruit is not ripe enough, boil them a little while in Water; then drain them very well, and put them into the Paste, with Sugar according to judgment, a few bits of preserved Lemon, and half a kernel upon each Piece; cover it with the same sort of Paste, and strew a little powder sugar over it to give it a glaze, which it will take in baking.

B. Clermont, *The Professed Cook* (1776).

Maitre d'Hotel Butter for Fish: see September 3.
Roast Grouse: see July 26.

## August 25

Hotel Dinner
Grand Hotel, Yarmouth, Nova Scotia, Canada, 1911

A thriving tourist industry in Nova Scotia in the late-nineteenth century was largely thanks to the Yarmouth businessman Loran Ellis Baker (1831–1899). He competed with established American railroad and steamship companies and kept all the business local by setting up the Yarmouth Steamship Company, which not only brought tourists into the province, but also provided them with accommodation and every other requirement of travel. His finest project was the Grand Hotel overlooking the Yarmouth harbour, which opened in 1894.

HOURS FOR MEALS

Breakfast 7.30 to 9.30

Luncheon 12.30 to 2

Dinner 6 to 7

Sunday—Breakfast 8.30 to 10

Dinner 1 to 2.00

Supper 6 to 7

GINGER ALE
AND
MINERAL WATERS
————————

| | |
|---|---|
| Coca Cola | 15 |
| Havelock Ginger Ale | 25c |
| White Rock Lithia, pints | 25c |
| "         "        splits | 15c |
| Apollinaris Water, pints | 25c |
| "         " | 15c |

Guests will please report at the office when having friends to meals. Meals served in room charged extra.

DINNER

Chicken Broth a la Riz      Cream of Celery

Olives      Lettuce

Pickled Walnuts India Relish      Pearl Onions

Worcestershire Sauce      Tomato Ketchup

Hot Beef Bouillon      Hot Clam Bouillon

Baked Fresh Halibut, Point Shirley Style

Boiled Boneless Salt Cod, Pork Scraps
Sliced Cucumbers          Italienne Potatoes

Baked Macaroni and Cheese

Corn Fritters, Maple Syrup

Roast Ribs of Beef, Pan Gravy
Roast Spring Lamb, Mint or Brown Sauce
Boiled New Potatoes          Mashed Potatoes
Green Peas          Ears of Corn          Mashed Turnip

Fruit Custard, Whipped Cream
Blueberry Pie          Pumpkin Pie
Pound Cake          Assorted Cakes
Peanut Butter
Vanilla Ice-Cream
Cream Sodas          Canadian Cheese
Watermelon          Apples          California Pears
Black Tea Oolong Tea
Black Coffee

---

This is as comprehensive and indulgent a dinner menu as any traveller could have wished for, but there are also two popular medicines hidden amongst its choices. Clam bouillon seems to have been a particularly popular remedy in the late-nineteenth century Canada. The *Canadian Druggist* of 1899, in its Hot Drinks Formulary, gave a recipe for clam bouillon with lemon. In an 1894 *Ontario Medical Journal* there was a testimonial from Dr. Hopewell of Canton, New Jersey, who said, "I have found Burnham's Clam Bouillon the best thing I have ever used in summer diarrhoea in children, and ask my fellow practitioners to give it a trial, given by itself or added to other food, its effect is wonderful."

The second "remedy" is the cream soda. Cream soda and ice cream soda are variations on the same idea of a milky/creamy/carbonated drink. The idea of serving a scoop or two of ice cream in a carbonated beverage seems to have come about in the 1870s in America, and there are several claimants for the honor of inventing it. In Canada, a patent for a cream soda recipe was granted to James William Black of Berwick in Nova Scotia in 1886, although it contained whipped egg whites instead of cream. Cream sodas were sold at drug stores and were often prescribed as medicine.

---

### Is Ice Cream Soda a Medicine?

On October 27, 1899, the final hearing was given to a charge brought by the Morality Department of the City of Toronto against W. J. Urquhart who

formerly kept a drug store at the corner of Yonge and Gerard Sts. in this city. The information, which was laid on behalf of the Lord's Day Alliance, charged the defendant with having sold two glasses of ice cream soda, on Sunday, thereby violating the Lord's Day Act. The only evidence submitted was that of Constable Guthrie, who testified to having made the purchase of ice cream soda as a beverage, Police Constable Ironsides have also made a similar purchase at the same time. For the defence, Dr. Mennie, Dr. Noble, and Mr. Geo. A. Bingham, druggist, were called. Their evidence was to the effect that Cream Soda was a medicine, and that its constituents were frequently prescribed by physicians. . . . After hearing argument on both sides, the Magistrate stated his desire to have the case go to a higher court, in order to have an interpretation of the law. He accordingly fined Mr. Urquhart $1 and costs, or ten days. Subsequently, Police Magistrate Dennison gave the following written judgement: " I find upon the evidence that Soda Water and Ice Cream are sometimes sold as medicine. In my opinion, sale of these articles mentioned in the evidence, was not made as a sale of medicine, although nothing was said by either party on the subject. I fine the defendant $1, and costs, or ten days."
*Canadian Druggist*, 1899.

## Recipes
~~~

### Corn Fritters

To a can of corn add two eggs well beaten, two tablespoonfuls of flour, one teaspoonful of salt, one half-teaspoonful of pepper; mix thoroughly; have the pan hot; put in two tablespoonfuls of lard, and drop in the corn in large spoonfuls. Cook brown.

B. F. Austin, *Woman, Her Character, Culture and Calling: A Full Discussion of Woman's Work in the Home, the School, the Church and the Social Circle, with an Account of Her Successful Labors in Moral and Social Reform* (Brantford, Ontario 1890).

### Canadian Pumpkin Pie

1 cup strained or mashed pumpkin
1/2 cup syrup [presumably maple]
1/4 cup brown sugar
1 beaten egg
1/2 teaspoon salt
1/4 teaspoon ginger or cinnamon
1/4 cup cream

Mix in order given, and bake until firm in a tin lined with pie dough.
Ottawa Ladies Hebrew Benevolent Society, *The Economical Cook Book* (1915).

Pound Cake: see April 19.

## August 26

Breakfast and Dinner on Mont Blanc
Switzerland, 1825

Mont Blanc is the highest peak in the Alps, at 15,781 feet (4,810 meters). By mountaineering standards, it is not a difficult climb; nevertheless, it has claimed many lives since its summit was first reached in 1786. Ascending the mountain hardly seems the sort of thing anyone would do virtually spontaneously, "for no other motive but that of curiosity." Nevertheless, that is what Edmund Clark and Captain Markham Sherwill did in August 1825.

The party (Clark, Sherwill, guides, and porters) spent one night on the way up at the usual camp site of Grand Mulets Rocks. They set off for the summit early in the morning of August 26, returning to the same camp for the night. The men, according to a widely published report of the feat, were "in hourly and imminent danger of their lives." They were in no danger of going hungry, however, to judge by their provisions list. Their "bill of fare" also provides an interesting comparison with modern camping and mountaineering food.

> twenty-one bottles of vin ordinaire,
> one bottle of Cognac brandy,
> one bottle of vinegar,
> one toupelle of syrup,
> two of sirop de vinaigre,
> two bottles of old Neuchatel wine,
> two bottles of claret,
> seven loaves,
> five pounds of cheese,
> two pounds and a half of sugar,
> and lemons,
> three pounds of raisins and prunes,
> nine cold fowls,
> eight joints of veal and mutton.
>
> "These provisions," he adds, "were all packed in haversacks and sent on by porters to the edge of the glacier, where we were to breakfast. These porters the guides thought proper to hire themselves, that they might be less embarrassed in ascending to the base of the mountain, and be ready to embark on the ice with unimpaired vigour."

There is no specific mention of camp stoves, and no suggestion of portable soup (see July 17) or other hot food, although it is most likely that some sort of stove was included—otherwise the cold fowls and joints would have been eaten nearly frozen. In any case, it appears from the list that the brandy may have been intended for a hot toddy of sorts—which would explain the lemons and sugar, and the necessity for the means to heat it.

## Recipes

~~~

---

### Undressed Meat
### (To Be Served Cold)

All meat that is dressed to be kept until cold, whether boiled or roast, should be over done, particularly in the summer, for if the gravy be left in either, it will not keep good more than two or three days, but if done quite dry it will keep a week or longer. Hot meat should be well sprinkled with salt before it is taken from the fire; and boiled beef that is intended to be eaten cold should be at least fourteen days in salt (if a few days longer it will eat all the better when boiled) on account that if not well salted, by being boiled rather longer than it would be to send to table hot, it will eat insipid.

John Simpson, *A Complete System of Cookery on a Plan Entirely New* (1816).

---

### Leg of Mutton

Cut off the Shank Bone, and trim the Knuckle, put it into lukewarm water for ten minutes, wash it clean, cover it with cold water, and let it simmer *very gently*, and skim it carefully. A leg of nine pounds will take two and a half or three hours, if you like it thoroughly done, especially in very cold weather.

William Kitchiner, *The Cook's Oracle* (1829).

---

## August 27

### ``Great Martial Banquet Alfresco,''
### Scutari, Crimea, 1855

Alexis Soyer (1810–1858) was a famous French celebrity chef of the Victorian era. He cooked for the most elite members of society, and created some of the most spectacular banquets of the nineteenth century (see July 3). He was also a great philanthropist and inventor as was demonstrated during his great contribution to relief work during the Irish potato famine of the 1840s. The Crimean War (1853–1856) offered him another opportunity to display his charitable and inventive traits.

The conditions at the front were appalling. More troops were dying of disease and malnutrition than in battle. In March 1855 Soyer traveled to the Crimea at his own expense and met with the famous nursing pioneer Florence Nightingale (1820–1910). He started by completely reorganizing the hospital kitchens at Scutari, and by the end of his time at the front every aspect of military victualling had benefited from his reforming hand. He taught soldiers to cook, reduced waste, invented new recipes using soldiers' rations, organized supplies of dried vegetables, and developed a new "bread biscuit." He also developed a new field stove which he demonstrated at a great outdoor "banquet" to which the senior officers of the English, French,

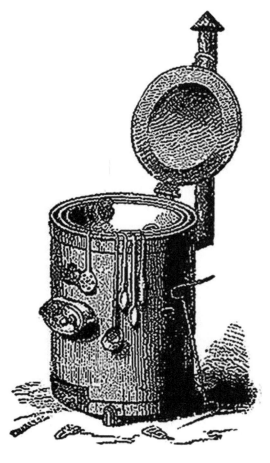

Field stove.

and Sardinian forces were invited. All of the dishes were based on soldiers' rations.

> The bill of fare consisted of plain-boiled salt beef; ditto with dumplings; plain-boiled salt pork; ditto with peas-pudding; stewed salt pork and beef, with rice; French pot-au-feu; stewed fresh beef, with potatoes; mutton ditto, with haricot beans; ox-cheek and ox-feet soups; Scotch mutton-broth; and common curry, made with fresh and salt beef.

The field stove was a portable steam boiler designed to give no signals to the enemy. It looked like a wastebasket, with a lid (no visible flames), a steam pipe (virtually no smoke), and a removable cooking pot. The design was so successful that it remained in use by the military, essentially unchanged, until the Gulf War during 1990–91.

## Recipes
~~~

Soyer kept up a correspondence with *The Times* (of London) newspaper while he was in the Crimea. He included many of his own ration ''receipts'' in his letters.

### French Beef Soup,
### Or Pot Au Feu (Camp Fashion)

Put in the kettle 6lb of beef, cut into two or three pieces, bones included; 1lb of mixed green vegetables, or 1/2lb of preserved, in cakes; 4 teaspoonsful of salt; if handy, 1 teaspoonful of pepper, 1 of sugar, and 3 cloves; and 8 pints of water. Let it boil gently 3 hours; remove some of the fat, and serve. The addition of 1½ lb. of bread, cut into slices, or 1 lb. of broken biscuits, well soaked, will make a very nutritious soup. Skimming is not required.

### How to Stew Fresh Beef, Pork, Mutton And Veal

Cut or chop 2lb of fresh beef into 10 or 12 pieces and put these into a saucepan with 1 1/2 teaspoonful of salt, 1 teaspoonful of sugar, 1/2 teaspoonful of pepper, 2 middle-sized onions sliced, 1/2 pint of water. Set on the fire for 10 minutes until forming a thick gravy. Add a good tablespoon of flour, stir on the fire a few minutes; add a quart and a half of water; let the whole simmer until the meat is tender. Beef will take from two hours and a half to three hours; mutton and pork, about two hours; veal, one hour and a quarter to one hour and a half; onions, sugar and pepper, if not to be had, must be omitted; it will then make a good dish; 1/2lb of sliced potatoes or 2oz of preserved potatoes; ration vegetables may be added, also a small dumpling.

## August 28

Lunch at Sea
SS *Königin Luise,* 1905

The SS *Königin Luise* (Queen Louise) was built in 1896 for the Norddeutscher Lloyd (North German Lloyd) line to carry immigrants from Bremen to New York or, until 1904, to Australian ports. The menu was written in German, with an English translation on the facing page.

Russian Cabbage soup      Consommé
Purée soup of lentils
—
Stuffed calf's breast
Succotash      Butter potatoes
—
Hunter Cake
—
Stewed Prunes
—
TO ORDER
WARM: Beefsteaks, broiled or fried
Mutton chops do.
Pork and beans, Boston style
Irish stew      Spaghetti au jus
Omelet with poultry liver
Poached eggs      Fried eggs
Baked potatoes

COLD
Turkey in aspic
Capon with stuffed green pepper
Fricadeau of veal, garnished
Roast beef, horseradish
Smok. Westphalia, & boiled ham
Fresh black and liver sausage      Corned beef
Salami      Sablath saus.      Smok. Beef      Tongue
Astrachan Caviare      Oil Sardines
Christiana anchovies
Delicatess Herrings in wine sauce

```
                            SALADS
              Potato Italian      vegetable
              Red beets      Salmon-Mayonnaise
                    Table celery Radishes

         CHEESE: Edam      Gorgonzola      Cream
                            Coffee
```

This is an exceedingly heterogenous menu. There is a strong core of simple, hearty food with a German and Eastern European slant. Russian cabbage soup, or *schi*, is a national staple, Irish stew is a one-pot dish of meat and potatoes, as is the pork and beans. There are a few fancy "made" dishes such as the *fricandeau* (see August 29), the stuffed capon, and turkey in aspic. There are, however, two strange anomalies. Amongst this European food there is one outstandingly American dish—succotash. "Succotash" comes from the Algonquian (Narragansett) word *msíckquatash*, meaning boiled corn, although generally now it is applied to a dish of corn and beans. It is said that the earliest settlers were shown how to make this by the Indians. The second oddity is that amongst all of this simple hearty fare is Astrakan caviare—an expensive delicacy even in 1905.

## Recipes

~~~

Black sausage is also called black pudding and blood pudding. It is a fresh sausage, and as its name suggests it is made from fresh blood taken at the time of slaughtering a beast (usually a pig). The "puddings of hogs or sheep" mentioned in the following recipe are the intestines, which are used as sausage skins.

---

### Blood Pudding—Boudin Ordinaire

Cook twelve onions in *bouillon* or *consommé* with parsley, young onions, thyme, basil, and a bay-leaf; hash them very fine; take four pints of blood that has been properly taken from the throat of the animal; put in a little vinegar to prevent it from curdling; cut a pound and a half of the caul in dices, put it into the blood with four pints of rich cream, hashed fine herbs, fine spices, salt, and pepper, mix all well together; take the puddings of hogs or sheep, which must be well scraped and cleaned; fill them with a filler; but do not make them too full, otherwise they might break; tie them into proper lengths; put them into a pot of warm water, and do them over a slow fire to prevent their breaking; turn them carefully with a skimmer; if they are pricked, and the fat comes out, they are sufficiently done; take them up upon a cloth and let them cool; when they are to be sent to table slit and grill them.

Antoine B. Beauvilliers, *The Art of French Cookery* (1827).

---

---

### Succotash

The delicacy of the year was the far-famed succotash, made by scraping the milky kernels from the ears, mingling them with little round beans, which had now come to be domesticated, and with bits of fresh meat, the whole being seasoned with salt, thickened with sunflower-seeds, *suthl'-to-k'ia*, or piñon-nut meal, and boiled until reduced to an almost homogeneous stew.

Frank Hamilton Cushing, *Zuni Breadstuff* (1920).

---

## August 29

### Daily Bill of Fare aboard the SS *Great Western*, 1844

The SS *Great Western* was the first steamship designed specifically for transatlantic crossing. She was a wooden side-wheel paddle steamer, with auxiliary sails, and at 236-feet long she was the biggest steamship ever built when she was launched in 1837. For a long time it had been believed that crossing the Atlantic by steam would never be feasible because of the huge volumes of fuel that would have to be carried—the increased size of the ship then limiting the speed. The engineering issues were solved by the famous railway engineer Isambard Kingdom Brunel (1806–1859), and the SS *Great Western* made her first crossing in an astoundingly short 15 days. The great age of transatlantic steamship races had begun.

---

### BREAKFAST.

| Dishes. | | Dishes. | |
|---|---|---|---|
| Beefsteaks | 4 | Omelets | 8 |
| Mutton Chops | – | Boiled Eggs | 100 |
| Pork Chops | 4 | Homony | 6 |
| Ham and Eggs | 0 | Hash | – |
| Fried Bacon | 6 | Mush | – |
| Fricasee Chicken | – | Fried Fish (Soles) | 5 |
| Veal Cutlets | 4 | Do. Potatoes | – |
| | Stews 6 | | |

### DINNER.

| | | | |
|---|---|---|---|
| Soup -Mock Turtle | 6 | Boiled Fowls | 3 pair |
| Boiled Fish – Salmon | | Corned Beef | 1 |
| and Lobster Sauce | 4 | Corned Pork | – |
| Baked Fish | – | Ham | 1 |
| Roast Beef | 3 | Tongues | 2 |
| Saddles of Mutton | 2 | Fricandeau | – |

| Roast Lamb | 2 | Mutton Cutlets | 8 |
| Roast Turkey | 2 | Macaroni | 4 |
| Roast Veal | – | Curry | – |
| Roast Pig | 1 | Irish Stew | – |
| Olive Ducks | 3 pair | Calf's Head | 2 |
| Roast Fowls | – | Roast Hare | 5 |
| Roast Geese | 1 | Lobster Patties | 6 |
| Boiled Mutton | 2 | Chicken Salad | 8 |
| Gullenteen Turkeys | 4 | | |

### PASTRY.

| Plum Pudding | 5 | Mince Pies | 6 |
| Apple Dumpling | 8 | Damson Pies | – |
| Raspberry Rollers | 2 | Cherry Pies | 4 |
| Baked Apple Pudding | 5 | Rice Pudding | 8 |
| Apple Pies | 7 | Orange ditto | 5 |
| Cranberry Pies | 7 | Custard ditto | – |
| Raspberry Puffs | 8 | Bergnets | – |
| Plum Pies | 7 | Brandy Fruits | 8 |

### WINES, JELLIES, AND BLANCHEMANGE.

The *Great Western* was a luxury ship. She could carry 148 passengers and there was no steerage class. The fare per person was 30 guineas for a cabin and 50 guineas for a stateroom. In August 1844, George Moore, Esq., made the crossing, and on the night before their arrival in New York he noted in his journal:

Had a grand state-dinner to-day; and the passengers appeared to do ample justice to the viands. Passed a pleasant evening. We presented Captain Mathews with a memorial, signed by all the passengers, on his first trip as commander, he having been first mate to Capt. Hoskin in the "Great Western" ever since she was launched. He richly deserved a more substantial mark of our regard for his unremitting attentions. The following was the Bill of Fare:

### Recipes
~~~

#### A Fricandeau of Veal

What is called a fricandeau of veal is simply a cushion of veal trimmed into shape, larded, and braised. Cut a thick slice (three or four pounds) from a fillet of veal, trim it around ... and lard it on top. Put some pieces of pork into a braising-kettle, or saucepan, if you have no braising-kettle; also slices of carrot, an onion with cloves stuck in, a stick of celery, and some parsley. Put in the meat, sprinkle over pepper and salt, and cover it with well-buttered paper. Now fill the pan with boiling stock, or water enough to just cover the meat. Put on a tight lid. If it is a braising-pan, set it upon the fire, with live coals on top. If a common saucepan, cover it, and put it into a hot oven.

It will take about two hours, or two hours and a half, to cook it. A professional cook would boil down the stock in which the fricandeau was cooked until reduced to a glaze, then with a brush would glaze all the top of the meat, placing it in the oven a moment to dry. However, it tastes as well without this extra trouble.

The best sauce for a fricandeau is tomato-sauce. It is often garnished with green pease, spinach, or sorrel; or a little wine (Madeira, port, or sherry) and roux may be added to the braising-stock for a gravy. The gravy should be strained, of course.

Mary Newton Foote Henderson, *Practical Cooking and Dinner Giving* (New York, 1877).

Calf's Head: see January 30.
Hominy: see May 9.
Mush: see January 27.

## August 30

### Medical Conference Dinner
### Bergen, Norway, 1885

When a professional or industry group gets together for a dinner, organizers often take particular pleasure in "themeing" the menu. At a medical conference in Bergen in 1885, the idea was interpreted slightly differently. The menu card itself was a tiny piece of "court plaster" in an envelope "just as it is sold by druggists." Court plaster was the precursor of modern adhesive dressing for small wounds. It was made from a piece of fabric, often silk, covered with isinglass—a gelatin-like material made from the swim bladders of fish. The intriguing name for this medicinal item comes from its previous use to make the "beauty spots" used as part of the fashionable makeup routine for court ladies.

One report of the dinner called it "the smallest menu in the world" (but did not record exactly how small this was) but noted that "it was rather an elaborate menu too, for so modest a space."

---

DINNER

Paté.      Madeira.
Potage de Tomate.
Poissons farci avec asperges.
Langues de boeuf grillé avec sauce d'olives.
Jambon avec choufleurs aux haricots.
Poules avec champignons.

> Homard à la mayonaise.
> Perdrix neige.
> Poulets avec salades aux cornichons.
> Dessert.      Champagne.
>
> Glacé
> Gateaux      Sherry
> Fruits

The menu was indeed elaborate enough to be entirely appropriate for a group of late-nineteenth century medical gentlemen at an international conference. It is a little unusual for the time that the menu items did not have classic names, but are mini-descriptions of the dishes.

One slight puzzle is the "snow partridge" on this menu. The snow partridge (*Lerwa lerwa*) is a native of the Himalayas, not the Arctic Circle. It may be that the birds for the dish were imported, or it may be that it was a more local species with the same common name. The true snow partridge feeds on moss and the shoots of mountain plants. It is said to be fat, tender, and tasting similar to grouse or ptarmigan.

## Recipes

~~~

There are an almost infinite number of interpretations of tomato soup, from the very simple to the very complex. This version is somewhere between the extremes and would be suitable for any dinner, casual or formal.

---

### Tomato Soup

> 2 quarts soup stock.
> 1 cupful stewed tomatoes.
> 1 small cupful of minced vegetables.
> 6 cloves.
> 1 tablespoon minced parsley.
> Salt and pepper to taste.
> Little flour for thickening.

Tomatoes stewed down after seasoning with salt, pepper and butter are a different article from the freshly prepared and impart a new richness to soup.

The soup stock may be the liquor in which a piece of beef or mutton is boiled for dinner, with the addition of other raw scraps and pieces, such as the bones and gristly ends of a beefsteak. An hour before dinner time take out the meat, strain the stock through a fine strainer and into the soup pot. Cut piece of carrot, turnip and onion into small dice and throw in and let cook till done and add the cloves and cup of tomatoes, pepper and salt, thickening and the parsley at last.

It is generally considered a reproach to say the soup is thin. A proper inulium should be observed. A spoonful of flour gives the smoothness and substance required without destroying the clearness of the soup.

Jessup Whitehead, *Cooking for Profit* (Chicago, 1882).

---

### Olive Sauce

Make a good brown sauce, mix it with stoned or turned French olives, season to taste and flavor with a little lemon juice. Serve hot.
  Charles Herman Senn, *The Book of Sauces* (1914).

---

A brown sauce is a basic sauce made with meat stock and thickened with a brown roux. Sauce Espagnole (see January 19) is a very elegant version.
  Lobster Mayonnaise: see March 31.

## August 31

### Second Cabin Tea
### aboard RMS *Saxonia*, 1910

The maiden voyage of the Cunard Line's RMS *Saxonia* was in May 1900. Apart from a wartime stint as a prisoner-of-war ship, she spent most of her working lifetime traveling the transatlantic route between Liverpool in England and Boston. She was fitted out to carry almost 2,000 passengers—the vast majority of them emmigrants who traveled in third ("steerage") class. As soon as the steerage passengers disembarked in their new land, the sparse furnishings "between the decks" were removed and the space filled with cargo for the return voyage to England.

The *Saxonia* left Boston on August 30, 1910, for England. The next afternoon, second-class passengers enjoyed their first "tea" at sea.

---

Grilled Hake Steaks
Grilled Beefsteak      Broiled Kidneys & Bacon
Poached Eggs on Toast
Mashed Potatoes
Cold:      Roast Beef      Brawn
Salad      Mixed Pickles
Compote Apricots & Rice      Rock Cakes
Marmalade      Preserves
Tea      Coffee

---

There is a great deal of misunderstanding about "tea." Cafés and tea shops often advertise "High Tea," at which they serve little sandwiches and cakes, or "scones" ("biscuits" in America) with jam and cream, and tea in fine china cups. This is not "high" tea, historically speaking. In the nineteenth century, high tea was a substantial meal taken in the early evening, by the lower classes, and it was served from the normal (i.e. "high") dining table. It was sometimes called "Meat Tea." Low tea was definitely high class. It was a mid-afternoon snack rather than a meal, and was intended to sustain and amuse the leisured class until their late and formal dinner—and of course it was served from the sort of low table that is now called a coffee table.

## "High Tea"

A well-understood "high tea" should have cold roast beef at the top of the table, a cold Yorkshire pie at the bottom, a mighty ham in the middle. The side dishes will comprise soused mackerel, pickled salmon (in due season), sausages and potatoes, etc., etc. Rivers of tea, coffee, and ale, with dry and buttered toast, sally-lunns, scones, muffins, and crumpets, jams and marmalade.

*The Daily Telegraph*, May 9, 1893.

"High teas" as a substitute for late dinners are not now so frequent as they used to be, but so long as our young people care to play tennis all evening in summer, they cannot quite go out of fashion. . . . In summer, cold fish and meats, mayonnaises, salads, fresh fruits, cream &c., are generally the rule; and in winter, besides such cold dishes as game pie, joints, and sweets, such things as rissoles, salmis and cutlets are given.

*Beeton's Household Manual* (1861).

## Recipes

~~~

## Rock Cakes

Whisk three whole eggs till light. Mix with them half a pound of powdered sugar, a quarter of a pound of flour, and a table-spoonful of currants. Beat all thoroughly together, drop the dough in lumps upon a buttered tin, and with a fork make them look as rough as possible. Bake the cakes in a moderate oven, and when they are done enough store them in a tin canister till wanted for use.

## Kidneys and Bacon

Trim away the fat from the desired number of kidneys, skin, and cut each into slices crosswise. Mix on a plate a table-spoonful of flour, a salt-spoonful of salt, and half a salt-spoonful of pepper. Dip each slice into the mixture. Melt a little bacon fat or butter in the frying pan, then put the required number of rashers of bacon, cut thinly, and fry very gently over a slow fire, turning them repeatedly. When sufficiently cooked, put them on the dish on which they are to be served, and fry the slices of kidney in the same fat. Turn them every minute, and in about five minutes they will be done enough, and may be put on the dish with the bacon. Pour off the superabundant fat; sprinkle a tea-spoonful of flour into the remainder, and mix it thoroughly; add gradually as much water as will make a somewhat thick sauce. Stir it over the fire till it boils, add a tea-spoonful of mushroom ketchup, and strain over the kidneys.

*Cassell's New Dictionary of Cookery* (1910).

Brawn: see April 28.
Poached Eggs: see June 20.

# September

### September 1

"First State" Banquet
Beijing Hotel, Beijing, China, 1999

In 1949, to commemorate the founding of the People's Republic of China, a great banquet was held at the Beijing Hotel. The hotel was designed for Western visitors and normally served only Western food, but for such an important national occasion Premier Zhou Enlai (1898–1976) insisted that the menu would be entirely Chinese. Nine famous chefs collaborated to chose the dishes that would best showcase Chinese cuisine. The food was chosen from the Huai Yang tradition of cooking. As the name suggests, this style of food comes from the region around the lower reaches of the Huai and Yantze rivers and features exquisite food carving.

Fifty years (less one month) later, on September 1, 1999, the hotel celebrated the anniversary of the "new" China by recreating the banquet for the enjoyment of ordinary citizens who could afford the 600 yuan price. The chef was the last apprentice of Zhang Fuzhi who had been responsible for the banquet in 1949.

---

COLD DISHES:
Spicy Duck
Spicy Chicken
Mushroom with Salt and Sesame Oil
Winter Bamboo Shoot with Shrimp's Roe
Cucumber with Salt and Sesame Oil
Spicy Fish
Pork Jelly in Zhenjiang Style

HOT DISHES:
Stewed Shark's Fin with Chicken
Sauce in Jar
Stewed Mixed Seafood in Chicken Sauce
Sauted Prawn with Red Sauce
Steamed Chicken with Mushroom
Sauted Vegetable and Mushroom
Braised Carp in Brown Sauce
Consomme of Swallow's Nest

---

PASTRY:
Steamed Dumpling Stuffed with Meat and Vegetable
Deep-fried Spring Rolls
Steamed Dumpling Stuffed with Mashed Red Bean
Steamed Chinese Bread

DESSERT:
Mashed Walnut
Chinese Date in Sweet Syrup

---

These dishes are familiar in one form or another to most Westerners who frequent Chinese restaurants—although their interpretation at this dinner was no doubt at an extraordinarily elegant level.

The Chinese date is not related to the date from the date palm. It is also called the "jujube," and comes from a tree (*Ziziphus zizyphus*) that is native to a wide area of North Africa, Northern India, and South and Central China. The berry-like fruit has a mucilagious texture which was thought to be soothing to inflamed throats and digestions, and it has a long history of medicinal use in both the East and the West. It is not eaten raw but is dried or—as in this menu, preserved in syrup like any other fruit.

## Recipes
~~~

---

### Steamed Chinese Bread

Method of Making Bread in China.

The Chinese method of making their bread is very curious—they neither make use of yeast or bake it in an oven. The shape and size of the loaves are not unlike the small bread made in this country. They are composed of nothing more than flour and water, and ranged on bars, which are laid across an iron hollow pan containing a certain quantity of water, which is then placed on an earthen stove. When the water boils, the vessel or pan is covered over with something like a shallow tub, and the steam of the water, for a few minutes, is all the baking, if it may be so called, which the bread receives. We understand, however, that it is by no means unpalatable;—in this state the Chinese consider it most nutritious.

*The Monthly Visitor and New Family Magazine* (London, 1801).

---

Birds' Nest Soup and Shark's Fin: see March 8.

## September 2

### Dinner aboard the First "Hebrew" Ship
### TSS *Kedmah*, 1947

Even before the modern state of Israel was proclaimed on May 14, 1948, post-World War II immigration, both legal and illegal, was well underway on a scale much greater than anticipated. The Zim Israel Navigation Company was incorporated in 1945 to find ships to carry these immigrants—not an easy task with so few vessels available after the war. The company's first purchase was the MV *Kedah* in 1947, which they refitted and renamed *Kedmah* (Hebrew for "eastward"). The first voyage of this "first Hebrew ship" ended with its arrival Tel Aviv on July 28, 1947. From then on the *Kedmah* regularly traveled the Marseilles-Haifa route, carrying many thousands of refugees and immigrants, many of them Holocaust survivors.

On November 29, 1947, the United Nations General Assembly passed the Partition Plan that would divide Palestine into Jewish and Arab states. A few months before this, on September 2, the *Kedmah*'s passengers sat down to the following dinner.

---

Potage Windsor

\*\*\*

Saucissons grilles
Puree de Pois-verts

\*\*\*

Saute de volaille Hongroise
Maccaroni
Haricots

\*\*\*

Triffle

\*\*\*

Café

\*

---

According to Jewish dietary laws (see July 11), dairy products cannot be used or served at meals containing meat. There are no fish choices at all on this menu, and the only possible vegetarian option is the macaroni, or the pea soup (providing it was made with vegetable stock). This was unequivocally a meat meal. This leaves the "trifle" problematic. Trifle generally contains cream or custard or both (see November 18), and clearly it could not be eaten at this dinner by observant Jews. Today a version could be made with soy milk and various artificial cream substitutes, but these were not common at the time. Jewish cookbooks offer alternatives for butter in cakes (margarine, chicken fat, ground almonds), so that these can be eaten at meat meals, but non-dairy trifle recipes seem to be absent. It is possible that it was provided for the non-Jews aboard, or for those who chose the macaroni (assuming it was a "vegetarian" recipe), or that the shipboard chefs had in fact managed a kosher variation.

Recipes

~~~

---

### Savory Macaroni

After baking some flour to a pale fawn color pass it through a sieve or strainer to remove its gritty particles. Break half a pound of macaroni into short pieces, boil them in salted water until fairly tender, then drain.

In a little butter in a saucepan brown a level tablespoon of very finely chopped onion, then add three or four sliced tomatoes, a half teaspoon of powdered mixed herbs, a little nutmeg, salt and pepper. When the tomatoes are reduced to a pulp add one pint of milk and allow it to come to the boiling point before mixing with it two tablespoons of the browned flour moistened with water.

Stir and boil till smooth, press the whole through a strainer and return to the saucepan. When boiling, add the macaroni and a few minutes later stir in two tablespoons of grated or finely chopped cheese.

It may be served at once, but is vastly improved by keeping the pan for half an hour by the side of the fire in an outer vessel of water. Or the macaroni may be turned into a casserole and finished off in the oven.

For a meat meal the onions may be browned in sweet drippings or olive oil and soup stock substituted for the milk.

Florence Kreisler Greenbaum, *The International Jewish Cook Book: 1600 Recipes According to the Jewish Dietary Laws with the Rules for Kashering* (New York, 1919).

---

Windsor Soup: see April 9.
Triffle (trifle): see February 7.

## September 3

### Cardinal's ''Fast''
### Dundalk, Ireland, 1858

His Eminence Cardinal Wiseman (1802–1865), the archbishop of Westminster, visited Ireland in 1858 as the representative of the newly reestablished Catholic hierarchy in England. The ''regal state'' in which he was received did not escape the notice of the English. No opportunity was missed on either side during the visit to reinforce the old political and religious enmity between the two countries. The English press drew some inferences from the bill of fare served to the Cardinal at the banquet given to him in Dundalk.

---

POTAGES.
L'huitres.     Meagre.

POISSONS.
Saumon au naturel, Saumon en matelote marinière, Saumon àl'admiral,
Saumon en matelote Saxone, Saumon à la crème (gratine), Saumon à l'ecillière,
Sole au gratin, Sole à l'Italienne, Sole fried, Sole à la Colbert, Filets de Soles à la

Maitre d'Hotel, Filets de Sole à la Hollandaise, Filets de Soles aux Huitres, Whiting au gratin, Whiting broiled à la Maitre d'Hotel, Fillets of Whiting fried, Dublin Bay Haddock à la Maitre d'Hotel, Dublin Bay Haddock baked, Haddock à la Maitre d'Hotel, Fillets of Haddock à la St. Paul, Côtelettes de Homard, Croustade de Huitres, Huitres au gratin.

HORS-D'ŒUVRES.
Petits vol-au-vents aux huitres, Petits vol-au-vents aux homards, Rissoles de homard.

SECOND SERVICE.
Homard, dressed, Huitres au gratin, Salade de Homard, Crême à la Vanille, Charlottes Russe, Gateaux de Millefeuilles, Nougat à la Parisienne, Jambon Surprise, Tartelletes aux Framboises, Tartelettes de Pommes, Pouding Chaud, Pâtisseries, Pouding Glacé, Fruit, Gateaux, Biscuits &c.

*The Times* newspaper reporter noted that the meal took place on a Friday when it was the Cardinal's duty "to appear unto men to fast," and that "the fast, the folk, and the fastee are all worthy of special mention." He followed his description of the meal with the wry comment that it was "a severely mortifying fast which must surely have tried his Reverence's stomach. If this be a Cardinal's fast, pray, Sir, tell us what must be a Cardinal's feast."

An immediate response to the article appeared a few days later in a letter from the slightly indignant member for the borough of Dundalk, who pointed out that "The day on which the dinner was given was not a fast day, but a day of abstinence from flesh meat." The good member missed the point: this was not a discussion about the rationale behind the Church's rules on fish and flesh days (see February 23) but was an opportunity to express an anti-Catholic sentiment by implying clerical gluttony.

The dining events of this visit had already caused controversy and accentuated the political and religious divide. A great banquet at Ballinasloe a few days previously had been boycotted by a number of civic leaders and prominent social figures when it was discovered that the representatives of the Church of Rome intended to omit the traditional toast to the health of the Queen of England. At the Dundalk event "the Queen's health was given, but in a manner more offensive than its omission. It was given after that of the Pope, thus plainly acknowledging the allegiance to the Pontiff as being paramount to that due to her Majesty" (*Nelson Examiner* and *New Zealand Chronicle*, December 11, 1858).

The political agenda aside, this menu is a fine litany of the classic ways of serving fish. Fish are usually fried or boiled—it is the garnishing and a sauces that define the dishes. The sole is served with the traditional sauce Colbert, and several of the dishes are served with the classic maitre d'hotel butter. The only oddity is the *jambon* (ham) surprise, but given its position towards the end of the meal it was most likely a cake decorated to look like a ham—a favorite type of Victorian dinner spectacle.

## Recipes

~~~

French chef Alexis Soyer in his famous book, *The Gastronomic Regenerator* (1847), wrote of the Dublin Bay Haddock: "This fish used to be very difficult to procure fresh in London, but the rapidity of steam conveyance by sea and land, brings it almost alive into the London markets. I must highly recommend this both for its firmness and its lightness."

---

### Haddock à la Maître d' Hôtel

Cut the fish open at the back on each side of the bone, season it with pepper and salt, dip it in flour, and lay it on a gridiron over a moderate fire, turning it very carefully; it will take about twenty minutes to cook, dress it on a dish without a napkin; then have ready a quarter of a pound of maitre d'hotel butter, put half of it in the back of the fish, and put the fish in the oven, put the remainder of the butter in the stewpan with six tablespoonfuls of rather thin melted butter; when quite hot pour it round the fish and serve.

---

### Maître d' Hôtel Butter

Put a quarter of a pound of fresh butter upon a plate, with two good tablespoonfuls of chopped parsley, the juice of two lemons, half a teaspoonful of salt, and half that quantity of white pepper; mix all well together, and put in a cool place till required.

---

### Cake in Imitation of a Ham

Put the yolks of fourteen eggs in a basin with 1 lb. of caster sugar, 1/2 saltspoonful of salt, and a few drops of essence of vanilla; beat them well until smooth and creamy. Whip the whites of the fourteen eggs to a firm froth, mix them gradually and lightly in with the batter, and sift in gradually 4 1/2 oz of cornflour and the same quantity of wheaten-flour. Procure a large and deep oval-shaped paper case, pour the batter into it, and bake. When cooked, take the Cake out of the oven, turn it out of the case, and leave till cold. Hollow out the under part of the Cake, and trim it all round with a sharp knife to the size and shape of a dressed ham. Coat the whole of the upper surface with dissolved apricot jam; coat also the part where the rind is generally left on the knuckle with some transparent chocolate icing, then place it where it may dry without being disturbed. Prepare some cream ice and flavour it with vanilla, then fill the interior of the ham with it. Ornament the ham with a design, piped on in royal icing; stick a fancy silver skewer in the knuckle end of the ham, and fix a paper ruffle round it. Put a lace-edged dish-paper on a dish, place the ham on it, and garnish with croûtons of red and yellow jelly. It is then ready for serving.

Theodore Garrett, *Encyclopaedia of Practical Cookery* (London, 1896).

Charlotte Russe: see September 4.
Hollandaise Sauce: see April 16.
Sole Colbert: see April 17.
Vol-au-Vents: see September 17.

## September 4

Dinner for the Governor-General
The Arlington, Cobourg, Ontario, Canada, 1874

The Irish peer, Frederick Hamilton-Temple-Blackwood, the Earl of Dufferin (1826–1902), was appointed as governor of the Dominion of Canada in 1872. He took to his role with enthusiasm and made a point of traveling to every province and meeting and speaking (in French and English) with Her Majesty's Canadian subjects with the aim of confirming the Imperial ties with Britain.

In 1874 it was the turn of Ontario to host the Dufferins. In Cobourg on September 4, they were taken by a special train to Rice Lake (so called because of the abundance of wild rice), where they visited the iron mines. A fine champagne lunch was served aboard the train, and in the tradition of intensive diplomatic tours, there was a full-scale formal dinner back in Cobourg that same evening.

---

MENU

Oysters on Shell.

SOUP.
Bisque a la Provencale. Printoniere.

FISH.
Saguenay Salmon a la Normande. Fillet of Trout a l'Anglaise.

RELEVES.
Oyster Pates. Vol au Vent a l'Imperiale. Pain a la Joinville.

ENTREES.
Supreme de Volaille. Lamb Cutlets a la Jardiniere.

ROAST.
Fillet of Beef. Turkey. Lamb.

GAME.
Partridge. Canard aux Olives. Snipe au petit Pois. Teal Duck.

COLD DISHES.
Galantine au Gelees.

VEGETABLES.
Potatoes. Corn. Tomatoes.

PASTRY.
Plum Pudding a l'Anglaise. Peach Pies. Apple Pies.
Blanc Mange. Monte aux Peche. Gelee au Madeira.
Gelee au Champagne. Charlotte Russe. Queen's Cake.
Kisses. Ladies' Fingers

ICES.
Vanilla Ice Cream. Lemon Ice.

DESSERT.
Grapes. Peaches. Apples. Melons. Pears. Figs.

WINES.
Sherry. Hock. Champagne. Claret.

LIQUEURS.

For the organizers of the dinner, it was no easy goal to impress the Dufferins, who were extravagant entertainers themselves. The plans must have been impressive, however, as Lady Hariot Dufferin (1843–1936), who was pregnant with her seventh child (born in February 1875) and too tired to attend the dinner after the exhausting day, was intrigued enough to want a sneak preview of the dining room. The dinner table was shaped like the deck of a yacht, and there was a nautical theme to the rest of the decorations in honor of the Earl's famous voyage in the North Atlantic to Iceland and Norway in 1856. The *pièce de resistance* on the table, although not listed on the silk menu, was a magnificent cake representing his yacht *Foam*.

## Recipes
~~~

### Queen Cake

Mix 1 pound of dried flour, the same of sifted sugar and of washed currants. Wash 1 lb of butter in rose-water, beat it well, then mix with it 8 eggs, yolks and whites beaten separately, and put in the dry ingredients by degrees. Beat the whole an hour, butter little tins, tea-cups, or saucers, filling them only half full. Sift a little fine sugar over just as you put them into the oven.
*The Dominion Cookbook* (Toronto, 1868).

### Charlotte Russe

1/2 lb. ratafia biscuits,
1/2 pint cream,
1 oz. sugar,
1 tablespoon sherry,
1 tablespoon raspberry jam,
1/2 oz. gelatine,
1 teaspoon vanilla.

Rub the jam through a sieve, dip the ratafias first into it, then into the sherry, and with them line the side of a plain Charlotte mould, the first row should be put in quite dry. Whip the cream to a stiff froth, add to it the sugar, vanilla, and melted gelatine. Fill the mould, when set, turn out and garnish the top with whipped cream.

Maud C. Cooke, *Cookery* (London, Ontario, 1896).

Soup Printoniere (Printanier): see February 28.
Vol-au-vents: see September 17.
Plum Pudding: see June 28.
Blanc Mange: see January 7.
Ladies fingers: see March 12.

## September 5

Ambigu for King James II
Bodley Library, Oxford University, Oxford, England, 1687

When King James II (1633–1701) visited Oxford for several days in 1687 a large number of sufferers of the disease known as scrofula (a tuberculous condition of the lymph glands in the neck) had a once-in-a-lifetime opportunity. The disease was also called "The King's Evil," and it was believed for centuries that it could be cured by the royal touch. On the morning of September 5, 1687, King James spent the hour or so after 8 A.M. at the Cathedral "touching for the evil," after which he was escorted to the Bodley Library, where some refreshment in the form of a breakfast "ambigu" was arranged.

### An Account of the Dishes wherewith the K. was Treated at the Publick Library

Dry Sweetmeats and Fruits 20 large Dishes piled high, like so many Ricks of Hay. Wet Sweetmeats 24 little flat Plates, like Trencher-plates, not piled; place among the greater dishes scatteringly in vacant Places to fill up the Vacances.

28 large Dishes of cold Fish and cold Flesh, as Westphalia Hams &c. Some whole, others cut into Slices and piled pretty high. 3 hot Dishes, viz. Shoulder of Mutton, Pheasant, Partridge and Quails; of these the K. did not eat, not medling with any Thing else, except only that he took one little piece of dry sweet Meat.

36 plates of Sallating piled high and copped with Oranges, Lemmons, Olives, Samphire, &c. Dems, Plums, &c.

The contemporary university historian who recorded the feast noted that the King ate very little, but in spite of the profusion of food "none did eat but he, for he spake to Nobody to eat." The strict protocol of the time prevented anyone else from eating until the royal personage indicated permission. It does not seem that this was arrogance on the King's part, as it was said that "he showed himself extremely courteous and affable to all."

Perhaps he was distracted by his scholarly conversation with the Library Keeper, Mr. Hyde.

The strict adherence to good manners disappeared in an instant when, after about three-quarters of an hour at the table, the King rose to leave. As he did so "the Courtiers fell to scramble after what was remaining, flung the wet sweet Meats on the Ladies Linnen and Petticoats and stain'd them." This sort of disorderly fight over royal leftovers was not unknown, and the King's passage being blocked by the greedy scholars and people, he stood by to watch for a few moments.

An ambigu was a single course meal of "flesh and fruit together," served when a full-scale dinner was not required. It commonly featured plenty of "banquetting stuffe"—which clearly appeared to be a major attraction for the scholarly rabble on this day. The word banquet at this time had two meanings. It meant, as it does now, a feast. It also referred to the final sweet course of such a feast, often taken in a separate room, or even a garden "banqueting house," and which developed into the course now called "dessert." "Banquetting stuffe" included sweetmeats, gingerbread, marzipan, jellies, comfits (sugared seeds and spices), "marmalade" (more like thick fruit paste, made from all sorts of fruit) small biscuits and wafers, and dried and fresh fruit. Sweetmeats, as in this menu, could be "wet" (in a sugar syrup) or "dry" (similar to crystallized or glacé fruit).

---

Scramble for Victuals at an Installation
of the Knights of the Garter
Windsor Castle, July 25, 1771

Two thousand beds were made in the Castle at Windsor, and two thousand tables were spread on Thursday. There were seventeen kitchens, and fifty cooks in each kitchen, beside other attendants. After dinner on Thursday, at Windsor, the new regulation of the Lord Steward took place about the scramble; as it was thought a better plan of economy to carry the victuals to the mob, than to let the mob come to the victuals. Accordingly the windows of the Castle were thrown open, and the provision tossed out to the gaping crowd below. A cloud of hams, chickens, pasties, haunches, and delicacies of every kind, with knives, forks, plates, tablecloths, and napkins, their companies, darkened the air. This was succeeded by showers of liquor; some conveyed in bottles, properly corked, but the greater part in rain. The scramble was more diverting than any other part of the preceding farce. You would see one stooping to a fowl and a great ham falling plump upon his back; another, having a fork stuck in his shoulder, and looking up to secure himself from more of the arrows thus flying by day, received a creamed apple-pye full in his face. A beef-eater having lost his cap in the scuffle had his loss repaired by a pasty falling inverted upon his head. A bargeman who had just secured a noble haunch of venison, was retiring as fast as he could with his booty, and ran with it full against the back of Lord—and made an impression on it so like a gridiron, that all the mob, after they ceased their laughter, cried out, smoak the Merry Andrew.

From the diary of an unknown Londoner, quoted by Stephen Collet in *Relics of Literature* (1823).

Recipes

~~~

There were examples of both "wet" and "dry" sweetmeats at this meal, and they would have been made from a wide variety of fruits. Cherries were an expensive delicacy and so would have been desirable at a royal meal, and ginger in both wet and dry forms was a favorite way to end a dinner for many centuries. The following examples of a wet sweetmeat (cherries) and a dry (ginger) are taken from *The Accomplished Ladies Rich Closet of Rarities* by John Shirley (London, 1691).

---

### To Preserve Black Cherries

Pluck off the stalks of about a pound, and boil them in Sugar and fair Water, till they become a pulp, then put in your other Cherries, with stalks, remembering to put half a pound of Sugar to every pound of Cherries; when finding the Sugar to be boiled up to that thickness that it will rope, take them off and set them by, using them as you see convenient.

[Note: "The thickness that it will rope" describes the appearance and behavior of the sugar syrup when it is ready. Today we would use a sugar thermometer.]

---

### To Candy Ginger

Take the fairest pieces, pare off the rind, and lay them in water twenty-four hours; and having boiled double-refined Sugar to the height of Sugar again; and when it begins to be cold, put in your Ginger and stir till it is hard to the Pain; when taking it out piece by piece, lay it by the fire, and afterward put it into a warm Pot, and tye it up close, and the Candy will be firm.

---

## September 6

### Dinner with the Moors
### Morocco, 1663

Lancelot Addison (1632–1703) was a chaplain in the British garrison at Tangier for seven years. Tangier ("the eye of Africa") was part of the dowry of the Portuguese Infanta, Catherine of Braganza (1638–1705), when she married King Charles II of England (1630–1685) in 1662. The British took control of Tangier in January 1662, on the basis of the marriage treaty, before the actual ceremony took place. They held it until 1684, intending to use it as a base for the colonization of Africa. The arrangement was not popular with the local population.

Addison later wrote about his experiences on the Barbary Coast in *An Account of West Barbary* (1671). In a chapter entitled *The Moresco Entertainment. Fashion of Travelling, Hospitals, Diet, Reverence to Corn, Forbidden Meats*, he described a dinner he had with some "Moors" that he thought was representative of the local hospitality.

IN the year of Salvation, 1663, September the sixth, at the going down of the sun, we came to an aldéa, called Angerà, at the utmost bounds of a mountain of that name, where we repaired to the house of Cidi Cassian Shat, whom we found sitting at his door, environed with about twenty aged Moors of the neighbourhood. Alighting from our horses, we delivered our segúra, or letters of safe conduct, to the old man, who, when he had perused, returned them with a grave nod, the testimony of his approbation, and the signal of our welcome. This done, we were called to a little upper room, which we could not enter till we had put off our shoes at the threshold, not for religion, but cleanliness, and not to prevent our unhallowing of the floor, but defiling the carpets wherewith it was curiously spread. At the upper end of the room was laid a velvet cushion, as large as those we use in our pulpits, and it denoted the most honourable part of the room. After we had reposed about an hour, there was brought in a little oval table, about twenty inches high, which was covered with a long piece of narrow linen; and this served for diaper. For the Moors, by their law, are forbidden such superfluous utensils as napkins, knives, spoons, &c.; their religion, laying down this general maxim, That mere necessaries are to be provided for: which caused a precise Moor to refuse to drink out of my dish, when he could sup water enough out of the hollow of his hand. But this straitness has of late years begun to be enlarged, and the prohibition is interpreted to reach no farther than their churchmen, and chief ministers of juftice; so that those who are able to provide handsome furniture for their tables, have a dispensation which they seem not prone to make use of, if the humour of the rest may be divined by that of this grandee; at whose house the table was adorned as before, and for supper there was placed upon it an earthen pot full of mutton, beef, cabbage, raisins, potatoes, berengénas [eggplants], &c. all boiled together, and extremely hot with dimicuto and garlic, which is their immutable sauce. This hodge-podge was in imitation of the Spanish olla podrida, excepting that it wanted bacon, an ingredient so indispensable to the Spanish olla, that there can be none without it, which occasioned this proverb, No sermon without St. Austin, nor olla without bacon: *Ny sermòn sin Agostino, ny olla sin locino.* But to proceed in our bill of fare: our next course was a single pullet cloven down the belly, with the four quarters spread out at large, by a way of cookery peculiar to the Moors. And these two dishes, with store of good bread, made up the feast. Our drink was strong wine newly brought from the press, which stood by us in a great stone jar, with a sort of wooden ladle in it, out of which we drank. Our posture was laying round about the table, according to the custom of the country. Our company was the second son of this family, a debonair Gentile person.

## Recipes
~~~

An *Olio,* or *Olla Podrida* is, according to the *Oxford English Dictionary,* "a dish of Spanish and Portuguese origin, composed of pieces of meat and fowl, bacon, pumpkins, cabbage, turnips, and other ingredients stewed or boiled together and highly spiced." The name comes from the cooking pot, and it was essentially a local version of the one-pot dinner found in one form or another in every culture (see *Pot au Feu,* April 7). The ingredients are as varied as circumstances allow, and there was sometimes a prodigious number, as this English interpretation from Robert May's *Accomplish't Cook*, published in 1660, shows.

---

### To Make an Olio Podrida

Take a Pipkin or Pot of some three Gallons, fill it with fair water, and set it over a Fire of Charcoals, and put in first your hardest meats, a rump of Beef, Bolonia sausages, Neats Tongues two dry, and two green, boiled and larded, about two hours after the pot is boil'd and scummed: but put in more presently after your Beef is scum'd, Mutton, Venison, Pork, Bacon, all the aforesaid in Gubbins, as big as a Ducks Egg, in equal pieces; put in also Carrots, Turnips, Onions, Cabbidge, in good big pieces, as big as your meat, a faggot of sweet herbs, well bound up, and some whole Spinage,

Sorrel, Burrage, Endive, Marigolds, and other good Pot-Herbs a little chopped; and sometimes French Barley, or Lupins green or dry.

Then a little before you dish out your Olio; put to your pot, Cloves, Mace, Saffron, &c.

Then next have divers Fowls; as first.

A Goose, or Turkey, two Capons, two Ducks, two Pheasants, two Widgeons, four Partridges, four stock Doves, four Teals, eight Snites, twenty four Quails, forty eight Larks.

Boil these foresaid Fowls in water and salt in a pan, pipkin, or pot, &c.

Then have Bread, Marrow, Bottoms of Artichocks, Yolks of hard Eggs, Large Mace, Chesnuts boil'd and blancht, two Colliflowers, Saffron.

And stew these in a pipkin together, being ready clenged with some good sweet butter, a little white wine and strong broth.

Some other times for variety you may use Beets, Potato's, Skirrets, Pistaches, PineApple seed, or Almonds, Poungarnet, and Lemons.

Now to dish your Olio, dish first your Beef, Veal or Pork; then your Venison, and Mutton, Tongues, Sausage, and Roots over all.

Then next your largest Fowl, Land-Fowl, or Sea-Fowl, as first, a Goose, or Turkey, two Capons, two Pheasants, four Ducks, four Widgeons, four Stock-Doves, four Partridges, eight Teals, twelve Snites, twenty four Quailes, forty eight Larks, &c.

Then broth it, and put on your pipkin of Colliflowers Artichocks, Chesnuts, some sweet-breads fried, Yolks of hard Eggs, then Marrow boil'd in strong broth or water, large Mace, Saffron, Pistaches, and all the aforesaid things being finely stewed up, and some red Beets over all, slic't Lemons, and Lemon peels whole, and run it over with beaten butter.

Robert May, *The Accomplisht Cook* (1660).

---

### September 7

Dinner for the Congress of Orientalists
Stockholm, Sweden, 1889

At the dinner at the eighth International Congress of Orientalists the menu was a magnificent testament to the skills of the "terribly learned" men present, rather than of the cooks, as is usually the case. It was in the form of a small octavo-sized booklet with twenty-eight pages. Each page had a different illuminated border and described a menu item in one of the "primitive and recondite languages" understood by the attendees. The mini-essays were in the appropriate script—cuneiform, hieroglyphs etc—and each was signed by the expert who had made the contribution.

---

POTAGE SUEDOISE.
Arabe vulgaire d'Egypte (Carlo Landberg)
Chinese (Gustave Schlegel)

RISSOLES A LA RUSSE.
Ge'z (A. Dilman)

SALMON A L'IMPÉRATRICE.
Sanskrit (F. Max Miller)

FILET DE BOEUF A LA PARISIENNE.
Malaisch

CHAUD-FROID DE SUPRÊME DE VOLAILLE A LA PERIGORD.
Syrisch (Th. Noldeke)

TIMBALE DE GÉLINOTTES A L'ORIENTALE.
Hebraisch (E. Kautzsch)

PATÉ DE FOIE GRAS.
Mandschu (Georg von der Gabelentz)

JEUNE COQ.
Javanais (A.C.Vreede)

SALADE.
Akkadian (A. H. Sayce)

AGNEAU AU RIZ A LA BÉDOUINE.
Langue Ottoman (Ahmed Midhat Bev)

ARTICHAUTS AU BEURRE.
Copte (E. Amélineau)

GÂTEAU A LA VICTORIA.
Hiéroglyphique (J. Lieblein)

GLACE.
Himyarish (D. H. Müller)

FROMAGES ASSORTIS.
Bichâri (H. Almkvist)

DESSERT INTERNATIONAL.
Classische Japanish (Dr. Isuboi)

FRUITS DIVERS
Djagtaï (A. Vambéry)

CHAMPAGNE.
Arab classique (De Goetje)

VIN DE BORDEAUX.
Langue de Babel (Paul Haupt)

## Recipes

~~~

"Swedish Soup" typically is either a fish soup containing dried pears, plums etc., or it is a thickened fruit soup, which may be served cold. The English and American interpretations can vary widely and include cold soups made with tapioca and flavored with cinnamon, to hot pea soup, to meat and vegetable soup.

### Swedish Soup

Cut up two quarts of apples and boil with two quarts of water until tender. Strain and put the juice on to boil again with a bit of stick cinnamon, lemon peel, and sugar to taste. Mix one tablespoon of cornstarch with one cup of water, and pour into the apple juice while it is boiling. Put in preserved cherries, which have been steeped in sugar and water, and add the apple pulp. Serve cold as soup, and put in cubes of lemon jelly when ready to serve.

Mary Johnstone Lincoln and Anna Barrows, *The Home Science Cook Book* (1902).

### Victoria Cake

| | |
|---|---|
| Flour, 3 lbs; | nutmeg, 1; |
| butter, 2 1/2 lb.; | mace, 1 blade; |
| sugar, 1 lb.; | eggs, 12 yolks, 6 whites; |
| citron and lemon peel 3/4 lb.; | yeast, 1/2 pint; |
| almonds (sweet) 1/2 lb.; | cream 1 1/2 pint; |
| currants 3 1/2 lb.; | orange-flower water, 1 tablespoonful. |

Take three quarters of a pound of flour well-dried, two pounds and a half of fresh butter, one pound of loaf sugar pounded, three-quarters of a pound of candied citron and lemon peel cut in thin strips, half a pound of sweet almonds, blanched and sliced, three pounds and a half of currants well dried and cleaned, one nutmeg grated, a blade of mace pounded, the yolks of twelve eggs, and the whites of six, beaten separately, half a pint of fresh yeast, a pint and a half of cream, and a tablespoonful of orange-flower water; first mix the spice with the flour, melt the butter and the cream together, and when cold, add it gradually to the flour; then add the other ingredients, and beat the whole together for half an hour; line a well-buttered tin with paper, also well-buttered, pour in the cake, and bake it in a moderate oven from an hour and a half to two hours.

Robert Kemp Philp, *The Dictionary of Daily Wants* (1861).

Chaud-froid: see July 28.
Pate de Foie Gras: see May 26.

## September 8

### Temperance Banquet
Metropolitan Hall, New York, 1853

The "Whole World's Temperance Convention" of 1853 had a "novel append-age" in the form of a Temperance Banquet held on September 8 in Metropolitan Hall, New York. There were many "reform" movements underway in the mid-nineteenth century, and they shared many adherents. The Temperance Banquet was held under the auspices of the New York Vegetarian Society, and several leaders of the women's rights movement were also present and vocal. Lucy Stone (1818–1893), the first woman to retain her own name after marriage, was there, as was Amelia Bloomer (1818–1894), the woman who created the outrageous but comfortable garment called "bloomers," and Susan B. Anthony (1820–1906), the renowned speaker on temperance and women's suffrage. The host for the "sumptuous banquet" was the newspaperman Horace Greeley (1811–1872) of the *New York Tribune*.

---

BILL OF FARE.

VEGETABLE SOUPS.
Tomato Soup, Rice Soup.

FARINACEA
Graham Bread,        Mixed Fruit Cakes,
Fruited Bread,        Apple Biscuit,
Wheat Meal Cakes,        Moulded Rice,
Corn Blanc Mange,        Moulded Farina,
Moulded Wheaten Grits.

VEGETABLES.
Baked Sweet Potatoes,      Stewed Cream Squashes.

PASTRY.
Mixed Fruit Pies,      Pumpkin Pies.

FRUITS.
Melons,       Apples,       Peaches,
Pears,       Grapes,       Pineapple

RELISHES.
Plum Jellies,      Baked Apples

COOKED FRUITS.
Cocoanut Custard,      Fruited Ice Cream.

BEVERAGE.
Pure Cold Water.

---

Naturally, the press had a field day. The responses to the event ran the gamut from cynicism to ridicule, with as much of the comment being directed to the women's rights campaigners as to the food. The author, Alfred Bunn, of *Old England and New England*, in a series of views taken on the spot (1853), wrote:

> Now, stewed squashes, sweet potatoes, wheaten grits, baked apples, and cocoa-nut custards, with songs, speeches, and prayers to match, are all very well in their way; and to some people's notions, may be said to comprise "all the delicacies of the season," and then again "pure cold water" is at all events a wholesome beverage; but when gentlemen are charged four shillings and twopence, and ladies two shillings and a penny, to enable them to partake of this sumptuous banquet; and when it is borne in mind that Metropolitan Hall will hold three thousand people, and that it was FULL, why it is pretty clear that Miss Lucy Stone must have made a very good thing of it. By her account, women are to have equal rights, and men are to have the exclusive right of paying for them.

A writer for the *Water-Cure Journal* and *Herald of Reforms* noted that the president of the New York Vegetarian Society was Dr. Trall, "who caters for the lovers of brown bread, douche baths, and wet shees (ugh!) at the Water-Cure Establishment, 15 Leight Street," and that "other worthy disciples of Sylvester Graham [see February 5]" were also officers. The writer determined to be in attendance, in spite of the full expectation that it would be far from being a "feast of fat things." He noted the welcoming feel of the Banquet Room, the "admirably arranged and beautifully ornamented tables," the number of spectators in the gallery ("who did not feel like risking more than the shilling charged for admission to that part of the house"), and he included the bill of fare as a "natural curiosity." The writer went on to note "the chilling announcement of "pure cold water" as the only beverage, which was "soon forgot amid the blaze and beauty of the women." The intrepid reporter found himself seated near several Bloomers (followers of Amelia)—including Amelia herself—and was curious to experience "how soon we got used to the Bloomer costume." He was so obviously distracted by the novelty of the occasion and the bloomer-clad ladies that he made no comment about the actual food.

## Recipes

~~~

### Cocoanut Custard

One cocoanut; one quart of milk; three eggs; one nutmeg; a little cinnamon; a little wine, brandy and rose water; a piece of butter size of an egg. Sweeten to taste; make like a custard; stir the cocoanut in; bake in a crust.

*Presbyterian Cook Book, Compiled by the Ladies of The First Presbyterian Church* (Dayton, Ohio, ca. 1873).

### Apple Biscuit

Boil apples in water until soft, then take them out and rub through a wire sieve; flavor with a drop or two of essence or of lemon, and, if you like the taste, a drop of the oil of cloves. Add lump sugar equal in weight to the pulp, and grind it with

> it; roll the sugared pulp into flat cakes about a quarter of an inch thick, and cut
> them into shapes. Finally dry them in a very slow oven, the heat not being
> strong enough to bake them or melt the sugar; they may be dried also by the
> summer's sun. They often require to be partially dried before they can be rolled
> out. They may, instead of rolling, be dropped on to paper, or put in a ring of
> paper upon a slightly greased iron plate.
> *Jennie June's American Cookery Book* (New York, 1870).

Baked Apples: see March 15.
Graham Bread: see February 5.

## September 9

Maiden Voyage Dinner
aboard the RMS *Lusitania,* 1907

When the *Lusitania* was launched in June 1906 she was the largest ocean
liner in the world, and one of the fastest. On her maiden voyage she left Liverpool, England, on September 7 and arrived in New York 4 days, 19 hours,
and 52 minutes later—a record transatlantic crossing. She was also "more
beautiful than Solomon's palace," and as luxurious as the luxury-loving
Edwardians could wish. The passenger classes were strictly segregated, and
second class was better than first class on other ships. Evenings aboard for
first class were about conspicuous consumption. Dressing for dinner meant
evening suits for men and fabulous gowns and brilliant jewels for ladies,
and dinner meant many courses of elegant food. A surviving menu for the
third day of the maiden voyage does not specify which class of passengers
enjoyed the dinner.

---

Hors d'oeuvres
Consomme Marguerite     Puree Musard
Halibut—Sauce Cardinal     Paupiettes of Whiting au Gratin
Calf's Head—Toulouse     Noisettes of Mutton a l'Italienne
Sirloin and Ribs of Beef—Yorkshire Pudding
Braised Gosling     Roast Capon
Saute of Mushrooms     Baked Tomatoes     Boiled Rice
Potatoes—Boiled, Duchesse, and Mashed
Baked York Ham
Victoria Pudding     Compote de Pruneaux     Marignan Chantilly
Gelee Oriental
Ice-Cream
Dessert
Tea     Coffee
Choice Cold Meats

---

*Lusitania.* Courtesy of Library of Congress.

The *Lusitania*'s career was glamorous but short. She was torpedoed by a German U-boat on May 7, 1915, and sank in 18 minutes, with the loss of 1,198 lives.

Many of those lost were Americans, and the event certainly precipitated the United States into World War I. Circumstances surrounding her sinking are still controversial, and rumors persist that she was sunk because she was secretly carrying ammunition for the war effort, and was thus a fair target for enemy action.

Recipes

~~~

*Paupiettes* or *polpettes* are sometimes called "headless birds." The name derives from the Italian word *polpetta*, referring to a meatball, but *paupiettes* are usually long, thin slices of meat or fish rolled around a stuffing (farce or forcemeat) and braised.

---

### Whiting, Paupiettes of

Fillet three or four full-sized whitings. Trim the fillets, season with pepper and salt, and spread upon each a little whiting forcemeat [below]. Roll them round, tie securely with twine, and wrap them in strips of oiled paper. Put them in the oven, and bake until done enough. Remove the paper, place the paupiettes upright on a dish, put upon the top of each a turned mushroom or a bunch of parsley, pour a little lobster sauce round them and serve.

---

---

### Whiting Forcemeat

Skin and fillet two or three whitings, scrape the flesh with a spoon, and rub it through a wire sieve. To twelve ounces of the fish thus prepared put half a pound of panada and six ounces of fresh butter. Season the mixture with pepper, salt, and grated nutmeg, mix the ingredients thoroughly, and add gradually three whole eggs and the yolks of two. Poach a small quantity of the forcemeat to ascertain whether or not it is firm, yet light and delicately flavoured. If too stiff, mix a little cream with it. Keep it on ice until required.

---

There are many different recipes for "Victoria pudding." There are moulded trifles, Christmas pudding-type puddings with fruit and spice, steamed bread puddings, and custards.

---

### Victoria Pudding

Boil a little piece of stick vanilla in a pint of milk till it is pleasantly flavoured, strain it upon six ounces of finely-grated bread-crumbs, and add three table-spoonfuls of sugar, one table-spoonful of brandy, and three well-beaten eggs. Butter a mould thickly, flour it, and ornament tastefully with dried cherries, slices of preserved citron, or stoned raisins. Pour in the pudding quite cold, put a plate upon it, and steam it over boiling water. Let it stand two or three minutes, turn it upon a hot dish, and serve with Victoria sauce, or with melted red currant jelly poured round it.

*Cassell's New Dictionary of Cookery* (1910).

---

Yorkshire Pudding: see December 24.
Duchesse Potatoes: see July 11.
Calf's Head: see January 30.

## September 10

### Fat Men's Club Clambake
### Power's Hotel, Dorlon's Point, South Norwalk, Connecticut, 1891

The famous Fat Men's Club started in South Norwalk in 1866. Over the next 25 years it used other venues, and inevitably it lost members—some moved away, some died, "and what was worse than either, some got thin on a foreign diet." The minimum weight required for membership was 200 pounds, and the great event on the club's calendar was its annual clambake.

On September 10, 1891, 23 members of this "affable asssortement of Brobdignanggian adiposity" returned to the birthplace of their club for its 25th anniversary. They sat in "enormous rustic chairs" on the porch of Power's Hotel, watching a huge pile of clams roasting under seaweed on the marshy land across the road. At 2:30 the feast was served in a large pavilion on the lawn. *The New York Times* reported that "Everything vanished as soon as it was brought, and clam and oyster and crab shells lay several inches thick on the floor."

25 bushels of hard and soft shell clams, roasted
10 bushels of oysters, roasted
100 Chickens,
Lobsters, crabs,
1 barrel of Potatoes, baked,
1/2 barrel of Sweet Potatoes
500 ears of Green Corn,
1 barrel of onions,
Tripe,
"and the other concomitants of the long-established
and highly-honoured bill of fare of the club."

The annual clambake was election day for the club. Judge Lockwood was reelected as president and "called attention to the increasing numbers of doctors in the society, and expressed the fear that it would be metamorphosed into a morgue or a medical society." It was also the time of the annual weigh-in. Judge Lockwood was the clear winner at 332 pounds, but several of those present were in danger of losing their membership when they only managed the minimum 200 pounds. In a very supportive gesture, at the request of the members, the wife of the hotel proprietor, Mrs. Power, also stepped on the scales, coming out at a very generous 273 pounds.

Recipes
~~~

### Roasted Clams

Roasted clams are served at Clam Bakes. Clams are washed in sea-water, placed on stones which have been previously heated by burning wood on them, ashes removed, and stones sprinkled with thin layer of seaweed. Clams are piled on stones, covered with seaweed, and a piece of canvas thrown over them to retain the steam.
Fannie Merritt Farmer, *The Boston Cooking-School Cookbook* (Boston, 1896).

### Roasted Oysters on Toast

Eighteen large oysters, or thirty small ones, one teaspoonful of flour, one tablespoonful of butter, salt, pepper, three slices of toast. Have the toast buttered and on a hot dish. Put the butter in a small sauce-pan, and when hot, add the dry flour. Stir until smooth, but not brown; then add the cream, and let it boil up once. Put the oysters (in their own liquor) into a hot oven, for three minutes; then add them to the cream. Season, and pour over the toast. Garnish the dish with thin slices of lemon, and serve very hot. It is nice for lunch or tea.
Maria Parloa, *Miss Parloa's New Cookbook* (New York, ca. 1880).

Tripe: see May 6.

## September 11

Day's Meals aboard an Airship
*R.33*, En Route from Norfolk, England, to Amsterdam, 1919

For the first few decades of the twentieth century, it seemed that airships—essentially steerable (or "dirigible") giant balloons—would be the answer to the prayers of those military or civic powers who wished to control the airspace of the world. The dream finally ended as a nightmare with a series of disastrous crashes and explosions in the 1930s, but for a brief time they were fascinating machines with limitless potential to provide adventure, excitement—and luxury.

The British airship R.33 was designed as a military flying machine, but some temporary adaptations were made to illustrate its commercial possibilities. A demonstration voyage with ten passengers aboard began on the evening of September 10, 1919, from Norfolk, England. No effort had been spared to ensure a comfortable journey to Amsterdam and return, with a viewing of the battlefields of Europe en route. A modest evening meal of drinks and sandwiches was served on the first evening, but the menu for the three meals the next day was more than adequate.

---

BREAKFAST: eggs and bacon, toast, hot tea or coffee.

LUNCH: Cold lobster, roast partridge, hot potatoes and French beans, iced pudding.

DINNER: Hot soup, salmon trout, roast lamb, potatoes, French beans, jam omelette, coffee.

---

The chef was a man called Cantaluppi—an Italian national who had served in the British Army before working at the Criterion Restaurant in London. Before the journey, Cantaluppi expressed some regret at the limitations imposed by the cooking facilities on board—there was a small electric stove, but cooking was also done on the exhaust pipes. He was confident, however, that he could alter the menu if required, and he took the precaution of taking extra eggs on board, so that he could whip up a soufflé if requested.

The military origin of the airship was still in evidence, and meals were served in the mess room in the keelway of the airship. There was no newspaper delivery in the air, but passengers were able to receive the news of the day over their breakfast, via wireless telegraphy.

### Recipes

~~~

---

### Cold Soufflé of Lobster

Choose a lobster weighing a little over 1 lb. for six or eight guests, take all the fish from the shell, saving fair slices of the best part for decorating the top. Chop the remainder very fine, and mix with 1/4 pint whipped cream and season to taste. Pound the shell well and add a little butter or margarine and simmer on the fire with about two tablespoonfuls of milk. Strain through a muslin, and when cold add to the cream and lobster, melt about four leaves of gelatine, and stir into the lobster cream. Have ready a round white china or silver soufflé dish with crisp shredded lettuce, hard-boiled egg, bits of skinned tomato, a little thin mayonnaise sauce passed through it all, reaching half-way up the dish, put the mixture of lobster in, and when set put over a thin layer of aspic jelly, slightly pink with cochineal, and the selected pieces of lobster, and serve very cold with bread and butter.

*The Times*, November 19, 1921.

---

### Sweet Omelet

Three Eggs.
Half an Ounce of Butter.
One tablespoonful of Castor Sugar.
One teaspoonful of Orange-Flower Water.
Salt.
(Jam.)

Put the orange-flower water and the sugar into a stewpan, and stir over the fire; let it boil quickly for three minutes, then put it into a basin to cool. When cool, add the yolks of egg and beat to a cream. Put a pinch of salt to the whites of egg, whip them to a stiff froth, and stir them lightly to the yolks of egg. Melt the butter in an omelet-pan, and pour in the eggs; put this on the fire for two minutes. Make some jam, about a dessertspoonful, quite hot; take the omelet out of the oven, and put it on a hot dish, spread the jam on the omelet lightly and quickly, fold it over like a sandwich, sprinkle a little castor sugar over it, and serve.

Mrs. Charles Clarke, *High-Class Cookery Recipes* (London, 1893).

---

## September 12

### Children's Meals
### aboard the SS *Strathaird,* 1957

The idea that children need a special, or at least different, diet from adults goes back to ancient times. The humoral doctrine (see February 23) proposed by the second-century Greco-Roman physician Galen held sway over medical thought and influenced dietary advice for all age groups for two millennia. It was believed that the body was made up of four "humors"—blood, phlegm, yellow bile, and black bile—and that imbalance in these created disease, and the most important way of maintaining or correcting balance was by diet. Each gender and age was dominated by a particular humor, which could itself be affected by disease, and the diet was modified accordingly.

Since the time of Galen there have been many, many theories about infant and child feeding, but in all of them the individual foods were selected from the range eaten by adults. It is only relatively recently that industry and marketing forces (particularly the media arm) have combined their power and expertise to promote processed food specifically to children, for profit rather than health reasons

The SS *Strathaird* regularly traveled the route between London, England, and Sydney, Australia. On September 12, 1957, she was somewhere in the region of the Suez Canal, having arrived in Port Said in Egypt on the previous day, on the eastward journey. The children's menu for the day shows the offerings for two meals.

---

| CHILDREN'S DINNER | CHILDREN'S TEA |
|---|---|
| Cream Soup | Cream of Vegetables |
| Grilled Fillets of Brill, Butter Sauce | Flaked Whitefish, Cream Sauce |
| Lamb Cutlets with Green Peas | Scotch Pie |
| Minced Lamb | Eggs to Order |
| Nature & Creamed Potatoes | Mashed Potatoes |
| Cauliflower | |
| Diplomate Pudding, Fruit Sauce | COLD SIDEBOARD |
| | Roast Beef      Pressed Tongue |
| | Lettuce and Beetroot Salad |
| | Gooseberry Pie |
| | Cream Ices |
| | Pastries and Cakes |
| | Bread      Butter      Jams |
| | Fruit |

---

There are no dishes on this menu that would suggest to an observer half a century later that the meal was specifically for children. At dinner there are four courses—soup, fish, meat, and dessert. There are no fish fingers, chicken nuggets, or fries. It is difficult to imagine a children's menu today that omits fries but proudly boasts cauliflower and pressed tongue. The food at this meal was simple, but elegant enough to have been served to the adults aboard without anyone thinking anything was amiss.

Diplomate pudding was enormously popular at fine dinners for adults since at least the 1890s. The exact origin and naming of its name are mysteries, although its roots do appear to be French. It is a moulded dessert made with cake and custard, decorated with dried fruit. Occasionally it is frozen in the manner of ice cream. Similar puddings go by the name of Cabinet pudding and Chancellor's pudding, so there appears to be some sort of political connection. One theory is that the diplomat in question was Count Karl Nesselrode (1780–1862), for whom the very famous (and similar) Nesselrode pudding was named (see June 30).

Scotch pie usually refers to a small individual mutton pie, and they are so called because of their long popularity in Scotland. A classic Scotch pie is made with mutton and is quite peppery. It is made with hot-water crust pastry (the sort used for "raised" pies since the Middle Ages), and the top crust is lower than the upper edge of the pie, forming a depression which can be filled with gravy or potato. One elderly correspondent to *The Times* in 1930 expressed some nostalgia for the mutton pies of his childhood. He described them as being "upright, of the size and shape of castle puddings, and the pastry was of the plainest, the interior being composed, as I understood it, of fat mutton, onion, and black pepper." Another reader obliged with a recipe which used puff pastry—which would probably be more acceptable to children (see the following).

Recipes

~~~

---

### Diplomate Pudding

Take sponge, or any kind of left over cake and cut in small pieces, using enough to fill a pudding mould. Add about a teaspoonful of chopped candied fruit to each person. Make a custard with one quart of milk, six eggs and a half pound of sugar; pour over the cake in the mould, and bake. Serve with brandy sauce with some chopped candied fruit in it.

Victor Hirtzler, *The Hotel St. Francis Cook Book* (1919).

---

### Mutton Pies

Remove all skin and fat from scraps of mutton. Mix with cooked potatoes, chopped onion and parsley. Grease patty pans and line with puff paste. Fill with meat and vegetable mixture well seasoned. Bake for a few minutes in a hot oven; then stand on a cooler shelf [in the oven] that the meat may stew nicely.

*The Times*, June 21, 1930.

---

## September 13

### Dinner Celebrating the Founding of Dulwich College
### Camberwell, Surrey, England, 1619

Edward Alleyn (1566–1626) was a famous actor during the time of Shakespeare, when the profession was considered rather disreputable. Alleyn was well liked, however, made a lot of influential friends, and became wealthy on account of his business acumen. Late in life, having no heir for his fortune, he decided to endow a "college"—which at that time was a charitable institution for the assistance of the poor. Dulwich College in southeast London was the result. The school began with "six poor brethren, and six sisters, twelve scholars, six assistants, and thirty out-members," and it is still in existence today—although as a rather more exclusive institution whose students pay fees to attend.

On September 13, 1619, Alleyn noted in his journal that the foundations of the building were completed, and a ceremony was held at which "ther wear present, the Lord Chancellor Bacon. Lord Arundel, Sir John Howland, high sheriff of the county, Inigo Jones, the king's architect and many other persons of distinction." After the sermon and anthem, Alleyn provided a fine dinner for the distinguished guests.

| 2 Mess of Meat. | 2 Course |
| --- | --- |
| Capons in whight broth | Rost godwith |
| Boyld pigions | Aytychok pie |
| Boyld venson | Rost partridges |
| Farct boyd meat | Wett leche |
| Could rost | Rost quayles |
| Gran salad | Codlyng targ |
| A chin of beef rost | Howse pigions |
| Shoulder of mutton w$^h$ oysters | Amber lech |
| Baked vensone | Rost rabbit |
| Rost neate tong | Dry neats tongs |
| A floringtyne | Pickle oysters |
| Rost capons | Anchoves |
| Rost ducks | So the other Mess. |
| Rost eel | |
| Westfalya bacon | |
| | |
| En | |
| | |
| So on the other Mess. | |

The foundation of any great dinner was a large amount and a great variety of meat, but this dinner also included vegetables. Vegetables were an integral part of many dishes, but were often not specifically listed. Alleyn included details of the expenses in his journal, and the "Gardyners Bill" included "2 colley storeys, 13 artichocks, 30 lettis, purslaine, beet roots, caretts, turneps."

It was also usual for there to be a final "banquet" course (see March 9), and this certainly took place at this dinner. The confectioners bill for "banquetting stuffe" included "wett suckett" (a "wet" sweetmeat, see September 5), almond past[e] (marzipan), colered biskett, wafers, and many dried fruits. The "amber lech" also indicates this was a fine and expensive dinner. A "leach" or leche was any dish that could be sliced, as a meatloaf today.

This one actually contained *ambergris* (*amber of grece*), the strange secretion from the digestive system of a whale that is used extensively in the fragrance industry and was once a prized ingredient in cooking and a valuable medicine.

Naturally also there was a good selection of beverages at the dinner. The Vintner's account listed "2 rundletts of clarett contayning 8 gall; A bottel of canory, 9 pints; 3 qts of sherry; 3 qts of whight wine." Alleyn also noted "of my owne . . . 2 hoggesheds of bere."

## Recipes
~~~

---

### To Boyle a Capon in White Broth

Boyle your Capon in faire liquor, and cover it to keep it white, but you must boyl no other meat with it, take the best of the broth, and as much vergious as of the broth, if your vergious be not too sowre, & put therto whole Mace, whole pepper and a good hand ful of Endive, Letuce or Borage, whether of them ye wil, smal Raisons, Dates, Marow of marow bones, a litle sticke of Sinamon, the peele of an Orenge. Then put in a good peece of Sugar, and boyl them well together. Then take two or three yolkes of egges sodden, and strain them and thick it withal, and boyl your prunes by themselves, and lay upon your Capon: powre your broth upon your Capon.

Thus may you boyle anie thing in white broth.

*The Good Huswifes Handmaide for the Kitchin* (1594).

---

A floringtyne (or florentine) was a type of flan or pie containing meat, especially veal.

---

### To Make a Florentine

Take the kidneis of a loyne of veale that is roasted, and when it is cold shredde it fine, and grate as it were half a Manchette very fine, and take eight yolkes of Egges, and a handfull of currans, and eight dates finely shred, a little senamon, a little ginger a litte suere and a litle salt, and mingle them with the kidneyes, then take a handfull of fine flower an two yolkes of egges and as much butter as two eggs, and put into your flower, then take a little seething liquor, and make your past and drive it as broad very thinne, then strake your dishe with a little butter, and lay your paste in and when it is halfe-baked drawe it out, and take two or three feathers, and a little rose-water, and wette all the cover with it, and have a handfull of suger finely beaten, and strawe upon it, and see that the Rosewater wet in every place, and so set it in the oven againe, and that will make a faire ise upon it, if your Oven be not hotte inough to reare by your ices, then put a little fire in the Ovens mouth.

Thomas Dawson, *Good Huswifes Jewell* (1596).

---

## September 14

Jane Austen's Dinner
Henrietta Street, Covent Garden, London, 1813

The English writer Jane Austen (1775–1817), who wrote enduringly popular novels including *Pride and Prejudice* and *Sense and Sensibility*, was also a prolific correspondent. Her letters show the same insight into and lively interest in human behavior as do her books. Jane stayed with her brother Henry (a banker) in London on several occasions between 1813–1815, and during that time she wrote regularly to her beloved sister Cassandra. She described the home (above his office) as "all dirt and confusion, but in a very interesting way" and was clearly made very welcome there. In her letter of September 14, 1813, she described dinner and supper on the day of her arrival.

> *Henrietta St.: Wednesday (Sept. 15, 1/2 past 8).*
> Here I am, my dearest Cassandra, seated in the breakfast, dining, sitting-room, beginning with all my might . . . We had a very good journey, weather and roads excellent . . . We arrived at a quarter-past four, and were kindly welcomed by the coachman, and then by his master, and then by William, and then by Mrs. Pengird, who all met us before we reached the foot of the stairs. Mde. Bigion was below dressing us a most comfortable dinner of soup, fish, bouillée, partridges, and an apple tart, which we sat down to soon after five, after cleaning and dressing ourselves and feeling that we were most commodiously disposed of . . . At seven we set off in a coach for the Lyceum; were at home again in about four hours and a half; had soup and wine and water, and then went to our holes.

The Mde. Bigion who prepared the dinner was her brother's housekeeper, and as much a family friend as servant (Jane left her a small legacy). She was French, or of French heritage, and had possibly accompanied Henry's wife Eliza who had lived in France and was the widow of a Frenchman who had been guillotined in 1794. The meal prepared by Mde. Bigion is a good example of an English middle-class family dinner of the time—quite plain and as Austen comments, "most comfortable."

Austen is often quoted as saying in another letter that "Good apple pies form a considerable part of our domestic happiness." It is certainly true that tart (or pie, Jane appears to have used the words interchangeably) is probably one of the oldest and best-loved sweet dishes in the Western world. Recipes for apple pie in one form or another appear in cookery manuscripts of the Middle Ages.

Recipes

~~~

### Apple Pie

Pare and core the fruit, after being wiped clean; then boil the cores and parings in a little water, till it tastes well. Strain the liquor, add a little sugar, with a bit of bruised cinnamon, and simmer again. Meantime place the apples in a dish, a paste being put round the edge; when one layer is in, sprinkle half the sugar, and shred lemon peel ; squeeze in some of the juice, or a glass of cider, if the apples have lost their spirit. Put in the rest of the apples, the sugar, and the liquor which has been boiled. If the pie be eaten hot, put some butter into it, quince marmalade, orange paste or cloves, to give it a flavour.

### Partridge Boiled

This species of game is in season in the autumn. If the birds be young, the bill is of a dark colour, and the legs inclined to yellow. When fresh and good, the vent will be firm; but when stale, this part will look greenish. Boiled partridges require to be trussed the same as chickens: from twenty to twenty-five minutes will do them sufficiently. Serve them up with either white or brown mush-room sauce, or with rice stewed in gravy, made pretty thick, and seasoned with pepper and salt. Pour the sauce over them, or serve them up with celery sauce.

Mary Eaton, *The Cook and Housekeeper's Complete and Universal Dictionary* (1823).

## September 15

### Masons' Banquet to Celebrate Their New Lodge
### Criterion Hotel, Taranaki, New Zealand, 1883

After the consecration of their new premises, the masonic brethren of the De Burgh Adams Lodge Rooms in Taranaki, New Zealand, adjourned to the nearby Criterion Hotel where they sat down to a "most excellent banquet . . . laid out in superb style."

Soups: Mulligatawny.

Table: Sirloin beef, braized ducks, roast fowls, ox tongues, ham, fowls, lobster patties, galantine of veal, pork pies, boiled turkey and aspic jelly, roast turkey, vol-au-vent of oysters, collared beef, roast ducks, roast lamb and mint sauce.

A boar's head formed a centre piece of the table.

Sweets, &c.: Apple souffle peach meringues, lemon sponge, vanilla cream, orange jelly, cheese-cakes, fruit jelly, pyramids of rice, compot of quince, tall cakes, rhubarb pies, blanc mange, ladies' fingers, Italian cream, custard in glasses.

Fruits in season.

Wines (assorted).

It is likely that most, if not all, of the brethren at this dinner were of British extraction. Most immigrants to New Zealand in the first half-century of its life as a colony came from Britain, and like immigrants everywhere they took their food ways with them. The gold standard for a civic dinner in a British colony was the style that it would have been at home (see also January 26, March 5). This dinner came complete with the boar's head (see January 4), a medieval relic that had already become something of an anachronism in Britain.

A different piece of colonial culinary history is represented by the Mulligatawny—a "curry" soup which gets its names from the combination of the Tamil words for pepper and water. It is decidedly Anglo-Indian, not Indian (see also kedgeree, June 27), a legacy of British colonial rule in India, so discussion about "authenticity" of recipes for the dish is meaningless. It began to be popular in Britain towards the end of the eighteenth century, in an almost infinite number of variations.

"Collaring" meat is another method of cooking which is now old fashioned. "Collared" meat (and fish) was boned, rolled up tightly (sometimes with a stuffing) and tied with string into a cylindrical shape before cooking (usually by boiling). In the case of pork, small pieces and scraps were sometimes pressed together then rolled up in the skin before tying. The advantage of "collaring" meat was that it was a way of using up awkwardly shaped pieces of meat, or scraps, and it was also easy to cut and serve.

## Recipes
~~~

---

### Mulligatawny Soup

2 tablespoonfuls of curry powder,
6 onions,
1 clove of garlic,
1 oz. of pounded almonds,
a little lemon-pickle, or mango-juice, to taste;
1 fowl or rabbit,
4 slices of lean bacon;
2 quarts of medium stock, or, if wanted very good, best stock.

Slice and fry the onions of a nice colour; line the stewpan with the bacon; cut up the rabbit or fowl into small joints, and slightly brown them; put in the fried onions, the garlic, and stock, and simmer gently till the meat is tender; skim very carefully, and when the meat is done, rub the curry powder to a smooth batter; add it to the soup with the almonds, which must be first pounded with a little of the stock. Put in seasoning and lemon-pickle or mango-juice to taste, and serve boiled rice with it.

*Beeton's Household Manual* (1861).

---

### Collared Beef

7 lbs. of the thin end of the flank of beef,
2 oz. of coarse sugar,
6 oz. of salt,
1 oz, of saltpetre,
1 large handful of parsley minced,

> 1 dessertspoonful of minced sage,
> a bunch of savoury herbs,
> 1/2 teaspoonful of pounded allspice;
> salt and pepper to taste.
>
> Choose fine tender beef, but not too fat; lay it in a dish; rub in the sugar, salt, and saltpetre, and let it remain in the pickle for a week or ten days, turning and rubbing it every day. Then bone it, remove all the gristle and the coarse skin of the inside part, and sprinkle it thickly with parsley, herbs, spice, and seasoning in the above proportion, taking care that the former are finely minced, and the latter well pounded. Roll the meat up in a cloth as tightly as possible, in the same shape as shown in the engraving; bind it firmly with broad tape, and boil it gently for 6 hours. Immediately on taking it out of the pot, put it under a good weight, without undoing it, and let it remain until cold. This dish is a very nice addition to the breakfast-table.
>
> *Beeton's Household Manual* (1861).

Ladies Fingers: see March 12.
Blancmange: see January 7.
Pork Pie: see November 3.
Vol-au-Vent: see September 17.

## September 16

### Induction Feast of the Bishop of Bath and Wells
### The Bishop's Palace, Wells, Somerset, England, 1425

John Stafford (later archbishop of Canterbury) was made bishop of Bath and Wells after the death of Nicholas Bubwith (see December 4). His inthronization feast was extraordinarily elegant.

| Le .j. cours. | Le .ij. cours. | Le .iiij. cours. |
| --- | --- | --- |
| Furmenty with venysoun. | Blaunche Mortrewys. | Gely. |
| Mammenye | Vyand Ryal. | Creme Moundy. |
| Brawnne. | Pecoke. | Pety Curlewe. |
| Kede Roste. | Conyng. | Egret. |
| Capoun de haut Grece. | Fesaunte. | Pertryche. |
| Swan. | Tele. | Venysoun Roste. |
| Heyroun. | Chykonys doryd. | Plovere. |
| Crane. | Pyions. | Oxyn kyn. |
| A leche. | Veysoun Rostyd. | Quaylys. |
| Crustade Ryal. | Gullys. | Snytys. |
| Frutoure Samata. | Curlew. | Herte de Alouse. |
| | Cokyntryche. | Smale byrdys. |
| A soltelte, a docter of lawe. | A leche. | Dowcet Ryal. |
| | Pystelade chaud. | Petelade Fryid. |

Pystelade fryid.

Frytoure damaske.


A sotelte, Egle.

Hyrchouns.

Eggys Ryal.

Pomys.

Brawn fryid.


A sotelte, Sent Andrewe.


Frute.

Waffrys.

Vyn dowce.

Even without knowing the circumstances of this feast, it would be clear from the dishes served that this was a fine meal for high class guests. The meal has the classic format of three courses, with richly symbolic *solteties* (see September 23) appearing after each course as both entertainment and expression of power. Most of the dishes on the menu are for some sort of bird—and birds, living in the air as they do, were considered closer to God than animals that walked the earth. As was usual for the time, lesser ranking guests in the lower part of the hall on this day were offered a mere fourteen dishes of less fine food spread over only two courses (see October 13).

The meal includes several dishes without which no feast of the time would have been complete—venison with frumenty, brawn (which would have been served with mustard), *crustades*, *leches*, and various fritters. The bill of fare also notes the wafers and sweet wine traditionally served as digestive aids at the end of a feast (but not usually formally recorded) and which are the forerunners of a modern dessert course.

One dish on this menu has no modern equivalent—an illusion food called a Cockentrice. Food made to look like something else was very popular in the middle ages. This menu for example includes *hyrchons* (yrchouns, "urchins" or "hedgehogs," see September 16), and the *pomys* may be *pommes doreng*, meatballs made to look like golden apples (see October 13). An illusion food was a fanciful dish made to amuse the guests and impress them with the skill of the cook (and by extension the wealth of the host), but unlike a *soltetie* (see September 23) it was meant to be eaten. A cockentrice was an extreme example of illusion food—a fantasy animal made by joining half a pig with half a capon—giving two possible versions of the beast.

## Recipes

~~~

### Cokyntryce

Take a Capoun, and skald hym, and draw hem clene, and smyte hem a-to in the waste ouerthwart; take a Pigge, and skald hym, and draw hym in the same maner, and smyte hem also in the waste; take a nedyl and a threde, and sewe the fore partye of the Capoun to the After parti of the Pygge; and the fore partye of the Pigge, to the hynder party of the Capoun, and than stuffe hem as thou stuffyst a Pigge; putte hem on a spete, and Roste hym: and whan he is y-now, dore hem with 3olkys of Eyroun, and pouder Gyngere and Safroun, thenne wyth the Ius of Percely with-owte; and than serue it forth for a ryal mete.

---

### Yrchouns

Take Piggis mawys, & skalde hem wel; take groundyn Porke, & knede it with Spicerye, with pouder Gyngere, Salt & Sugre; do it on the mawe, but fille it nowt to fulle; then sewe hem with a fayre threde, and putte hem in a Spete as men don piggys; take blaunchid Almaundys, & kerf hem long, smal, & scharpe, and frye hem in grece and sugre; take a litel prycke, & prykke the yrchons, An putte in the holes the Almaundys, every hole half, & eche fro other; ley hem then to the fyre; when they ben rostid, dore hem sum wyth Whete Flowre, & mylke of Almaundys, sum grene, sum blake with Blode, & lat hem nowt browne to moche, & serue forth.

Thomas Austin, *Two Fifteenth-Century Cookery-Books* (1430).

---

Brawn: see September 22.
Furmenty (frumenty): see February 23.

## September 17

### Centennial Dinner
### Exchange Coffee House, Boston, Massachusetts, 1830

The celebration of the 200th anniversary of the settlement of Boston began at 8 A.M. on the morning of September 17, 1830, and continued until late in the evening. After the meetings, processions, and military displays, a fine banquet was held in the evening at the Exchange Coffee House on Congress Street. One hundred twelve diners sat down to a substantial repast, at a cost of $3 each per person, including wine. The Lieutenant Governor of Massachusetts, Thomas L. Winthrop (1750 or 60 -1841), great-great-great grandson of John Winthrop (1587/8–1649) presided.

Fifty years later *The New York Times* considered the historic event and commented

But look at the bill of fare and see if it was not substantial. French dishes, too, with horrid French titles badly expressed, it is true—but no doubt well cooked. ... It will be noted that fifty years ago they had not brought the arrangement of bills of fare to that high perfection which present such divisions that in 1880 one is bewildered in selecting an ordinary meal.

There is no doubt that the banquet organizers went all out to impress, but this menu is hardly pretentious. Most of the main dishes were simply boiled or roasted, but on the other hand the glamor is often in the pastry work, and the details of the "puddings, pies, and custards" are unknown. The

Mock Turtle Soup;

Boiled Bass;

Baked Cod Fish;

Stewed Black Fish;

Anguille à la Tartare;

Boiled Hams;

Boiled Corned Beef;

Boiled Tongues;

Boiled Legs of Mutton;

Boiled Turkey, Oyster Sauce;

Beef Alamode;

Beef Bouillie

Chickens à la Supreme;

Vol au Vent aux Huitres;

Vol au Vent de Voláille;

Vol au Vent à la St. Lambert;

Vol au Vent Wild Pigeons;

Vol au Vent Poulettes à la Conti;

Puddings,

Pies,

Custards,

Perdrix au Choux;

De dindons à la Galentine;

Fricandeaux au Tomata;

Lobster Curried;

Roast Beef;

Roasted Legs of Mutton;

Roasted Mongrel Geese;

Roasted Tame Ducks;

Roasted Chickens;

Roasted Wild Pigeons, stuffed and larded;

Roasted Partridges;

Roasted Wild Ducks;

Roasted Wild Gray and Black;

Roasted Woodcocks;

Roasted Plovers;

Roasted Quails;

Roasted Snipes;

Turks Caps Ice Creams,

&c., &c.

DESSERT.

WILLIAM GALLAGHER.

range of vol-au-vents suggests the services of an experienced pastry cook, however. A vol-au-vent is, according to the *Oxford English Dictionary* "A kind of raised pie, formed of a light puff paste filled with meat, fish, or the like." They are most usually made as individual servings, sometimes bite-sized, as an *hors d'oeuvre*.

## Recipes

~~~

The name "vol-au-vent" means, more or less, "light as air." They are made from puff pastry shells which are filled just before serving. Puff pastry has a reputation for being difficult to make, and most cooks today purchase it from the freezer section of the supermarket. The following recipe for puff pastry is taken from the *Virginia Housewife*, first published in 1824. It is considered to be the first regional American cookbook, and it was, and still is, hugely popular, and was reprinted many times. For forming the *vol-au-vents* from the puff paste, see December 28 (where they are referred to as "patties").

---

### To Make Puff Paste

Sift a Quart of Flour, leave out a Little for rolling the Paste, make up the remainder with cold Water into a stiff Paste, knead it well, and roll it out several Times; wash the Salt from a pound of butter, divide it into four Parts, put one of them on the Paste in little Bits, fold it up, and continue to roll till the Butter is well mixed; then out another portion of Butter, roll it in the same manner, do this till all the Butter is mingled with the Paste, touch it very lightly with the hands in making; bake it in a moderate Oven that will permit it to rise but will not make it brown. Good Paste must look white, and as light as a Feather.

Mary Randolph, *The Virginia House-wife* (1831).

---

A Turk's Cap, in this context, was an ice-cream in a "turban" of pastry, which was often highly decorated.

---

### Turk's Cap, with Ice Cream

Make a clear paste, or batter, as the former; and butter the mould, so called, in which it is to be baked; when it is cold, cut off the top gently, and a good deal of the inside; which dry in the oven, till it can be reduced to powder or crumbs: boil a pint of cream and sugar according to judgment; reduce it to half, and add the crumbs to it: mix it well, to ice it to a certain degree, that you may put it in the cap, and cover it over with the top to hide the cream: you may masquerade the outside as you think proper, or serve it plain, if of a good colour.

B. Clermont, *The Professed Cook; Or, The Modern Art of Cookery, Pastry, & Confectionary* (1812).

---

Beef Alamode (à la Mode): see March 6.
Mock Turtle Soup: see July 4.
Sauce Tartare: see December 11.
Vol-au-Vent: see September 17.

## September 18

### Meals in the Pullman Dining Car
### in the Funeral Train of President William McKinley, 1901

William McKinley (1843–1901), the twenty-fifth president of the United States, died on September 14, 1901, from gunshot wounds received in an assassination attempt on September 6 in Buffalo, New York. His body was taken by train—the pilot locomotive draped in black—from Buffalo to Washington, DC, two days later for a formal funeral service there before being returned to his hometown of Canton, Ohio, for burial.

The Pullman Dining Car on September 16 offered the following meal selections for those accompanying the president's body to Washington.

## BREAKFAST

Fruit        Cantaloupe

Oatmeal with Cream

Malt Breakfast Food with Cream

Fried Pan Fish        Salt Mackerel

Sirloin and Tenderloin Steak, Plain or with Mushrooms.

Ham        Breakfast Bacon

Lamb Chops

Broiled Young Chicken

Eggs—boiled, fried, scrambled

Omelettes—plain or with rum

Potatoes, any style

Griddle Cakes, Maple Syrup

Corn Muffins, Rolls, Toast

Coffee        Cocoa        Tea


## LUNCHEON

Puree of Turnips with Sago

Raw Tomatoes        India Relish

Roast Fillet of Beef

Scrambled Eggs With Mushrooms

### COLD

Roast Beef        Tongue        Ham        Sardines

Pickled Lamb's Tongues

Boston Baked Beans

Baked Potatoes        Browned Potatoes

Stewed Tomatoes        Boiled Rice

Chicken Salad

Ice Cream        Cake        Marmalade

Preserved Fruits        Golden Gate Fruits

English And Graham Wafers

Fresh Fruit

Canadian and Edam Cheese

Bent's Water Crackers

Coffee        Tea

DINNER

Blue Points

Bisque of Lobster        Consomme

Celery        Cucumbers

Boiled Cod, Egg Sauce

Potatoes Hollandaise

Chicken Croquettes

Apple Fritters, Wine Sauce

Roast Beef

Roast Mutton with Jelly

Mashed Potatoes        Boiled Potatoes

Pickled Beets        Boiled Onions

Lettuce Salad

Tapioca Pudding

Ice Cream        Cake

Preserved Fruits        Marmalade        Dry Canton Ginger

English and Graham Wafers

Fresh Fruit

Roquefort and Canadian Cheese

Bent's Water Crackers

Coffee

This set of menus nicely demonstrates the defining features of the three main meals of the day. Plenty of meat and potatoes were offered at each meal, but eggs only at breakfast and lunch (they have never been considered "proper" at dinner). Breakfast has cereal, griddle cakes, muffins, and bacon. Ice cream appears at lunch and dinner, but never at breakfast. Cocoa is only offered at breakfast, and the only hot beverage after dinner is coffee. The only real oddity is that marmalade—usually considered exclusively a breakfast preserve, is on the lunch and dinner menus, in the apparent absence of bread in any form.

The Canton ginger served at the end of dinner was not some special recipe in honor of the president's home town. It is simply an alternative name for gingerroot, which originated in China, and much of it exited the country through the port of Canton (Guangzhou), hence the name. Ginger, like mint, has been a traditional end-of-meal digestive for centuries. It is preserved, for this purpose, in sugar, either in dry form or in syrup, and is eaten like candy.

Recipes

~~~

Egg Sauce has been a traditional accompaniment to cod for centuries.

---

**(Egg) Sauce for Boiled Cod**

To one gill of boiling water add as much milk; stir into this while boiling two tablespoonfuls of butter gradually, one tablespoonful of flour wet up with cold water; as it thickens, the chopped yolk of one boiled egg, and one raw egg beaten light. Take directly from the fire, season with pepper, salt, a little chopped parsley and the juice of one lemon, and set covered in boiling water (but not over fire) five minutes, stirring occasionally. Pour part of the sauce over fish when dished; the rest in a boat. Serve mashed potato with it.

F. L Gillette and H. Ziemann, *White House Cook Book* (1887).

---

Potatoes Hollandaise: see April 16.
Candied Ginger: see September 5.
Chicken Croquettes: see August 21.
Tapioca Pudding: see September 26.

## September 19

Patriotic "Hooverized" Dinner
Daniel's and Fisher's Tower, Denver, Colorado, 1918

The menu for the dinner prepared for the Sixteenth Annual Convention of the American Institute of Banking in Colorado on September 19, 1918, was a patriotic statement as much as a listing of dinner dishes. On a white background the red and blue wording proclaimed this to be a "Patriotic 'Hooverized' Dinner," although there was no explanation on the menu as to how this "Hooverizing" was achieved. To "Hooverize" was to economize, and it was the powerful words of the wartime Food Administrator Herbert Clark Hoover (1874–1964) that had led to his name being adapted as a verb. Hoover's catchcry was "Food will win the war!" and he implemented many campaigns and ensured that much legislation was enacted to save food for the war effort. A large part of saving anything is not wasting it, and housewives were exhorted to buy and cook economical dishes and to use all leftovers (see box).

This dinner may not have been extravagant, but it was hardly frugal. For the organizers, it was certainly an economical dinner in one respect. No beverage costs had to be factored in. There was no alcohol, because Colorado had been a "dry" state since the first moments of 1916—it was one of the first states to enact Prohibition laws. The alternative beverage—the loganberry juice of the Phez brand—also came free, too, being donated by the manufacturers.

Food poster for war. Courtesy of Library of Congress.

Fruit Cocktail

—

Chicken-with-Noodles-Soup and Breadsticks
Mixed Olives

—

Roast Duckling with Apple Sauce
Sweet Potatoes          New Spinach with Egg
Watermelon Pickle          Pascal Celery
Hot Rolls

PHEZ (Pure Juice of the Loganberry)

—

Tomato Salad
Cheese Straws

—

Cream Bisque
Mints          Cake          Salted Nuts
Coffee

Cigars          Cigarettes
(Philip Morris)

*Courtesy of The Pheasant Northwest Products Co. Salem, Oregon.

## Waste Not, Want Not in Wartime

According to a well-known domestic scientist, the only things which should find their way to the garbage pail are: Egg shells—after being used to clear coffee. Potato skins—after having been cooked on the potato. Banana skins—if there are no tan shoes to be cleaned. Bones—after having been boiled in soup kettle. Coffee grounds—if there is no garden where they can be used for fertilizer, or if they are not desired as filling for pincushions. Tea leaves—after every tea-serving, if they are not needed for brightening carpets or rugs when swept. Asparagus ends—after being cooked and drained for soup. Spinach, etc.—decayed leaves and dirty ends of roots. If more than this is now thrown away, you are wasting the family income and not fulfilling your part in the great world struggle. Your government says that it is your business to know what food your family needs to be efficient; that you must learn how to make the most of the foods you buy; that it is your duty to learn the nature and uses of various foods and to get the greatest possible nourishment out of every pound of food that comes to your home. The art of utilizing left-overs is an important factor in this prevention of waste. The thrifty have always known it. The careless have always ignored it. But now as a measure of home economy as well as a patriotic service, the left-over must be handled intelligently.

*Foods That Will Win the War and How to Cook Them* (1918).

## Recipes

~~~

## Chicken Soup, No. 1 (with Noodles)

Take one large chicken, cook with four quarts of water for two or three hours. Skim carefully, when it begins to boil add parsley root, an onion, some asparagus, cut into bits. Season with salt, strain and beat up the yolk of an egg with one tablespoon of cold water, add to soup just before serving. This soup should not be too thin. Rice, barley, noodles or dumplings may be added. Make use of the chicken either for salad or stew.

## Watermelon Pickle

Do not throw away the rind of melons. It can be preserved and will make a delicious relish. Remove the green rind of watermelon and the inside pink portion that is left on after eating it. Cut it into two-inch pieces and pour over it a weak brine made in proportion of one cup of salt to a gallon of hot water. Let this stand overnight, then drain and add clear water and one level tablespoon of alum. Boil in this water until the rind has a clear appearance. Drain and pour ice water over the rind and allow it to stand a short time. In a bag put one teaspoon each of cloves, allspice, cinnamon and ginger and place this in the preserve kettle with the vinegar and sugar. Allow one cup of sugar and one cup of vinegar (dilute this with water if too strong) to every pound of rind. Thin slices of lemon will give it a pleasant flavor—allow one lemon to about four pounds of rind. Bring this syrup to the boiling point and skim. Add the melon and cook until tender. It is done when it becomes perfectly transparent and can be easily pierced with a broom straw. A peach kernel in the cooking syrup will improve the flavor. Housewives who object to the use of alum can omit this and merely wash the rind after removing from brine to free it from all salt and then cook it slowly as per directions given above. The alum keeps the rind firm and retains its color. In this case the rind will require long and steady cooking, say three-quarters of an hour or longer. As soon as rinds are cooked they should be put into the containers and covered with the syrup.

Florence Kreisler Greenbaum, *The International Jewish Cook Book* (New York, 1919).

Cheese Straws: see April 22.

## September 20

### Library-Themed Dinner for the American Library Association Annual Conference, Grand View House, Lake Placid, New York, 1894

The American Library Association, founded in 1876, held an annual conference and dinner. In the 1890s, new and interesting ideas were afoot in library science, and the menu for the dinner that year demonstrated two of them.

| MENU | MENU KEY |
|---|---|
| a la Dewey and Cutter | |
| 613.38 plus 596.48 a Eu 398.923.144 | Consomme a l'Imperatrice |
| RN plus MJB a la eu8 | |
| 614.394 of 583.32 a la 944.36 | Cream of Peas a la St. Germain |
| RNC of RGP a la 39 | |
| — | |
| 974.16 597.5    D944.37e | Kennebec Salmon Dartoise |
| 841K    PBS    D13 | |
| 588.32    a la 944 | Peas a la Francaise |
| RGP a la 39 | — |
| — | |
| 636.2—591.49 a la G54 | Filet de Boef a la Godart |
| RM a la G54 | |
| 583.79 944.36 | Potatoes Parisiennes |
| RGP 39P | |
| — | |
| 957    621.96    RRLP 65 | SIBERIAN PUNCH |
| — | — |

| | | | |
|---|---|---|---|
| 598.6 plus 614.132 plus 536.46 | | | Roast Squab |
| RJND plus REQ | | | |
| 583.55 plus 665.3 plus 664.5 | | | Lettuce Salad |
| RGL plus RRBV plus RRBO | | | |
| — | | | |
| 945.73 642 | RZU 35N | | Neapolitan Ice Cream |
| 618.19 in 641 | MHJ RZT | | Sunshine Cake |
| — | | | |
| 634 | 613.38 | RH and R8BC | Fruit and Coffee |

The menu was "written" in a combination of the two brand new and competing library classification systems—the Dewey Decimal System and the Cutter Expansive Classification system. The system designed by Melvil Dewey (1851–1931) allocated books according to subject into one of ten major categories, each of which was subdivided into ten divisions, and each of these into ten sections. Numbers were assigned to each category, division, and section. Charles Ammi Cutter's (1837–1903) system was inspired by Dewey's, but the twenty major subject categories were denoted by letters, and author's names according to alpha-numeric tables.

The 1890s were good years for American libraries. Wealthy Golden Age philanthropists such as Andrew Carnegie were funding libraries across the country, and two brilliant library scientists lent their intellectual muscle to this financial brawn. Both Dewey and Cutter were founding members of the American Library Association, and it is almost certain that they were both at Grand View House on the night of this dinner.

It is unknown who had the idea to present the menu in code, with a key, but no doubt it gave the attending librarians great pride and delight.

Some menu items are easily translated from the Dewey code on the menu. Peas, potatoes, and lettuce are classified botanically as dicotyledons, meaning they have two prominent embryonic leaves. The Dewey number for the subject Dicotyledons is 583, hence dishes containing these include this code. Other straightforward examples are squab, which is a bird (598) and fruit is simply fruit (634).

The numbers reveal other information about the dishes than the ingredients. Kennebec salmon is a fish (597) from the river of that name in Maine (Northeastern United States: 947) cooked as in the Artois region of France (944). The method of preparation of some dishes is indicated by the "code" too. The squab was cooked by the application of heat (536), and the punch chilled by Applied Physics (621).

It was common in the nineteenth century for chefs to name dishes after famous or important people, and there are two examples on this menu. The "Godart" is most likely a "typo" for the classic beef garnish "à la Godard," said to be named after the French composer Benjamin Godard (1849–1895), and described by the *Larousse Gastronomique* as a mixture of *quenelles* (see October 15), small whole truffles, and mushroom caps. However, the French minister of justice at that time was famous for his personal library, and his name was Justin Godart. It is possible that the Library Association commissioned the creation of a dish especially in honor of such a man.

Dishes called "*à l'Imperatrice*" always contain rice and are named in honour of Eugénie de Montijo (1826–1920), the Spanish wife of Napoleon III of France. In this menu, the clear soup with rice would have been light, not rich, hence the code 613 for Promotion of Health.

Cutter's classification system was not ultimately as widely adopted as Dewey's due to Cutter's earlier death, although some aspects of it have been absorbed into other systems, such as that used by the Library of Congress. It is more difficult, therefore, to interpret the Cutter numbers on this late-nineteenth century menu. The letters RG are applied to all of the vegetables, and P specifically stands for peas and potatoes, and L for lettuce. The salad dressing is made from oil (O) and vinegar (V). All of the banquet items (apart from the Sunshine Cake: see Recipes) appear in Charles Ranhofer's famous work *The Epicurean*, which was published in the same year. Ranhofer was the enormously influential chef at Delmonico's in New York for over three decades and was responsible for virtually all of the important banquets in the city during that time. If the letter "R" which features so prominently in this menu represents an author's name, then it could perhaps be Ranhofer.

## Recipes
~~~

Sunshine cake was popular and recipes for it appeared in many cookbooks of the time. It is presumably so called because of the bright yellow color produced by the number of egg yolks used.

---

### Sunshine Cake

Make the same as Angel Cake, using one teaspoonful of orange extract instead of vanilla, and adding the well-beaten yolks of six eggs to the beaten whites and sugar before adding the flour.

---

### Angel Cake

One cup of flour, measured after one sifting, and then mixed with one teaspoonful of cream of tartar and sifted four times. Beat the whites of eleven eggs, with a wire beater or perforated spoon, until stiff and flaky. Add one cup and a half of fine granulated sugar, and beat again; add one teaspoonful of vanilla or almond, then mix in the flour quickly and lightly. Line the bottom and funnel of a cake pan with paper not greased, pour in the mixture, and bake about forty minutes. When done, loosen the cake around the edge, and turn out at once. Some persons have been more successful with this cake by mixing the sugar with the flour and cream of tartar, and adding all at once to the beaten egg.

Mary Johnson Bailey Lincoln, *Mrs. Lincoln's Boston Cook Book* (Boston, 1884).

## September 21

Daily Diet of the "American Pedestrian"
Cambridge Park Trotting Course, Boston, 1842

There was a vogue for unusual or extended walking feats during the nineteenth century, and one of the most famous pedestrians was Thomas Elworth (1816–unknown). In 1842 he accepted a challenge to walk 1,000 miles in 1,000 consecutive hours—something that he had boasted he could do. The venue was the trotting track in Boston, which was exactly one mile in length. He completed his "arduous task" in forty-one days and sixteen hours, stating that he felt as well, if not better, at the end of it than at its commencement. Elworth kept a detailed record of his feat—his times and speeds, the weather conditions, his occasional aches and pains, and his daily diet.

> Sept. 21st—Breakfast, fried fish and shells; Dinner, mutton broth and shells; Supper, beef and shells.

Elworth was described as not carrying a pound of superfluous flesh, and modern science would agree. At 5 feet 9 inches in height and 150 pounds, his body mass index (BMI) today would be calculated at slightly over 22, which is within a normal range. He attributed his ability to his being "inured to hardship from an early age" and to his plain and temperate mode of living.

There was little variation in his diet over the 41 days. Several dishes occurred regularly—mutton, fried pork, fried eggs, beef steak, fish and "shells," with only occasional sweet dishes such as custard, "thickened milk," rice pudding, or apple sauce.

The most frequent item is the "shells," which he enjoyed at 36 of the 118 meals. There is no further exploration of his dietary preferences or beliefs, save the comment "N.B. At every meal used potatoes" and one reference to his "partiality for salt food."

It is unknown whether Elworth ate so many "shells" (presumably oysters) because he enjoyed them, because they were cheap and available, or because he believed they would assist his endurance. Since the ancient Greeks, oysters have been associated with enhancing strength, stamina, and overall performance—the explanation of their reputation as aphrodisiacs. Hippocrates (c. 460—370 BCE), the Greek often referred to as "the father of medicine," considered that they were "soon turned to blood", hence strength. There has been universal agreement over the centuries on one thing—that oysters need to be consumed raw for best benefit.

Sports nutrition may appear to be a new science, but in fact since ancient times people have sought to improve performance through dietary means, whether this be for sport or fighting purposes. Many, many dietary regimes have been claimed at one time or another of being ideal for those undertaking feats of physical endurance—a lot of meat, no meat, high protein, low protein, high carbohydrate, or low carbohydrate have all had their time in the dietary limelight. Specific performance-enhancing foods or nutrients are also not a new idea. The ancient Greek Olympians tried a potion of asses' hooves ground up in oil, the Aztecs ate the living heart pulled out of their sacrificial victims, and nineteenth-century athletes took a variety of substances now either banned or far too dangerous such as mixtures of strychnine and brandy or wine and coca leaves. Sports nutrition is now a lucrative industry, and athletes invest their hopes in large amounts of sports drinks, energy bars, and vitamin and mineral supplements.

## Recipes

~~~

The following recipes are from a famous cookbook writer of the time, Sarah Josepha Buell. They appear in *The Good Housekeeper, Or The Way to Live Well and to Be Well While We Live*, published in Boston in 1839.

On the topic of shellfish she said, "Shell fish have long held a high rank as restorative food; but a well-dressed chop or steak is much better to recruit the strength and spirits."

---

### To Fry Cod or Other Fish

It is much more difficult to fry fish than meat. Lard or dripping is better than butter, because the last burns so easily. The fat fried from salt pork is best of all. The fire must be clear and hot but not furious; the fat hot when the fish is put in, and there should be sufficient to cover the fish. Skim the fat before laying in the fish. Cut the cod in slices half or three quarters of an inch thick; rub them with Indian meal to prevent breaking, fry it thoroughly. Trout and perch are fried in the same manner; only do not rub Indian meal on them—dip in white of an egg and bread crumbs or dust with flour.

---

### Mutton Leg to Boil

Mutton must be boiled the same as other meats—that is, simmered very slowly, and the scum carefully removed. Always wash it before cooking and put it in cold water. Only allow water sufficient to cover it, and the liquor makes excellent broth, with a little rice and a few carrots, &c.

Cut off the shank bone and trim the knuckle—if it weigh nine pounds it will require three hours to cook it. Parsley and butter, or caper-sauce should be served with it—onion sauce, turnips, spinage and potatoes are all used.

---

## September 22

### Installation Feast of the Archbishop of York
### Cawood Castle, York, England, 1465

George Neville (ca. 1432—1476) was the younger brother of the "King-maker," Richard Neville, the 16th Earl of Warwick. As one of the younger sons of a noble family, George was destined for a position in the Church, regardless of his own feelings for the religious life. In an age when spectacular feasts were indications of great power, the celebrations that accompanied his enthronement as archbishop of York surpassed all that had gone before, including royal coronations. There were in fact a whole series of feasts and entertainments over many days—each feast having several alternative bills of fare for the various social ranks. The bill of fare for the Archbishop's table was particularly fine.

It was the sheer size and duration of the event that made it exceptional: it was a clear statement to the assembled nobles of the wealth, power, and influence of the Neville family. Sixty-two master cooks and an untold number of kitchen workers fed between 2,000–3,000 people at each meal for a week. The guest list included 28 peers, 59 knights, 10 abbots, and 7 bishops. One of the invited nobles was the Duke of Gloucester, the future Richard III (see July 6).

| THE FIRST COURSE. | THE SECOND COURSE. | THE THIRD COURSE. |
| --- | --- | --- |
| Braun with mustard | Gilly parti riall | Bland desere |
| ffurmente with venyson | viand rasens | dates in comfet |
| hert poudred | venison in brakes | neutes vert |
| ffessand in brayn | pecock in trapille | Bittur rofstid |
| Swan rost | cony roste | Curlew rofstid |
| Ganetz | roo reversed | fessand rofstid |
| Gullez | lardes de venison | Railes rost |
| capon de haut grece | pertuches | Egret rost |
| heron roste | wodcok | Rabettes |
| carpet in venison | plouer | quailes |
| pik in ereblad | Goodwitts | poums vert |
| leshe caute rialle | red shankes | Grt whelpes rost |
| ffritur boyse | yarowe helpes | dotterelles rost |
| venyson bak | knottes | martynets rost |
| custad planted | Oxene | Gret birds |
| chewetts riall with a suttellte | Creme in purpull | larkes rost |
| | leshe cipirs | sparowes |
| | ffritur napkyne | ffreche sturgion |
| | tarte in molde | lesshe blaunche |
| | chatowe dyuers riall with a suttelte | ffritur cuspe |
| | | quinces bak |
| | | rosestis florishid |
| | | chamlettes withe a sutteltte |

All were seated according to rank in four dining halls and a gallery—with one hall for the "Gentlemen, Franklins, and Yeomen" being "twyce filled and served." Every moment was choreographed down to the last detail: the laying of the tablecloths, the folding of the napkins, the placing of the salt (see October 13), the exact procedure for "assaying" (checking for poison) the dishes, and the serving of the food. Honored noblemen performed the traditional roles of carver, panter or pantler (in charge of bread), royal cup-bearer, ewerer (bearer of the water for hand washing), sewer (in charge of the tasting and serving of dishes), stewards and marshalls. The role of carver was the most honored: he was expected to perform his role with great skill and artistry and contribute to the theatrical aspect of the feast. The panter's role was also highly ritualized, and his instructions to cut and serve the "upper crust" to his lord have supplied another metaphor for the social elite.

Frontispiece of 1513 carving book.

The food of course was designed to contribute to the great spectacle. The feast began with the customary brawn (see February 23) and mustard, one of the most ancient and popular condiments, followed by venison with frumenty (see February 23), and would have ended with wafers, fruits, and sweet wine. There were the obligatory subtelties (see September 23), the illusion and symbolic foods such as the *roo* (roe) *reversed* (lying as if asleep), the venison in brakes (a deer, seeming to be hiding in the bushes), a peacock in its plumage (see November 6), and *poums vert*, presumably the green version of pommes doreng (see October 13), as well as a huge array of game and birds, fritters, *leches*, custards, etc.

The *whelpes rost* are problematic: Does this mean puppies? A dish called *Scotwhelps rost* appears on the menu for the coronation feast of Richard III (see July 6). The English have never been known to choose to eat man's best friend (apart from occasionally for medicinal purposes), and "whelps" occasionally meant the young of other animals.

## Recipes

~~~

"Brawn" is usually taken to mean a "potted" dish made from the flesh of a boar or pig, and it could be made and decorated in an almost infinite number of ways, as the following recipe shows.

### To Mak Braun Rialle (Royal Brawn)

To mak braun rialle tak and boille freche braun in faire water till it be som dele tender then tak blanched almondes and grind them and draw them up with som of the sam brothe and apart of wyne as hoot as ye may then mak the mylk hot and do the braun in the strener hot and drawe it with the mylk het, put therto grece and venyger and set it on the fyere to boile and salt it and put it in a vesselle and when it is cold take it out or chauf the vesselle with out with hoote water or againste the fyere and when ye haue it out cutt it in thyn shyves and lay iij lesks in a disshe aftur the quantite and tak pouder of guinger or pared guinger mynced with annes in comfettes and ye may draw it with som of the same with a parte of the wyne or els thou may cutt it in lesks and serue it furthe, or els ye may tak it into another colour what ye wille, and ye will haue it grene draw it with mylk of almondes and grind leke leves in a mortair and put ther to saffron and when it is ground myche or litille coloure it ther with, when ye tak it from the fyere and do as ye did the tother tym and ye may do ther to a quantite of canelle guinger or sanders and mak it broun and serue it furthe, or els ye may tak turn sole and wesshe it and wringe it well in wyn that ye sesson it up with, and when it is boiled colour it up blew or sangwene whedur ye wille and do ther with as ye did be for, or when ye tak it from the fyer and hath bene sessoned then tak freche braune sodyn tender and cutt it in thyn lesks or dice smalle and cast it into the pot and stirre it welle to gedure then put it unto another vesselle and when it is cold leshe it and serue it.

*Noble Boke Off Cookry ffor a Prynce Houssolde or Eny Other Estately Houssolde*, MS 674 in the Holkham collection (late-fifteenth century).

Ffurmente (frumenty): see February 23.
Cony Roste [roast rabbit]: see August 16.
Bland Desere: see September 23.

## September 23

### Feast for King Richard II
### Durham House, London, England, 1387

John Fordham, Bishop of Durham and secretary and adviser to King Richard II (1367–1400) held a great feast on September 23, 1387, at his official residence in London (a site now occupied by the Adelphi Theatre in The Strand). The guests of honor were the King and the King's uncle, John of Gaunt, Duke of Lancaster. They sat down to an extraordinarily refined and sophisticated meal, composed as was usual for a grand feast of the time of three courses (a lesser feast might only have two) with a gradual progression towards the finer ingredients, but without the clear distinction between savory and sweet dishes that are familiar today.

At the time of this feast Richard had not yet attained his majority, but he had already made himself unpopular with many of the established aristocracy. There can be little doubt that, as was also usual for the times, there was a powerful political agenda associated with this feast. One of the

| THE FIRST COURSE. | THE SECOND COURSE. | THE THIRD COURSE. |
|---|---|---|
| Veneson with Furmenty. | A potage called Gele. | Potage. Bruete of almondes. |
| A potage called viaundbruse. | A potage de Blandesore. | Stwde lumbarde. |
| Hedes of Bores. | Pigges rosted. | Venyson rosted. |
| Grete Flessh. | Cranes rosted. | Chekenes rosted. |
| Swannes rosted. | Fesauntes rosted. | Rabettes rosted. |
| Pigges rosted. | Herons rosted. | Partrich rosted. |
| Crustade lumbard in paste. | Chekens endored. | Pejons rosted. |
| | Breme. | Quailes rosted. |
| A soltetie. | Tartes. | Larkes rosted. |
| | Broke braune. | Payne puff. |
| | Conyngges rosted. | A Dissh of Gely. |
| | | Longe Frutours. |
| | A soltetie. | |
| | | A soltetie. |

mechanisms of propaganda was the *soltetie* or *subtelty*—a food "sculpture" which was paraded around the hall with much fanfare at the end of each course. They were wrought with great skill in the form of such things as saints, kings, dragons, and castles—sometimes with moving parts, fountains of wine, noise making, and strategic fires. They were not intended to be eaten, but to deliver a specific message of political or religious significance and to inspire awe at the power and wealth of the host.

Political machinations aside, Richard almost certainly appreciated the fine food at this feast. He was known to be a fastidious man with refined and sophisticated tastes, who collected fine objects such as monogrammed spoons and elegant dishes. He also probably encouraged the culinary arts, for the first actual cook book in the English corpus, *The Form of Cury*, was written by his own master cooks in about 1390. It is ironic that he probably died from starvation in prison—by order of the Henry Bolingbroke, the cousin who deposed him to become King Henry IV.

## Recipes

~~~

Many of the dishes on this bill of fare appear throughout the medieval era and are to be found in other menus in this book (see January 23 and April 4).

"White dishes" such as blancmange (see January 27) and the similar blank dessore (a sort of white soup) were very desirable because they were fine, elegant, labor-intensive, and expensive and therefore demonstrated the wealth and sophistication of the feast provider.

> ### Blank Dessore
> ### (Blandesore, Blaund Surrey,
> ### or "White Dish from Syria")
>
> Take Almandes blaunched, grynde hem and temper hem up with whyte wyne, on fleissh day with broth. and cast þerinne flour of Rys. oþer amydoun, and lye it þerwith. take brawn of Capouns yground. take sugur and salt and cast þerto and florissh it with aneys whyte. take a vessel yholes and put in safroun. and serue it forth.
> *Forme of Cury* (ca. 1390).
> *Interpretation*: Take blanched almonds, grind them and mix them up with white wine [or] on a flesh day with broth and add to it rice flour or wheat starch and cook it [to thicken], add ground chicken and season it with sugar and salt. Strain it and garnish it with white candied aniseed and saffron and serve it.

Furmenty (frumenty): see February 23.
Rabettes Rosted: see August 16.

## September 24

### Prison Dinner
### Leavenworth State Penitentiary, Kansas, 1928

When investigators visited the penitentiary at Leavenworth on September 24, 1928, to report on the conditions, the prison population was 3,146—which was 1,716 over capacity. Seventy-four inmates were under life sentences, and 120 were military prisoners. To supervise and control this number were 122 guards ("not many more than when there was a smaller population"), although an increase to 128 had been authorized.

The investigators reported that the inmates were clean in spite of poor bathing facilities, and in good general health, and they noted the meals served that day.

> The general dining room has a capacity of 1,632. It is necessary to serve three tables each meal. They are installing new tables with metal tops and seats. There was a complaint of dust from coal going into the nearby bakery and kitchen.
> The food is satisfactory. The following was the bill of fare for today: breakfast—oatmeal mush, hot muffins, butter, syrup, coffee; dinner—frankfurters and cabbage, steamed potatoes, bread, water; supper—baked spaghetti and cheese, stewed fruit, bread, tea.

Leavenworth was built 25 miles north of Kansas City as a high security jail for male prisoners. Construction was still going on in 1928, although this was in the form of factory buildings, not more cell blocks. Due to the pressure of numbers, recreation facilities were insufficient. Punishment consisted of "isolation, restricted privileges and loss of credits."

Assuming that this menu was representative of the normal bill of fare (and no special culinary effort was made on account of the presence of inspectors)

Leavenworth prisoners march to dinner. Courtesy of Library of Congress.

and the quantity was not restricted, it appears that the food was substantial and filling enough, but rather lower in vegetables than modern guidelines would recommend. Food means more to humans than mere calories and nutrition points, however, and it is now accepted that the quality and variety of food in prisons has a great bearing on inmate behavior and prison discipline issues.

## Recipes
~~~

There are two distinct types of muffins. In the old English sense, they are "raised" with yeast (see March 15) and thus are similar to sweet bread. In the early American sense the mixture is essentially like that of small cakes raised with baking powder. To make a sufficient amount of these muffins to serve the Leavenworth population would have required 178 quarts of flour.

---

### Muffins

Sugar 3/4 qt.,
Flour 5 qt.,
Baking Powder, 3/4 c.,
Salt 2 tbsp.,
Eggs, 8,
Milk 3 1/4—3 1/2 qt.,
Butter substitute, melted, 1/4 lb.

---

Mix and sift the dry ingredients. Beat the eggs, add the milk and pour the liquid over the dry ingredients. Add the melted fat and pour the mixture into well-greased muffin tins to bake.

Number of servings: 96

Lenore Richards, *Quantity Cookery: Menu Planning and Cookery for Large Numbers* (ca. 1922).

---

### Baked Spaghetti with Cheese and Eggs

Four hard cooked eggs,
one cup broken spaghetti,
4 tablespoons grated cheese,
2 tablespoons butter,
1 tablespoon flour,
3/4 cup milk,
1/2 teaspoon salt,
1/8 teaspoon each pepper and mustard, parsley.

To hard cook the eggs put them into about 1 quart cold water. Bring to the boiling point, reduce heat and simmer without bubbling for 15 minutes. Plunge at once into cold water and let stand five minutes. Remove shells and cut in thin slices crosswise. Cook spaghetti in a rapidly boiling salted water for 15 minutes. Drain and dip in cold water.

Melt butter, stir in flour and slowly add milk, stirring constantly. Mix salt, pepper and mustard and stir into sauce Bring sauce to the boiling point. Put a layer of spaghetti into a well buttered baking dish add a layer of sauce and cover with a layer of eggs. Continue layer for layer of spaghetti sauce and eggs until all are used making the last layer of spaghetti. Cover with grated cheese and baked 25 minutes in a moderately hot oven. Garnish with sprigs of parsley and serve from baking dish.

*The Port Arthur News* (April 8, 1927).

---

## September 25

Hotel Dinner
Hôtel Hochschneeberg, Schneeberg, Austria, 1907

Hotels catering for tourists often try to provide menus that will enable every guest to find something acceptable for dinner. In the process they often sacrifice their own national cuisine. Guests who stayed at the Hôtel Hochschneeberg in the Austrian Alps in 1907, however, could be sure of getting a typically Austrian meal.

---

Hühnerpüreesuppe
Forelle blau sauce Mouseline
Gedämpfer Tafelspitz
Warme und kalte Gemüse
Steiner-Kapaun

Salat
American Compote
Äpfelstrudel
Kaiserschmarrn und Röster
Käse
Obst
Coffee
Bier
Kahlenberger 1905
Kalterer-See-Auslese
Liquere

The only exception to the thoroughly Austrian cuisine is the "American Compote." *Tafelspitz* is a traditional Austrian dish of boiled beef with vegetables, typically served with *Apfelkren* (apple and horseradish sauce.) The name means "the point of the table," and refers to the cut of meat used—the pointed end of a rump of beef. It is said that Tafelspitz was the favorite dish of Emperor Franz Joseph I (1830–1916), and it was always present on his table.

Another dish on this menu associated with the Austrian Emperor Fran-Joseph is the *Kaiserschmarrn und Röster*, thick caramelized pancakes shredded and served with stewed fruit, especially plums. *Kaiserschmarrn* literally means "the Emperor's mish-mash" or "rubbish." There are a number of stories about how the dish got its name. One story is that the cook made a mess of some pancakes and quickly and creatively dressed them up as a new invention. Another is that the Emperor named them "rubbish" sarcastically when his wife, the Empress Elisabeth (1837–1898) refused to eat them (she was constantly concerned about her figure). The most likely is of course that it simply refers to the chopped up nature of the pancake.

## Recipes

~~~

*Apfelstrudel* (apple strudel) is an Austrian version of apple pie which is familiar all over the world. It is made with extraordinarily thin pastry—so thin it is almost transparent. Very few people make their own strudel pastry today, as it is easy to buy. The following recipe shows how it is done. The use of chicken fat or oil in this particular version is suggested in order to allow this dish to be eaten with a meat meal, and comply with Jewish food law (see July 11). Non-Jews would use butter.

### Apple Strudel

Sift two cups of flour, add pinch of salt and one teaspoon of powdered sugar. Stir in slowly one cup of lukewarm water, and work until dough does not stick to the hands. Flour board, and roll as thin as possible. Do not tear. Place a tablecloth on table, put the rolled out dough on it, and pull gently with the hands, to get the dough as thin as tissue paper.

Have ready six apples chopped fine, and mixed with cinnamon, sugar, one-half cup of seedless raisins, one-half cup of currants. Spread this over the dough with plenty of chicken-fat or oil all over the apples. Take the tablecloth in both hands, and roll the strudel, over and over, holding the cloth high, and the strudel will almost roll itself. Grease a baking-pan, hold to the edge of the cloth, and roll the strudel in. Bake brown, basting often with fat or oil.

Florence Kreisler Greenbaum, *The International Jewish Cook Book* (New York, 1919).

## September 26

### Dinner Out Hunting with Buffalo Bill
### near Fort McPherson, Nebraska, 1871

General Philip Henry Sheridan (1831–1888) became famous for his role as a union general during the American Civil War, and infamous for his part in the Indian Wars of the Great Plains (see November 26). When the general and Indian hunter expressed a wish to hunt game, the obvious guide was William Frederick Cody (1846–1917), better known as Buffalo Bill.

Buffalo Bill. Courtesy of Library of Congress.

Sheridan arrived at Fort McPherson on September 22 and immediately reviewed the troops of the Fifth Cavalry. The next day they set off on a ten-day hunting expedition. Buffalo Bill was a great showman, and he made sure he looked the part as they set off. He wrote,

So I dressed in a new suit of buckskin, trimmed along the seams with fringes of the same material; and I put on a crimson shirt handsomely ornamented on the bosom, while on my head I wore a broad sombrero. Then mounting a snowy white horse—a gallant stepper, I rode down from the fort to the camp, rifle in hand. I felt first-rate that morning, and looked well.

Other arrangements were also first rate. Sixteen wagons

carried supplies—including one solely for ice. Three other wagons were set up so that members of the party could travel easily, should they become fatigued. Sufficient linen, china, glassware, and wine was taken to ensure that dining standards were maintained.

On the night of September 26, Buffalo Bill recorded the splendid dinner, saying "I considered this a fairly good meal for a hunting party. Everybody did justice to it."

---

BILL OF FARE

Soup
Buffalo Tail

Fish
Broiled Cisco, Fried Dace

Entrees
Salmi of Prairie Dog, Stewed Rabbit, Filet of Buffalo aux Champignons
Vegetables
Sweet Potatoes, Mashed Potatoes, Green Peas

Dessert
Tapioca Pudding

Wines
Champagne Frappe, Champagne au Naturel, Claret, Whisky, Brandy, Ale

Coffee

---

The hunters themselves obviously provided much of the produce for this dinner, and it seems a little odd that these tough hunting men chose a nursery pudding to follow their large feed of game.

## Recipes

~~~

---

### Tapioca Pudding

Six table-spoonfuls of tapioca
one quart of milk,
three eggs,
sugar and spice to your taste;

Heat the milk and tapioca moderately; bake it one hour.
*The New England Economical Housekeeper, and Family Receipt Book* (Cincinnati, 1845).

---

Buffalo is more properly named bison.

---

### Buffalo

Like bear-meat, buffalo resembles beef, when it is in prime condition. The flesh
is darker than beef, and the fat has a reddish color; the heart, liver, and marrow
are like those of beef; the latter is delicious; the tongue, and flesh of the hump
are the choice portions; buffalo-meat may be cooked like beef, and should be
rather well done.

Juliet Corson, *Miss Corson's Practical American Cookery and Household
Management* (1886).

---

### How to Cook Bison (``Buffalo'') Hump,
### after the Manner of the Indians

Cooked for dinner the entire hump of a bison, after the manner of the Indians; this favourite part of the animal was dissected from the vertebrae,
after which the spinous processes were taken out, and the denuded part
was covered with skin, which was firmly sewed to the back and sides of
the hump; the hair was burned and pulled off, and the whole mass exhibiting something of a fusiform shape, was last evening placed in a hole dug in
the earth for its reception, which had been previously heated by means of a
strong fire in and upon it. It was now covered with cinders and earth, to the
depth of about one foot, and a strong fire was made over it. In this situation
it remained until it was taken up for the table today, when it was found to
be excellent food.

*James' Expedition to the Rocky Mountains* (1825).

---

## September 27

Traffic Association Banquet
Café Nat Goodwin, Crystal Pier, Santa Monica, California, 1913

When the Los Angeles Traffic Association held their annual business meeting and banquet on September 27, 1913, they chose the "Most beautiful café
over-the-sea in the world." The Nat Goodwin café was named for the actor
and comedian Nathaniel Goodwin (1857–1919), and it was a haunt of movie
stars, music lovers, and gourmets.

The café was well known for its cabaret music, and the guests at the dinner
on this night enjoyed a fine musical program as well as the following dinner.

---

MENU

Martini Cocktail
Celery en Branch        Olives

Consomme St. Xavier
Haute SauterneFilet of Flounder, Vin Blanc
Pommes Parisienne
St Julien          Spring Chicken Saute Sec
Potato Croquettes          Petit Pois
Stuffed Tomato Surprise
Ice Cream and Cake
Café Noir
Cigars and Cigarettes

It is interesting that the first item on this menu is not oysters or *hors d'oeuvres*, but a Martini cocktail. The first documented use of the word "cocktail" in the sense of a mixed drink is in 1803, in a context that suggests it was taken for medicinal purposes. Three years later it is used clearly in the sense of a mixed drink made from a base of spirituous liquor. There are more myths and stories as to how, exactly, the cocktail got its name than there are about almost any other beverage or food. There are almost as many stories about the origin and naming of the Martini.

The Martini cocktail is unequivocally American in origin, but everything else about it is disputed. It probably originated in the 1870s and really came into its own in the first two decades of the twentieth century, but debates about its true history and authentic original recipe are not in any danger of being solved in the near future. The classic martini is a mixture of gin and vermouth, and most aficionados would agree that the garnish is an olive. The relative quantities of the ingredients are hotly disputed, however, with everything from simply saluting the vermouth bottle with the glass of gin to a five-to-one ratio of gin to vermouth being said to be correct. Even the method of mixing the two basic ingredients is disputed, with James Bond famously preferring his "shaken, not stirred." Nevertheless, the martini cocktail has become firmly entrenched in American folklore and literature—and even politics. The period of U.S.-Soviet relations during the presidency of Franklin D. Roosevelt (1882–1945) was once jokingly referred to as the "four martinis and let's have an agreement" era, and the Soviet leader Nikita Khrushchev (1894–1971) once called it "America's lethal weapon."

## Recipes

~~~

### Spring Chicken Fried
### (Spring Chicken Saute Sec)

After the chicken has been cleaned and singed lay it in salt water for half an hour. Cut it up as for fricassee and see that every piece is wiped dry. Have ready heated in a spider some goose fat or other poultry drippings. Season each piece of chicken with salt and ground ginger, or pepper (I prefer the ginger, it is also more wholesome than pepper). Roll each piece of chicken in sifted cracker

crumbs (which you have previously seasoned with salt). Fry in the spider, turning often, and browning evenly. You may cut up some parsley and add while frying. If the chicken is quite large, it is better to steam it before frying.
"Aunt Babette," *Aunt Babette's Cook Book* (Cincinnati, ca. 1889).

---

### Tomatoes, Surprise

Peel four tomatoes, cut off the tops, and scoop out the centres with a small spoon. Season the inside of the tomatoes with salt and pepper, and turn upside down so the water will run out. Cut some celery in small dices, wash well, and mix with mayonnaise sauce, season with salt and pepper, then fill the tomatoes. Serve on lettuce leaves.
Victor Hirtzler, *The Hotel St. Francis Cook Book* (1919).

---

Pommes Parisienne: see June 23.
Potato Croquettes: see December 7.

## September 28

"Menu for Jews"
aboard the SS *Majestic*, 1929

The magnificent White Star Line's SS *Majestic* left Southampton, England, on September 25, 1929, on one of her regular transatlantic voyages and arrived in New York on the morning of October 1. Aboard were well over 2,000 passengers in three classes. In first class there was at least one countess, one baroness, and one viscount—plus Prince and Princess Matchabelli. The Princess, born Norina Gill (1889–1957), was an Italian actress who later started a perfume company with her husband, Georges Matchabelli (1885–1935), a prince from Soviet Georgia and previous ambassador to Italy. Norina was en route to Detroit, where she was once more to play the role of the Madonna in a production of "The Miracle"—a play written by her previous husband Karl Vollmöller—which she performed over 2,000 times.

The biggest percentage of the passengers aboard the SS *Majestic* were in third class, and many were emigrants from Europe—and many of these were Jewish. Somewhere in the mid-Atlantic, on September 28, the following "Special Menu" was served. The menu was handwritten, and on the reverse, in a different hand, is written "Menu for Jews."

---

Special Menu.

Salt Herring.     Bismarck Herring.
Tomato Soup.
Grilled Halibut.
Grilled Lamb Chops.
Beef Goulash.
Spinach.     Mashed Turnips.

Baked Jacket Potatoes.
Salad.
Compote of Pears & Pineapple.
Tea.          Coffee.

This was a simple meal of simple food. It included meat, so it would have been dairy-free in accordance with Jewish dietary laws (see July 11). The herrings and "goulash" would have presumably been familiar and comforting to the European Jews aboard.

There are many different forms of prepared herring (see May 6). Bismarck herring is the name given to unskinned filets pickled in a mixture of vinegar, sugar, salt and onions. They are said to have been a particular favorite of the German Chancellor, Otto von Bismarck (1815–1898), who allowed the producer (who regularly sent them to him) to give them his name.

The story of *goulash* is not so straightforward. The word comes from the Hungarian *gulyás* meaning herdersman (or cowboy), and *hús* meaning meat. It is a meat stew, flavored with paprika, and traditionally cooked in a cauldron called a *bogracs*. There is no more a single authentic recipe for goulash than there is for *pot-au-feu* (see April 7) or hot-pot (see March 29). In practice, every region, and every individual cook in every region, insists that his or hers is the only genuine *goulash*. Many purists say that tomato and sour cream are not traditional, that in recipes where the meat is fried as a first step, it is with lard, not oil, and the consistency should be soupy rather than stew-like.

## Recipes

~~~

### Hungarian Goulash

Cut one pound of lean stewing beef in pieces and place in a saucepan and cover with boiling water. Cook slowly until tender then add
One-half cup of onions
One carrot, diced,
One faggot of soup herbs.

When the meat is tender, season with
One teaspoon of salt,
One and one-half teaspoons of paprika

Thicken the gravy with browned flour and then add one-half cup of sour cream.
Garnish with finely chopped parsley.
Mrs. Mary A Wilson, *Mrs. Wilson's Cook Book* (1920).

Jacket Potatoes: see March 4.

## September 29

### Supper with the King
*Château de Choisy*, France, 1757

Louis XV (1710–1774) was king of France from the age of five years. He was greatly interested in food, and it is said that he personally perfected a recipe for an asparagus-tip omelette, and that he was responsible for the popularization of the *chaud-froid* (see July 25)—a dish that was originally a mistake.

Since medieval times there was a tradition in France of public dining on the part of the king. The king had to be seen—it was part of his kingly duty —and to be seen dining allowed a public display of his wealth and power. This was called *grand couvert* (grand dining) to distinguish it from private meals of *petit couvert*. Although he loved eating, Louis was less enamoured of dining in public than his father, the "Sun King" Louis XIV (1638–1715), and he did less and less of it.

Louis was at the *Château de Choisy* on the outskirts of Paris on the evening of September 29, 1757. It may be that his supper was taken as a petit couvert.

---

A SOUPER
Deux oilles,
Une aux gros oignons,
Une à l'espagnolle;
Deux potages,
Un de santé,
Un a la purée de navets.

ENTRÉES
De petits pâtés à la balaquine,
De filets de lapereaux à la genevoise,
De filets mignons de mouton sauce-piquante,
De filets de faisans en matelotte,
De cailles au laurier,
De tourtereaux à la vénitienne,
De perdreaux à l'ancien salmy,
De petits pigeons acccompagnés,
Une blanquette de poularde aux truffes,
Une marinade de Campines,
D'ailerons de poullardes en hatelets,
De noix de veau glacées dans leur jus.
Un hachis de gibier à la turque,
De ris de veau à la sainte-menehould,
De canetons de Rouen à l'orange,
Un haricot velouté brun.

QUATRE RELEVÉS
Un rost de bif de mouton de Choisy,
Une pièce de bœuf à l'écarlatte.
Un aloyau, le filet mincé à la chicorée,
De poulles de Caux à l'oignon cru.

QUATRE GRANDS ENTREMETS
Un pâté de faisands,
Un jambon au perdroüillet,
Une brioche,
Une croquante.

DEUX MOYENS ROST
De petits poulets,
De campines,
De pigeons ortolans,
De grives,
De guignards,
De perdreaux rouges,
De faisands,
Un caneton de Rouen.

SEIZE PETITS ENTR[EMETS]
Une crème à l'infusion de café.
D'artichaux à la Baligoure,
De cardes à l'essence,
De chouxfleurs au parmesan,
D'œufs au jus de perdreaux,
De truffes à la cendre,
D'épinards au jus,
De crètes,
D'animelles,
D'haricots verts au verjus,
Une omelette au jambon,
De pattes de dindons à la Duxelle,
Un râgout meslé,
De profiterolles de chocolat,
De petites jalousies,
Une crème à la Genest.

A glance at this modest supper menu shows the great symmetry and regularity of numbers that was a feature of French meals in the eighteenth (and on into the nineteenth) centuries. It also shows how many French culinary words have entered the English language essentially unchanged—such as marinade, profiteroles, piquant, and omelette. There is one example of the reverse influence: the *rost de bif* (sometimes written *rosbif*).

The English were the acknowledged masters of the art of roasting large pieces of meat, and roast beef became so closely associated with the English that they became known abroad as *rosbifs*. The phrase in France also came to apply to the *method* of cooking, so that there could be a *rosbif de mouton*, for example (see January 18).

## Recipes

~~~

*Animelles* are testicles (see May 29), usually of lamb, and they were a "dainty dish," as were cocks' combs.

---

### Animelles or Lambs Stones

Take two or three pairs of Lambs Stones, and being ready to serve, cut them in four or eight Pieces, take off the skin, throw some fine Salt over them and wipe them dry; flour them without touching them with your Hands, and fry them immediately in very hot Hogs Lard, make them crisp, then dish them up, and serve them up hot for a dainty Dish.

---

### A Ragôut with Cocks Combs with a White Sauce, for a Dainty Dish

Put in a stew-pan a Bit of Butter and a Bunch of Sweet Herbs, with some Mushrooms cut in Bits, and Truffles if you have any; toss it up, put in about half a spoonful of fine Flour, moisten it with a little Broth, season it with Salt and Pepper, and let it stew over a slow Fire. Now put in your Cocks Combs, and thicken your Ragôut with Yolks of Eggs and Cream, mixed with a little Nutmeg; let your Ragôut be palatable, and serve it up hot for a dainty Dish or for what you think fit.

*The Modern Cook*, a translation of Vincent la Chapelle's *Cuisine Moderne* (1742).

---

Potage de Sante: see March 28.
Brioche: see February 24.

## September 30

### Sheriff's Dinner
### Hall of the Fishmongers' Company, London, England, 1847

The newly elected sheriffs for the city of London and county of Middlesex "by ancient custom" were chosen on the 28th of September, and on the 30th were sworn before the Cursitor-Baron of the Court of Exchequer. The Cursitor-Baron would at this time also officially approve the choice (by the livery companies, see October 28) of Lord Mayor for the year. A strange custom whose original meaning is obscure was enacted at this time too. The senior alderman would formally count six horseshoes and sixty-one hobnails, and chop two bundles of sticks, thereby fulfilling the conditions by which the Corporation of London held "certain estates in Shropshire."

Naturally, the ceremonies were wound up with a banquet. Messrs. Bath and Breach of the London Tavern catered the dinner, and 240 worthy civic leaders sat down in the Fishmongers' Hall to a dinner of a particularly "grand and *recherché* character, comprising every kind of delicacy."

---

FIRST COURSE.—Turtle, pieds de tortue a la matelotte, vol-au-vent au gras, escallopes a l'Italienne, pieds de tortue a l'Espagnol, turbots, dories, Gloucester salmon, mullets, crimped cod, saute whitings with oysters, smelts, matelotte of tench, spitched eels, boiled and roast chickens, raised pies, venison pasties, stewed rumps of beef, sauce a l'Espagnol, roast capons, roast rumps of beef, hams, tongues, saddles of mutton, tendrons de veaux aux champignons, cotelettes de mouton a la Soubise, compote de pigeons a la Victoria, ris de veau aux tomattes, cotelettes d'agneau aux concombres, filets de lapereaux a la Sultan, fricandeau de veau au sorel, vol-au-vent with ragout, quenelles de poulardes aux champignons, filets de canetons a la puree de pois.

REMOVES.—Haunches of venison.

SECOND COURSE.—Ptarmigans, partridges, pheasants, grouse, turkey poults larded, leverets, mayonnaise of lobsters, prawns, croustade of oysters, gateau a la Duchese, apple tarts, fanchonettes; Italian, noyeau, and Rhenish creams; nugat with cream; maraschino, Dantsic, noyeau, and apple jellies; gateau of apple, boudin St. Clair; raspberry, apricot, and greengage tourtes; trifles, soufles, plum and cabinet puddings.

DESSERT.—Pineapples, hot-house grapes, peaches, nectarines, melons, apples, pears, gages, plums, filberts, walnuts, almonds and raisins, ornamented cakes, brandy cherries, ginger, olives, and ices.

WINES.—Champagne, sherry, hock, Sauterne, Moselle, Bucellas, Madeira, claret, and Port; milk punch.

At the end of the dinner, the "loving cup" went round, "according to ancient civic custom." A loving cup is a large, two-handled cup of silver, often highly ornate. The passing around of the loving cup in a highly formal manner, each person in turn taking a draught, is a ceremony with very ancient roots. It was intended to demonstrate friendship—or at least the absence of imminent aggression, the "weapon hand" being clearly in view the whole time.

## Recipes
~~~

### Fanchonettes a la Vanille

Break into a stewpan six yolks of eggs, four ounces of powdered sugar, with an infusion of vanille, two ounces of fine sifted flour, work these well together, and by degrees, add one pint of cream; put the stewpan over a slow fire, and stir it continually till it boils thick; cover twenty or thirty tartlet moulds, and fill each with the cream; bake them in a slow oven, and when they are cold whip two whites of eggs very strong, and mix them with four ounces of sifted sugar for a maringue, and with a paper funnel garnish the fanchonettes neatly; sift sugar over them, and put them again into the oven to dry. These may he flavored with orange or lemon, and to which may be added currants that have been washed and dried, or the cream may be intermixed with almonds cut fine.

I. Roberts, *The Young Cook's Guide* (1841).

---

### Milk Punch

Rub off on lumps of sugar the zest of a dozen lemons; pare off what you do take off on the sugar, but take none of the white stuff; infuse in two quarts of brandy; strain off in two days, and add of clarified sirup two pounds, and of water two quarts, with half a pint of hot new milk; strain through a jelly bag, and keep in a close jar or small cask till it fines, which will be in six weeks or less. Milk punch may be made extempore by adding a little hot milk to lemonade, and straining through a jelly bag; it is generally drunk cold.

Thomas Webster and William Parkes, *An Encyclopædia of Domestic Economy* (1855).

---

Cabinet Pudding: see June 30.

# October

## October 1

### Dinner in Utopia
### Red Bank, Monmouth County, New Jersey, 1854

A large number of "experimental colonies" or "utopian societies" were formed in the nineteenth century in response to a growing belief in the breakdown of community and the associated increase in social evil and sinning. Many, but not all, had a common religious foundation. Some were exclusively vegetarian. Several, including the "North American Phalanx" which is the source of this day's menu, were based on the ideas of the French social philosopher Charles Fourier (1771–1837).

The actual physical conditions in many of the communities were far from utopian, which explains why so many of them lasted such a short time—the enthusiasm and energy of the recruits quickly fading in the harsh reality of awful accommodation, grueling labor, and inadequate food. Fourier's philosophy of cooperative living (in communities called "phalanxes") allowed for a more liberal approach, with individual variations in wealth being quite acceptable. The Fourier followers who founded the North American Phalanx in fact made a deliberate attempt to recruit wealthy members, and as part of their strategy did away with the usual shared food system and replaced it with a "restaurant" with a daily bill of fare, table service, and every item ordered being charged against the patron's labor account.

---

| SOUP | PASTRY |
|---|---|
| Rice Soup | Naples Biscuit |
| Beef Soup | Gingerbread |
| | Sugar Cakes |
| MEATS | |
| Roast Veal | |
| Ragout | Squash Pie |
| Corned Beef with Cabbage | Apple Pie |
| Boiled Ham | Squash Pudding |
| Cold Roast Beef | |

VEGETABLES

Boiled Potatoes

Boiled Sweet Potatoes

Vegetable Gumbo

Stewed Tomatoes

Pickled Beets

Tomato Sauce

Squash

FRUIT

Apple Sauce

Preserved Peaches

Apples

BREAD

White Bread

Crackers

Graham Bread

MISCELLANEOUS

Chocolate

Coffee

Black Tea

Hot and Cold Milk

Sugar

Syrup

Butter

Cheese

TO ORDER

Dry and Wet Toast

Cottage Cheese

Pickles

Molasses

There is a fine range of choices in this menu—substantial meat dishes as well as vegetables (squash appears to be in good supply), cakes and pies, condiments and beverages. Perhaps its more liberal food policy assisted this group to survive for 15 years (1841–1856)—significantly longer than many similar societies.

## Recipes

~~~

### Pumpkin and Squash Pie

The usual way of dressing pumpkins in England in a pie is to cut them into slices, mixed with apples, and bake them with a top crust like ordinary pies. A quite different process is pursued in America, and the editor can testify to the immense superiority of the Yankee method. In England, the pumpkin is grown for show rather than for use; nevertheless, when properly dressed, it is a very delicious vegetable, and a universal favourite with our New England neighbours. The following is the American method of making a pumpkin pie: Take out the seeds, and pare the pumpkin or squash; but in taking out the seeds do not scrape the inside of the pumpkin; the part nearest the seed is the sweetest; then stew the pumpkin, and strain it through a sieve or colander. To a quart of milk for a family pie, three eggs are sufficient. Stir in the stewed pumpkin with your milk and beaten-up eggs till it is as thick as you can stir round rapidly and easily. If the pie is wanted richer make it thinner, and add another egg or two; but even one egg to a quart of milk makes "very decent pies." Sweeten with molasses or sugar; add two tea-spoonfuls of salt, two table-spoonfuls of sifted cinnamon, and one of powdered ginger; but allspice may be used, or any other spice that may be preferred. The peel of a lemon grated in gives it a pleasant flavour. The more eggs, says our American authority, the better the pie. Some put one egg to a gill of milk. Bake about an hour, in deep plates, or shallow dishes, without an upper crust, in a warm oven. There is another method of making this pie, which, we know from experience, produces an excellent dish: Take out the seeds, and grate the pumpkin till you come to the outside skin. Sweeten the pulp; add a little ground allspice, lemon peel, and lemon juice; in short, flavour it to your taste. Bake without an upper crust.

J. M. Sanderson, *The Complete Confectioner, Pastry-Cook, and Baker* (ca. 1849).

---

### Squash Pudding

Run your stewed squash through a sieve; take four eggs, one pint of milk; sweeten it thoroughly; add a little rose-water and cinnamon. Make a good paste, and pour the above ingredients into a deep pudding dish.

Esther Howland, *The New England Economical Housekeeper, and Family Receipt Book* (1845).

---

## October 2

### Banquet for the 75th Anniversary of the Biltmore Hotel
### Los Angeles, California, 1998

Everything about Los Angeles was booming in the early 1920s. There was prosperity and a mood of great optimism. It was the Roaring Twenties and the Jazz Age, and a great movie industry was developing around Hollywood. The town was ready for a large and glamorous hotel. When the Biltmore Hotel opened on October 1, 1923, the newspapers were already calling it "fashionable." It was the biggest hotel west of Chicago, with over a thousand rooms, all with private baths, and it instantly became a landmark and an irresistible venue for the rich and famous.

The opening banquet was a spectacular affair. Three thousand guests attended (seven thousand hopefuls did not make the list), and dined in eight dining rooms full of flowers, to the combined music of seven orchestras and a host of live canaries. It was the beginning of a long relationship between the hotel and the motion picture industry. Many of the guests on the night were involved in movie making, including Cecil B. de Mille, Douglas Fairbanks Sr., and Mary Pickford. A few years later the Academy of Motion Picture Arts & Sciences had its beginnings at the Biltmore, and the first awards night (the "Oscars") was held in the hotel's Crystal Ballroom (see May 16).

For the 75th anniversary the menu of the grand opening banquet was re-created, the proceeds of the $75 a head charge going to benefit the Los Angeles Conservancy.

---

ESSENCE OF TOMATO AUX QUENELLES
Tomato Bisque with Spinach and Chicken Dumplings
*

CRABMEAT EPICURIENNE
Crab and Cream Cheese Mousse
with Shallots and Fine Herbs wrapped in a Crepe Purse
*

INTERMEZZO
Cognac Granite
*

ENTRÉE
Choice of

CHICKEN A LA BILTMORE
Free range Breast of Chicken Stuffed with Spinach, Pine Nuts,
and Mascarpone with Cabernet Sauce

NOISETTES OF LAMB
Domestic Lamb, Rosemary Garlic Mashed Potatoes and Garlic Cream
Seasonal Vegetables

PAN ROASTED SEA TROUT WITH CAPERS
Presented with Parsley Boiled Potatoes and Seasonal Vegetables
*

ANNIVERSARY SALAD
Spring Field Greens and Teardrop Tomatoes with Champagne Vinaigrette
*

DESSERT
Choice of

FRESH PEACH HILDA
Fresh Peaches with Hazelnut Ice Cream,
Chartreuse Anglaise and Whipped Cream.

BERNARD's SIGNATURE ''BLACK PLATE''
INDIVIDUAL BAKED ALASKA
*

PETIT FOURS SECS
COFFEE/TEA

---

The dishes may have been the same as at the dinner in 1923, but the menu card itself demonstrates some interesting changes in dining behavior in the intervening 75 years. This menu shows the modern trend to describing dishes in detail—almost to the extent of giving recipes. There are a number of possible explanations for this. The gold standard of a fine dinner used to be a superb rendition of classic dishes—and every reasonably sophisticated consumer knew the classic names. Today the desire is for constant novelty, so a chef's creations must be described in detail so that diners know what they are getting. It may be that this trend has caused a "dumbing down" of diners who no longer understand the classic culinary language. A diner in 1923 would not need to have been told that *quenelles* are "dumplings." Alternatively, of course, this could be viewed as finally moving away from French as the language of menus, and the sense of snobbery that this implied.

The only dish on this menu that is not described in detail is the bombe Alaska, because it is enduringly popular and familiar. Bombe Alaska is a dish of sponge cake and ice cream coated in a meringue mixture and quickly cooked in an oven to slightly set the meringue but without melting the ice cream. There are a number of stories about its origin, from the fanciful to the possible. The most popular story is that it was invented by Charles Ranhofer of Delmonico's in New York to celebrate the purchase of Alaska in 1867. One problem with this theory is that in his book *The Epicurean*, Ranhofer calls it "Alaska, Florida." The other is that the idea is not new at all. Thomas Jefferson (1743–1826) served an ice cream in a crust in 1802 (see February 6), and in 1866 the French Baron Brisse (possibly the first food journalist) noted in his newspaper column that at a dinner of a Chinese delegation at the Grand Hotel in Paris, "baked ices" were served. The only real question is—who *named* the dish?

## Recipes
~~~

---

### Baked Alaska

Whites 6 eggs.
6 tablespoons powdered sugar.
2 quart brick of ice cream.
Thin sheet sponge cake.

Make meringue of eggs and sugar as in Meringue I [see below], cover a board with white paper, lay on sponge cake, turn ice cream on cake (which should extend one-half inch beyond cream), cover with meringue, and spread smoothly. Place on oven grate and brown quickly in hot oven. The board, paper, cake, and meringue are poor conductors of heat, and prevent the cream from melting. Slip from paper on ice cream platter.

---

### Meringue

Whites 2 eggs.
2 tablespoons powdered sugar.
1/2 tablespoon lemon juice or
1/4 teaspoon vanilla.

Beat whites until stiff, add sugar gradually and continue beating, then add flavoring.

Fannie Merritt Farmer, *The Boston Cooking-School Cookbook* (Boston, 1896).

---

## October 3

### Dinner on the Inaugural Flight
### Super Constellation, KLM Airlines, 1953

Royal Dutch Airlines (or KLM from its name in Dutch) has been flying international routes since May 17, 1920, making it the oldest airline in the world still operating under its original name. The company has a long association with another famous product of Holland—the blue and white china called Delftware. KLM has a tradition of presenting its first-class passengers with miniatures made of Delft china, filled with yet another product originating in the Netherlands—gin. On the occasion of the airline's first flight aboard the Super Constellation, from Amsterdam to Johanessburg, South Africa, on October 3, 1953, the theme was varied slightly. There was no gin, and the Delft souvenir was a tiny square of china on which was painted the menu for the "Trans-Saharan" dinner.

---

Homard en Bellevue
Tomatoes farcies aux Champignons
Velouté Dame Blanche
Tournedos Rossini
Céleri en branche
Pommes Château
Coupe Jamaïque
Fromages Assortis
Corbeille de Fruits
Café—Liqueur—Cognac

---

Airline food has become the butt of many jokes over the years. In the early years, airlines went to a great deal of trouble to provide inviting, elegant food because it was all first-class travel (see timeline, January 21). The only people who could afford to fly were wealthy and were used to fine dining and would not have tolerated anything less.

In-flight catering poses many challenges. There is limited space for storage and cooking of food, but passengers from many different ethnic, cultural, and religious backgrounds have to be supplied. Turbulence can complicate serving and eating, and at high altitudes food tastes more bland, so seasoning has to be adjusted.

Over recent decades many airlines have progressively reduced or completely ceased in-flight catering, particularly on short-haul and domestic flights in economy class, pleading rising costs. There has been a parallel move, however, to have celebrity chefs involved in meal-planning, particularly for those offered in first and business class, in an attempt to attract the more wealthy passengers.

Recipes

~~~

Tournedos Rossini was created by the famous chef Auguste Escoffier (1846–1935) in honor of the composer Gioachino Rossini (1789–1868).

---

### Tournedos Rossini

Seasoning: 4 tournedos, butter, 4 croûtons, fried in butter, meat jelly, 4 slices foie gras, Madeira, 12 slices truffle, dem-glace sauce. Season and sauté the tournedos in butter. Cover each crouton with a little meat jelly and place the tournedos on top. Arrange on a serving dish. Sauté foie gras in butter and place a slice on each tournedos. Add a little Madeira to the pan in which the tournedos were cooked, boil, add the slice of truffle and the very well reduced demi-glace sauce. Pour over the tournedos. Serve with a dish of noodles, mixed with butter and Parmesan cheese.
  Auguste Escoffier, *Ma Cuisine* (1934).

---

*Pommes chateau* are a traditional garnish for grilled meats. Their being presented as a side dish to the tournedos Rossini suggests that this was not served with the usual noodles.

---

### Pommes Chateau

Take twenty potatoes, turn them with a knife into olive shape, boil them in salted water for five minutes; drain them and put them on a baking-tin with salt and butter or dripping. Cook them in a very hot oven for thirty minutes, moving them about from time to time. Sprinkle on a little chopped parsley before serving.
  Mrs Brian Luck, *The Belgian Cookbook* (1915).

---

### Velouté Dame Blanche

A basic velouté (thickened white sauce or soup) with diced chicken, chicken quenelles, tapioca, and almonds. It is named for the opera *White Lady*, by François-Adrien Boïeldieu (1775–1834).

---

### Coupe Jamaique

Coffee ice cream, cream, pineapple, rum-apricot sauce, decorated with a crystallized violet.

## October 4

Insurance Company Dinner
Copenhagen, Denmark, 1896

When the Hafnia Life Insurance Company in Copenhagen held a company dinner on October 4, 1896, for some reason not made clear on the menu, it was decided that it would be written in Latin.

---

Hafniæ, anno MDCCCLXXXXVI
Octbr. IV
—

ORDINATIO COENAE
IN DIE CONFIRMATIONIS "FILIOLÆ"

*Rep.*

Sorbitionis homari
q. s. ad "Madeira"

Leporis in crusto volante
q. s. ad "Bordeaux"

Linguea bovinæ cum oleribus
q. s. ad "Sauterne"

Gelatinae vini albi
q. s. ad "florem Lactis vanillatum"

Anatis assæ cum solano
q. s. ad "Bourgogne"

Casei gallici cum pane et butyro
q. s. ad "Oporto"

Glaciei gallicæ novæ
q. s. ad "Xeres"

Crusti saccharati amydalum
q. s. ad "Champagne"

Infusi faborum Coffeæ
q. s. ad liquorum benedictum "D.O.M."

D. S. *Nydes* cum apetitu et ad libitum.

---

"Hafnia" is the Latin name for Copenhagen. It is also the name of a large Danish insurance company that was founded in the nineteenth century. The menu is in the Buttolph collection of historic menus at the New York Public Library, and many of the items have notations on them in what is presumably the hand of the collector, Miss Frank E. Buttolph (1850–1924). The only indication that "Hafniæ" refers to the insurance company rather than simply the location is a note to that effect on the reverse of the menu in the same handwriting, so it is reasonable to assume that it is correct.

It must have been an interesting challenge for the organizers of the dinner to try to translate "modern" dishes that did not exist in ancient Rome into the Latin language. It also makes for an interesting challenge to both Latin scholars and culinary historians to try to interpret the items on the menu.

*Leporis in crusto volante* for example translates approximately as "hare (or rabbit) in a flying crust." The most likely is that these were what would now be called *vol-au-vents*—which are puff pastry cases that "fly in the wind" or are as "light as air" (see September 17). There are mentions, but not actual recipes in the fourteenth-century European cookery manuscripts for "Payn Puff," which may have been something similar, but it is certain that the ancient Romans did not make puff pastry. Good, light pastry is made with hard fats such as lard—or in the case of puff pastry, butter—and the Romans found the use of animal fat disgusting and used olive oil for every culinary purpose.

The *solano* served with the roast duck is a small mystery. The word is Latin-like and is the name of the hot summer wind of Spain, and a word associated with several wine-growing areas around the world, but these do not seem likely. The word order suggests a side dish, and if this is the case then it probably means potatoes, which are of the botanical family *Solanum*. Potatoes, of course, are a New World plant only known in Europe from the early sixteenth century, and the Romans could not have known about them.

A reasonable translation of the menu is lobster soup; rabbit vol-au-vents; beef tongue with vegetables; white wine jelly; roast duck with potatoes; French cheese with bread and butter; novel French ices; almond tart; coffee; and Benedictine liqueur.

## Recipes

~~~

The following recipes are taken from *A Practical Dictionary of Cookery: 1200 Tested Recipes* by E. S. Meyer (London, 1898). Puff pastry is a component of many of the recipes in this book. It is not commonly made in the home today, as it is perceived as being complicated, and it is easy to purchase frozen.

---

### Almond Tartlets

4 oz. pounded almonds,
2 oz. butter,
2 oz. pounded sugar,
the yolks of 2 eggs,
1 oz. crushed ratafias,
1 tablespoonful cream.
Crust No. 400 [see below] . . . made with 8 oz. flour, and other ingredients in proportion.

Put the butter and sugar into a basin, and beat them together with a wooden spoon until the mixture becomes smooth and creamy. Add the pounded almonds and ratafias, and the eggs, which must be beaten and strained. Whip the cream to a stiff froth, and mix it thoroughly with all the other ingredients. Butter some patty pans, line them with the paste, put some of the mixture in each, and bake carefully in a moderately quick oven.

---

### Crust, Puff

1 lb. flour,
1 lb. butter,
yolks of 2 eggs,
juice of 1 lemon,
1/4 tea-spoonful salt,
7 or 8 table-spoonfuls water.

Put the flour in a basin and make a hollow in the centre, in which place the yolks of the eggs (first removing the speck), salt, lemon juice, and sufficient very cold water to make a smooth paste, mixing the dough with a wooden spoon as the water is added. Turn the crust on to a floured pastry-board, and leave for 5 minutes, then roll it out into a sheet 1/2 an inch in thickness, and sift a little flour on it. Press the butter into a sheet about an inch thick, and lay it in the centre of the paste, fold over each end on to it, entirely hiding the butter, sift a little flour over, and roll the paste out into a long sheet 1/4 of an inch thick. If this is properly done the paste and butter will flatten out without the butter breaking through the paste. Sift a little flour on the board and on the paste between each rolling-out. Fold the paste in three, and roll out; fold again in three, roll out a second time, then put the paste on a floured dish, and leave it in a very cool place, or, in summer, over ice for 1/4 of an hour. At the end of that time fold and roll out twice again, set it aside for 1/4 of an hour, then fold and roll out twice making 6 rollings-out in all and it is ready for use. It is most important to have the butter thoroughly cold and hard, as if it is at all soft and greasy it is impossible to prevent it breaking through the paste, which will then not rise properly. Should it seem at all watery, wring it dry in a cloth, or the paste will be heavy, but if good fresh butter is used this ought not to be necessary.

Vol-au-vents (see September 17).

## October 5

### Druggists' Luncheon
### Steamboat *Sandy Hook*, New York, 1894

The National Wholesale Druggists' Association Convention of 1894 ended with an excursion that was, according to *The New York Times*, "unequalled in the history of trade gatherings or gatherings of any kind in point of magnificence and completeness." The steamboat *Sandy Hook*, which was capable of the great speed of 20 knots, was chartered by the Entertainment

Committee to take the delegates and their wives and daughters (clearly, none of the delegates themselves were women) on a trip around the harbor, during which time they were to enjoy luncheon catered for by the famous restaurant Delmonico's and music from the full band of the Seventh Regiment. The weather was clear and bracing, but the sea a little choppy, resulting in some of the passengers becoming seasick, so the boat was quickly ordered about, and the cruise continued on the calmer waters of the Hudson River. All passengers recovered thanks in part to "judicious doses of champagne" and were able to enjoy their luncheon.

---

Huitres

Consommé en tasses.

Homard à la Newberg.

Filets de boeuf aux olives farcies.

Haricots verts sautés.

Cotelettes de volaille à la crème.

Petits pois à l'Anglaise.

Sorbet Romaine.

Perdreaux au cresson.

Foies gras à la gelée.       Salade de laitue.

Croute aux ananas.

Gelée aux pistaches,      Orientale. Charlotte vanille.

Glaces fantaisies.

Fruits.       Petits Fours.

Café

---

The luncheon was a masterpiece of organizing, particularly on the part of the staff of Delmonico's. Every single piece of tableware including the tablecloths for 520 guests had to be carried from the restaurant to transform the entire lower deck into a dining room. One hundred uniformed waiters were in attendance, and the meal was served with amazing efficiency. The hot dishes were served smoking hot, the chilled dishes thoroughly cold, and the wine was "handled in the most artistic manner." It was no mean feat for the restaurant to provide such an excellent service for such a large number on an unfamiliar and constantly mobile venue far from its own premises, and the visitors were unstinting in their praise.

New York had come to expect such service from Delmonico's restaurant. It had catered for virtually every great dinner in the city for decades.

## Recipes

~~~

### Croûtes aux Ananas, Sauce d'Abricots

Cut from cooked savarin some slices three-eighths of an inch thick; from these remove some rounds three inches in diameter; divide these in two through the center and notch them on their convex side. Arrange these slices shaped like cocks'-combs on a baking sheet, dredge them over with sugar, and glaze in a brisk oven; cover them on the unglazed side with strawberry marmalade strained through a sieve, and lay on each one a fine slice of preserved pineapple; decorate the borders of the crusts reaching out beyond the pineapple with angelica lozenges and candied cherries cut in four, then dress them on a dish in a circle, one overlapping the other. Fill the hollow of the circle with candied fruits cut in dice, such as apricots, pears, greengages, green almonds, candied cherries, orange peel and angelica, the whole washed in warm water, and then mingled with apricot marmalade flavored with kirsch; heat the dish after it is dressed in the oven for ten minutes. Serve an apricot kirsch sauce (below) separately.

Apricot Kirsch Sauce: Put three gills of apricot pulp into a copper pan, with as much water and half a pound of sugar; let boil up once or twice, then strain the sauce through a fine sieve and add one gill of kirsch to it.

Charles Ranhofer, *The Epicurean* (1894).

Savarin: this is a sweet yeast cake made the same way as brioche (see February 24), but baked in a ring mold.

Lobster Newberg: see April 16.

Petits pois à l'Anglaise: see November 27.

Petits Fours: see November 14.

## October 6

### Remarkable Fish Banquet
### Lafayette Restaurant, Centennial Grounds, Philadelphia, 1876

The American Fish Culturists' Association gave "one of the most novel dinners which has ever taken place in this country" during the Centennial International Exhibition (World's Fair) in Philadelphia in 1876. The American Fish Culturists' Association was started in 1870, in response to awareness of declining populations of some fish—proving that concern about the environmental damage done by recreational and commercial fishing is not a new issue. They proved to be a powerful lobby group, but their interest was not purely altruistic. They saw fish as a commodity and hoped to replenish depleted waterways with the products of their own fish hatcheries.

The exhibition provided the association with a fine opportunity for promoting its main product. *The New York Times* reported that the intention was that "every variety of fish caught on the Atlantic or Pacific coast of the United States will be presented, supplemented by European fish." The job of sourcing and preparing the supplies fell to Eugene C. Blackford of Fulton Market, New York City, and he acquitted himself superbly, sourcing 58 varieties from around the world.

Blackford sought far and wide for his supplies and his advice. The English sole and turbot were brought over on the SS *Brittanic*, and the Japanese seaweed was courtesy of the cook of the Japanese Commission at the exhibition. His brief was also made easier by extending the definition of "fish" for the purposes of the banquet to include many other aquatic creatures such as

### SOUPS.

Green turtle, a la Blackford.

Bisque of Lobster, Seth Green Style.

### HORS D'ŒUVRE CHAUD.

Bouchees of Craw Fish,      Fried Oysters,

A la Remy.      Ferguson Style.

Fried Scallops, á la Edmunds.

### HORS D'ŒUVRE FROID.

Mackerel in Oil.—Norway      Mackerel, Fried.—Norway.

Halibut.—Norway      Salmon.—Norway.

Pluck Fish.—Norway      Canned Mackerel.

Anchovies.—Sweden.      —Norway.

Conger Eel.—Portugal.      Mackerel.—Sweeden.

Sardines in Oil.—Portugal      Squid in Oil.—Portugal.

Conger Eel with Tomatoes.      Mackerel in Oil.—Spain.

—Spain.      Sardines in Oil.—Spain.

Miilion.—Spain.      Sardines in Vinegar.—Spain.

Fried Bass.—Spain.

Botargo, (Mullet Roes.)—Turkey.

Cray Fish, Cape of Good Hope.—Africa.

Shake, Dried Salmon.—Japan.

Sardines.—France      Anchovies.—France.

Tunny.—France

Salmon.—Holland.

Shark Fins, Black.—China.      Shark Fins, White.—China.

Oolachans.—Alaska.      Sardines.—Italy.

Caviar.—Russia.      Poisson au Blanc.—Russia.

Caviar.—California.

Dried Octopus Eggs.—China.      Dried Fish Maws.—China.

Sword Fish.—Portugal.

### RELEVEES.

Striped Bass, a la Brevourt.      Pompano, a la Reeder.

### ENTREES.

Caisse of Terrapin, a la Norris.

Deviled Crabs, Gill's style.

Filet of English Soles, a la Buckland.

Turbot a la Whitcher.      Timball of Frogs, a la Cost.

VEGETABLES.

Potatoes, Parisienne.     French Peas.

French String Beans.     Stuffed Egg Plants.

ROAST.

Sheep's Head, Agassiz Sauce.     Blue Fish, a la Goode.

COLD PIECES.

Aspic of Eels, a la Huxley.

Buison D'Ecrevisses, a la Atkins.

Saumon, a la Baird, Beurre de Montpelier.

Lobster Salad.

DESSERT.

Pudding, a la Neptune.     Napolitan Ice Cream.

ORNAMENTAL PIECES.

Bateau de Pecheur, a la Roosevelt.

"Fisherman's Luck," a la Shepherd Page.

Kan-ten Japanese Sea-weed, a la Sekizawa Akekio.

Fruits.     Cheese.     Coffee.

---

terrapin, frogs, and octopus eggs. The use of some preserved products also must have helped in the catering: as well as the canned fish and fish in oil, there was *botargo*—the roe of fish (usually mullet) pickled or dried.

A large number of foreign commissioners to the exhibition were invited, and the advance publicity of the "icthyc feast" excited much curiosity. The propaganda opportunity was greatly increased by the honoring of many of the guests and those prominent in the fisheries business in the names given to the dishes.

## Recipes

~~~

---

### Fried Scallops

Clean one quart scallops, add one and one-half cups boiling water, and let stand two minutes; drain, and dry between towels. Season with salt and pepper, roll in fine cracker crumbs, dip in egg, again in crumbs, and fry two minutes in deep fat; then drain on brown paper.

Fannie Merritt Farmer, *The Boston Cooking School Cook Book* (1896).

---

---

### Deviled Crabs

Boil them, take the meat out of the bodies, and large claws; put it into stew pan with half a pint of claret, spoonful of eschalot vinegar, a little cayenne, some salt, piece of butter. Stew for an hour over a gentle fire until they are almost dry. Then add small quantity of fish stock, or gravy, a tablespoonful of essence of anchovy, and small piece of butter rolled in flour. Serve with sippets of fried bread around the dish.

    Carrie V. Shuman, *Favorite Dishes. A Columbian Autograph Souvenir Cookery Book* (1893).

---

Napolitan [Neopolitan] Ice Cream: see December 20.
Turtle Soup: see November 10.
Sharks Fins: see March 8.

## October 7

### Esperanto Society Meeting Dinner
### New England, 1911

A group of students and enthusiasts of the constructed language Esperanto met on this day over a fine meal. Presumably they had no problem interpreting the menu, which was written in the language that they studied.

---

TAGMANĜETO

La 7an de Oktobro, 1911

MENUO

Buljono
Salaj Biskvitoj
Celerio      Hispanaj Oilivoj
Viandfritaĵo de Kokido
Vakcinia Ĵeleo
Pistitaĵo de Terpomoj
Nematura Maizo     Trančitaj Tomatoj
Valdorfa Salato
Varmegaj Bulkoj
Vanila Glaciaĵo     Diverospecaj Kukoj
Kafo

—

A. S. Coldwell
La Ulmoj

---

Esperanto was designed as a neutral international language by L. L. Zamenhoff in 1889, and there are estimated to be about two million speakers worldwide. Seventy-five percent of its vocabulary comes from Latin and Romance languages, and about 20 percent from Germanic languages, so it is possible for native speakers of these (and Slavic languages) to guess many of the words.

This lunch (tagmanĝeto) was held at "La Ulmoj" ("The Elms") in Novan-glujo ("New England"). The menu does not specify the country where this meal took place. In addition to the northeastern corner of the United States, there are areas named New England in Cambridgeshire in the United Kingdom and in inland northern New South Wales in Australia. A translation of the menu and a study of the food served shows unequivocally that this meal took place in the United States.

---

Bouillon
Salted Biscuits
Celery      Spanish Olives
Roast Chicken
Whortleberry Jelly
Mashed Potatoes
Fresh Corn (on the Cob)      Sliced Tomatoes
Waldorf Salad
Hot Rolls
Vanilla Ice cream      A Variety of Cakes
Coffee

---

Salted biscuits, celery, and olives were almost obligatory on American menus of the era; maize was never eaten fresh from the cob in England in the early-twentieth century, although maize flour was used in baking; whorteberries (*Vaccinium myrtillus*) would have been called bilberries or blueberries in England, and were not grown in Australia until the 1950s. The final convincing dish is the Waldorf Salad—an unequivocally American salad traditionally understood to include apples, celery, and walnuts in a mayonnaise dressing.

As well, a resort called "The Elms" in Manchester, New Hampshire, at this time, was run by Archie Coldwell.

## Recipes

~~~

The Waldorf Salad was invented by chef Oscar Tshirky ("Oscar of the Waldorf") for the opening of the hotel by that name in New York in 1893. Oscar included his recipe for it in the cookbook he published in 1896—called simply *The Cook Book*. His original recipe did not contain walnuts.

---

### Waldorf Salad

Peel two raw apples and cut them into small pieces, say about half an inch square, also cut some celery the same way, and mix it with the apple. Be very careful not to let any seeds of the apples be mixed with it. The salad must be dressed with a good mayonnaise.

Within a very short period of time, multiple variations of the salad were to be found in many cookbooks, and one appearing in 1905 did include nuts.

---

### Waldorf Salad

Three-fourths cup chopped nuts,
half cup chopped celery;
one cup apple cut fine,
dash of paprika,
and salt to taste.

Mix with mayonnaise or any other salad dressing as preferred. Enough for six persons.
*The Times Cook Book, No. 2* (1905).

---

## October 8

### Chicago Fire Centennial Anniversary Banquet
### Conrad Hilton Hotel, Chicago, Illinois, 1971

Chicago was booming in 1871 when a disastrous fire razed the city. It began on October 3 and burned until October 10, destroying four square miles of the city, damaging $200 million in property, killing hundreds, and leaving a third of its citizens homeless. The rebuilding began immediately, continued at a rapid pace, the new face of the city emerging, it seemed, even stronger. One hundred years later Chicago commemorated the anniversary of the fire with a series of special events, including the obligatory parade and series of banquets.

The largest banquet was sponsored by the mayor and members of the City Council and took place at the Hilton Hotel. Guests totaling 1,400 sat down in the International Ballroom to a menu that was a mini-history of the fire itself.

---

Fire House Double Strength Beef Bouillon
Corn Sticks
Roast Prime Rib of Beef
Mrs. O'Leary's Baked Beans with Salt Pork
Little Giant Company Glazed Carrots
Caesar Salad
Assorted Muffins and Soda Bread
Tub Butter
Mayor Mason Bombe—Rum Sauce
Coffee—Old Fashioned Cube Sugar—from Kettle
*Clement Columbet Pinot Noir*

---

The fire is said to have begun in the barn belonging to a Catholic immigrant called Mrs. O'Leary, when her cow kicked over a lamp. The Little

Giant No. 6 Fire Company was the first on the scene with its horse-drawn steam engine capable of pumping 600 gallons a minute in four streams. The heroic firemen from the Little Giant fought the fire single-handedly for 20 minutes before support arrived. Mayor Mason took decisive action and placed the city under Marshall law in an attempt to control the inevitable looting.

## Recipes

~~~

Caesar salad is a classic American salad. It was created relatively recently in historic terms (well before the fire), yet its exact origins and authentic original recipe are still much disputed. Most stories about its invention say it was created in the 1920s, in Tijuana, Mexico—the great place of refuge from the restrictions of Prohibition (see April 1). The great cook and food writer Julia Child (1912–2004) gives an exact date—July 4, 1924. She says that some of the escapees from Prohibition who were staying at Caesar's Palace in Tijuana called for a late-night snack, and the proprietor Caesar Cardini assembled a salad from what he could find in the depleted pantry.

---

### Caesar Salad

| | |
|---:|---|
| 3 anchovies | 2 cups iceberg lettuce |
| 1/4 teaspoon dry mustard | 1/2 teaspoon salt |
| 1/4 teaspoon prepared horseradish | black pepper, freshly ground |
| 1 teaspoon fresh lemon juice | 1/2 cup croutons, plain or garlic |
| 1 tablespoon red wine vinegar | 3 to 4 tablespoons Parmesan cheese |
| 3 tablespoons olive oil | 1 egg, coddled. |

Place anchovies on a small plate; sprinkle with mustard, horseradish, lemon juice, vinegar and oil. Mash with a fork into a smooth paste. Make sure lettuce is crisp and dry; break into 1-inch pieces and place in a large salad bowl. Sprinkle with salt and a generous grinding of pepper. Add anchovy paste and croutons. Sprinkle cheese on top. Drop coddled egg on top of cheese. Toss salad gently until greens are well coated with dressing. Makes 2 servings.
*Albuquerque Journal*, May 2, 1975.

---

### Glazed Carrots

2 tablespoons butter
1 pound small whole carrots, scraped, boiled, and drained.
1 ounce cognac
2 tablespoons brown sugar
dash of ground ginger

Melt butter in medium saucepan, add carrots and pour cognac over vegetable. Sprinkle with sugar and ginger and cover. Cook slowly 10 minutes and uncover.

Continue cooking, stirring several times 10 more minutes or until carrots are glazed. Serves 4.
*The News and Tribune*, Jefferson City, April 10, 1975.

Baked Beans: see
Bouillon: see

## October 9

Eggless, Poultryless Meals for President Harry S. Truman
The White House, Washington, DC, 1947

In the first week of October 1947 the Citizens Food Committee released the White House menus for the first few days of the proposed Food Conservation Program. The publicity was intended to provide an example from the top: even President and Mrs. Truman would abide by the designated meatless day (Tuesday) and eggless and poultryless day (Thursday).

| LUNCH | DINNER |
|---|---|
| Corn Soup. | Melon Balls. |
| * | * |
| Peppers stuffed with Rice and Mushrooms. | Baked Ham. |
| Lima Beans, Glazed Carrots. | Baked Sweet Potatoes, Asparagus, Cauliflower. |
| * | * |
| Baked Apple. | Green Salad. |
| | * |
| | Coffee Mallow. |

The aim of the campaign was to reduce home wheat consumption to allow America to be "The Granary of Hope" for post-World War II Europe. The campaign to save wheat had been ongoing since the war ended, but with a second drastic winter and poor harvests set to push Europe closer to starvation, it was given new impetus with the formation of the Citizens Food Committee.

No campaign is without its critics, and this one was no exception. The Secretary of Agriculture Clint Anderson claimed it was merely a symbolic sacrifice, "like going to church on Sunday and then raising hell all week"; *Time Magazine* wondered whether perhaps the sensible place to start saving grain was with the nation's farms, not the consumer; and many argued that there was no gain if chicken saved on Thursday was swapped for meat saved on Tuesday. Whatever the attempted arguments against the campaign,

World War II food poster. Courtesy of Library of Congress.

propaganda and patriotic fervor won out, and it seems that the nation took to it with enthusiasm.

The job of persuading 140,000,000 people to change the eating habits of a lifetime went to architect and businessman Charles Luckman. His minimum goal was to save 100,000,000 bushels of wheat, and this would be done by "bringing International diplomacy in as an unseen guest at the table of every American family."

The campaign was voluntary: saving wheat was a patriotic duty not an enforceable law. For several years Americans had been urged to save wheat by reducing bread consumption, but even under the new scheme a specific "wheatless" day was not regulated on the basis that far more wheat was consumed by farm animals than directly in the form of bread.

Aside from the wheatless and poultryless days there were other points to the campaign. Wheat bread consumption was still to be kept to a minimum, and the public was advised that "one slice of bread saved per person each day means seven million 1-lb. loaves a day for Europe." It had been estimated that 10% of the food bought for American tables was wasted, and a considerable part of the advertising effort went towards what would now be called "awareness raising" of the problem, with widespread use of slogans such as "Don't start the next war in the garbage can," "you strike a blow for peace when you save food," "Food Is Life—Save It," and "Make One out of Seven Leftover Day."

---

The Housewife's Pledge, 1946

1. I will do my utmost to conserve any and all foodstuffs which the starving millions of the world need today so desperately.

2. I will buy only the food my family actually needs for its proper nourishment and health.

3. I will neither waste nor hoard nor discard any article of food in cooking or in serving and will ask my family for the fullest possible cooperation.

4. I will be particularly watchful in the use of wheat and cereals, fats and oils, and will try to make certain that not a scrap of bread is wasted in my home.

5. I will make these little sacrifices gladly for the sake of those who cannot enjoy my God-given right to live and give as an American.

*First signator*: Eleanor Roosevelt, June 6, 1946.

## Recipes

~~~

The Citizens Food Committee included several White House recipes along with the menus. The jellied salad was part of the meatless Tuesday menu, the coffee mallow is from the Thursday menu given here.

---

### Perfection Salad

1 tablespoon granulated gelatin soaked in
1/4 cup cold water
1 cup boiling water
1/4 cup sugar
1/4 cup vinegar
2 tablespoons lemon juice
1 teaspoon salt.

As jelly begins to thicken fold in 1 1/2 teaspoons chopped onion, 1/2 cup shredded cabbage, celery and 1 1/2 tablespoons pimiento of green pepper, finely cut.

---

### Coffee Mallow

16 marshmallows
1/2 cup hot coffee
1 cup heavy cream
1/2 teaspoon vanilla.

Cut marshmallows in quarters with wet scissors. Add coffee. Cook in double boiler until melted. Cool. When beginning to thicken, fold in cream, beaten stiff, and add vanilla. Mold in dessert glasses. Serves six.
*The New York Times*, October 7, 1947.

---

Baked Apple: see December 14.

## October 10

International Lunch Menu
International Casino, Times Square, New York, 1938

In spite of its name, the International Casino in Times Square was a theatre-restaurant, cocktail bar, and nightclub all rolled into one, and for the briefest of times it provided the most dazzling venue in New York. When the Casino finally opened in mid-September 1937 after months of delays, there were still mechanical problems with the complicated stage and sets for the opening show "Bravo!" Patrons were not perturbed however as there was one other huge attraction at the Casino—the bar. The law at the time specified that only one "stand-up" bar was permitted at each establishment, but the architects and designers got around this inconvenient rule in a very creative way. They built the Spiral Bar—a beautiful mahogany feature that curved upwards two stories, from the ground floor to the mezzanine.

A few months after the Casino's opening, at luncheon on October 10, 1938, patrons were offered the following menu.

---

LUNCHEON
(Choice of Entree Determines Price of Lunch)
—
Chicken Giblet and Noodle Soup
—
Spaghetti with Meat Balls and Fresh Mushroom Sauce 75
Frankfurters and Boston Baked Beans 75
Minced Filet of Beef a la Deutsch 90
Moussaka of Lamb a la Moldave 75
Baked Sugar Cured Ham au Sherry 80
Fresh Creamed Spinach
—
Apple Pie     Cocoanut Custard Pie     Swiss Pastry
Whole Stewed Pear     Cheese Tray
Chocolate Fudge Cake
Coffee

---

Restaurants and other dining establishments have several ways of charging for meals. In the case of a hotel, meals sometimes used to be included in the tariff—the so-called American Plan (see May 29). Sometimes a hotel or other hostelry would have a *table d'hote* (see also August 19), at which a meal was provided for a fixed price, and the customer simply chose what they wanted from the list. This idea has morphed (or degenerated) into the "all you can eat" buffet system found in many places today where quantity seems to be valued more than quality. More upmarket restaurants have an *à la carte* menu, in which each item is individually priced. Historically, some of the most glamorous and expensive restaurants even provided two menus—one with prices (given to the host, or the gentleman), and one without (for the guests or the lady). Another method is shown here, a compromise between individually priced items and fixed-price meals. The entrée, usually being the most expensive part of the meal, determines the cost of the whole meal, guests having no, or restricted, alternatives in the other courses. The system allows guests to feel that they have a choice and management to control work and costs. The International Casino certainly lived up to its name in presenting a range of internationally inspired choices.

In early January 1940 the casino closed as a theatre-restaurant, with plans for it to reopen as a ballroom. The plans all came to an ignominious end in June when its president Chester H. Canning was charged with embezzlement and tax evasion.

## Recipes
~~~

Moussaka is a "Greek" or Middle Eastern dish, and as with so many national dishes there are endless arguments about the authenticity of recipes for it, even within its country of origin. This is one American version.

---

### Moussaka

1 pound lean beef, ground
1 teaspoon salt
1/2 teaspoon pepper
1 small eggplant thinly sliced
1 can tomato paste
1/2 cup bread crumbs
grated cheese

Season meat with salt and pepper and press into bottom of greased casserole. Lay eggplant slices over meat and spread with tomato paste.

Top with breadcrumbs and bake, covered, in a moderate oven (350 deg.) for 30 minutes. Remove, cover and bake 15 minutes longer or until crumbs are brown and eggplant is tender. Serve with grated cheese.
*Oakland Tribune*, October 7, 1940.

---

### Chocolate Fudge Cake

| | |
|---|---|
| 2 cups sifted Swans Down cake flour | 2 egg yolks beaten light |
| 3 teaspoons baking powder | 3 squares Baker's unsweetened chocolate |
| 1/2 teaspoon soda | 1 1/4 cups milk |
| 1/4 teaspoon salt | 1 teaspoon vanilla |
| 1/2 cup Crisco or butter | 2 egg whites stiffly beaten |
| 1 cup sugar | |

Sift flour once, measure, add baking powder, soda and salt. Sift three times, cream butter and sugar thoroughly until light and fluffy. Add egg yolks and chocolate, then flour and milk alternately. Beat after each addition until smooth. Add vanilla.

Fold in egg whites. Bake in 2 greased 9-inch layer pans in moderate oven (350° F.) for 30 minutes. Put layers together with fudge frosting. Double recipe to make 3 10-inch layers. All measurements level.

---

### Fudge Frosting

All measurements level
2 cups sugar
2 sqs. unsweetened chocolate
2 tablespoons corn syrup
2/3 cup milk
2 tablespoons butter
1 teaspoon vanilla

Cook sugar, chocolate corn syrup and milk, stirring until all are dissolved. Then stir occasionally to prevent burning. Cook until syrup forms a very soft ball when tested in cold water. Remove from fire. Add butter and cool slightly. Add vanilla and beat until frosting is creamy and ready to spread.
*Chilicothe Constitution-Tribune*, May 10, 1935.

---

Boston Baked Beans: see June 11.

## October 11

### Dinner for Princess Elizabeth
### Ottowa, Canada, 1951

The organization of the arrangements for the visit of a head of state of another country is a challenging undertaking for officials and protocol advisers. The temptation to bang the national drum too loud has to be tempered by the need to be open to be welcoming and mindful of any significant cultural differences. If there are diplomatic or political tensions in the background, so much more the difficulty. When Princess Elizabeth (b. 1926) visited Canada in October 1951, there were few such issues. Canada was a former colony of Britain, and still linked with it via the British Commonwealth. It was appropriate and desirable for her Canadian hosts to show the Princess the bounty of the nation that still formed part of her dominion. The members of the Ottawa City Council demonstrated their national pride at the dinner they gave in her honor, as the Quebecois had done when her parents visited Canada in 1939 (see May 17). Less than five months later, on the death of her father, the Princess became Queen of England and "Supremed Liege Lady in and over Canada," reported *The Times*.

A luncheon was given today in their honour by the city council. The menu included dishes from all 10 provinces: there were Nova Scotia and Prince

Edward Island maritime oysters; cream of peas *Québecoise*; Newfoundland salmon; Alberta elk; Saskatchewan grouse; New Brunswick potatoes; Manitoba wild rice; British Columbia candied fruits; and Ontario cheese *fleurons*. No alcohol was served.

With the exception of the wild rice and elk, the dishes at this dinner could as easily have been served at a dinner in England. At an English dinner the oysters might have come from Colchester, the salmon and grouse from Scotland, and the cheese from Stilton, or Cheddar, for example, but the style and method of cooking would have been identical. The cheese fleurons are a variation of a savory cheese pastry, and the English have always loved small savory dishes, cheese or otherwise, at the end of a meal.

## Recipes

~~~

### Crème de Pois

1 pint green peas;
1 1/2 pints white stock;
1 gill cream;
2 yolks of eggs;
1 spray of mint.

Simmer stock and peas twenty minutes, rub through a sieve. Mix together cream and yolks of eggs, add them to the stock and stir all together over the fire until it begins to thicken. Serve at once.
Amy G. Richards, *Cookery* (Montréal, 1895).

### Wild Rice Casserole

1 1/2 cups wild rice
6 cups boiling water
6 beef bouillon cubes
1 onion
1 green pepper
1/2 lb mushrooms
1/2 cup butter

Preheat oven to 350 degrees F. Wash rice in several waters. Place in 2 quart casserole. Combine boiling water and boullion cubes. Pour over rice. Cover casserole. Bake 1 1/4 hours. Pare and chop onion. Removes seeds and white vein from pepper, chop. Slice mushrooms. Saute vegetables in 1/4 cup butter until tender. Stir into rice, dot with remaining butter. Bake uncovered 20 minutes longer.
*Winnipeg Free Press*, June 23, 1962.

### Canadian Cheese Fleurons

1/2 lb. soft Canadian white cheese.
1/2 lb. soft Canadian yellow cheese.
1/2 teaspoon of dry mustard.
4 oz. Dry White Canadian wine.
4 oz. Light Cream Sauce.
Dash of Worcestershire Sauce.
Dash of Cayenne Pepper.

Dice cheese in small cubes. Put wine in sauce pan on open fire and dissolve mustard. Add a few drops of Worcestershire Sauce to taste, and a dash of Cayenne pepper to taste. Finally, add hot cream sauce and beat up together. Let boil for a minute making a cream paste.

The Fleurons are made with flaky puff paste cut in moon shapes. Patty shells are also used. Fill the Fleurons up and serve hot.

*Lethbrige Herald* (Alberta), October 27, 1951.

## October 12

### Columbus Day Dinner
### aboard the SS *America*, 1962

It probably seemed fitting for a ship named *America*, of the United States Line, to celebrate Columbus Day in 1962 with a special dinner. Columbus Day celebrates the arrival of Christopher Columbus (1451–1506) in the Americas in 1492, and the beginning of what came to be called the Columbian Exchange. The exchange of people (settlers and slaves), plants, animals, and diseases between the Old and the New Worlds wreaked changes so profound that they are difficult to comprehend, even 500 years later. That the exchange is thought to have been unequal is at the root of much of the controversy about the celebration of the day.

Iced Table Celery    Jumbo Shrimp Cocktail    Assorted Spanish Olives
Cherrystone Clams on the Half Shell    Cornets of Prosciutto Ham
Fresh Fruit Cocktail Columbus    Pâté de Fois Gras aux Truffes
Beluga Massolol Caviar on Ice    Smoked Irish Salmon

*

Bisque de Castilian    Consommé Isabella    Green Turtle Soup au Jerez
COLD:   Cream Vichyssoise    Consommé Madrilene

*

TO ORDER, 20 MINUTES:   Broiled Live Maine Lobster, Seville Butter
Poached Fresh Salmon, Hollandaise Sauce

*

Assorted Vegetable Dinner à la Cadiz
Sauté of Kidneys au Santa Maria
Globe Artichoke Hollandaise
Raviolis Neapolitan

\*

REFRESHMENT:   Genevoise Sherbert, Wafers

\*

Roast Young Turkey, Giblet Gravy, Cranberry Sauce
Baked Sugar-cured American Ham, Alcantara Sauce
TO ORDER FROM THE GRILL:   Prime Cut Sirloin Steak, Bordelaise Sauce

\*

COMPOTE:   Preserved Black Bing Cherries

\*

Steamed Rice Romano
Lima Beans Sauté      Minted Green Peas      Corn on the Cob, Melted Butter
California Asparagus Sevigne      Brussels Sprouts Sauté Milanaise
POTATOES:   Parsley, Mousseline, French Fried or Candied Sweet

\*

Salad Espagnole, Special Dressing

\*

Coupé Glacé Neapolitan      Petits Fours      Mignardises
Gâteau Catalane      Caramel Glacé Porto Nuevo

\*

Provelone Cheese and Toasted Crackers

\*

Assorted Nuts      After Dinner Mints      Table Raisins
Tunis Dates      Crystallized Ginger      Table Figs

\*

Fresh Fruit Basket      Grapes on Ice

\*

Demi Tasse

---

The exchange of food was certainly unequal. What are now considered the national dishes of many countries that were part of the Old World contain ingredients from the New. It is almost impossible to conceive of Italian food without tomatoes, or Indian without chillies, or English without potatoes—yet tomatoes, chillies, and potatoes are New World foods.

It is unlikely that the passengers aboard the SS *America* paused to consider their dinner menu in the light of how different it might have been without the ingredients from the Americas.

The *vichyssoise* soup (and its hot cousin, *potage Parmentier*, see October 21, January 12) perhaps symbolizes best the thoroughly harmonious synthesis of the food of the two hemispheres. It combines the Old World leek with the New World potato into an intermittently fashionable soup, served chilled, as if to purposely stimulate discussion. It was the invention of Louis Diat (1885–1957), the French chef at the Ritz-Carlton in New York in 1917. The recipe, he said, was based on the soup of his childhood, as prepared by his mother. The reason for serving it chilled in its new American incarnation is disputed. It may have simply not been reheated in time, or it may have been a last-minute inspiration on a hot day.

## Foods from the New World

| | |
|---|---|
| Maize (corn) | Tomato |
| Wild rice | Black walnuts |
| Quinoa | Hickory nuts |
| Beans (navy, cranberry, black, kidney, lima) | Beechnuts |
| Peanuts | Hazelnuts |
| Potatoes | Pecans |
| Sweet potatoes | Cashew Nut |
| Squash, Pumpkins | Pine nuts |
| Blueberries, huckleberries, blackberries | Sunflower |
| Cranberries | Turkey |
| Persimmons | Allspice |
| Papaya (Paw-Paw) | Juniper |
| Guava | Sassafras |
| Avocado | Cacao (Cocoa and Chocolate) |
| Bell peppers and chilies | Vanilla |
| Pineapple | Maple sugar |
| | Cassava (manioc) |

## Recipes

~~~

### Vichyssoise

| | |
|---|---|
| 4 large potatoes | 1/4 teaspoon white pepper |
| 3 leeks with tops, chopped | 2 cups milk |
| 2 cups chicken stock | 1 cup cream |
| 1 tablespoon butter | 4 tablespoons minced chives |
| 2 teaspoons salt | |

> Peel and dice potatoes and cook with leeks in the stock until very soft, about 20 minutes. Strain through a fine sieve. Add butter, salt, pepper, milk and cream and reheat. Serve chilled garnished with chives.
> Adapted from a recipe in the *New York Times*, July 13, 1943.

Consommé Madrilène is a clear soup with chopped tomatoes and sometimes bell peppers and other finely chopped vegetables. It should be thick and syrupy, on the verge of gelling.

### Consommé Madrilène

Slice a handful of sorrel and cook for five minutes in consommé. Add vermicelli and one tomato cut in small dices. Serve grated cheese separate.
Victor Hirtzler, *Hotel St. Francis Cook Book* (1919).

Candied Sweet Potatoes: see December 20.
Foie gras: see May 26.
Parsley potatoes: see December 6.
Petits fours: see November 14.

## October 13

### Coronation Feast of King Henry IV
### Great Hall of Westminster, London, England, 1399

Henry IV (1367–1413) was crowned in Westminster Abbey only two weeks after he formally deposed his cousin Richard II. After the ceremony, there was the usual "honourable feaste" in Westminster Hall.

This was the bill of fare that was set before the king himself: three courses of increasingly elegant food, each followed by a *soltety* (see September 23). The lesser ranking guests would have been presented with a progressively smaller number of choices of the less refined dishes, some only receiving two courses. One's station in the court and country's hierarchy was not just denoted by the range of food choices at a feast such as this. The table at which one sat, and the exact position on the table, was also determined by rank, with higher ranking guests closer to the guest of honor who sat at the "high table" (often literally elevated on a dais, in full view of the other diners). At this feast, at the right hand of King Henry, sat the archbishop of Canterbury and several prelates, and at his left the archbishop of York and several other prelates. At lower tables at progressively greater distances sat the principal citizens of London, the newly created knights, and the existing knights and squires.

A further detail of the seating protocol provides the phrase "above the salt" for a person of distinction. Salt was a vital commodity in medieval times because of its vital role in food preservation—and by extension, he who controlled the supply of salt controlled the people who needed it. It was therefore accorded great honor on the table, being placed in an intricately decorated

| FIRST COURSE. | SECOND COURSE. | THIRD COURSE. |
|---|---|---|
| Braun en peuerarde. | Venyson en furmenty. | Blaundesorye. |
| Viaund Ryal. | Gely. | Quyncys in comfyte. |
| Teste de senglere enarme. | Porcelle farce enforce. | Egretez. |
| Graund chare. | Pokokkys. | Curlewys. |
| Syngnettys. | Cranys. | Pertryche. |
| Capoun de haut grece. | Venyson Roste. | Pyionys. |
| Fesaunte. | Conyng. | Quaylys. |
| Heroun. | Byttore. | Snytys. |
| Crustade Lumbarde. | Pulle endore. | Smal byrdys. |
| Storieoun, graunt luces. | Graunt tartez. | Rabettys. |
| | Braun fryez. | Pome dorreng. |
| A Sotelte. | Leche lumbarde. | Braun blanke leche. |
| | | Eyroun engele. |
| | A Sotelte. | Frytourys. |
| | | Doucettys. |
| | | Pety perneux. |
| | | Egle. |
| | | Pottys of lylye. |
| | | A Sotelte. |

receptacle close to the most important people at the feast. Those who were seated "below" the salt were in no doubt as to their lower rank.

Medieval feasts were not just elaborate meals, they were highly theatrical events with a great deal of ceremony and ritual. Traditional ceremonial roles were taken by various noblemen. Henry's own eldest son, the twelve-year old Prince of Wales (the future Henry V), stood by his father during the feast holding the Sword of Mercy, one of the five ceremonial swords that formed part of the coronation regalia. On the King's other hand stood the Earl of Northumberland with the Sword of Justice. At the appropriate point in the feast, the hereditary King's Champion rode into the hall on horseback to make the traditional challenge to any dissenters to the King's right to rule by literally throwing down his gauntlet (the origin of the phrase)—a ceremony last performed at the coronation of George IV in 1821 (see July 19).

## Recipes

~~~

The following recipes are taken from *The Form of Cury* (ca. 1390), the manuscript written by the Master Cooks of Richard III. The language and instructions are difficult to follow, and the recipes are open to interpretation.

"Pety perneux" (*pernantes, pernollys, peruant*) were small pies or pasties made with minced meat or marrow, sweetened and spiced in a similar way to mince pies. The marrow provided fat, in the same way as the Victorians would use suet and we would now use butter.

---

### The Pety Peruaunt

Take male Marow. hole parade and kerue it rawe. powdour of Gynger. zolkes of Ayrenn, dates mynced. raisouns of coraunce. salt a lytel. & loke þat þou make þy past with zolkes of Ayren. & þat no water come þerto. and forme þy coffyn. and make up þy past.

[*Interpretation*: Take marrow, cut it up, add ginger powder, egg yolks, minced dates, currants, salt; make a crust with egg yolks and make a coffin, and put the mixture in the crust and bake it.]

The instruction to use egg yolks in the crust suggests that a "short," edible pastry was intended. Pies, particularly large pies, were made with very thick hard pastry and functioned more like serving dishes, the contents being scooped out as if from a casserole dish. The comment "that no water come thereto" probably refers to the need to keep the baked crust dry, which preserved the contents, sometimes for a very long time.

---

"Pome dorreng" (*pommedory* and other spelling) were a favorite at feasts. They were meatballs cooked on skewers and "gilded" with a coating of egg yolks so that they suggested golden apples, or coated with parsley for the green apple version.

---

### For to Make Pommedorry

Tak Buff and hewe yt smal al raw and cast yt in a morter and grynd yt nozt to smal tak safroun and grynd therewyth wan yt ys grounde tak the wyte of the eyryn zyf yt be nozt styf. Cast into the Buf pouder of Pepyr olde resyns and of coronse set over a panne wyth fayr water and mak pelotys of the Buf and wan the water and the pelots ys wel yboylyd and set yt adoun and kele yt and put yt on a broche and rost yt and endorre yt wyth zolkys of eyryn and serve yt forthe.

[*Interpretation*: Take raw beef and chop it small and grind it in a mortar not too small. Take saffron and grind it with the beef. When it is ground, take the white of the egg, if it is not stiff enough, add raisins and currants. Set over a pan with water and make balls of the beef; and when the balls are well boiled [poached], cool them. Put them on skewers and coat them with yolks of eggs and roast them and serve them.]

---

Furmenty (frumenty): see February 23.
Brawn: see September 22.

## October 14

### Banquet to Celebrate the Persian Empire
Persepolis, Iran, 1971

The official celebration of the 2,500-year history of the Persian monarchy was conducted on such an epic scale that, ironically, it was instrumental in contributing to its demise. The festivities were held over a five-day period, with the center of the activity being in a magnificent "tent city" erected in the desert at Persepolis, the historic birthplace of the Persian Empire. The site was cleared of snakes and other unpleasant desert creatures, and avenues of trees, a perfumed garden, and a beautiful floodlit fountain were installed. Fifty "tents" (actually prefabricated apartments with marble bathrooms and Persian carpets, built under blue and yellow canopies) accommodated the most important guests, with the lesser guests being obliged to stay in two new purpose-built hotels nearby. The largest tent (at 68 by 24 meters) was the pink and blue canopied banqueting hall. It was here that the single most spectacular, most publicized, and most controversial event was held.

The banquet was catered by Maxim's of Paris, and the menu heading read:

Banquet offered by Their Imperial Majesties the Shahanshah Aryamehr and the Empress of Iran in honour of Their illustrious guests taking part in the ceremonies of the 2500th anniversary of the foundation of the Persian Empire by Cyrus the Great.

Six hundred guests (including 37 heads of state) representing 69 nations attended. Guests were seated according to rank, as they have been since medieval times. Almost 100 of the most important sat at one long zigzag table, the remainder at tables of 12. The tables were set with Limoges china, Baccarat crystal, and gold-plated cutlery.

---

Quails' Eggs stuffed with Golden Imperial Caviar.
*Champagnean Chateau de Saran*

Mousse of Crayfish Tails in Nantua Sauce.
*Haut Brion Blanc, 1964*

Roast Saddle of Lamb with Truffles
*Chateau Lafite Rothschild, 1945*

Sorbet of Moët et Chandon, 1922

Peacocks stuffed with foie gras
*Musigny Conte de Vogue, 1945*

Oporto glazed figs with raspberries
*Dom Perignon, 1959, reserve vintage*

Coffee and *Cognac Prince Eugène*

---

Persepolis banquet tent. (AP Photo/Staff)

There was much that was medieval in style about this banquet. It was accompanied by spectacular entertainment. It was preceded by a parade of over 1,700 soldiers, chariots, and three replica ships illustrating the glorious history of the Persian Empire, and it was followed by a sound and light show out in the cold desert air, which in turn was followed by a fireworks display.

As for the banquet itself, the only quintessentially Iranian food was the caviar—and a massive 2,000 pounds were used. Caviar is the roe of some species of fish, particularly the sturgeon, and the finest is sourced from the Caspian Sea. Its consumption has long been associated with luxury, but it was noted that the Shah himself did not care for it, and was served artichokes instead. The peacock—a bird prized at banquets since medieval times for its regal colors—was a symbol of Persian royalty and was served as it would have been at a medieval banquet, for its decorative and symbolic value, in full plumage (see November 6).

The events were ten years in the planning, and although the official cost was given as $16.8 million, some estimates went as high as $2 billion. The lavishness of the occasion caused outrage amongst those who noted that many Iranians were living in poverty, and it became a powerful propaganda tool. It was called "The Devil's Festival" by the Ayatollah Khomeini (1902–1989), the leader of the 1979 revolution which led to the overthrow of the Shah and the establishment of the Islamic Republic of Iran, with himself as Supreme Leader.

Recipes

~~~

Nantua Sauce is a classic accompaniment to lobster and crayfish.

---

### Nantua Sauce

Nantua Sauce: Heat up 11/2 gills Bechamel sauce, and stir in 1/2 gill of cream, then finish with 1 1/2 oz. of crayfish butter. Crayfish tails may if liked be mixed with this sauce just before serving.

---

### Crayfish Butter

1/2 pint of picked shrimps or prawns,
3 oz. of fresh butter,
and 1/2 oz. of anchovy paste.

Pound the picked shrimps or prawns in a mortar till smooth, add the fresh butter, and anchovy paste; mix thoroughly and rub through a fine sieve. Keep on ice till wanted. A little liquid carmine or cochineal may be added to color if found necessary.

Charles Herman Senn, *The Book of Sauces* (Chicago, 1915).

---

Bechamel Sauce: see January 18.

## October 15

### Banquet for the Commissioner General
### Hotel Continental, Paris, France, 1898

From the mid-nineteenth century until the First World War, a series of international expositions were held in Europe and the United States. It was an era of massive industrial and agricultural development, and the world fairs presented an unparalleled opportunity for both host and visitor countries to promote their products and increase trade at the same time as showcasing various aspects of their cultures. Hosting an exposition was an enormously expensive undertaking, and host countries lobbied hard to ensure the participation of as many exhibitor countries as possible

The planning and promotion for the Exposition Universelle in Paris in 1900 began years beforehand with a huge building program. The railway system was improved with the building of new stations and the Metro system was begun. New buildings went up to house the exhibits—a glass exhibition hall (the *Grand Palais*), an octagonal wine pavilion called La Ruche, a smaller pavilion (the Petit Palais), and a wonderful Art Deco bridge, the *Pont Alexandre III*.

The economic potential of an interesting and successful exhibit for a visitor country too was enormous, and planning began early for visiting nations. In July 1898, President William McKinley (1843–1901) appointed Ferdinand

Wythe Peck (1848–1924) of Chicago, the wealthy patron of the Chicago Auditorium Building and vice president of the 1893 World's Columbian Exposition (see March 20) as commissioner general of the United States to the exposition. The new commissioner began lobbying for an increase in the allotted 150,000 feet of space allocated by the exposition directors. He and his family and staff arrived in Paris on September 13 and took up temporary residence at the Continental Hotel.

On October 15 the American Chamber of Commerce gave a banquet in his honor. Peck, in his speech, noted that the French authorities were "most cordial" but "did not realize the relative importance of American manufactures, which amounted to 35 percent of the whole world, while the agricultural products were even greater" and that the space granted so far was "glaringly disproportionate to America's needs."

---

### MENU

Crème de Laitues aux Quenelles de Volaille
Bisque d'Ecrivisses

—

Petits Bouchées aux Huitres
Turban de Sole à l'Amiral

—

Filet de Bœuf Renaissance
Poularde braisée aux Truffes

—

Marquise au Kirsch
Perdreaux flanqués de Cailles sur Canapé
Salade
Pâté de Foies Gras à la Gelée

—

Petits Pois à la Parisienne
Gâteau aux Avelines

—

Corbeille de Fruits, Bonbons, Petits Fours

—

### VINS
Madère vieux     Château Lagrange 1881
Haut Sauternes Supérieur     Pomarde Boucherottes 1878
Saint-Emilion en carafes     Champagne frappé
"Crême Montabello"

### CAFÉ ET LIQUEURS

---

The banquet itself, held by an American organization at a Paris hotel, was of the sort of fine, classic food that could just as easily have been served at a fine American restaurant of the time. There would have been no surprises for men accustomed to dining at such restaurants as Delmonico's in New York.

Recipes

~~~

---

### Crème de Laitue, Romaine ou Chicorée à la Evers

Procure two pounds of lettuce, romaine or chiccory, and proceed exactly the same for either. Wash them in several waters after removing the greenish leaves, then cook them in boiling, salted water, until the hardest parts yield under the pressure of the finger, then drain and cool them off; squeeze out all the water, and chop them up coarsely. Put into a saucepan four ounces of butter, and when very hot, add the lettuce and let fry for a few minutes; moisten with two quarts of broth, then boil and simmer for fifteen minutes, adding one quart of velouté, strain through a sieve or tammy, heat it up again, and when the soup is near boiling point, thicken with egg-yolks, cream and butter, seasoning with salt, sugar, and nutmeg.

Charles Ranhofer, *The Epicurean* (New York, 1894).

---

In this dinner, the soup was served with chicken quenelles. Quenelles are lightly poached dumplings made from forcemeat (a finely minced or pounded meat mixture) and were a common garnish at elegant dinners. There are many recipes, some of which are very complex, but the basic concept is the same whether meat or fish is used. The following recipe is a simple version.

---

### Chicken Quenelles

Mix together half a cupful each of the soft part of bread and of finely chopped or pounded chicken-meat cooked; season the mixture highly with salt and cayenne, and moisten it with enough raw yolk of egg to bind it so that little olive-shaped pieces can be moulded between two small spoons; either roll the *quenelles* in egg and cracker dust and fry them, or poach them until they float in boiling broth or water, and then use them.

Juliet Corson, *Miss Corson's Practical American Cookery and Household Management* (New York, 1886).

---

### Filbert Cakes with Rum (Petits Gâteaux d'Avelines au Rhum)

Roast half a pound of filberts; clean them well by removing their outer reddish skins, then pound with three-quarters of a pound of sugar, two eggs and half a gill of rum, making it into quite a fine paste; lay this in a vessel and soften it gradually with eight egg-yolks, continuing to beat until it is frothy, then add two ounces of finely shredded citron, four ounces of potato fecula, four ounces of melted butter and lastly six firmly beaten egg-whites. Pour this paste on a buttered sheet covered with paper, spread it out to half an inch in thickness and cook in a slow oven. Turn the cake over on a grate when done and leave to cool and set until the following day. Pare and cut it either in lozenges, oblongs or other shapes; steep each one slightly in Jamaica rum and ice over, dipping

> them into Jamaica rum fondant bestrew the cakes with chopped-up roasted
> filberts.
>   Charles Ranhofer, *The Epicurean* (New York, 1894).

Marquise au Kirsch: a Marquise is a frozen custard dessert, in this case fla-
vored with kirsch (cherry liqueur).
Fish Turban: see April 24.
Diplomate pudding: see September 12.

## October 16

Tribute Dinner for a Cow
Red Deer, Alberta, Canada, 1912

A very unusual guest was honored at a banquet in the town of Red Deer,
Alberta, on the evening of October 16, 1912. The Red Deer Board of Trade
invited local officials, politicians, businessmen and members of the press to
pay tribute to "a money-making milker"—Rosalind of Old Basing, "the
champion butter cow of the British Empire."
   Rosalind had produced in one year 15,700 pounds of milk, with an average
butterfat content of 5.7 percent, and three calves for which the owner turned
down an offer of $3,000.

---

Oyster Stew

Red Deer Celery     Olives     Pickled Walnuts

Fresh Salmon

Wild Duck
Partridge
Prairie Chicken

Roast Beef

"Woodvale" Potatoes     Red Deer Peas     Red Deer Beans

Salad

Deep Apple Pie     Ice Cream     Mince Pie

Cheese

Nuts and Raisins     Fruit

Tea
Coffee

Rosalind's Milk     Laurentia Milk

---

Rosalind had her own stall, in the place of honor near the head table. Her own dinner menu is not recorded, but the human guests sat down to a meal which included Rosalind's own milk, meat from her own species, and other local produce. The alternative beverage offered was bottled "Laurentia" milk (the "milk for the 20th century") from the first homogenizer in Canada.

---

### Toast to Rosalind

*Let us drink to the health of Rosalind, the cream of all the kine,*
*Let us rise and join in a real milk toast, instead of sparkling wine,*
*For there ne'er was a cow like Rosalind, Old Basing's pride and boast,*
*And she is our honoured guest tonight, together we'll play the host.*

*Such a banquet board as the one that night Red Deer had never seen,*
*Where men of state and untold wealth paid homage to one bovine;*
*Oh, the things they said about Rosalind would have caused that cow to blush,*
*If she could have heard her praise sung as she quietly ate her mush.*

*Tregilius was there with a gallant speech that would flatter a fairy queen,*
*While Duncan Marshall in dulcet tones depicted a charming scene,*
*Of a kind-faced cow in a clover patch on a balmy day in June,*
*Telling her calf a nursery rhyme or humming a lullaby tune.*

*But Rosalind is a cow with sense, her head wasn't turned at all,*
*She actually looked a trifle bored as she lolled in her big box stall;*
*The silvery phrases of compliment fell flat as a cake of mud,*
*And big-eyed Rosie switched her tail as she solemnly chewed her cud.*

*It must be great to be a cow in one of those Pullman pens,*
*With lots to eat and a jointed name like Alice of Old Vincennes;*
*To have a record of fifty pounds of milk in a single day,*
*And a college man with a big degree to slip you a shot of hay.*

*To be petted and praised by a cultured crew of learned men and great,*
*Who journey for miles at great expense to honor you at a fete,*
*That's sure some life, so when I die—and this is an honest vow,*
*I hope the Moulder will make of me a high class Jersey cow.*

Harry Burmester, recited at the dinner.

---

### Recipes

~~~

Pickled walnuts have been a favorite English condiment since the eighteenth century. The nuts were eaten as a relish, and the liquid was added to stews, as a sort of catsup.

---

### Pickled Walnuts

The fruit should be obtained before the shell is hard. Prick the walnuts with a fork, and place them in a jar filled to the top with white vinegar. They should be closely covered, so that the air is entirely kept out.

Let the walnuts stand so for two days, then, draining off the vinegar, fill the jar again, and this time let it stand a fortnight. Then place the walnuts in a jar, and cover as follows:

Add salt to the white vinegar until an egg will float in the solution. Simmer with two ounces of mace, a quarter of an ounce of cloves, the same of nutmeg, and a head of garlic that has been peeled and sliced.

Cook this mixture for twenty minutes, then, while still hot, pour it over the walnuts.

The pickle should be kept some little time before using to insure the walnuts being soft and edible.

*The Trenton Times*, October 22, 1904.

---

### Recipe for Cooking Prairie Chicken

First dip bird in scalding water so husbands will not tear bird's skin when plucking. Draw. Drench with salt water. Allow to stand 12 hours with sliced lemon inside to reduce gaminess. Before cooking, rub well with bacon fat. Cover bird with bacon strips. Put small amount of water in bottom of roaster to prevent burning, and roast at 375 degrees in covered pan. Baste during last half hour with bacon fat, and (if you have a little gypsy in you) claret or sherry.

*Winnipeg Free Press*, September 19, 1949.

---

## October 17

### Hotel Supper
#### New Denison Hotel, Indianapolis, Indiana, 1888

The menu for supper at the New Denison hotel in Indianapolis on October 17, 1888, is interesting in that it provides some insight into the vastly different social rules of the late-nineteenth century and the naming of meals in different times and places.

---

FRUIT
Bartlett Pears     Stewed Apples

—

Oyster Stew

—

BROILED
Sirloin Steak Mutton Chops Sugar Cured Ham
English Bacon Veal Cutlets
Salt Mackerel Beef Steak

—

FRIED
Fresh Fish    Bacon
Veal with Salt Pork

—

POTATOES
Saratoga    Stewed in Cream    Lyonnaise
Minced    Baked

—

EGGS
Fried    Boiled    Poached    Scrambled    Shirred

—

COLD
Roast Beef    Corned Beef    Ham    Dried Beef
Chicken Salad    Potato Salad
Beef Tongue

—

MISCELLANEOUS
Tea Rolls    Plain Bread    Graham Bread
Mush and Milk    Corn Cakes    Oat Meal
Buttered Toast
Flannel Cakes
Cheese    Cerealine    Crackers

—

HOURS FOR MEALS
Breakfast 6.30 to 10.30 Dinner 12.00 to 3.30 Supper 6.30 to 8.00
NURSES AND CHILDREN
Breakfast 7.30 Dinner 12.00 Supper 5.00 6.30

Well-to-do families who had children and needed or wanted to travel took their nurses (nannies) with them. Nurses and children took their meals at different times, which had a number of advantages to everyone else. Parents and other adults could dine in peace while the children were supervised by their nurses, and nurses of the frail or indisposed had their meals out of the way early to allow them to focus on their patients. And of course, nurses were not the same *class* of person and could not be expected to dine with those of a higher social standing.

The menu is for "supper," which at this hotel was the third meal of the day.

## Recipes

~~~

Flannel cakes or velvet cakes or crumpets are a variation on a theme of griddle cakes (hot cakes, etc.); yeast is risen like the original English muffins (see March 15). The name is related to flannen cakes or flannen biscuits. They are eaten with sausages or other meat, or with syrup etc. at the end of the meal.

## Flannel Cakes or Crumpets

Two pounds of flour, sifted. Four eggs. Three table-spoonfuls of the best brewer's yeast, or four and a half of home-made yeast. A pint of milk. Mix a tea-spoonful of salt with the flour, and set the pan before the fire. Then warm the milk and stir into it the flour, so as to make a stiff batter. Beat the eggs very light, and stir them into the yeast. Add the eggs and yeast to the batter, and beat all well together. If it is too stiff, add a little more warm milk. Cover the pan closely, and set it to rise near the fire. Bake it, when quite light. Have your baking-iron hot. Grease it, and pour on a ladle-full of batter. Let it bake slowly, and when done on one side, turn it on the other. Butter the cakes, cut them across, and send them to table hot.

## Minced Potatoes

This likewise has been a restaurant specialty and has been known as of great effect in drawing trade. It ought to be observed however, that it takes a considerable allowance of butter in the pan to give the potatoes the fine yellow-brown, and appetizing flavor that will draw the people from a distance of many blocks to breakfast or supper.

Chop cold boiled potatoes quite fine and season with salt. Spread a spoonful of drippings or butter in an omelet-pan or small frying-pan and place the minced potatoes about an inch deep. Cook on top of the range like a cake, without stirring. Invert a plate that just fits the pan over the potatoes. Let them brown nicely and slowly, then turn over on the plate. Push in the edge a little around and serve on the same plate with the brown on top. There are oval shaped pans that make these suitable for a platter, and even in the round frying-pan it can be managed to give the cake the platter shape.

Jessup Whitehead, *Cooking for Profit* (1886).

## Lyonnaise Potatoes

Three tablespoons of butter put in a frying-pan, and when the butter is melted a tablespoon of chopped onion fried till it is a pale straw-color, then add a quart of cooked potatoes, sliced, and thoroughly seasoned with salt and pepper. When they are hot a tablespoon of chopped parsley added and cooked two minutes. The onions may be omitted.

Eliza Leslie, *Seventy-five Receipts for Pastry, Cakes, and Sweetmeats* (1830).

Graham Bread: see February 5.

## October 18

### Snacking at the Siesta Drive-In Movie Theater
### Sarasota, Florida, 1959

On October 18, 1959, the Siesta drive-in movie theater in Sarasota, Florida, was showing the Academy Award-winning *Woman Obsessed*, starring

**AT OUR SNACK BAR**

CLEAN, MODERN, COURTEOUS

| | |
|---|---:|
| BUTTERBURGER, Pure, Ground Beef (and a lot of it!) | .35 |
| CHEESEBURGER, Tangy Cheese with our Pure, Ground Beef | .45 |
| HOT DOG—"Toasted to a Turn"—Zestful and Tasty | .25 |

PIZZA—OUR SPECIALTY

| | |
|---|---:|
| Made To Your Order—Big 10-inch | .75 |
| With Pepperoni | .90 |

| | |
|---|---:|
| GRILLED AMERICAN CHEESE | .35 |
| BARBEQUE BEEF Famous "Smithfield" Old Hickory Smoked | .40 |
| BARBEQUE HAMBURGER—Cooked in "Smithfield" Special Sauce | .40 |
| FRENCH FRY BOAT—Cooked Immediately to Crispy Golden Brown | .25 |
| LARGE POTATO BOAT—Enough For The Entire Family. Just | .60 |
| SHRIMP ROLL—Full of Meaty Shrimp and Seasoning, Wrapped in Egg Roll | .35 |
| HOT DEVILED CRAB ROLL—Tangy and Spicy | .25 |

CHICKEN Box Dinner—1/2 Chicken "Southern Fried"
—Served With French Fries, Hot Buttered Roll, Catsup, Sauce                    1.50

SHRIMP Box Dinner—Eight Jumbo Florida Pinks,
Served With French Fries, Hot Bun, Catsup, Tartar Sauce                    1.25

| | |
|---|---:|
| COLD DRINKS—Coca-Cola, Root Beer, Orange, Grape, | .10, .25, and .30 |
| We Use MAXWELL HOUSE Coffee—with Pure Cream | .10 & .20 |
| NESTLE'S Hot Chocolate. A Big Cup. At Your Request We Will | |
|     Add An Ounce Of Pure Cream At No Charge | .15 & .25 |
| Our Candy and Gum Vended From Machines | .01, .05, .10 |
| Cigarettes (All Your Favorite Brands) | .30 |
| ICE-CREAM—Cup, Sandwich, "On a Stick"—All | .15 |

| | |
|---|---:|
| Hot Buttered POP CORN | .15 |

For Your Convenience We Have Clean Tiled Men's and Ladies'
Lounges Located In The Main Building.

Susan Hayward, in Cinemascope, plus *Love is a Many-Splendored Thing*, starring William Holden and Jennifer Jones. Patrons could make the evening complete by purchasing treats or a full dinner from the snack bar.

The snack bar menu shows that the fast-food industry was well and truly established by this time. Most of the current modern favorites are there in one form or another, although the prices are considerably different from those today.

## Recipes
~~~

---

### Egg Rolls

Boil a quart of new milk with a quarter of a pound of butter, the same of lard, and a little salt; beat up two eggs, and pour the boiling milk on them, stirring all the time; when nearly cold, add a tea-cup of yeast, and as much wheat flour as will make a thick batter; when quite light knead it up as bread, and let it lighten before moulding out; grease the pans, and bake them with a moderate heat. A little sugar and water rubbed on just before baking rolls makes them glossy.

Elizabeth Lea, *Domestic Cookery* (1869).

---

## October 19

### Testimonial Dinner for Charles Lindbergh
### Hotel Chelsea, Atlantic City, New Jersey, 1927

Charles Lindbergh (1902–1974) became an instant hero when he piloted the first solo nonstop transatlantic flight from New York to Paris, on May 20–21, 1927, a feat for which he was awarded the Medal of Honor. It was this achievement and the resulting huge popularity with the general public that was responsible for the enormous development in the aviation industry over the next few decades. International flights suddenly became a possibility for everyone, not just a handful of wealthy enthusiasts or intrepid adventurers.

Almost immediately after his famous flight, Lindbergh embarked on a tour that took him right across the United States. He was treated as a celebrity and was banqueted wherever he went. On October 19 it was the turn of Atlantic City, where a testimonial dinner was held in his honor at the Hotel Chelsea.

---

Tomato Favorite
Clear Green Turtle, aux Quenelles
Celery        Olives        Salted Almonds
Cassolette of Lobster, Mornay

Breast of Chicken,      Virginia Ham
New Peas      Parisienne Potatoes
Endive with Orange Salad
Neapolitan Ice Cream
Cakes
Coffee

The menu shows the strange hybrid names of dishes that appeared as the move away from French as the language of choice progressed as the twentieth century wore on. The turtle soup is named in English, but it is "aux quenelles" which then looks odd. The residual French phrases sometimes represent economy of language. Classic styles of presentation, such as Parisienne in respect of the potatoes were so well known even to non-French speakers that there was no need to "translate" them—and indeed the only translation is a mini-description. The name of the potato dish is a half-translation, and the word order Anglicized by being transposed—in French the dish would be *Pommes de Terre à la Parisiènne*. Eventually French disappeared from all but the most formal menus, and the description-type menu is the modern norm.

Mornay sauce is the most interesting thing on this menu from a historic point of view. It is relatively new but documentation about its origins is scarce, and consequently there are as many stories about its provenance as there are about much older recipes. It seems to have appeared towards the end of the nineteenth century, almost certainly in France (Mornay is a French region). Mornay is based on a Béchamel (see Recipes). It is a cheese sauce, useful on everything from eggs, to vegetables, to fish.

## Recipes

~~~

### Mornay Sauce

Reduce by one-third 1 cup of Béchamel Sauce mixed with 1/2 cup cream. Add 1/2 cup grated Gruyère and Parmesan cheese, mix. Incorporate 3 tablespoons of butter and strain.

For fish, replace the cream with light chicken stock.

Adapted from *Larousse Gastronomique*, 1961 edition.

Bechamel Sauce: see January 18.
Green Turtle: see November 10.
Quenelles: see October 15.
Potatoes Parisienne: see June 23.
Neapolitan Ice Cream: see December 20.
Salted Almonds: see April 3.

## October 20

### Dinner with the British Secret Service
### Claridge's Hotel, London, England, 1944

The Special Operations Executive—Britain's wartime covert operations organization, commonly known as The Secret Service—was formed in July 1940. The mission set for it by Prime Minister Winston Churchill (1874–1965) was "to set Europe ablaze."

Ten of its senior members met on this day in 1944 over a dinner organized by Brigadier Eric Mockler-Ferryman (1896–1978), the head of operations, North West Europe. The discussion, if it was recorded at all, may still be top secret, but the menu survives. It was a fine dinner by any standards, in spite of the wartime restrictions under which the hospitality industry had to work.

---

La Supreme de Turbotine Antiboise

—

La Poularde du Surrey à la Broche
La Pomme Anna
Les Haricots Verts Frais
Le Chouxfleurs Polonaise
Le Coeur Laitues

—

La Peche Ambassadrice

—

Le Café

---

The budget allowed the Secret Service appears to have been generous. The spies would hardly have been aware of rationing, and certainly did not go thirsty. The order to the hotel Banqueting Department allowed 21 shillings a head, with "extras" being cocktails, wines, liqueurs, and cigarettes. Cocktails were three shillings and sixpence apiece ("not more than two each, or whisky if preferred"), and two bottles of St. Julien were ordered (but three eventually drunk), as well as Port and Cognac.

The letter accompanying the account is an interesting example of commercial "manners" of the time.

I beg to enclose herewith an account for the dinner held here on Friday, 20th October, and trust that you will find it correct.

I would like to point out that although you only reserved two bottles of St. Julien for the dinner, the Head Waiter took the liberty of opening and serving a third, as the two bottles were used during the two first courses. I hope that this is in order.

Thank you for your valued patronage, and always at your disposal,
I am, dear Sir,
Yours faithfully,
H. A. Van Thuyne.
General Manager.

The total bill came to £30.4.6., was paid "without demur," and an official receipt was requested by the brigadier.

## Recipes
~~~

Dishes styled "à la Polonaise," or "in the Polish style," are garnished with buttered breadcrumbs and hard boiled eggs.

---

### Chou-Fleur à la Polonaise

Cauliflower
Sieved yolk of 1 hard-boiled egg
2 oz. butter
1 heaped tablespoon dry white breadcrumbs
chopped parsley

Prepare and cook the cauliflower in the French way [i.e. cut into florets]. Heat the butter and cook crumbs to a golden brown. Dish the cauliflower, pour over the butter and crumbs, sprinkle over the egg yolk and parsley.
Constance Spry. *The Constance Spry Cookery Book* (1956).

---

Sauce Antibois (Antibes Sauce) has a mayonnaise and tomato purée base, flavored with anchovy and tarragon.
Pommes (potatoes) Anna: see June 21.

## October 21

### All-Potato Dinner
### Les Invalides, Paris, France, 1787

The French pharmacist and chemist Antoine-Augustin Parmentier (1737–1813) almost single-handedly ensured the acceptance of the potato as suitable food for humans in eighteenth-century Europe. The potato was a New World food (see October 12) and had been known about in Europe since the sixteenth century, but unlike chocolate it was a long time before it was accepted. It attracted suspicion from the beginning as it is from the highly poisonous and deadly nightshade family. Every expert soon had an opinion on its undesirability. Medical men declared it caused leprosy (because it was white), clerical men said it was an indecent Protestant vegetable that incited lust, cooks and gourmets thought it was tasteless and flatulent, and just about everyone thought it coarse fodder suitable only for pigs, prisoners, and desperate peasants.

Parmentier had personal experience that convinced him otherwise. He had joined the army in 1757 and spent several years as a prisoner of war in Germany, where potatoes were the main feature of the prison diet. He returned to France determined to promote and popularize the potato and was truly tireless and creative in his efforts. He gave a bouquet of potato flowers to

Marie Antoinette (1775–1793) which she wore in her bosom at court. He had plots of the new "secret" vegetable heavily guarded—by day only—to ensure that its value would be suspected and the plants would be pilfered at night. Finally, he held a number of dinners at which every dish was made with potatoes, and invited important and influential people. Amongst those invited at one banquet or other were Benjamin Franklin (1706–1790), who was U.S. minister to France between 1778–1785, and the aristocratic scientist Antoine Lavoisier (1743–1794).

One of the dinners took place on October 21, 1787. The artist Paul Heuzé attended, and he recorded the dishes.

> There were two soups to start with—a potato purée soup, a meat bouillon [simmered rather well with potato bread, "which did not crumble"], a matelote [fish stew] followed by a dish with a white sauce [presumably of potatoes], then another *maître d'hôtel*, and a fifth in red sauce. The second service consisted of five other dishes, not worse than the first, initially a pie, then fried, a salad, *beignets* [donuts or fritters] and a *gâteau économique* [economical cake]. The remainder of the meal included cheese, preserves, a plate of biscuits, another of tart, and finally a potato *brioche*. After that was coffee, also of potatoes. There were two kinds of bread, one a soft white bread of potato pulp and wheat, the other a firm bread of potato pulp and potato starch.

Parmentier was a man with a strong social conscience, and he was certain that the potato—being easy to grow on a small plot of land and highly nutritious—would buffer the peasant class against hard times. He succeeded, and Louis XVI supposedly said, "France will thank you some day for having found bread (i.e. potatoes) for the poor." Parmentier is honored forever in dishes given his name—which always contain potatoes—such as the well-known *potage Parmentier* (see January 12).

## Recipes
~~~

The "meat bouillon which simmered rather well with the potato bread" refers to a crust soup or *mittonage* (see April 4).

---

### Potato Bread

Boil thoroughly, and mash fine, mealy potatoes; add salt and a very little butter; rub them with twice their quantity of flour; stir in your yeast, and wet up with lukewarm milk or water, till stiff enough to mould up. It will rise quicker than common wheat bread; and it should be baked as soon as risen, for it soon sours.
   A. L. Webster, *The Improved Housewife, Or, Book of Receipts* (1853).

---

### Potato Cake

Bake eighteen large York potatoes, and when done, rub their pulp through a wire sieve; put this into a large basin, add four ounces of butter, eight ounces of sifted sugar, a spoonful of pounded vanilla, a gill of cream, the yolks of six eggs and the whipped whites of two, and a little salt; work the whole well together, and then place it in a mould previously spread with butter, and strewn with bread-crumbs; bake the cake for about an hour, and when done, dish it up with a fruit sauce poured round the base.

Charles Elmé Francatelli, *The Modern Cook* (1860).

---

### Potatoes à la Maître d'Hôtel

Wash the potatoes clean, and boil them with the skin in salt and water. When they are done, let them cool, then turn them in the shape of big corks, and cut them into slices as thick as twopenny pieces, for if the slices were too thin, they would break in the sauce. If you should have no [*Maître d'Hôtel*] sauce ready, make a butter sauce, and instead of water, moisten with milk, mix with it a little chopped parsley, pepper, salt, a little glaze, and the juice of a lemon, if acid is required. Mind that the sauce is neither curdled nor too thick.

Louis Eustache Ude, *The French Cook* (1822).

---

Maître d'Hôtel Sauce [Butter]: see September 3.

## October 22

### Women Suffragists's Dinner
### New York City, 1913

The militant English suffragette Emmeline Pankhurst (1858–1928) visited the United States in 1913 on a lecture tour. Her hostess was her American counterpart Alva Belmont (1853–1933), the socialite turned suffragist who ran a restaurant at 13 East Fortieth Street in Manhattan where women could gather in safety and talk out the issues over inexpensive meals. Newspaper editors clearly thought that Mrs. Pankhurst's choice of vegetarian food on this day was noteworthy.

---

Vegetable soup
Home-made gingerbread
Charlotte russe
Raspberry preserve
Cocoa

---

The article in *The New York Times* said,

Mrs. Pankhurst is not a vegetarian by principle, but largely so by force of circumstances, as are a great number of the English militants. In serving their terms in prison in England, one of them said yesterday, found that the vegetable food was much better than the meat, so they confined themselves entirely to it while serving their sentences, and many continued to do so afterward. Some are vegetarians by principle ... Miss Joan Wickham, Mrs. Pankhurst's agent in this country, is a vegetarian, as is Miss Elsie McKensie, an English militant, who has served a sentence in the English prisons, and is now in Mrs. Belmont's employ.

There was a common philosophical underpinning to many of the reform movements of the nineteenth century, so it was not uncommon for followers of one movement to feel sympathy with another. An individual might therefore be allied with more than one of the pacifist, temperance, suffragist, vegetarian, anti-vivisectionist, trade-union, and anti-slavery groups. Mrs. Pankhurst's choice may have another explanation, however, albeit one still related to her prison experience.

The suffragettes (as distinct from their less assertive sisters, the suffragists) were the militant arm of the women's movement in England, and as such they often fell foul of the law and were imprisoned. They continued to protest in prison by going on hunger strikes, and were then force-fed by the authorities. The result was bad publicity for the government in general, and the prison system in particular, and increasing

Mrs. Pankhurst. Courtesy of Library of Congress.

sympathy for the suffragettes. To counter this the so-called Cat and Mouse legislation was enacted in April 1913. It was more properly known as The Prisoners Temporary Discharge for Ill-Health Bill: it banned the force-feeding of prisoners and allowed their release for 15 days to enable them to recover their health, after which they were arrested again and re-imprisoned.

Emmeline Pankhurst—in her mid-fifties—had been imprisoned on over a dozen occasions in 1912–13 and had experienced the cat-and-mouse game firsthand. Her visit to America came between "games," and her choice of food on this day may represent the attraction of sweet, comfort foods to one who had experienced real hunger and poor health many times.

One of the fund-raising methods used by the Women's Suffrage movement was the production and sale of cookbooks. It was an idea that would have horrified the women's libbers of half a century later, but at the time it was a clever example of "start where you are and use what you have." The women of the early-twentieth century had, by definition, very few ways to produce an income. And what better way to spread the message subversively than via an apparently innocuous domestic text such as a cookbook?

Recipes

~~~

---

### Parliament Gingerbread

(With apologies to the English Suffragists)
1/2 lb flour
1/2 lb treacle
1 oz. butter
1/2 small spoon soda
1 dessert spoon ginger
1 dessert spoon mixed spices
1/2 cup sugar
A bit of hot water in which soda is dissolved.

Put flour in a basin, and rub in butter, and dry ingredients; then, soda and water; pour in treacle, and knead to smooth paste. Roll quite thin and cut in oblongs. Bake about 1/4 hour.

Mrs. L. O. Kleber, *The Suffrage Cook Book* (Pittsburgh: Equal Franchise Federation of Western Pennsylvania, 1915).

---

Charlotte Russe: see September 4.

## October 23

``Thousand and One Nights'' Dinner
Château de Bellevue, France, 1787

The Château de Bellevue was built for Madame de Pompadour (1721–1764), the mistress of King Louis XV (1710–1774) in 1750. On the King's death, it passed into the hands of Louis's unmarried daughters Marie-Adélaïde (1732–1800), Victoire-Louise (1733–1799), and Sophie-Philippine (1734–1782). On October 23, 1787, the surviving aunts Adélaïde and Victoire entertained their nephew King Louis XVI (1754–1793) at an entertainment they called ``Mille et Une Nuits.'' The dinner was of the usual two services (courses), and that it was as extensive and expensive as only royalty can be is obvious by the fact that the following menu is of the first service only.

---

Premier service
—
Le Dormant
Quatre hors-d'œuvre d'office

Deux potages

La garbure, la faubonne
—
Deux grosses pièces

L'aloyau à la broche—Le rot de bif de mouton de Bellevue

—

Deux relevés

—

Les Poulardes en casserole au riz—Le cochon de lait à la broche

—

Doux entreés

Le caneton de Rouen, grillé à la Mirepoix
Les perdreaux rouges du Roi, en salmis
Les filets de poulardes au beurre et en truffes
La noi de veau piquée et glacée
Les poulets gras en marinade
Les cailles en selle aux écrivisses
Les langues de bœuf à la Maréchale
Les pigeons à la Gautier en papillotes
Les lapereaux en blanquette
Les quenelles de poulardes au velouté
Les pluviers à la Bourguignotte

—

Quatre hors-d'œuvre pour le Roi
Les foies gras
Les lapereaux au gratin
Les côtelletes de mouton grillés

The even number of dishes and the symmetry of numbers were typical of grand dinners of the time. All of the elegant and expensive ingredients are here—the *foie gras*, plover, quail, suckling pig, and baby rabbit, in the most refined presentations—the meat was larded, glazed, truffled, and on skewers, *en papilotte* (see December 9). There are two slightly unusual-sounding dishes. The *ros de bif de mouton* (roast beef of mutton) sounds very strange indeed, but is explained at the menu for April 9. The *garbure* sounds close to garbage, and the word is in fact related. It refers to a thick soup of vegetables, especially cabbage and beans—a one-pot dinner—and was a staple dish for peasants. Marie Antoinette (1775–1793) famously loved playing at the country life and dressing as a shepherdess at the Trianon (see July 24), so perhaps the garbure was fashionable at the court—in an upmarket version of course.

The Thousand and One Nights was not just a dinner, it was a theatrical experience with entertainment. No doubt the participants were not aware that it was the end of an era. The storming of the Bastille that was the conscious beginning of the French Revolution was less than two years away, and on January 21, 1793, Louis XVI was dead, executed by guillotine as a traitor.

## Recipes

~~~

Garbure is a thick French country-style soup based on cabbage. Depending on wealth and circumstances it can be very simple (little else but cabbage)

or very rich due to the inclusion of such things as goose and duck fat or ham or other meats. The royal family of France would have been more likely to have the expensive version, such as in the following recipe from *The French Cook ... Adapted to the Use of English Families* written by Louis Eustache Ude in 1829.

---

### The Garbure, with Brown Bread

Take a knuckle of ham, perfectly sweet, a knuckle of veal, and about six pounds of flank of beef, which put into a pan, with an onion stuck with two cloves, a few carrots, &c.; pour over the above two ladles of broth, and let the whole sweat over a slow fire. When the meat is done through the middle, cover it entirely with boiling broth, and let the whole stew for three hours. Then take one or more cabbages, which are to be washed clean and blanched. Braize them between layers of bacon, and moisten them with the liquor in which the sweating has been made, strained through a silk sieve. You must observe, that if the cabbages are not made rich and mellow, they are good for nothing. Add to the above, either sausages, bacon, or stewed legs of geese: mind above all things that the cabbage be not too briny, for the soup then would not be eatable. When the cabbage and broth are stewed enough, cut very thin slices of rye-bread: drain the cabbage in a cloth, so that there be no fat left, then take a large deep silver dish, lay a bed of bread, and over that, one of cabbage, and moisten them with a little broth; let them stew on a slow fire. When the cabbage and bread are sufficiently moistened, lay on six or eight beds more of each, and let it simmer on the stove. Send up with the ham on the middle; the bacon, the legs of geese, and sausages on the borders, and some broth separately*.

*This soup is never seen in this country [England]; it requires a very deep and very large dish.

---

## October 24

### Medical Dinner
### Bergen, Norway, 1891

Theme menus seem to be popular amongst professional groups at conferences. There is none so apparently repulsive and obscure as the one for a dinner held by a group of medical doctors (probably obstetricians) in Bergen in 1891.

The menu items themselves are written in Latin, and the document is rich with puns and other word plays. It is certain that it demonstrates the sort of black or "gallows" humor common amongst those who work in areas where human distress or disease is prominent.

---

*Aabnings
-tidsrummet*

Liquor ptomaini
*Madeira*

—

Filaria phlyndroica

Furiones viciles
*Chât. Grillet*

—

*Udsidnings – og*
*fremgangstidarummet*

Rupia, not luetica, ut
pasta servata
*Fleury*

—

Lingua, nates
*Ol et Dram*

—

*Udskjæringstidsrummet*
Fas-i-anus
Psoas in pure bono et
laudabile servata
*Chât. La Laguna*

—

*Efterbyrd*
Peri-Ost, Panis & foetus
*Champagne Moet et Chandon*

(OBS)COENA MEDICORUM

[pig illustration]

The linguistic aspects of the menu could be fodder for some long and interesting discussions between linguists and culinary historians, but ultimately it is impossible to know what exactly the dishes were at this dinner.

The meal began with *Aabningstidsrummet*—from *aabnings* meaning "opening" or bodily orifice (presumably the intended meaning here), and *tidsrummet* means period, so "time for openings"—in other words the first course. This was a *liquor* (a liquid—a cocktail or a soup, perhaps), called *Ptomaine*—an indefinite word meaning something highly toxic and often used to refer to a particularly virulent form of food poisoning. The other dish in this course is *Filariae*—parasitic worms such as those causing Elephantiasis—perhaps a joke name for a dish of eels, or noodles? In the second course are *Nates* (buttocks, or rump?) and *Lingae* (tongues)—probably some innocuous cold meats. There is also a very repulsive-sounding dish. *Rupia* are pus-filled eruptions that are particularly associated with syphilis, although the menu thankfully specifies that these are *non luetica*—that is, not syphilitic. Whatever this represented, it was served with pasta.

The Fas-i-anus may be a play on the Latin for pheasant—*fasianus*. The *psoas* is a large muscle in the lumbar region, so the dish was probably a large piece of meat from the back of an animal—a cut such as a chine (see January 2) or saddle perhaps. Whatever it was it was served plain, good, and with great praise. A final word play is the peri-ost. *Periosteum* is the fibrous sheath that covers bone (*peri* meaning around), but *ost* is cheese, so this course represented the cheese and what was served around it. The *panis* is straight-forward, as it means bread, but the *foetus* represents some sort of joke no doubt obvious to the guests at the dinner. Perhaps some sort of dish of eggs? Perhaps fish eggs such as caviar?

That this menu was for a dinner of obstetricians is suggested by the final course—the *Efterbyrd* or afterbirth (which includes the mysterious *foetus*), and the "Obs" in front of Coena (supper)—which also suggests things "obscene." Most bizarrely, there is a drawing of a pig below this phrase, at the bottom of the menu.

## Recipes
~~~

Bread is the only menu item that has avoided being made into a joke or word play.

---

### Nordskbröd (Norway Bread)

... is made either entirely of rye flour, or of barley with a third part rye. The dough is prepared with cold water, and kneaded a long while till it does not stick to the hands. Afterwards it is flattened with a rolling-pin of a round shape, but furrowed longitudinally, which is turned by the hands as fast as possible. The edges of the dough, thus spread out, are repeatedly turned in, and the whole laid carefully on a table, though smoothed with such a rolling pin. It is baked on an iron made on purpose, being moved about and turned during the process, and subsequently smoothed and polished with a bunch of the heads of rye straw dipped in water.

Carl von Linné, *Lachesis Lapponica, or a Tour in Lapland* (written in 1732; published in 1811 by the Linnaean Society).

---

## October 25

### Dinner for the Royal Horse Guards
### Town Hall, Holborn, London, England, 1882

The Royal Horse Guards were entertained at dinner on the night of October 25, 1882, by the residents of the Albany-street barracks. Many of the men had recently returned from the campaign in Egypt, which was of great strategic and economic importance to Britain. Egypt was unstable following the completion of the Suez Canal, and Britain was intent on protecting its interests there.

The original plan had been to hold the dinner in a great marquee set up in the barracks' square, but it blew down in a storm the previous day, necessitating a last minute move to the Town Hall building. Of the 750 men who sat down to this dinner, 400 were troops.

The meal was described in *The Times* newspaper:

The *menu* was suggestive of the occasion. After "the roast beef of Old England" came "Egyptian boar's head," then Kassassin slices, bastions of galantine à *l'Alexandria*, Arabi brawn, Wolseley's Cairo game pie, some roast venison, the gift of Lord Fitzhardinge, rounds of Scotch beef, pyramids of briskets, Cumberland hams, English fighting cocks, Tel-el-Kebir salad, and "Household" plum pudding.

The menu card itself may have been suggestive of the specific occasion, but undoubtedly the actual dishes served were the same as at any other similar dinner of the time. The British had a reputation for meat-heavy meals, and this was never more true than in the case of dinners for military men. The names given to the dishes were in honor of the campaign, the dishes themselves would almost certainly have been very simple—mostly plain roasts and a few prepare-ahead dishes such as game pie, brawn (see February 23), and a galantine (jellied meat, see June 19).

The boar's head since medieval times had traditionally represented the head of Satan (see January 4). On this occasion it was clearly symbolic of defeat of the earthly enemy of the British. The "fighting cocks" would certainly have been in name only—true fighting birds were not bred for eating and made a poor feed. The dish was undoubtedly an ordinary chicken dish; choosing to name them in this way on the menu was in tribute to the fighting men of the battalion.

The names of several dishes were in acknowledgement of the campaign. "Wolseley" was Lord Wolseley (1833–1913), commander of the British forces in Egypt and the most famous British soldier of the time. He is considered to be the inspiration for Gilbert and Sullivan's "very model of a modern Major-General" in their comic opera *The Pirates of Penzance*. Tel-el-Kebir and Kassassin were the sites of famous battles, and Alexandria is the major seaport of Egypt and was the point of entry of the British in July 1882.

## Recipes
~~~

Game pie has been made essentially the same way since medieval times. It is a "raised" pie—that is, it is made with a special hot water crust pastry that can be "raised" or molded like clay into a freestanding crust (or "coffin"). In more recent times the pastry was used to line shaped metal molds, some of which were very elaborate indeed. The pastry when made very thick and hard—so long as it did not get damp or cracked and remained airtight—would keep the contents edible for long periods, which was important in the days before refrigeration. The instructions seem fairly lengthy but raised pies are of such historic interest, and appear in so many menus in this book, that they are worthy of consideration. Obviously the exact filling can be as varied as circumstances allow, but the pastry has been made the same way for hundreds of years.

### Game (Raised Pie of)

2 brace of partridges, grouse, or other birds,
forcemeat [below],

raised crust [see November 3] made with 1 Ib. flour, and other ingredients in
proportion,
1/2 pint gravy jelly [i.e. thick gellied stock],
2 hard-boiled eggs,
seasoning pepper and salt,
yolk of an egg.

Butter a raised pie-mould and line it with crust, reserving sufficient for the
cover. Spread a very thin layer of forcemeat at the bottom of the pie, and place
on it some of the pieces of game, which must be cut into small neat joints, sprinkle them with pepper and salt, and build the pie up in a dome shape, filling the
interstices with more forcemeat until all the pieces are used. Cut the eggs into
slices, lay them round the edge of the pie, and pour in the gravy jelly, which must
be warmed just enough to become liquid. Roll out the cover, place it on top, fasten the edges together securely, and ornament them neatly. Make a wreath of
small pastry leaves, and decorate the top of the pie with these, slightly moisten-
ing their underside, that they may adhere properly. Brush the pie with a pastry-
brush dipped in beaten egg-yolk, and bake in a good oven for 3 hours. A buttered
paper should be laid over the top of the pie to protect the crust as soon as the pie
is nicely coloured. The pie should be left in its mould until cold, when the mould
must be carefully undone and lifted away, and the pie garnished with very fresh
parsley before it is sent to table. If liked, the lid of the pie may be removed, and
replaced by a thick layer of very fresh and delicately made aspic, lightly chopped.

## Forcemeat (For Cold Savoury Pies)

1/2 Ib. lean raw veal,
1/4 Ib. fat bacon,
2 oz. butter,
yolks of 2 eggs,
panada [below] made with 1/4 Ib. breadcrumbs, and other ingredients in proportion,
seasoning pepper and salt.

Remove all skin and fat from the veal, cut it and the bacon into dice, and
pound them to a smooth paste with the butter; then add the panada and pound
again, add the yolks of the eggs, season with pepper and salt, mix well, and
pound until perfectly smooth, then rub the whole through a fine sieve, and it is
ready for use.

## Panada

4 oz. fresh breadcrumbs
1/4 pint light veal stock,
1/4 pint cream.

Have the breadcrumbs in a basin, pour the veal stock, which must be boiling,
over them, cover, and let them remain 1/2 an hour, then turn the soaked bread
into a very clean cloth, and wring it well to press out the liquid. Put the bread

into a lined saucepan, pour the cream on it, and stir them constantly with a
wooden spoon over a gentle fire until the cream is absorbed and the panada
forms a dryish paste, adheres to the spoon, and leaves the sides of the saucepan.
It is then ready to be used where directed.
  Ethel Myer, *A Practical Dictionary of Cookery: 1200 Recipes* (London, 1898).

Brawn: see April 28.

## October 26

### French Exhibition Banquet
### Hotel du Louvre, Paris, France, 1867

The second half of the nineteenth century saw a series of international expositions, and the competition was particularly fierce between England and
France in the wake of the huge success of London's Great Exhibition of
1851. After the London Exhibition of 1862, it was again France's turn with
the Paris Universal Exposition of 1867.

In the last few days of the exposition a banquet was held at the Hotel du
Louvre. The 320 guests included ladies, although it was unusual at the time
for women to attend public banquets. In spite of the beautiful venue, the
impressive guest list, and the obvious attention to detail, it seems that the
banquet was not an unqualified success. *The Times* reporter noted:

> Amongst the decorations of the table not the least brilliant was the bill of fare
> itself—a beautiful work of De La Rue, in gold and colours, about as broad and
> long as an alderman's back, and if the waiters had only kept the word of its
> promise to the eye to any considerable degree there would have been a feast wor-
> thy of Belshazzar, although it may be that the guests ought to be thankful they
> had not occasion to tempt their stomachs with all the various dishes and culi-
> nary combinations set forth on the broad sheet before them when cool reflection
> and cool heads came in the morning. Here is the text of the document that was
> perused with such abortive interest and expectancy.

1. Hors d'Œuvres—Huitres "Natives" Angleterre; Huitres d'Ostende, Belgique;
St. Peray, France; Rüdesheimer Hinterhaus, Allemagne; Salade d'Anchois, Ita-
lie; Saucisson de Nuremberg, Allemagne; Harengs, Hollande; Caviar, Russie;
Crevettes, Angleterre; Olives, Espagne; Pickles, Indes Orientales; Pain de
Vienne de Toutes Espèces.

2. Potages—A l'Impératrice, France; Tortue à l'Anglaise; Russe à la Purée de
Gibiere; Sauterne, France; Punch Glacé à l'Anglaise; Madère, Portugal; Xérès,
Espagne; Moselle Mousseu Sharzhofberger, Allemagne.

3. Relevés—Filets de Sole à la Normande, France; Turbot Sauce Hollandaise et
Ecrivisses, Hollande; Rougets Grillés de Malte, Angleterre; Château d'Yquem,
France; Steinberger Cabinet, Allemagne; Dindes, des Mans à la Royale, France;
Roast Beef, Angleterre; Haunches of Venison, Angleterre; Chambertin, France;
Vöslau, Autriche.

4. Entrées—Côtelettes de Pré-sale aux Pointes d'Asperges, France; Pilaff de Volaille, Turquie; Jambon de Westphalie, Allemagne; Carrick de Crevettes, Indes Orientales; Salmis de Bartavelles, Espagne; Timballe de Macaroni, Italie; Côtelettes de Homards, Amérique; Poitrine d'Oie, Choux Rouge de Vienne, Autriche; Champagne, Cliquot, France; Montrachet, France; Rauenthaler Berg, 1862, Allemagne; Sorbet à la Romaine.

5. Rôts—Poulardes Truffées, France; Faisans de Boheme, Autriche; Grousse d'Ecosse, Angleterre; Becasses, Angleterre; Gelinottes et Coqs de Bois, Russie; Salades Diverses, France; Ermitage blanc, 1846, France; Château Margaux, 1858, France; Schloss Johannisberg, 1862, Allemagne.

6. Entremets—Petits Pois, France; Artichauts de Catalogne, Espagne; Plum Pudding, Angleterre; Bavaroise aux Pistaches, Bavière; Gelée au Marasquin, France: Bombe Italienne, Italie; Glaces; Château Lafitte, Retour des Indes, France.

7. Dessert—Fruits, Biscuits, Gateaux, Fromages; Porto Royal blanc, Portugal; Tokai, Hongrie; Lacrima Christi, Italie; Liqueurs de tous les Pays; Café, Turquie; Cigars, La Havane; Vevey Fins, Suisse; Cigarettes, Russie.

There had clearly been a great deal of attention given to sourcing the food from the individual countries that had participated (16 represented in the menu), but insufficient quantities had been allowed—an unforgiveable situation for such a prestigious event. The newspaper went on to say

...the dining commenced and continued for a long time. Perhaps the nations feasted on their own comestibles, so that the Russians had all the gelinottes, the Austrians the Bohemian pheasants, the Indians the curried prawns, the Italians the macaroni timbals, the Germans the Westphalia hams and the English their roast beef and plum pudding, but "Brun, Chef de Cuisine" took liberties with the latter delicacy in form and subtance quite out of bounds, and demands for various viands were met by the assurance that there were no more.

## Recipes

~~~

In all of the varied dishes from so many countries, one dish at this banquet would have been at home at any English or European table since medieval times. The *Pain de Vienne de Toutes Espèces* (Viennese spice bread) is essentially a type of gingerbread. Gingerbread is one of the oldest sweets known, and the recipe is almost infinitely variable, yet still remains recognizable. In its earliest form it was a thick dry paste of breadcrumbs (and sometimes ground almonds), honey, and spices. Over the centuries it changed to become a yeast-risen sweet bread, and after the development of baking powders in the early-nineteenth century into the "cake" that is known today.

### Pain d'Epices

Mix some flour with some honey and a little orange-flower water; add some yeast, ginger, and allspice, and make it into dough and knead it well; let it rise an hour in a warm place, then make it into cakes of different sizes; bake them; when cold they are fit for use. They require to be well kneaded.

Frances Crawford, *French Confectionary Adapted for English Families* (1853).

Turtle Soup: November 10.
Hollandaise Sauce: see April 14.

## October 27

### Dinner with a Tibetan Monk
### Gyantsé, Tibet, 1936

In July 1936 British career diplomat Basil Gould (1883–1956) was asked to head a mission to Tibet to assist with the finding of a peaceful solution to the internal conflict in the country. Tibet had been without a spiritual leader for three years, since the death of the thirteenth Dalai Lama in 1933 (his replacement, the current Dalai Lama was not chosen until 1937, as a two-year old), and the Regent Panchen Lama was at odds with the Tibetan government, who considered him to be the protégé of the ruling Chinese.

The official diary of the mission was kept by the photographer Frederick Spencer Chapman (1907–1971), and on October 27 he noted "We all lunched with the Chikyab Khempo ["Lord Chamberlain"], a mild and courteous white haired monk who is the head of the Ecclesiastical party." He attached the bill of fare to the diary.

Tibetan or Chinese names of dishes.

On arrival—Indian tea with Jacob's biscuits and hard dried apricots.

Later—Bowl containing three sweet rose-flavoured dumplings in warm sweet milk. (Tung-yan.) Chopsticks, and squares of Tibetan paper on which to put the chopsticks, were provided and renewed after this course.

After another interval many small dishes were put on the table. These contained:

Stewed mutton in gravy with onion and carrots.
Tinned herrings.
Halved green peaches.
Stewed peaches.
Tinned pineapple slices.
Dried dates.
Chinese sweets. (Koten)
Melon seeds.
Peanuts.
Mongolian ham.
Yak tongue.
Pressed beef.
Plain beef.

Small dishes of sauce and a Chinese spoon were brought for the above and were retained for the rest of the meal. (Tsu-de':)

A Continuous supply of chang (Tibetan barley-beer) was provided.

Then the main course followed. The above small dishes were left on the table until the last course (15th) appeared and there was no longer room for them.

These courses appeared in one or two large China bowls which were put in the middle of the table so that each person could take what he wanted with his chopsticks or spoon.

The dumplings (courses 3, 6, 9, 14)—two or three on a small dish—were brought round to each guest.

1. Shark's fins and minced mutton in gravy. (Yu-ti.)
2. Fine mince rolled in butter with vermicelli, celery and cabbage. (Chi chou.)
3. Firm mince meat in pastry. (Sha-pa-le.)
4. Slices of a very firm fleshed fish (rather like tunny) with onion, carrot, and boiled bacon. (Bou-yu.)
5. Sea slugs in soup, with boiled pork. (Hay-sing.)
6. Round meat dumplings. (Rupoutsi.)
7. Green peas and mince. (Tre-ma.)
8. Hard boiled eggs, quartered and attached to a similar quarter of mince, in sauce. (Bo-bo-yun-tse.)
9. Pastry dumplings. (Chou-tse.)
10. Bamboo roots with boiled pork in soup. (Sin-tse.)
11. Eels in Soup with pork and Onion. (Chang-yow-tse.)
12. Rice with raisins, cherries, etc. (chu-mi).
13. Small squares of sweet fried bread.
14. Jam dumplings with sponge cake. (Meko-pin lama cow.)
15. (a) Shark's stomach. (Yuto) (b) Boiled Pork and carrot. (Hlobay) (c) Minced yak. (Teru) (d) Pieces of mutton. (Hor-ru) (e) Steamed rice with four varieties of white bread-pastry in the form of flowers, peaches horse-shoes and also soup. (Ti-mo-mo)

The range of natural food resources in Tibet itself is very restricted due to the high altitude and cold climate. The basic diet is based on barley, particularly in the form of *tsampa* (toasted flour), and the products of the yak, especially yak milk and butter. There are few vegetables. Imported tea is an essential luxury and is mixed with yak butter to make *tsocha* (buttered tea). There are few vegetables and no fish.

The menu for this seven-hour lunch (and discussion) shows the Chinese influence and the large range of imported foods. Theos Bernard (1908–1947), an American student of yoga and Tibetan Buddhism who met with Gould later, made the point in his book *Penthouse of the Gods* that

> A meal such as this is, of course, to be had only in the homes of the wealthy; for most of these ingredients have to be imported from India and China, and some of them come in sealed tins. But these importations are no more extraordinary than our own from Europe or from the Orient.

The round meat dumplings that Chapman called *rupoutsi* may have been the same as *momo*, the well-known steamed Tibetan dumplings filled with finely ground meat and vegetables.

---

### Sea-Slugs or Beche de Mer
#### (*Holuthuria* species)

The Trepang, biche de Mer, Morntia, balaté, or sea snail, is, like the birds nests, found principally upon the reefs of the Paracels and Malay islands. The trepang is brought up by divers, and the preparation consists in opening and cleaning them, then boiling, and, finally, smoking them with green wood.

James Hingston Tuckey, *Maritime Geography and Statistics* (London 1815).

Bêche-de-mer requires extended soaking before cleaning and use, and has a jelly-like texture, a fishy odor, and little taste. Though it may serve as the main ingredient in a Chinese soup or stew, its role is that of imparting and harmonizing the flavors of other ingredients. Recipes for its preparation are legion.

Frederick J. Simmons, *Food in China* (1991) .

---

### Recipes
~~~

---

### Tibetan Buttered Tea

The tea is made in two different ways; first as an infusion with hot water, as in Europe, and this preparation is called Cha-chosh "tea water"; secondly in a very peculiar manner, which I will describe in detail from a recipe obtained by my brothers at Leh:

The tea—loosened brick-tea—is mixed with nearly half its volume of soda, in Tibetan called Phuli. The mixture is then thrown into a kettle filled with the necessary quantity of cold water, the proportion varying as in our mode of making tea. When the water is about to boil, the mixture of tea leaves and soda is stirred, an operation continued four to six minutes after the boiling of the water. The kettle is then removed from the fire and the tea is filtered through a cloth into a round, wooden cylinder about three to four inches in diameter and two to three feet high; the tea leaves are generally considered as useless and are thrown away. The tea is vigorously queried in a wooden tub (called in Tibetan Gurgur), like chocolate; a large amount of clarified butter is then added (generally double the quantity of the brick tea), and some salt; when the operation of querling is continued. Finally the tea is again thrown into a kettle, mixed with milk, and heated anew, as it has generally greatly cooled down during all the operations just described. This tea, called "Cha," strongly resembles a kind of gruel, and is taken, together with meat or pastry, at dinner or supper; but it is not allowed to be taken during the performance of religious ceremonies, when tea-water alone, Cha-chosh, is handed round as refreshment.

Emil Schlagenweit, *Buddhism in Tibet* (1863).

---

Sharks' Fin: see March 8.
Chinese Steamed Bread: see September 1.

## October 28

### Dinner of the Worshipful Company of Wax Chandlers
### Newcastle-upon-Tyne, England, 1478

A livery company is an occupational guild or trade association, and many of them have very ancient roots. Some, such as the Worshipful Company of Wax Chandlers, which began in 1358, continue to exist only as charitable institutions, and some have been granted their charter as recently as the end of the twentieth century. In 1515 when the existing 48 livery companies were listed in order of importance, the wax-chandlers came out at number 20, just ahead of the tallow-chandlers, reflecting the status of the two sorts of candles—fine beeswax for the church and noble households, and tallow candles made from fat for the ordinary home.

In Newcastle-upon-Tyne in the northeast of England in the fifteenth century, both groups of chandlers were combined with the Barber-Surgeons. On Lord Mayor's Day in 1478, 124 men from the combined companies sat down to their annual dinner, at a total cost of seven shillings and sixpence.

---

Two loins of veal
Two loins of mutton
One loin of beef
One leg of mutton
One dozen pigeons
One dozen rabbits
One pig
One capon
One goose
100 Eggs
2 gallons of wine
1 kilderkin of ale

---

At first glance at this bill of fare, there is no indication of the actual method of cooking of each of the dishes. It seems likely that the meats were simply roasted or boiled. The eggs are more of a mystery, as custards or similar dishes in which they might have been used are not on the menu—and with 124 guests, there was not one egg per person. The shortfall was not as great as it seems, however, as "a hundred" in this instance actually meant 120 eggs. Up until the eighteenth century, a "hundred" had different meanings depending on the commodity being discussed. A "short hundred" was the number recognized today, but there was also a measure called the "long hundred" which was usually six score (120), but occasionally nine score, or even 124. The "long hundred" applied particularly to fish, as well as eggs.

There are other traps in trying to determine from historic menus or provisions lists the amounts of a particular item served. A gallon, for example, is not, and has never been, a fixed amount, but varies from country to country and time to time, and also varies according to whether a dry or wet material is being measured. Also, some ancient units of measurements are now obsolete, such as the "kilderkin" in this bill of fare. A kilderkin was a cask of a specific capacity, but again the exact amount depended on the commodity. By a statute of 1531 a kilderkin of beer was 18 gallons, of ale 16 gallons, and of butter 112 pounds.

There would have been no confusion for the medieval provider, who would have known exactly how many articles he would receive for each commodity.

## Recipes
~~~

---

### Pegions Stewed

To mak pegions stewed hew pegions small and put them in an erthen pot then tak erbes and pilled garlike and chope them to gedur and put them in good brothe put ther to whit grece poudur and vergious colour it with saffron and salt it and stew it well and serue it.

---

### Capon or Goos Roste

To rost capon or gose tak and drawe his leuer and his guttes at the vent and his grece at the gorge and tak the leef of grece parsly ysope rosmarye and ij lengs of saige and put to the grece and hew it smale and hew yolks of eggs cromed raissins of corans good poudurs saffron and salt melled to gedure and fers the capon there withe and broche hym and let hym be stanche at the vent and at the gorge that the stuffur go not out and rost hym long with a soking fyere and kep the grece that fallithe to baist hym and kepe hym moist till ye serue hym and sauce hym with wyne and guingere as capons be.

*A Noble Boke off Cookry ffor a Prynce Houssolde or Eny Other Estately Houssolde* (ca. 1500).

---

Cony Roste (roast rabbit): see August 16.

## October 29

### Dinner for the Worshipful Company of Barbers and Surgeons
### The Barber-Surgeons Hall, Monkwell Square, London, England, 1742

In medieval times there was no real distinction between the occupations of barbers and surgeons (see October 28)—they were one and the same thing. When the Barbers' Company was formed in 1461, it was they who performed surgery. Some time later a group that was particularly concerned with the more serious surgical operations, such as amputations, split off into a voluntary society called the Company of Surgeons of London. Barbers continued to perform minor procedures such as bloodletting (a common cure-all), lancing abscesses and pulling teeth. In 1540 the two groups were combined again into the Company of Barber-Surgeons—it still being considered that they were two halves of the same profession. This professional guild continued until they were formally separated again in 1745.

Three years before the two professional groups went their separate ways, on Lord Mayor's Day (October 29) in 1742, the bill of fare (and costs) for the Worshipful Company of Barbers and Surgeons annual dinner was as follows:

|  | £ | s | d |
|---|---|---|---|
| Seventeen Dishes of Fowles, Oysters, Sauceages and Bacon. | 8 | 1 | 6 |
| Three Large Sir Loynes of Beef. | 1 | 16 | 0 |
| Eleven Tongues, Eleven Udders. | 3 | 6 | 0 |
| Eleven Cock Turkeys and Sauce. | 3 | 1 | 6 |
| Eight Chines, Sauce, and Dressing. | 2 | 4 | 0 |
| Twelve Geese and Sauce. | 2 | 8 | 0 |
| Twelve Dishes of Mincepyes. | 3 | 0 | 0 |
| Eleven Custards and Florindines. | 2 | 4 | 0 |
| Three Dishes of Chickens, three each. | 0 | 15 | 0 |
| Nine Dishes of Rabitts, two each. | 1 | 4 | 0 |
| Nine Dishes of Chickens, three each. | 1 | 7 | 0 |
| Twelve Large Pippin Tarts. | 2 | 8 | 0 |
| For the Musicks [Musicians] dinner | 0 | 0 | 5 |
| For Wood and Coales | 0 | 12 | 0 |
|  | 33 | 2 | 0 |

This was a typical English corporate or other formal dinner of the time—lots of meat, and several choices of pies and tarts. The particular way that the "sirloin" is recorded is interesting. There is a popular belief that the sirloin got its name when a particularly impressive "joint of goodly presence" was ceremonially given a knighthood—thus becoming "Sir Loin"—by either King Henry VIII, or James I, or Charles II, depending on the source of the story. However, the sirloin is simply "above the loin"—*sur longe* in French. Many food words in English show the enduring legacy of that French invasion in 1066. Words for livestock retained their English roots, for example, cows and pigs—yet the words for the food derived from those animals show the French influence—beef (*boeuf*) and pork (*porc*). The English aristocracy, who were reared to speak French for hundreds of years after the Norman conquest—did not need to know, nor presumably did they care, what the live animals were called that were the source of their meat—that was the job of peasants and farmers.

## Recipes

~~~

"Pippins" are old-fashioned apples. The word was generally applied to particularly late-harvest apples with good flavor and good keeping qualities.

---

Pippin-Tart

Cut some Golden-pippins in Halves, pare them, and take out the Cores; and stew them with half their Weight of Sugar, and some Lemmon-peel cut in thin long Slices, and Water enough to cover them. When they are clear, they are enough; then set them by to cool, and strain off the Liquor, or Syrup, and put that in a Pan to stew gentl, with some candied Lemon and Orange-peel in Slices; then have a sweet Paste prepared in a Dish, and lay in your Pippins, and bake them in a gently Oven; and when it is hot, pour in some Cream, either pure or artificial, and serve them to the Table.

Richard Bradley, *The Country Housewife and Lady's Director* (1732).

---

Mince Pies: see January 9.
Florindines (Florentines): see September 13.
Udder: see November 1.

## October 30

### Dinner with Sir Morton Peto
### Delmonico's, New York, 1865

Sir Morton Peto (1809–1889) was an English railway entrepreneur, and it was only natural that he would be drawn to visit the United States, where the railway system was expanding at an enormous rate in the second half of the nineteenth century. The time came to be known as the "Gilded Age" because of the vast amount of wealth that was generated during the post-Civil War reconstruction, and the very conspicuous consumption that accompanied it.

At the end of his visit, Peto entertained his American friends and contacts at a splendid banquet at Delmonico's—the finest restaurant in New York, thanks in no small part to its famous chef Charles Ranhofer (1836–1899). When an extraordinarily wealthy man presents a *carte blanche* to the gifted chef of a top-class restaurant to provide a dinner for 250 guests, the result must be spectacular. Even the menu was printed in gold leaf on satin. The cost was reported to be $200 a head (at a time when the average wage was $5 a week), for which the restaurant provided the following bill of fare.

---

MENU.
*Barsac.*    Huitres.

POTAGES.
*Xérès F.S. 1815.*    Consommé Britannia.
Purée à la Derby.

HORS D'ŒUVRE. Variés
Cassolettes de foies-gras    Timbales à l'écarlate.

## POISSONS.

*Steinberger Cabinet.*     Saumon à la Rothschild.

Grenadins de bass, New York.

## RELEVÉS.

*Champagne Napoleon.*     Chapons truffés.

Filet de bœuf à la Durham.

## ENTRÉES.

*Château Latour.*     Faisans à la Londonderry.

Côtelettess d'Agneau Primatice.

Cromesquis de volaille à la purée de marrons.

Aiguillettes de canards à la bigarade.

Rissolettes à la Pompadour.

## ENTRÉES FROIDS.

*Côtes Rôtis.*     Volière de gibier.

Ballotines d'anguilles en Bellevue.

Chaudfroid de rouges-gorges à la Bohémienne.

Buisson de ris d'agneau Pascaline.

*Sorbet à la Sir Morton Peto.*

## RÔTIS.

*Clos-Vougeot.*     Selle de chevreuil, sauce au vin de Porto groseilles.

Bécassés bardés

## ENTREMETS.

Choux de Bruxelles     Haricots Verts.

Artichauts farcis.     Petits Pois.

## SUCRÉS.

*Tokai Imperial.*     Pouding de poires à la Madison.

Lousiannais à l'ananas.

Gelée aux fruits     Pain d'abricot à la vanille.

Muscovite fouettée.     Gelée Indienne.

Vacherin au marasquin.     Cougloff aux amandes.

Mazarin au pêches.     Mousse à l'orange.

Caisses jardinière.     Glacées assorties.

Fruits et Desserts.

## PIÈCES MONTÉES.

| | |
|---|---|
| *Madère Faquart.* | Cascade Pyramidale. |
| Corbeille arabesque. | Ruines de Poëstum. |
| Le Palmier. | Trophée militaire. |
| Corne d'abondance. | Nougat à la Parisienne |

The newspapermen ran out of superlatives in describing the "sumptuous richness and elegance of the banquet." The decorations included a floral mosaic of the "Star-Spangled Banner" and the Union Jack, the table service was the one made especially for the Prince of Wales' visit in 1860, the men were "brave" and the women were "fair" (it was most unusual for women to dine in public at the time), and the music charming. The food, of course, was perfect.

Ironically, the following year Peto was a victim of the financial crisis of 1866, was declared bankrupt, and lost his seat in Parliament.

## Recipes

~~~

Charles Ranhofer was the chef at Delmonico's from 1862–1876 and again from 1879–1896. His comprehensive cookbook *The Epicurean* was published in 1894 and remains a classic. The recipes are from the classic French repertoire and most are complex and are built on multiple subsidiary preparations (stocks, sauces, farces, etc.).

---

### Rissolettes

[Basic] Rissolettes are made with very thin pancakes, cutting them into round pieces two and a half inches in diameter, the salpicon ball to be an inch; they are fastened together by a string of chicken forcemeat [see October 15 for a simple version], a quarter of an inch thick, and laid on one-half of the circles. The paste for the pancakes is composed of half a pound of flour, stirring gradually into it, five eggs, a little milk, salt and two ounces of melted butter; the paste must be liquid. Put some clarified butter into small frying pans, add a little of the paste and spread it around so as to form very thin pancakes; when done lay them on a cloth, and cut from them with a round two and a half inch in diameter pastry cutter, pieces for the rissolettes.

---

### Rissolettes à la Pompadour

Have a small Julienne salpicon of beef palate and mushrooms mixed with a little well-reduced and well-seasoned béchamel [see January 18 for a basic version] set into a vessel to get cold. Make a ball of this preparation one inch in diameter, and lay it on the center of one of the pancake rounds, two and a half inches wide;

> fold the pancake and fasten the two edges together with a string of chicken que-
> nelle forcemeat; dip them in eggs and bread-crumbs and fry them to a fine color.
> Serve on folded napkins.

Saumon à la Rothschild is salmon poached in champagne with truffles.
Chaud-Froid: see July 25.

## October 31

### Dinner for the Palace Workmen
### King's Hall Restaurant, Holborn, London, England, 1913

In 1913 the whole façade of Buckingham Palace was remodeled in the astonishingly short period of 13 weeks—which included the removal of the scaf-
folding and cleaning up of the forecourt. King George V (1865–1936) gave
"personal directions" for a dinner to be given for everyone who had had a
part in the work, in gratitude for their "remarkable achievement" and also
as "a well-deserved tribute to the craft and discipline of British workmanship." A total of 500 guests attended the dinner, at one of the largest dining
rooms in London, although the King and Queen were, regretfully, unable to
be present themselves.

*The Times* reporter noted that "the spirit of the entertainment was simple
and sincere. . . . There was no ceremony or formality." The workmen came
"in their best clothes, and though black coats and linen collars were predomi-
nant, many were to be seen in tweeds, corduroys, and woollen mufflers, for
there were labourers of all kinds in the company as well as masons and carv-
ers." The men sat down at tables decorated with smilax and chrysanthe-
mums, to a "substantial British dinner." It was undoubtedly a dinner such
as many if not most of the men had never had in their lives.

---

Scotch Broth.
Boiled Turbot with Hollandaise Sauce.
Roast Saddle of Mutton.
Roast Beef.
Baked Potatoes.
Brussels Sprouts.
Cauliflower.
Saxon Pudding.
Dessert.

---

The beverage offered was an "abundant supply of good ale," but the newspaper reporter noted that "quite a considerable number of the men drank
water or mineral water." After the dinner, pipes and tobacco were handed
around, the tobacco packets being specially printed with the Royal Arms in
gilt and the words "From H. M. the King, 31st October, 1913"; these were
observed to be greatly appreciated as mementoes of the occasion. Finally,

there was musical entertainment to end the event which the men "will long remember with pride and joy."

---

### The Roast Beef of Old England

Roast meat is the Englishman's delice and principal dish. . . . The English men understand almost better than any other people the art of properly roasting a joint, which also is not to be wondered at; because the art of cooking as practiced by most Englishmen does not extend much beyond roast beef and plum pudding.

Pehr Kalm (1716–1779), a Swede, from *An Account of His Visit to England on His Way to America in 1748.*

When mighty roast beef was the Englishman's food
It enobled our hearts and enriched our blood.
Our soldiers were brave and our courtiers were good.
Oh! The roast beef of England, Old England's roast beef.
Henry Fielding (1701–1754) in *Grub St. Opera* (1731).

---

## Recipes
~~~

---

### Beef, Sirloin of, Roast

Choose the middle of a sirloin, with as much undercut as possible. Roast it before a nice clear fire, or in a good oven. Cook it quickly for 15 minutes, then move it a little farther away, and let it become thoroughly done without risk of burning. Baste it continually the whole time. Put the joint on a hot dish, and cover it over. Strain off the dripping, put a little salt in the bottom of the pan, and pour on it 1/4 pint of boiling water. Strain this round the meat, garnish with scraped horse-radish, and serve with horseradish sauce and Yorkshire pudding handed round.

Time 2 to 2 1/2 hours. Sufficient for 9 or 10 persons.

Ethel S. Meyer, *A Practical Dictionary of Cookery: 1200 Tested Recipes* (London, 1898).

---

### Scotch Barley-Broth, With Boiled Mutton Or Beef, as *Bouilli Ordinaire*

From three to six pounds of beef or mutton, according to the quantity of soup wanted, put cold water in the proportion of a quart to the pound—a quarter-pound of Scotch barley, or more or less as may suit the meat and the water, and a spoonful of salt, unless the meat is already slightly salted. To this put a breakfast-cupful of soaked white or split peas, unless in the season when fresh green peas are to be had cheap, a larger quantity of which must be put in with the other vegetables, using less barley. Skim very carefully as long as any scum rises; then draw aside the pot, and let the broth simmer slowly for an hour, at which time put to it two young carrots and turnips cut in dice, and two or three onions sliced. Ten minutes before the broth is ready, add a little parsley, picked and chopped,—or the white part of three leeks may be used instead of onions, and a head of celery sliced, instead of the parsley seasoning; celery requires longer boiling. For beef-broth a small quantity of greens roughly shred, and the best part of four or five leeks cut in inch lengths, are better suited than turnip, carrot, and parsley, which are more adapted to mutton. If there is danger of the meat being overdone before the broth is properly *lithed*, i.e. thickened, it may be taken up, covered for a half hour, and returned into the pot to heat through before it is dished. *Garnish the bouilli* with carrot and turnip boiled in the broth, and divided; or pour over it caper-sauce, parsley and butter, or a sauce made of pickled cucumbers, or nasturtiums heated in melted butter, or in a little clear broth, with a tea-spoonful of made mustard and another of vinegar. Parsley, parboiled for two minutes and minced, may also be strewed over *bouilli*—or a sprinkling of boiled carrots cut in small dice.

Christian Isobel Johnstone, *The Cook and Housewife's Manual* (Edinburgh, 1828).

Saxon Pudding: see March 22.
Hollandaise Sauce: see April 14.

# November

## November 1

### All Hallow's Day Dinner
### New College, Oxford, England, 1624

There are two consecutive days in the Christian calendar in which the dead are commemorated and honored. November 1 is All Hallow's Day (or Hallowmas or All Saints Day or the Feast of All Saints) when, as its name suggests, all saints (officially recognized or not) are celebrated. It is followed by All Souls' Day, when the faithful dead are honored. All Hallow's day was a day of particular celebration at New College in Oxford, England. An old account book provides an interesting description of the meals provided in 1624 by the warden for the various residents, and it clearly shows the college hierarchy.

All Hallow's Day. For Mr. Sub-Warden. First course: mutton and white broth; rost beefe, 1s.6d.; 2 minced pies, 2s.; a pig, 1s.6d.; udder and tongue, 8d.; 1 capon, 1s.6d; a custard, 1s.6d.; veale, a breast, 1s.6d. Second course: 2 rabbets, 1s.3d.; 1 partridge, 1s.; 4 snipes, 1s.; 12 larkes, 6d.; 1 warden pie, 2s.6d; 1 tart, 1s.6d.; in wine, viz., a pint for grace-cup, 2s.2d., in sugar, a quarter, 4d.

For Mr. Deanes. First course: mutton and white broth; rost beefe, 1s.6d.; 2 minced pies, 2s.; 2 forequarters of a pig, and a head, xd.; 1 custard, 1s.6d.; a mess of veale, 8d. Second course: a capon, 1s.6d.; 2 rabbets, 1s.3d.; 12 larks, 6d.; a tart, 1s.6d.; wine, a quarte of sacke, 1s.; claret, 8d.

For Masters and Bachelors of Law: stewed mutton and broth; roaste beefe, 1s.6d.; a minced pie, 1s.; halfe a pig, 9d.; and a head; a mess of veale, 8d. Second course, a capon, 1s.6d.; two rabbits, 1s.3d; a custard, 1s.6d.; a tart, 1s.6d.; wine, 1s.8d.

A number of the dishes listed here would hardly make the dinner table at all today, never mind at a special dinner. Offal is a general word for the "waste" when an animal is butchered, and there is much on this menu that would now be called offal—the udder and head, certainly, and the tongue, possibly. In the past, people were not so squeamish and every part of the animal was eaten, including feet, ears, cocks' combs and testicles (see September 29)—and many parts were considered prize morsels. Expensive animal protein is still not wasted today of course; it is disguised in sausages and luncheon meats and pies.

The warden pie provided for the sub-warden does not simply refer to the fact that it was given by the college warden, nor are there any macabre overtones (even though this dinner was the day after Halloween). Wardens were an old variety of pear that was very common, kept well, and was particularly good for cooking—like its apple counterpart, the pippin (see October 29). The sub-warden was also favored by being provided with "a pint" (of what, exactly, is not stated) for a grace cup (or loving cup) which, by definition, he shared (see September 30.)

Recipes
~~~

---

### To Roast a Cows Udder

Take a Cows Udder, and first boyl it well: then stick it thick all over with Cloves: then when it is cold spit it, and lay it on the fire, and apply it very well with basting of sweet Butter, and when it is sufficiently roasted and brown, then dredge it, and draw it from the fire, take Venegar and Butter, and put it on a chafing dish and coals; and boyl it with white bread crum, till it be thick: then put to it good store of Sugar and of Cinnamon, and putting it into a clean dish, lay the Cows Udder therein, and trim the sides of the dish with Sugar, and so serve it up.

Gervase Markham, *The English House-wife* (1683).

---

"Neat's Tongue" was calf's tongue. It was often preserved by drying and had to be soaked before cooking.

---

### To Roast a Neates Tongue to Be Eaten Hot

Boyle a faire Neates Tongue tender, blanch it and lard it on one side, pricke in some Cloves: then cut out the meate at the great end, and mince it with a little dubbing suet, as much as an Egge, then season it with a little Nutmeg, and Mace, and Sugar, three or four Dates minct, a handfull of Currans, halfe a preserved Orenge minct small, about halfe a graine of Muske: worke up your meate with the yolkes of two raw Egges, and stuffe it hard into the Tongue; then pinne over the end a peece of a Caule of Veale, or a skinnie peece of Beefe suet, then put it on a small spit, thorow both ends, set a Dish under the meate to save the gravie, baste it with sweete Butter, and put to the gravie a little Sacke, or Muscadine, and the yolke of an hard Egge minct, and the coare of a Lemmon minct; when your Neates Tongue is roasted, take it up and put it in a dish fitting for it, and put a little Sugar into the sawce, and powre it all over the Tongue, and serve it hot to the Table.

John Murrell, *Murrell's Two Books of Cookerie and Carving* (1638).

---

Mince Pies: see January 9.

## November 2

Dinner with Emily Dickinson
Mount Holyoke Female Seminary, South Hadley, Massachusetts, 1847

The American poet Emily Dickinson (1830–1886) enrolled at Miss Mary Lyons' Seminary at the age of 17. Miss Lyons's aim—although perhaps not overtly stated—was to provide suitably educated wives for missionaries. It turned out not to fulfil Dickinson's expectations—whatever they might have been—or perhaps she was sick, or homesick, for she stayed there only ten months before returning home forever. In a letter written to her brother Austin on November 2, shortly after her arrival, she sounded quite content, describing the seminary dinner in detail and saying "Isn't that a dinner fit to set before a king?"

---

Roast Veal
Potatoes
Squash
Gravy
Wheat and Brown Bread
Butter
Pepper and Salt

*Dessert*
Apple Dumpling
Sauce
Water

---

Dickinson remained at home in Amherst for the rest of her life, becoming increasingly reclusive and perhaps eccentric, but keeping up a prolific correspondence with friends and family. She appeared to fill her life with her letter writing and domestic duties, and the full extent of her creative writing —over 800 poems, carefully copied out and bound into small books—was not discovered until after her death. Instead, during her lifetime, she was known in her neighborhood for being a fine baker of bread and cakes.

## Recipes

~~~

### To Roast Veal

Be careful to roast veal of a fine brown color; if a large joint, have a good fire; if small, a little, brisk fire. If a fillet or loin, be sure to paper the fat, that you lose as little of that as possible: lay it at some distance from the fire till it is soaked, then lay it near the fire. The breast must be roasted with the caul on till it is done enough; skewer the sweetbread on the back side of the breast. When it is nigh done, take off the caul, baste it, and dredge it with a little flour. Veal takes about the same time in roasting as pork.

---

### Cooking Potatoes

Select the potatoes you design for dinner the day previous; pare them, and throw them into cold water, and let them stand three or four hours; then, at a proper time before dinner, put them into boiling water; and when they have sufficiently boiled, turn off all the water, leave off the cover, and hang them over the fire to dry. When the steam has passed off, they will then be in the best possible condition for eating. By this mode, potatoes even of a watery and inferior quality become mealy and good.

---

### Apple Dumpling

Select large, fair, pleasant sour, and mellow apples; pare them, and take out the core with a small knife, and fill up the place with sugar; prepare some pie-crust, roll it out quite thick, and cut it into pieces just large enough to cover one apple. Lay an apple on each piece, and enclose them entirely; tie them up in a thick piece of cloth that has been well floured, put them in a pot of boiling water, and boil them one hour; if the boiling should stop, they will be heavy. Serve them up with sweet sauce, or butter and sugar.

*The New England Economical Housekeeper, and Family Receipt Book* (Cincinnati, 1845).

---

## November 3

### "All-Red Route" Luncheon
### aboard the RMS *Miowera,* 1896

The *Miowera* was one of two steamships operated by the Canadian Australian Steamship Company between Vancouver and Sydney, via Honolulu and Brisbane. When the service began in May 1893 it became possible for the English to travel right around the world without leaving British soil, solely on British ships and trains. It used to be said that "the sun never sets on the British Empire," because British colonial possessions spanned the globe—and this service became known as the "All-Red Route" from the traditional color of British colonies on maps of the time.

On November 3, 1896, the *Miowera* was northbound, and a few days out from Vancouver, having left Sydney on October 13 and Honolulu on October 20. The British citizens aboard also did not need to venture far from their accustomed culinary empire. The bill of fare offered a broad choice of comfortingly British food, with only a few dishes from "elsewhere."

---

SOUP
        Barley.

  FISH
        Potted Salmon and Walnuts.

HOT

Stewed Steak.     Braized Tomatoes.

Ceylon Curry and Rice

Macaroni Cheese.     Boiled Indian Corn.

COLD

Roast Beef and Horseradish.     Melton Mowbray Pie.

Corned Beef.     Pressed Ox Tongue.     York Ham.

Potted Meats and Fish.

POTATOES

Mashed.

SALAD

Plain.     Tomato.     Cucumber.

SWEETS

Tapioca Custard.

Banana Fritters.     Coventry Puffs.

CHEESE

Gruyere     Cheddar     Stilton     Fruit

---

The only dishes without a clear British Empire heritage are the Boiled Indian Corn (from the Americas) and the Gruyere Cheese (from Switzerland). Boiled corn, or corn on the cob, never took off in Britain, perhaps for reasons of transport and storage, or perhaps for reasons of national pride— America rather embarrassingly being lost to the Empire in 1776. For reasons of pragmatism, corn (in the form of maize flour) was accepted as famine food during the Irish potato famine, but it was never accepted as a real substitute for wheat in Britain.

The "curry" would have been as much British as "Ceylonese." The British have had a love affair with "curry" for centuries as a result of their very long colonial occupation of the Indian subcontinent (see January 1). The "Ceylon curry" served on the *Miowera* would have been a decidedly Anglo-Indian interpretation, and probably unrecognizable to any native of Ceylon (Sri Lanka).

The most unequivocally British things on this menu are the cold dishes, particularly the Melton Mowbray Pie. This is a large "raised" pork pie (see October 25), intended to be eaten cold, and made in exactly the same manner as it has been since medieval times. Many hundreds of years ago, before developments in metal technology made shaped baking containers possible, food was cooked in pastry "coffins." These were constructed from special pastry made with hot water and fat (ideally lard) which could be moulded like clay (or "raised") into freestanding containers. These were then filled as we would fill a casserole dish today, lidded with more pastry, and baked. The town of Melton Mowbray in Leicestershire has been famous for its pork pies for centuries. They are now subject to a protected geographical indication (PGI) to ensure that only the genuine product is given the name.

## Recipes

~~~

The following instructions for a raised pork pie to be served cold, in the manner of a traditional Melton Mowbray pie, are taken from *Cassell's Dictionary of Cookery*, published about 1870.

---

### Pork Pies, Pastry for
### (Hot Water Crust for Raised Pies)

Put a quarter of a pound of finely-shred beef suet—or five ounces of lard, or a quarter of a pound of mutton suet—and an ounce of fresh butter into a saucepan with half a pint of boiling water and a pinch of salt. Stir the mixture until the fat is dissolved, and pour it boiling hot into a pound and a half of flour. Knead it well to a stiff paste, and add a little more warm water if required. Shape the dough, and get it into the oven while it is warm. If the pie is to be baked in a mould, lay a piece of the proper shape in the bottom. Press long pieces into the sides, and fasten these to the top and bottom with the white of an egg. If a mould is not to be used, cut off as much pastry as will make the cover, and wrap it in a cloth to keep it warm. Mould the rest with both hands into the shape of a cone, and make the sides smooth and firm. Press the top down with the knuckles of the right hand, and with the left press the outside closely to keep it firm and smooth. Be careful that the walls are equally thick in every part. Fill the pie, put on the cover, pinch the edges, fasten securely with the white of egg, ornament the outside in any way that may suit the fancy, brush over with yolk of egg, and bake in a slow oven if the pie be large, in a quicker one if it be small.

---

The same cookbook advises elsewhere that ``those who are not particularly experienced in the work may mould the pie round a jelly-pot or bottle, which has been made warm by being immersed for some time in warm water. To fill the pie, the book gives the following advice.

---

### Pork Pies

Cut the meat into pieces the size of a small nut, and keep the meat and fat separate. Season the whole with pepper and salt, half a dozen young sage leaves, finely shred, or half a teaspoonful of dried powdered sage, one ounce of salt, two and a quarter ounces of pepper, and a pinch of cayenne may be allowed for a pie containing three pounds of meat. Pack the fat and lean closely into the pie in alternate layers until it is filled. [Cover, seal, glaze, and bake as above]. Neither water nor bone should be put into pork pies, and the outside pieces will be hard unless they are cut small and pressed closely together. The bones and trimmings of the pork may be stewed to make gravy, which should be boiled until it will jelly when cold, and when this has been nicely flavoured, a little may be poured into the jar after it is baked through an opening made in the top.

---

Tapioca Custard: see September 26.

# November 4

Common Hospital Diet
Devon and Exeter Hospital, England, 1829

Joseph Bennett, a shoemaker in the parish of Linkinhorne in Southeast Cornwall, was admitted to the Devon and Exeter Hospital with a "complaint in his back" on October 15, 1829. He must have been feeling better a couple of weeks later, because he recorded in his diary on November 4 (a Wednesday) the "common diet" for patients of the hospital for the week.

---

Mon. Wed. Fri.
Breakfast. One pint of water gruel. Bread for day 15oz.
Dinner. One pint of rice milk.
Supper. One pint of milk pottage on Monday. Cheese 2oz on Wednesday and One oz butter on Friday.

Tues. Thur. Sat. Sun.
Breakfast. One pit of water gruel with 11oz. of bread for day.
Dinner. One pint of broth, 4 oz. Mutton, 1lb potatoes.
Supper. Cheese 2oz.

---

Hospitals have only recently become expensive residences for the sick of all classes. Until relatively recently, the wealthy remained at home, hiring nurses to live in if necessary, and their physicians visited regularly. When King Edward VII developed appendicitis just before his coronation in 1902, it would have been unthinkable for him to go to a hospital frequented by the general public, and an operating theatre was set up in the palace. At the other end of the scale, the poor when they got sick managed as best they could without paid leave from work or any form of insurance for their medical expenses. Hospitals catered for some of those between the wealth extremes, such as the tradesman Joseph Bennett.

Hospital dietaries were planned according to ideas of nutrition for the sick, with consideration of hospital economics, and both tended to suggest bland diets of cheap food. Nurses in private homes were the nutritionists and cooks for their patients—or the housewife if a nurse was not available—and cookbooks commonly had chapters on invalid cookery. The author of *The English Cookery Book, Receipts Collected by a Committee of Lladies*, published in 1859, stated that in cooking for the invalid

> great art is required, because the palate is morbidly acute, or disinclined to strong flavours of any kind. Thus it often happens that seasoning which is relished in a state of health is loathed under disease; and the cook who is not aware of this fact will be almost sure to displease her employers. Hence it is that the nurse who understands the kind of cookery which is fitted for the sick will generally succeed better than the most finished cook, because she knows by experience that all rich flavours are sure to turn the stomachs of her charge. Chicken is for this reason so generally liked by the sick, because its flavour is mild; while the dark and high-flavoured meat of game or ducks would be turned out of the

room as soon as submitted to the nose, without even having the honour of a taste. Fat should be most carefully avoided in all animal broths, such as mutton-broth or beaf-tea; onions, garlic, and other herbs, except perhaps parsley, are also objectionable in the sick-room; and even the faintest flavour of the first in bread sauce will seldom be tolerated. Pepper may be used to some extent when not forbidden, and also salt, but beyond these seasonings it is seldom safe to venture far.

## Recipes

~~~

The following recipes are taken from a *New System of Domestic Cookery*, written by Maria Rundell (1824). In her general remarks in the chapter of "Cookery for the Sick and for the Poor" she wrote,

> The following pages will contain cookery for the sick; it being of more consequence to support those whose bad appetite will not allow them to take the necessary nourishment, than to stimulate that of persons in health. It may not be unnecessary to advise that a choice be made of the things most likely to agree with the patient; that a change be provided; that some one at least be always ready; that not too much of those be made at once which are not likely to keep, as invalids require variety; and that they should succeed each other in different forms and flavours.

---

### Water Gruel

Rub smooth a large spoonful of oatmeal, with two of water, and pour it into a pint of water boiling on the fire; stir it well, and boil it quick; but take care it does not boil over. In a quarter of an hour strain it off; and add salt and a bit of butter when eaten. Stir until the butter be incorporated.

---

### Ground-Rice Milk

Boil one spoonful of ground rice, rubbed down smooth, with three half-pints of milk, a bit of cinnamon, lemon-peel, and nutmeg. Sweeten when nearly done.

---

## November 5

### Dinner aboard a Clipper Ship
*Ringleader,* 1855

Nineteen-year-old Edward P. Sargent set off from Boston, Massachusetts, on October 27, 1855, on the trip of a lifetime. He was aboard *Ringleader*, one of the exciting, fast, new clipper ships bound for London, England, via San Francisco and China, an 8–10-month trip. Within less than 24 hours the ship was in seas so rough that the captain had to lash himself to the rigging, and on November 3 a sailor was lost overboard. On the 5th of November, Sargent noted in his journal:

The crew are repairing the rigging and sails. For dinner to-day we had roast and curried chicken and boiled salt beef with beets, turnips, potatoes, rice, apple-pudding. At the first table the captain, chief mate, & myself sit; at the second, the 2nd & 3d mates; the carpenter and boatswain eat bv themselves in their room.

Two days later, after enjoying a dinner of "chicken-pie, roast chicken, beef, ham and apple-pudding," young Sargent wondered, "What shall we do when the apples and chickens are gone?" Ships embarking on long voyages at this time (before refrigeration) set off with as much livestock and fresh food aboard as they could carry and replenished at each port. When the fresh food ran out, crew and passengers had to rely on what could be preserved—salted meat, preserved potatoes, ships' biscuits and so on, the diet becoming progressively more monotonous and unhealthy. Food is important to morale, however, and seafarers and explorers often hoarded a few animals or longer-keeping foods such as apples for special occasions.

Sargent's journal shows the progression of the food supplies as the weeks of the voyage went by. At the Thanksgiving dinner, he made a point of noting that the pork was fresh (i.e., not salted), suggesting that there were still pigs aboard. His complete menu was "Mock Turtle Soup, Roast Pork (fresh), Cranberry and Mince pies." Fresh meat was getting scarce by this time, but on Christmas Day he commented on "an unusually nice dinner of fresh pork." By January 27 they had rounded Cape Horn and were still two weeks away from San Francisco. Sargent noted on that day that "the goat was killed, or rather murdered." One man who had grown fond of it refused to eat the meat, but to Sargent the loss was of the final source of fresh milk.

## Recipes

~~~

### Boiled Salt Beef

Salt beef should be put on with plenty of cold water, and when it boils the scum removed. It is then kept simmering for some hours. A piece weighing fifteen pounds will require three hours and a half to boil. Carrots and turnips for garnishing should be put on to boil with the beef. If in the least tainted, a piece of charcoal may be boiled with it.

   N. K. M. Lee, *The Cook's Own Book and Housekeeper's Register* (1842).

### Turnips, to Dress Young White

Wash, peel, and boil them till tender in water with a little salt; serve them with melted butter poured over them. Or, they may be stewed in a pint of milk thickened with a bit of butter rolled in flour, and seasoned with salt and pepper, and served with the sauce.

   N. K. M. Lee, *The Cook's Own Book and Housekeeper's Register* (1842).

---

### Boiled Apple Pudding

Pare, core, and quarter, as many fine juicy apples as will weigh two pounds when done. Strew among them a quarter of a pound of brown sugar; add a grated nutmeg, and the juice and yellow peel of a large lemon. Prepare a paste of suet and flour, in the proportion of a pound of chopped suet to two pounds of flour. Roll it out of moderate thickness; lay the apples in the centre, and close the paste nicely over them in the form of a large dumpling; tie it in a cloth and boil it three hours. Send it to the table hot, and eat it with cream sauce, or with butter and sugar.

H. W. Derby, *The New England Economical Housekeeper, and Family Receipt Book* (Cincinnati, 1845).

---

Compost: see February 23.
Frumenty: see February 23.

## November 6

### Coronation Feast of King Henry VI
### Great Hall of Westminster, London, England, 1429

Henry VI (1421–1471) was only nine months old when he became King of England. His coronation as King of England was held on St. Leonard's Day in 1429, a month before his eighth birthday. His second coronation, as king of France, took place in December 1431.

The ceremony at his first coronation must have been arduous for a small child, but he apparently demonstrated "great humility and devotion." It must also have been lonely, sitting in state at the high table, at the ensuing "honourable feast in the great hall".

| FIRST COURSE. | SECOND COURSE. | THIRD COURSE. |
|---|---|---|
| Frumenty with Venison. | Grand blank barred with gold. | Quinces in compost. |
| Vyand royall planted with losynges of gold. | Gely party wrytten and noted with Te deum laudamus. | Blaund sure powdered with quarter foyles guylt. |
| Bores hedes in castelles of golde and enarmed. | Pygge endored. | Venyson. |
| Befe with motton boylyd. | Crane rosted. | Egrettes. |
| Capon stewed. | Byttore. | Curlew. |
| Sygnet rosted. | Conyes. | Cock and partriche. |
| Heyron rosted. | Partriche. | Plover. |
| Great pyke or luce. | Pecok enhakill. | Quailes. |
| A rede leche with lions corvyn therein. | Great Breme. | Snytes. |
| Custarde royall, with a lyoparde of golde sitting their, and holding a fourdelyce. | A white leche planted with a red antelope with a crown about his necke with a chaine of gold. | Great birdes. |

Frytour of sunn facion, with a floureldyce therein.

Flampayne powdered with leopardes and flouredelyce of gold.

Larkis.

Fritour garnished with a leopardes hede and twoo Estryche feathers.

Carpe.

A sottite of Saint Edwarde and saint Louis . . .

Crabbe.

A sotlytie, an emperor and a kynge . . . and the king who is now . . .

Leche of three colours.

A bake meate like a shiled, quarterid red and whit, sette with losynges gylt and floures of borage.

Frytour crispid.

A sotyltie of oure Lady syttynge with her chylde in her lap . . .

---

This must have been a spectacular meal. In addition to the obligatory *subtelties* (see September 23), there was a boar's head in a castle of gold, a peacock *enhakill* (cooked then refitted into its skin and feathers), a *bake meate* (a pie) shaped like a shield, colored red and white and decorated with real gold, a fritter "like the sun," and another decorated with a leopard's head and ostrich feathers. Almost every dish was colored, carved, and decorated in some way: a jelly with musical notation, a red *leche* (see October 13) carved with lions and a white one with an antelope with a chain of gold about its neck, and a custard decorated with a gold leopard.

The decorative food was not designed to amuse the child king. This was no children's party. This was a political statement. Every single color and motif was rich with symbolism. The gilding with real gold of many of the dishes bespoke the wealth and power of a king, and this was reinforced by the use of the King's heraldic colors. Many of the dishes were decorated with the fleur de lys—the stylized lily that was the symbol of the French monarchy since the fifth century, many with the lion of England (synonymous with the leopard in heraldry), and many—quite tellingly—with both. The message was unequivocally that this king was king of France as well as England.

## Recipes

~~~

Birds with spectacular feathers such as swans and peacocks were often cooked then reinserted into their skin to be served with great effect. Birds (especially those with regal plumage) were considered fine food suitable for nobility. They also played an important symbolic role in the ancient code of chivalry, when a vow spoken over a bird was absolutely binding.

In the following recipe for Pecok Enhakill, from the sixteenth-century alchemist Giambattista della Porta, the bird can also be made to appear to breathe fire. In spite of the recipe title, the instructions are clearly that the bird is roasted.

---

### A Boiled Peacock May Seem to Be Alive

Kill a Peacock, either by thrusting a quill into his brain from above, or else cut his throat, as you do for young kids, that the blood may come forth: then cut his skin gently from his throat unto his tail; and being cut, pull it off with his feathers from his whole body to his head: cut off that with the skin, and legs, and keep it: Rost the Peacock on a spit: his body being stuffed with spices and sweet herbs, sticking first on his brest cloves, and wrapping his neck in a white linnen cloth; wet it always with water, that it may never dry: when the Peacock is rosted, and taken from the spit, put him in his own skin again; and that he may seem to stand upon his feet, you shall thrust small iron wires, made on purpose, through his legs, and set fast on a board, that they may not be discerned, and through his body to his head and tail. Some put Camphire in his mouth; and when he is set upon the table, they cast in fire.

John Baptista Porta, *Natural Magick* (1669 [1558]).

---

### November 7

Dinner by Numbers
Grand Hotel, Yokohama, Japan, 1919

The Grand Hotel in Yokohama opened on August 16, 1873, with 30 rooms and seven employees. In spite of its small beginnings, management had big ideas and immediately began promoting the style and quality of the hotel as being equal to the European and American standard. The hotel's catering ability and flexibility were promoted with the advice that in addition to regular meal offerings, special menus for up to a hundred people could be prepared at short notice. The special services continued to be promoted over the next decades—everything from the provision of picnic baskets to rooms for women travelers to party catering. Everything possible was done to position the hotel as *the* place to stay for Westerners visiting or working in the country, right down to the provision of famous English brands of pickles and breakfast marmalade. By 1914 the hotel could accommodate 150 guests, and it had succeeded in becoming one of the best in Japan—until it was destroyed by an earthquake in 1923.

Hotels in the Orient overcame the potential embarrassment of incorrect meal orders occurring due to language difficulties by hitting upon the idea of numbered menu items (see the tiffin menus, March 31, April 25, and July 20) which clearly left less room for error. The dinner menu for November 7, 1919, shows how the system worked—although the numbering errors may have been a little confusing to guests.

## DINNER

### RELISHES

1. Fruit Cocktail

2. Radishes     3. Olives.     4. Salted Peanuts

5. Sardines in Oil     6. Tuna Salad     7. Anchovies

—

### SOUP

8. Bisque of Oysters     10. Consomme Royal

—

### FISH

11. Red Tai Sante Meuniere Julienne Potatoes

—

### ENTREES

12. Sweetbreads Braise L'Ancienne     13. Chicken a la King

14. Spaghetti au Gratin

—

### ROASTS

15. Prime Ribs of Beef au Jus     16. Roast Leg of Mutton Currant Jelly

—

### VEGETABLES

17. String Beans     18. French Peas     19. Mashed Turnips

20. Boiled Potatoes     21. Roast Potatoes

—

### SALAD

22. Pomelo Salad

—

### DESSERT

23. Walnut Ice-Cream     24. Chocolate Eclairs

25. Hawaiian Pineapple

—

### CHEESE

27. Edam     28. Canadian     29. Fresh Cottag

—

### FRUITS

29. Assorted Fruits in Season     31. Nuts     32. Chinese Ginger     33. Preserves

—

34. Coffee     35. Tea     36. Milk

—

Dishes ordered not on the Bill of Fare will be charged extra.

—

An extra charge of fifty yen per person will be charged for all meals served in Room.

The most intriguing aspect of this menu is that amongst the great range of international foods—French classic soups and sauces, English roasts, Italian spaghetti, Hawaiian pineapple, Canadian cheese, and Chinese ginger—there is not one token Japanese item. The only dish that might have been unfamiliar to some Western visitors is the pomelo salad. The pomelo (*Citrus maxima*) is a large citrus fruit, believed to be the ancestor of the grapefruit. It originated in Southeast Asia and was said to have been introduced to the West Indies in the seventeenth century by a Captain Shaddock—hence its alternative name of *shaddock*. The flesh is quite coarse and dry and it is sweeter than the grapefruit, and is widely used in Southeast Asia in salads—although not the highly constructed decorative variety popular in America in the first half of the twentieth century.

## Recipes

~~~

---

### Pomelo Salad

On each plate put a crisp white lettuce leaf with six lobes of a large rose-tinted pomelo, pointing to the center. Between each section of pomelo, near the center, put the blanched half of an English walnut, and in the center put a good spoonful of mayonnaise sprinkled with finely chopped maraschino.

   Frances Barber Harris, *Florida Salads: A Collection of Dainty, Wholesome Salad Recipes That Will Appeal to the Most Fastidious* (1918).

---

Chocolate Eclairs are finger-shaped, cream or custard-filled cakes made from *choux* paste—the same paste as used for *profiteroles, croque-en-bouche* (seeMay 18), and small savory pastries. The paste is piped onto greased trays in whatever shape is desired—small balls for profiteroles or elongated fingers for eclairs. When baked they are split open while hot and any remaining uncooked soft paste in the center is removed. When cool they are filled and iced as desired just before serving.

---

### Pâté à Choux

Weigh four ounces of flour, to which add half a teaspoonful of sugar. Put two gills of cold water in a tin saucepan with two ounces of butter, and set it on the fire, stir a little with a wooden spoon to melt the butter before the water boils. At the first boiling of the water, throw into it the four ounces of flour and stir very fast with the spoon, holding the pan fast with the left hand. As soon as the whole is thoroughly mixed, take from the fire, but continue stirring for about fifteen or twenty seconds. It takes hardly half a minute from the time the flour is dropped in the pan to that when taken from the fire. The quicker it is done, the better. When properly done, nothing at all sticks to the pan, and by touching it with the finger it feels as soft as velvet, and does not adhere to it at all. Let it stand two or three minutes, then mix well with it, by means of a spoon, one egg; then another, and so on; in all four. It takes some time and work to mix the eggs, especially to mix the first one, the paste being rather stiff. They are added one at a time, in order to mix them better. If the eggs are small, add half of one or one more. To use only half a one, it is necessary to beat it first. Let the paste stand half an hour, stir again a little, and use. If it is left standing for some time and is found rather dry, add a little egg, which mix, and then use.

Pierre Blot, *Hand-Book of Practical Cookery* (1867).

Currant Jelly: see January 5.

## November 8

### Duchess of Buccleuch and Monmouth's Table
### Dalkeith Castle, Scotland, 1701

Aristocratic homes on landed estates have been self-supporting communities for centuries (see January 5, January 12, and August 2). Ownership of great tracts of land and supremacy over tenant farmers allowed the rich to provide their own meat, game, grain, dairy products, fruit and vegetables, and sometimes fish. Great wealth meant that whatever else was needed—wine, sugar, spices, dried fruit, and so on—could be purchased from near and far and delivered to the door. Bread and ale were made on the premises, hams and bacon cured, meat salted down, and surplus produce preserved in various other ways. Household guests were frequent, and traveling strangers had to be fed on short notice. Running a stately household was a formidable task, and the organization fell to the steward, who had to track the movement of supplies and keep meticulous accounts in great ledgers.

The surviving records of the household of the Duchess of Buccleuch and Monmouth in Scotland at the beginning of the eighteenth century describe the meals for the day for Her Grace and her staff. The meals for November 8 were probably typical, and the daily plan included that for breakfast next morning, as the preparation had to be done the evening before.

DINNER.
First Course. 200 oysters, bacon and pease pottage, haggis, with a calf's pluck, beef collops, mutton roasted, three joints, fricassee of five chickens; remove, a roasted goose. Second Course, six wild fowl and six chickens, buttered crabs, collard beaf, tarts, four roasted hens. *Steward's table.* Beef, one piece, roasted mutton, two joints. **Officers table**. Beef, two pieces, roasted mutton, two joints. *Last table.* Beef, three pieces, mutton roasted, six joints.

SUPPER.
One joint of mutton in stakes, fried toast, broiled whitings, two roasted rabbits. *Steward's table.* Mutton roasted, three joints. *Officers table.* Mutton roasted, three joints, two hens. *Last table.* Mutton roasted, eight joints.

BREAKFAST.
Two joints of mutton in collops, four quarters of roasted lamb, two roasted capons.

The menus for the various groups show the typical hierarchy of the meal table since medieval times, with more courses and more choices the higher up the social scale. It also mentions a "remove" in the first course for the top table. The dining table from medieval times until well into the nineteenth century was set up with all of the dishes in their allotted place before the diners sat down. By the eighteenth century the table arrangement was of such consequence that cook books contained illustrations of exactly where to place each dish so that the whole impression was of great symmetry and abundance. Dishes that were not inherently impressive to look at, such as soups, or dishes expected to be eaten early in the meal were removed at a certain point during the course, because the remnants spoiled the overall appearance. A gap on the table was equally undesirable for the same reason, so a new dish was placed in the same spot. This dish was called a "remove" (although the nomenclature gets confusing because occasionally it was the dish that was taken away that was given the name). In the case of Her Grace's table, the "remove" of roasted goose probably took the place of the oysters or the peas pottage.

## Recipes

~~~

The following recipe is taken from the first printed Scottish cookery book, *Receipts for Cookery and Pastry-Work*, by Mrs. McLintock, published in 1736.

---

### To Dress Scots Collops

Take a leg of Veal, and cut away the flesh from the Bones, and pare away all the skin, cut them in thin slices, beat the collops with the Back of a Knife to make them tender, then fry them; take two Beef Pallates, boil them till the skin comes off them, then cut them in Pieces, and take forced Meat in small Balls, and fry them brown in a Pan; take three Veals sweet Breads, boil them with a piece of Butter in a sauce Pan, and put a little Flower in it; shake it about, and put to it a Pint of strong Broth, and half a Mutchkin of Claret, or white Wine; then put in the Pallats, and sweet-breads, Anchovies, Capers, pickled Oysters, some whole Onions, Pepper, Salt, a little Nutmeg; put in the Collops, and boil all together a Quarter of an Hour, then take out the Onions, and take some Yolks of Eggs, and a whole Lemon, and squeeze into the Eggs, and put them into the collops, and toss them, till they be thick; garnish the Dish with sippets of Bread, Lemon Peill, and serve them up.

---

Fried toast is a "made dish" as can be seen from its position on the menu; it is not an alternative to plain bread. It is a sort of French toast, made with cream.

---

### Fried Toast

Cut a slice of bread about half an inch thick, steep it in rich cream, with sugar and nutmeg to your taste, when it is quite soft, put a good lump of butter into a tossing-pan, fry it a fine brown, lay it on a dish, pour wine sauce over it, and serve it up.

   Elizabeth Raffald, *Experienced English Housekeeper* (1769).

Collared Beef: see September 15.
Collared Meat: see September 15.
Haggis: see January 25.
Pease Pottage: see March 7.

## November 9

### Quiet Dinner for Two in Paris
### *Chez Denis*, Paris, 1975

In June 1975 *The New York Times* food critic Craig Claiborne (1920–2000) placed a bid in a fund-raising auction being run by the Public Broadcasting System's Channel 13. His $300 stake won him a dinner for two with no ceiling price, at any restaurant in the world that accepted the American Express credit card. Claiborne was uniquely qualified for the challenge, and finally redeemed his prize on November 9. Over a five-hour meal at the Paris restaurant *Chez Denis* on the Rue Gustave Flaubert, he and his partner Pierre Franey got through 31 dishes and 9 wines at a cost of $4,000—equivalent to the buying power today of almost $15,000. He had not expected to win the auction, and neither he nor the newspaper expected the outrage that followed his reports of the meal.

---

### HORS D'OEUVRE
Beluga Caviar, in crystal, enclosed in shaved ice, with toast.
*1966 Champagne Comtesse Marie de France*


### FIRST SERVICE
Consommé Denis: wild duck consommé with shreds of fine crêpes and herbs,
lightly thickened with fine tapioca.
Crème Andalouse: cream of tomato with shreds of sweet pimento and *fines herbs*.
Cold Germiny soup—cream of sorrel.
Parfait of Sweetbreads
Mousse of Quail in small tart.
Tart of Italian ham, with mushrooms and a border of truffles.
*1918 Chateau Latour.*


Belon Oysters, broiled quickly in the shell, and served with a pure *beurre blanc*.
Lobster in a cardinal-red sauce with truffles.
Provençale Pie of red mullet, baked with tomato, black olives, and herbs.
*1969 Montrachet Baron Thénard.*

Filets et sot l'y laissant de Poulard Bresse: the filet strips and "oysters"
from the backbone of the chicken in a cream sauce containing wild mushrooms.
Chartreuse of Partridge: roasted partridge in a bed of cabbage, baked in a mosaic
pattern, intricately styled, with carrot and turnip cut into fancy shapes.
Fillet of Limousin Beef with a thick truffle sauce.
*1928 Chateau Mouton Rothschild*

Raspberry sherbert
Orange sherbert
Lemon sherbert

SECOND SERVICE
Ortolans en brochette.
Fillets of wild duck *en salmis*, in a rich brown game sauce.
Rognonade de veau: roasted loin of veal wrapped in puff pastry with fresh
black truffles "about the size of golf balls."
Pommes Anna
Purée Rachel: artichoke purée

Cold dishes:
Foie Gras in clear aspic
Breast of Woodcock (rare) with a natural chaud-froid.
Another Aspic
Cold Pheasant with hazelnuts.
*1947 Chateau Lafite-Rothschild*
*1961 Chateau Petrus*
*1929 Romanée Conti*

3 sweets:
A cold glazed Charlotte with strawberries.
Île Flottante
Poire Alma
*1928 Chateau d'Yquem*

THIRD COURSE
Pastry confections
Fruit
*1835 Madeira*

Coffee with 100-year-old Calvados or an *hors d'age* cognac.

*The New York Times* received almost a thousand letters in response to the report, four fifths of which expressed outrage at the demonstration of conspicuous consumption in a world when so many were starving. Even the Vatican apparently weighed in on the debate with its own newspaper condemning the gluttony and ostentation.

Although Claiborne later noted that the meal was not perfect in all respects, on the night he was not disappointed; he wrote, "Over all it was an unforgettable evening, and we have high praise for Claude Mornay, the 37-year-old genius behind the meal." Most of the cost was in the wine, and written into this was the fact that three bottles of the *Latour* had to be opened to find one that was drinkable. The restaurant proprietor, Denis Lahana was at pains to point out that because of the quantity required to create some of the dishes, there was enough food for ten people, and not all the food was expected to be eaten. Even allowing for a tiny portion of each of the 31 dishes and 9 bottles being consumed, it is still amazing that Claiborne was able to comment that he did not feel "all that stuffed" and was "laudably sober" at the end of the meal.

## Recipes

~~~

The dishes on this menu come from the classic French repertoire. Many of them are highly complex and time consuming. An example is the *chartreuse* —an ornamental, highly decorated dish made in a mold, and a great favorite in Victorian times. The following recipe is from *The Modern Cook*, published in 1860 by Charles Elmé Francatelli, who was for a short time the chef to Queen Victoria.

---

### Chartreuse of Vegetables, Garnished with Partridges

Scrape eight large carrots, and parboil them in water with a little salt for ten minutes; then put them to boil in some broth with a little sugar and salt, and a small pat of butter; when done, place them on a dish in the larder to get cold. In the mean time, eight large turnips should be peeled, and boiled in the same way as the carrots, and then put on a dish to cool. Next, a plain round mould must be lined with buttered paper, and the prepared carrots and turnips cut into appropriate forma or shapes for the purpose of arranging them over the bottom and round the inside of the mould, taking care that they fit in with each other, so as to represent any of the foregoing designs. Meanwhile parboil three large savoy cabbages in water; then immerse them in cold water, after which squeeze the moisture from them; spread them upon a napkin on the table, take out the cores, season with minionette-pepper and salt, and tie each up with string. Then, put the cabbages into a large stewpan with three partridges trussed with their legs inside, one pound of streaky bacon (previously parboiled), and two large saveloys; season with two onions stuck with four cloves, two carrots, and a garnished faggot; moisten with three pints of stock, cover with a buttered paper, put on the lid, and set them to braize gently for about two hours, if the birds are young, or three hours if not. When done, drain the cabbage into a colander, put the partridges, bacon, and saveloys on a dish to cool; squeeze the broth from

---

the cabbage by pressing it tightly in a strong kitchen rubber; then chop it and afterwards put it into a stewpan with a spoonful of brown sauce, and stir it quickly over a brisk fire until it resembles a somewhat firm paste. Use this preparation to garnish the bottom and sides of the chartreuse, about an inch thick. The partridges must be cut up neatly into small members, tossed in enough brown sauce to moisten them, and then placed in the cavity of the chartreuse in close order, so as to give it solidity when turned out of the mould on its dish; a layer of prepared cabbage should be placed over these, and the whole covered with a circular piece of buttered paper. An hour before dinner, the chartreuse must be placed in a stewpan with sufficient water to reach up only one-third the height of the mould; then set the lid on, and put the stewpan near or upon a slow fire to keep the water gently simmering, so that the steam may warm the chartreuse through. When about to serve, turn the chartreuse up-side-down in the dish, and draw the mould off with care, remove the paper, and garnish the base with a close border of the bacon and saveloys cut into scollops; pour some brown sauce (worked with essence of vegetables) round the entree, glaze the chartreuse carefully, so as not to disturb the order of the vegetables, and serve.

Ortolans: see December 31.
Pommes Anna: see June 21.

## November 10

### Lord Mayor's Dinner
### Guildhall, London, 1828

From the time of King John (1167–1216), the newly elected Lord Mayor of London was required to present himself to the Royal Courts of Justice, who would then inform the King as to his identity. From 1751 until 1959 this ceremony took place on November 9 (unless that day fell on a Sunday, as it did in 1828, when it was held the following day), and over the centuries it developed into a great pageant.

The parade and presentation were followed by the Lord Mayor's dinner, and over the centuries this also became more and more grand. By well into the nineteenth century this still retained its medieval character. There were several different menus for the different ranks of officials, who were seated according to their status. At the dinner in 1828 there were six different menus served. The greatest selection of the finest dishes went to the top table in the Hustings, at which the Lord Mayor and Aldermen sat. Slightly different menus were served to the five long tables in the Hustings, the four short tables in the hall next to the Hustings, the four tables in the body of the hall, the five side tables in the hall, and the Court of the King's Bench.

### Hustings Table
(At which the Rt. Hon. the Lord Mayor presides.)

7 tureens of turtle, 2 dishes of fowls, 2 roasted capons, 2 hams (ornamented), 1 tongue, 2 raised French pies, 1 pigeon pie, 1 dish shell-fish, 1 dish prawns, 1

roasted pullet, 2 dishes mince pies, 2 tourtes, 2 marrow puddings, 3 marbré jellies, 3 blancmanges, 4 dishes of potatoes, 2 salads, 2 chantilly baskets.

*Removes*. 2 roasted turkeys, 2 pheasants, 1 goose, 1 dish of partridges, 1 dish
wild fowl, 1 leveret, 2 dishes pea-fowl.

*Dessert*. 6 pineapples, 6 dishes grapes, 2 dishes apples, 3 ice-creams, 2 dishes
pears, 1 dish dried fruit, 2 dishes walnuts, 2 dishes brandy cherries, 2 dishes
Savoy cakes, 2 dishes rout cakes, 2 dishes filberts, 2 dishes preserved ginger.

Many of the dishes on this menu made regular appearances at the Lord
Mayor's dinner for well over a hundred years. French and pigeon pies, hams,
mince pies, Savoy and Rout cakes, hot-house fruit (especially pineapples),
and preserved ginger were standard items—but above all, it was turtle soup
that symbolized civic banqueting. It was reputed to have the ability to prepare the stomach for the digestive stress that was an inevitable feature of
such banquets, but this was a secondary medicinal justification for the expensive, exotic delicacy.

Turtles were shipped live in vast numbers, in specially built tanks on the
decks of ships, from the West Indies to supply the demand. It was a very
lucrative trade for a while in the eighteenth and nineteenth centuries, but
its success held the seeds of its own destruction. Inevitably, turtles were
hunted almost to extinction, and the supply dropped off. It was unthinkable
to have an important banquet without turtle soup—and anyway, people had
gotten to like the slightly gelatinous texture—so a substitute had to be found.
Mock-turtle soup made from calf's head (which created a similar gelatinous
texture) became so worthy a substitute that in a short time it became a worthy soup in its own right, with no shame in placing it on any menu.

## Recipes
~~~

### Turtle Soup

Cut the head of the turtle off the day before you dress it, and place the body so as
to drain it well from blood, next day cut it up, dividing the several parts, viz., the
back, belly, fins, and head from the intestines and lean meat, taking care to cut
the gall clean out without breaking it; scald in boiling water the firstnamed
parts so as to take off all the skin and shell, cut them in pieces small enough to
stew, and throw them into cold water, boil the back and belly in water till you
can extract the meat from the bones, not longer; put the meat on a dish, then
make a good stock with leg of veal, plenty of lean ham, the flesh of the inside of
the turtle, draw it down to a colour, and fill it up with beef stock and the liquor
and bones of the boiled turtle, season it with the stalks of the basil and marjoram, plenty of onions, bay leaves, bunch of parsley, cloves, mace, and whole
pepper, skim it well, and let it boil gently for four hours, and then strain it to
the pieces of fin, back, belly, and head of the turtle, which when they are done
tender take out into dishes; take out the bones of the pieces of fins and cut the
rest in neat square pieces with as little waste as possible. Thicken the stock with

roux and boil it to cleanse from grease and scum, adding mushroom trimmings, and then strain it through a tammy; in the mean time boil your herbs that have been washed and picked in a bottle or two of Madeira wine with a little sugar, and rub them through a tammy. The herbs are basil, marjoram, thyme, parsley; the two former of which must not be spared, for on them much depends the flavour of the soup. Now add altogether soup, herbs, meat, and some forcemeat and egg balls, boil for a short time and put it away in clean pans till the following day, as the rawness goes off, and you improve the flavour by so doing; boil it again the next day, and a little before serving season it with lemon juice, Cayenne, salt, and a bottle of Madeira.

N.B. The fat should he taken great care of, separated on cutting up the turtle; blanched, cut in neat pieces and stewed tender in a little soup separate, and then divided at last as the tureens require.

Richard Dolby, *The Cook's Dictionary and Housekeeper's Directory* (1833).

Raised Pies: see October 25.
Savoy Cakes: see August 1.

## November 11

### Staff Meals
### Hotel Pennsylvania, New York, 1919

The Hotel Pennsylvania was the world's largest hotel when it opened in New York in January 1919. To service its 2,220 rooms (and 2,200 baths), pamper and feed its guests, and manage the various amenities such as the Turkish baths, library, swimming pools (separate pools for men and women) to the desired high standard required an army of staff. Almost 2,000 staff, in fact —including 60 "girls" to manage the telephone system—and all had to be fed while on duty. Where these "girls" fitted in the staff hierarchy is uncertain, but what is certain is that there was a hierarchy. One's position in the hierarchy determined where and what one ate—even down to whether or one got cream or merely top-of-the-milk on breakfast cereal. The menu for this day in November reveals it all.

|  | OFFICERS HALL | MAIDS CAFETERIA | HELPS CAFETERIA |
|---|---|---|---|
| BREAKFAST, 6:30 to 8:30 A.M. | Apple sauce. Malt breakfast food, or dry cereal & cream. Baked eggs. Rolls & butter. Coffee, Milk. | Apple sauce. Malt breakfast food, or dry cereal & top milk. Bread and butter. Coffee, Milk. | Stewed prunes. Malt breakfast food, or dry cereal & top milk. Boiled eggs. Rolls & butter. Coffee, Milk |
| LUNCH, 11 A.M. to 1 P.M. | Barley Soup. Roast Loin of Pork. Pot Roast of Beef. Boiled Potatoes Creamed Turnips. Lettuce Salad. Bread and Butter. Rice Pudding. Tea, Coffee, Milk. | Barley Soup. Pot Roast of Beef. Boiled Potatoes. Chicory Salad. Bread and Butter. Rice Pudding. Tea, Coffee, Milk. | Barley Soup. Pot Roast of Beef. Boiled Potatoes. Chicory Salad. Bread and Butter. Rice Pudding. Tea, Coffee, Milk. |

| DINNER, 5 P.M. to 7 P.M. | Fricassee of veal & biscuits. Scalloped ham. Mashed potatoes. Fried Parsnips. Bread and butter. Ice cream. Tea, Coffee, Milk. | Fricassee of veal & biscuits. Mashed potatoes. Fried Parsnips. Bread and butter. Ice cream. Tea, Coffee, Milk. | Fricassee of veal & biscuits. Mashed potatoes. Fried Parsnips. Bread and butter. Ice cream. Tea, Coffee, Milk |
|---|---|---|---|
| SUPPER, 9 P.M. to 10 P.M.. | | Breaded veal cutlet Boiled potatoes. Stewed tomatoes. Assorted pastry. Bread & butter. Tea, Coffee, Milk | Breaded veal cutlet Boiled potatoes. Stewed tomatoes. Assorted pastry. Bread & butter. Tea, Coffee, Milk |
| LATE SUPPER, 12 to 1 A.M. | | Mixed meat sandwiches. Coffee | |

The dietitian employed by the hotel noted, and clearly intended to address, that "too much meat has been used, but traditions are easier to build up than broken down, and the elimination of part of the meat is necessarily a slow process." The maids no doubt noted that the only beverage offered to them at the "late supper" was coffee—presumably to keep them awake on the late shift, as they appear to be the only staff on duty at that time of the night.

## Recipes

~~~

---

### Veal Fricassee

Take a knuckle of veal; boil two hours in sufficient water to cover it, when thoroughly cooked, remove the meat, and thicken the gravy with one tablespoonful of flour; add a little salt and one egg, well beaten; pour over the meat and serve hot with slices of lemon.

Carrie V. Schuman, compiler, *Favorite Dishes* (Chicago, 1893).

---

### Pot Roast

For six people buy 3 pounds of meat to allow for loss of weight in cooking, or, if possible, a heavier piece, which will cook better and allow for left-over scalloped meat or meat pie. In this case the additional cost may be figured on the next meal. Buy the top of the round, as it is clear meat and there is no waste.

Sear the meat on all sides in fat; add water, cover the pot, and cook on the back of the stove or in the oven for 3 hours.

Vegetables may be added for flavour.

---

Scotch Barley Soup: see October 31.
Rice Pudding: see January 12.

## November 12

### 20th Anniversary Banquet of the Scottish Geographical Society
### North British Station Hotel, Edinburgh, Scotland, 1904

The Royal Scottish Geographical Society was founded in 1884, with the aim of supporting geographical education, research, and exploration. In 1904 the society celebrated its anniversary by celebrating the success of two antarctic expeditions—the British Antarctic Expedition of 1901–04, which had been led by Robert Falcon Scott (1868–1912), and the Scottish National Antarctic Expedition of 1902–04, led by William Speirs Bruce (1867–1921).

Both Scott and Bruce were present at the banquet, as was the president of the Royal Geographical Society of London, Sir Clements Markham (1830–1916). Clements had been a member of one of the expeditions sent in search

|  |  |
|---|---|
|  | Huitres Natives |
| Amontillado | — |
|  | Consommé à la "Discovery" |
|  | Velouté de Volaille |
| Liebfraumilch | — |
| 1893 | Filets de Sole à l'Antarctique |
|  | Eperlans frits, Sauce Chivry |
|  | — |
|  | Terrines de poulardes Alexandra |
| San Marceau | — |
| 1893, or | Selles de Pré Salé à la *Carême* [?] |
| Deutz & | Pommes Grand'mere |
| Geldermann | — |
| 1893 | Punch à la Romaine |
|  | — |
|  | Faisians bards à la Broche |
|  | Salade de cœurs de laitues |
|  | — |
|  | Pêches Framboises |
| Chât. Margaux | Glaces Polaires |
| 1899 | Corbeilles de Friandises |
|  | — |
| Sandeman's | Paillettes à la "Scotia" |
| Port, 1891 | — |
|  | Dessert |
| Café—Liqueurs |  |
|  | CIGARS |
|  | CIGARETTES |

of John Franklin (1786–1847) who had gone missing while searching for the Northwest passage in the Canadian Arctic in 1847. There had been some friction between Clements and Bruce for some time, with Clements impugning the latter's motives, for which he later apologized.

The names of several of the dishes on the menu are in celebration of the Antarctic and its explorers. The fish is styled *Antarctique*, and the ices are very appropriately styled *Polaires*, the *Discovery* was Scott's ship, and the *Scotia*, Bruce's. The basic presentations were classic—filets of sole, saddle of lamb, chicken terrine, and pheasant on skewers, but the dishes were especially modified and renamed for the dinner, and exactly what they contained is unknown. Usually, for an occasion such as this it was sufficient for a minor change in a sauce or garnish to justify a new name.

The *Paillettes* are intriguing. Paillettes are fine flakes of metal used decoratively, such as sequins, or the gold specks in Dantziger liqueur (see December 11) and some confectionery. The word sometimes also refers to the small savory pastries called cheese straws (see April 22), perhaps on account of the golden flakes of Parmesan cheese with which they are often sprinkled before baking. This latter use would fit their position on this menu, as it was usual for British dinners of the time to end with a small savory.

## Recipes
~~~

The word *terrine* comes from the same root as the word *tureen* and originally meant the same thing—a container for food. *Tureen* has retained its meaning as the large, glorified lidded bowl for serving soup. A terrine was originally the earthenware container for a paté-like, layered or jellied dish but can now also refer to the contents themselves. A terrine is the same as a "potted" dish or a "shape"—the meat being compressed into a dish or mold and allowed to chill. The following is a simple version.

---

### Shape of Chicken

A good-sized fowl.
4 breakfast-cupfuls water
1 teaspoonful Peppercorns
A blade of Mace
Salt and Cayenne Pepper.

Break the bones well, and return them to the pan, and boil for 3 hours or longer; the legs should be scalded and scraped, and all the giblets used, as well as the skin.

When this has all been boiled, strain (there should be 2 breakfast-cupfuls of stock); season nicely, and return to the pan, with the chopped chicken and seasonings, to boil up for 10 minutes; put this into a mould to get cold. Turn out and decorate with parsley. The giblets, legs, and skin are all boiled as long as the bones.

Mrs. Black. Glasgow, *Choice Cookery "La Bonne Cuisine": A Selection of High-Class and Household Recipes* (ca. 1890s).

---

Punch a la Romaine (Roman punch): see July 1.

## November 13

### Dinner with Pablo Casals
### The White House, Washington, DC, 1961

The great Spanish-Catalan cellist Pablo Casals (1876–1973) went into self-imposed exile in protest against the Spanish Civil War (1936–1939) and the dictatorship of General Franco (1892–1975) that followed. He also refused from that time to give concert performances in any country that recognized Franco's government. It was a great coup for President John F. Kennedy (1917–1963) when Casals accepted his invitation to perform at the White House for the second time—the first occasion being over half a century earlier, for President Theodore Roosevelt (1858–1919) in 1904.

The occasion was a State Dinner for Governor Luis Muñoz Marin (1898–1980) of Puerto Rico. Casals, the pianist Mieczysław Horszowski (1892–1993), and violinist Alexander Schneidner (1908–1993) performed an hour-long concert of chamber music in the East Room before the dinner. There were 153 guests including musicians, politicians, diplomats, newspaper editors and journalists, and patrons of the arts—too many for the State Dining Room, necessitating extra tables to be set up in the Blue Room and the Oval Room.

At the Casals dinner. (AP Photo)

French was still the language of White House menus until the Clinton Administration (and it still is for the British royals), but by the 1960s the style of dinners had changed significantly since the early part of the century. In place of multiple courses each with several elaborate, intricately sauced or garnished dishes there is lightness and elegant restraint.

---

**DINNER**

---

| | |
|---|---|
| *Inglenook Pinot* | Mousse de Sole Admiral |
| *Chardonnay* | |
| | Filet de boeuf Montfermeil |
| *Almaden Cabernet* | |
| *Sauvignon* | Galantine de Faisan au Porto |
| | Salade verte |
| *Piper-Heidsieck* | |
| *1953* | Sorbet au Champagne |
| | Pâtisserie |

---

## Recipes

~~~

Admiral sauce is a traditional sauce for fish or fish dishes. The basic flavorings of anchovies, chives, and capers are added to a base of melted butter or rich white sauce.

---

### Admiral Sauce

To one pint of rich white sauce (Velouté or Allemande) add 1 dessertspoonful of finely chopped capers, 1 teaspoonful of chopped parsley, one of chopped lemon rind, the juice of half a lemon, and a teaspoonful of anchovy essense. Reheat and serve hot.
   Charles Herman Senn. *The Book of Sauces* (1915).

---

### Montfermeil

A warm salad of potatoes, salsify, white of hard-boiled eggs en julienne, the yolk being rubbed through a sieve to decorate; mayonnaise sauce.
   J. Berjane, *French Dishes for English Tables* (1931).

---

### Champagne Sorbet

To 1/2 pint of syrup [see note below] add 1/4 bottle of champagne, the juice of half a lemon and of two oranges. Let some peel of both lemon and orange soak in the syrup as it boils for about ten minutes, then strain carefully and freeze,

> working it with a paddle to make it smooth, and when the ice is set, add another 1/4 bottle of champagne.
> *The Times*, June 24, 1922.

Note: A basic sorbet syrup is made from sugar and water in the ratio 2:1. Velouté and Allemande sauces: see January 18.

## November 14

### Lunch for the King and Queen of Greece
### Ambassador Hotel, Los Angeles, California, 1953

King Paul (1901–1964) and Queen Frederika (1917–1981) of Greece visited the United States in 1953 on a goodwill tour. The diplomatic "thank you" implicit in the visit was for the six years of assistance given to Greece under the Truman Doctrine. The visit lasted from October 28 to December 3 and was "the most varied tour any royal couple has made in the United States" and promised, said the newspapers, to be pleasant for all concerned. It certainly appeared that the royal couple were happy, and happily received, wherever they went. The royal schedule at times looked very hectic—as royal tours often are as each community demonstrates its best assets to the visitors. By mid-November the King and Queen were in California. On November 13 they had a day in Hollywood, where it became immediately obvious that they were movie fans. They attended a luncheon for 300 guests put on in their honor by the Association of Motion Picture Producers and held on a stage at R.K.O. Studios. The following day they attended a football game between the University of Washington and the University of Los Angeles, then were feted at dinner at the Ambassador Hotel in Los Angeles. The menu for the dinner paid tribute to the visitors with some Greek-inspired dishes.

---

Hawaiian Pineapple
Filled with Fresh Fruit Illuminee

Hearts of Celery      Colossal Ripe and Green Olives
Consomme Royale—Golden Cheese Straws

Roast Tenderloin of Beef—Chasseur

Rice Pilaff
Zucchini a la Greque

Hearts of Romaine
Roquefort Dressing

Crown Athenia Flambe
Sauce Marron

---

Petits Fours

Coffee

Paul Masson Rose Wine

*Petits fours* are small, often merely bite-sized sweet cakes served at the end of dinner, with coffee. Like *hors d'oeuvres* (see January 20) there is really no adequate translation in English. The name "petits fours" comes from the French words meaning "little oven." Once upon a time brick ovens were heated by having a fire built right inside (like wood-fired pizza ovens today). The ashes were then raked out, and the large items such as bread, pies, and large cakes were placed in the oven, to be cooked by the heat radiating from the bricks. After these were taken out, there was enough residual heat to cook little cakes as the oven cooled down. There are two classic types of petits fours—plain, dry (*sec*) cakes such as biscuits, meringues, and perhaps *madeleines*, and iced or decorated (*glacé*) cakes made from a pound-cake type base.

## Recipes
~~~

Here is a recipe for petits fours of the glacé type (see January 20 on the various types), with the subsidiary recipes, from the *New York Times*, May 24, 1964.

## Petits Fours

1 recipe almond butter cake.
1 recipe hot apricot glaze.
1 recipe mock fondant.
1 recipe butter cream frosting.

1. Slice the cake into two layers using a long serrated knife.
2. Spread one layer with a thin coating of apricot jam. Top with the second layer. Brush the loose crumbs from the surface.
3. Brush the surface with hot apricot glaze. Allow to set twenty to thirty minutes. Cut into small rounds, crescents, oblongs, and triangles. Place the cakes far apart on a cake rack placed over a piece of waxed paper.
4. Pour the warmed mock fondant over the cakes to coat all sides evenly. The excess will run down onto the paper and may be scraped back into the pan and rewarmed to use again. Do not overheat the fondant or it will lose its shine.
5. Allow the cakes to harden. Cut off the rack and place in small paper cases. They may be decorated with butter cream frosting forced through a parchment paper cornucopia fitted with a decorating tube.

Yield: three dozen petits fours.

## Almond Butter Cake

3 whole eggs
2 egg yolks
1/2 teaspoon vanilla
1/2 cup sugar
1 teaspoon grated lemon rind
1/4 cup almond paste
1/4 cup butter, melted and clarified (see note)
3/4 cup sifted flour.

1. Pre-heat oven to 350 degrees.
2. Line jelly roll pan [swiss roll pan] with parchment paper.
3. Combine the whole eggs, one egg yolk, vanilla, sugar, and rind. Heat over hot water until lukewarm.
4. Cream the almond paste with remaining yolk.
5. Beat the warm egg mixture, preferably in an electric mixer, until tripled in bulk.
6. Add the melted butter to the almond paste and fold into the egg mixture with the flour. Fold gently. Pour into the prepared pan. Bake fifteen minutes or until lightly browned and firm to the touch.

Yield: one 10 by 15 by 3/4 inch cake.
Note: to clarify butter, melt until foamy and pour off clear yellow liquid. Discard milky residue.

## Apricot Glaze

1 cup apricot jam, sieved.
1 tablespoon cognac.

Heat the sieved apricot jam and stir in the cognac.

## Mock Fondant

1 cup simple syrup.
3 cups sifted confectioners sugar (icing sugar), approximately.
2 teaspoons melted butter
2 teaspoons egg white
1 ounce unsweetened chocolate, melted.

1. 1. Place the simple syrup in a pan and gradually stir in the sugar until a stiff paste is formed.
2. 2. Warm the mixture to lukewarm while stirring. Add the butter and egg white. Adjust the consistency if necessary for coating the petit fours by adding more simple syrup or confectioners sugar.
3. 3. Add the chocolate to half the mixture. Use other half white.

Yield: one and one half to two cups.

---

### Simple Syrup

2 1/2 cups sugar
3/4 cup white corn syrup
1 1/4 cups water.

1. Combine the ingredients in a large pan.
2. Heat gently while stirring to dissolve the sugar. Brush the sides of the pan with plain water to wash any undissolved sugar crystals down.
3. Raise the heat and boil rapidly without stirring for five minutes.
4. Cool. Store in a jar in the refrigerator until needed.

---

### Butter Cream Frosting

4 tablespoons soft butter
2 cups confectioners' sugar (icing sugar), sifted
1 teaspoon vanilla.

1. Beat the butter with half the confectioners' sugar until light and fluffy.
2. Gradually add the remaining sugar and vanilla until the desired consistency is reached.

The frosting may be flavored and colored if desired.

---

Roquefort Dressing: see December 27.
Pilaf (pilau): see March 30.

## November 15

### Gilbert and Sullivan Dinner
### Park Central Hotel, New York, 1936

The American Gilbert and Sullivan Association celebrated (three days in advance), the 100th anniversary of the birthday of Sir William Schwenk Gilbert (1836–1911), the librettist of the famous Gilbert and Sullivan musical partnership, by giving a grand dinner.

Four hundred members attended, and the special guests were the cast of the English D'Oyly Carte Gilbert and Sullivan Company which was currently performing at the Martin Beck Theatre. Inspiration for the menu was taken from the musical offerings of the famous partnership.

---

FRESH FRUIT COCKTAIL

CELERY     OLIVES
"From the greengrocer you get grapes
and green pea, cauliflower, pineapple
and cranberries."—Iolanthe.

MOCK TURTLE SOUP A LA RUDOLPH
"There's rich mock-turtle—thick and clear—
Perhaps we'll have it once a year."
—Grand Duke.

BUTTERCUP SPRING CHICKEN
"I've chickens and conies."
—H.M.S. Pinafore.

POTATO RISSOLE A LA BUNTHORNE.
"An attachment a la Plato for a bashful
young potato."—Patience.

REGINALD BEANS AU BEURRE
"Or a not-too-French French bean."
—Patience.

DON ALHAMBREA DEL BOLERO
ASPARAGUS
"Grew like the asparagus in May."—Gondoliers.

TESSA AND GIANETTA ICE CREAM
"Does your human being inner
Feed on everything that nice is?
Do they give you wine for dinner,
Peaches, sugar-plums and ices?"
—Gondoliers

PRINCESS ZARA MACAROONS.
"Who thinks slightingly of a cocoanut
because it is husky?"—Utopia Ltd.

MRS. CRIPPS' COFFEE
"I've treacle and toffe, I've tea and I've
Coffee."—HMAS Pinafore.

FITZBATTLEAXE ROLLS—MELBA TOAST
"His sensitive palate as dry as a crust is,
A tenor can't do himself justice."
—Utopia Ltd.

The dishes were in all probability made according to basic recipes in the hotel's repertoire, and merely renamed for the occasion. As for the accompanying beverages, for some unrecorded reason the obligatory toasts to the appropriate recipients—the president of the United States, to King Edward VII, and to Rupert D'Oyly Carte, the impresario who started the company —were drunk in plain water. Homage was also paid to the man who had inspired the whole evening by one of the special guests, Sir Gerald Campbell, the British Consul General, who summed up his contribution not just to music, but to life in general, by noting that the world stood in need of a person who could "debunk the problems of the present like Gilbert did those of his day."

## Recipes
~~~

Melba toast was invented and named for the Australian opera singer, Dame Nellie Melba, by the famous French chef Auguste Escoffier.

---

### Toast Melba

Cut bread in one-eighth-inch slices and toast until it is crisp.

---

### Steamed Whole Spring Chicken

| | |
|---|---|
| 1 chicken | Salt and pepper |
| 1 cup oysters | 1/2 cup cream or milk |
| 1 tablespoon fat | 3 hard-cooked eggs |
| 1 tablespoon flour | Minced herbs |

Prepare a full-grown Spring chicken as for roasting, season inside and out with salt and pepper, stuff with whole, raw oysters and place it in a steamer with a close-fitting cover, and steam until the chicken is done, then place the chicken on a warm dish and make a gravy as follows: Put the fat into a saucepan with the minced herbs and flour and stir until the mixture bubbles; add the liquor in the kettle below the steamer, the cream or milk, and cook, stirring constantly, until the mixture boils. Add the eggs, chopped fine, let the whole boil, pour it over the chicken and serve at once.

Ruth Berolzheimer, *The American Woman's Cook Book* (1939).

---

Macaroons: see February 17.

## November 16

### Dining with James McNeill Whistler
### Chelsea, London, England, 1875

The artist James McNeill Whistler (1834–1903) was born in Massachusetts but lived for long periods of his adult life in London. He bought a home in sight of the River Thames, first at number 2, then at number 7 Lindsey Row (now Cheyne Walk), and entertained frequently. His friend Alan Summerly Cole (1846–1934), the Assistant Secretary at the South Kensington Museum and a textiles expert, recorded in his diary on November 16, 1875, "Dined with Jimmy: Tissot, A. Moore and Captain Crabb. Lovely blue and white china—and capital small dinner. General conversation and ideas on art unfettered by principles. Lovely Japanese lacquer." Whistler (his friends never called him "Jimmy" to his face) meticulously wrote out and stored the menus for his dinner parties, signing each one with his monogram of a butterfly with a stinging tail. The menu for the "capital dinner" enjoyed by Cole was typical for one of Whistler's small parties.

---

Potage tomate, à l'Americain
Sole frite
Côtelettes de Mouton soutise
Poulet à la Baltimore
Homony
Bifteck à la Francaise
Compote de Poire
Café

---

Whistler's lifestyle was lavish, and often beyond his means. He was as meticulous about food as he was about his appearance—and he was proud of his reputation as a dandy. He did much of the preparation himself for his dinner parties and his legendary Sunday breakfasts—a most unusual thing for a man of his time—and he referred to the cookbook as the family Bible. He had a poor opinion of British food, describing a typical meal as "Beef, the people or the rats had been gnawing, beer, and cheese rinds, salad without dressing and tarts without taste. Quite British!" Perhaps this was the reason that he made a point of featuring American dishes at his dinners (as on this menu), and in particular his own specialty of buckwheat pancakes.

Whistler arranged his dining table with an artist's eye, gracing it with beautiful pieces of china and glassware, flowers, and goldfish in bowls. He frequently borrowed suitable pieces from friends, and the Japanese laquerware mentioned by Cole was almost certainly borrowed from his brother's wife, whose collection he coveted. His artistic impulses occasionally got the better of him, however, such as when he tinted the food to harmonize with the dinner plates.

## Recipes
~~~

The "soutise" on the menu is almost certainly meant to be "soubise"—a classic sauce made from onion purée, and a traditional accompaniment to lamb or mutton cutlets.

Eliza Acton (1799–1859) in her *Modern Cookery for Private Families* (1845) gives two versions, an English and a French. The French version is based on a *béchamel* (see October 19) instead of cream and does not contain cayenne.

---

### Soubise

(*English Receipt*)

Skin, slice, and mince quickly two pounds weight of the white part only of some fine mild onions, and stew them in from two to three ounces of good butter over a very gentle fire until they are reduced to a pulp, then pour to them three-quarters of a pint of rich veal gravy; add a seasoning of salt and cayenne, if needed; skim off the fat entirely, press the sauce through a sieve, heat it in a clean stewpan, mix it with a quarter of a pint of rich boiling cream, and serve it directly. Onions, 2 lbs.; butter, 2 to 3 oz.: 30 minutes to 1 hour.

Veal gravy, 3/4 pint ; salt, cayenne: 5 minutes. Cream, 1 pint.

---

### Chicken, Baltimore Style

Split a young chicken down the back as for broiling; take out the breastbone and cut off the tips of the wings. Cut into four pieces, dredge with salt and pepper, dip them in egg and crumbs and put in a pan with enough melted butter poured over each piece to moisten it. Roast in a hot oven about twenty minutes. Make a rich cream sauce or Bechamel sauce, pour on a dish and place the chicken on it. Garnish with slices of fried bacon.

Isabel Gordon Curtis, *The Good Housekeeping Woman's Home Cook Book* (Chicago, ca. 1909).

---

Hominy: see May 19.

## November 17

### Humble Meal
### Café Royal, London, England, 1937

The Wine and Food Society of England was founded in the 1930s and over its first few years focused its demonstrations first on English, then on Continental and International cuisine (see January 15). The society found new inspiration in 1937 when they held a dinner "to show how foodstuffs within the reach of the humble can be transformed by the culinary arts into a meal acceptable to the most delicate palate."

---

Giblet Soup.
Huss (Dogfish) on a crabmeat foundation.
Mock Chicken Pie (made from rabbit).
Apple Charlotte.

---

*The Times* newspaper described the meal under the heading "Lucullus on the Dole."

Lucius Licinius Lucullus (ca. 118–56 BCE) was a Roman general who amassed a fortune during his military campaigns and became so famous for the lavishness of his table that his name has become a synonym for obscenely extravagant consumption. One famous tale about him is that one day when he had no guests for dinner, his servant served only one course, whereupon he was reprimanded by his master who said, "Did you not know? Today Lucullus dines with Lucullus." In recognition of Lucullus's unstinting expenditure in the area of food, dishes styled "Lucullan" usually contain several (sometimes many) expensive ingredients such as truffles.

The chairman at the dinner was M. Beaumont, president of the True Temperance Association, who said his association was trying to spread among the frequenters of the public house and the inn the principles that were fostered elsewhere by the Wine and Food Society. Beaumont's presence did not prevent alcoholic beverages being served with this humble meal. There were two inexpensive wines, according to *The Times*, "such as could cheer the table of all but the humblest homes, if taxation and transport did not make wine a luxury as well as a necessity."

Nowadays we usually purchase our chickens plucked and cleaned ready for cooking, and without the offal that we seem to be so squeamish about. Not so long ago, to purchase a chicken without its giblets would have been unthinkable, because they were so useful. Giblets are the "garbage or entrails" of the fowl, the term often including the feet and wing tips, and they were a tasty base for soup or gravy.

Apple charlotte is a homely dish, a sort of poor relation of the *Charlotte russe*, and a cross between an apple pie and a bread pudding. The name is somewhat of a mystery. The *Oxford English Dictionary* suggests that it may refer to the feminine name, but far more likely it has its roots in the ancient charlet—a sort of thickened custard originally made with ground pork.

## Recipes
~~~

The following recipes are from *A Year's Dinners: 365 Seasonable Dinners and How to Cook Them* (1934) by May Little. It was published by Harrods of London, and was subtitled "A Handy Guide for Worried Housekeepers"—the worry being addressed was the daily problem of "what shall we have for dinner?"

---

### Giblet Soup

| | |
|---|---|
| 3 pints of stock. | Bouquet garni. |
| 2 sets of fowls' giblets. | 1 1/2 oz. butter. |
| 2 onions. | 1 oz. flour. |
| 1 carrot. | 2 oz. rice. |
| 1 leek. | Chopped parsley |
| 1 stick of celery. | Salt and pepper. |

Carefully clean the giblets (heart, gizzard, liver, wings, and neck) and cut into small pieces. Prepare and slice the vegetables, melt the butter in a saucepan, add the onions and giblets, fry a nice brown, stir in the flour, cook gently for three or four minutes, add the stock and vegetables, boil up and simmer gently for 40 minutes, skimming occasionally. Cook the 2 oz. rice, drain and add, remove some of the giblets and keep to garnish, pass through a sieve, return to the pan, season well and add a little sherry if liked, reheat and put in pieces of giblets and chopped parsley and serve.

---

---

### Apple Charlotte

| | |
|---|---|
| Apples. | 2 oz. butter. |
| Stale bread. | Sugar. |
| 3 or 4 cloves. | Custard sauce. |

Stew the apples (peeled and cored) till tender with sugar and cloves. Line a cake tin with bread dipped in clarified butter, join the edges together with egg. Pour in the stewed apples, cover with a round of bread dipped in butter, cover with buttered paper and bake in a quick oven, turning round to brown on all sides alike, turn out carefully and pour custard sauce round.

---

## November 18

### Dining on a Clock Face
### Trades Hall, Leicester, England, 1910

Dinners and luncheons have been held in some strange places over the last few hundred years—often to commemorate the completion of a great project. In May 1862 a celebration with plenty of refreshments was held in a new sewerage tunnel in London, prior to it being handed over to the Metropolitan Board. Less than 12 months later, in January 1863, a great banquet was held on the platform of the Farringdon Street station to celebrate the opening of the London Underground Railway for business the following day. At other times and places manufacturers have celebrated in, for example, chimneys, huge boilers, a brewery "copper of astonishing magnitude," and the top of Nelson's column in Trafalgar Square in London.

On November 18, 1910, it was the turn of Messrs Gent & Co. Ltd. at the Faraday Works, Leicester, to celebrate. They had just completed the four clock faces for the dials of the world's largest electric clock for the premises of the Royal Liver Insurance Company at Liverpool. Until then the largest clock in the world had been "Big Ben" at the Houses of Parliament, but the new monster was two feet larger in diameter. To mark the occasion, a luncheon was held on one of the clock faces before it was delivered. The menu was strictly in theme.

---

Mock Turtle Soup
(served in face-plates)

Mutton Cutlets
(Bread-crumb insulation)

Galantine of Tur(n)key
(A la Ding-Dong)

Pressed Beef
(Use both hands)

York Ham
(From the "big-end")

Salad
(Without the clock-oil)

Raspberry Trifle
(A trifle larger than Big Ben)

Apple Tart
(Cores removed, Hands off)

Mince Pies
(Currents alternating)

Cheese and Celery
(A la counterweight, from the cast-iron *bed*)

What the diners probably did not realize was that they were dining on top of one of the most useful pieces of kitchen equipment ever invented. Clocks are so taken for granted nowadays that it is almost impossible to consider managing day-to-day life without them. In medieval times literacy rates were very low, and technology nonexistent. Most cooks could not read, so recipe books were redundant, and such as have survived are very minimalist because they assumed a lot of knowledge and were intended as memory aids for master cooks, not detailed instruction manuals. There were no clocks, thermometers, or weighing scales in kitchens. So how did cooks measure and time their recipes? Mostly they learned by experience, judging the appearance and texture of the food, or the sounds it made as it cooked. There were some tricks of the trade—holding a hand in the oven and judging how hot it was and whether the coals needed to be stoked, judging the number of "walms" (boilings up) that a dish required—or by praying. Occasionally a recipe specified that something should be cooked as long as it took to say a number of repetitions of a particular prayer, such as an "Ave-Maria while" (about 12 seconds), a "Pater Noster while" (about one minute), or the time to say the Miserere Psalm "very slowly" (perhaps 3 minutes).

## Recipes

~~~

A trifle is a thing of little importance, something trivial and inconsequential. By the end of the sixteenth century *trifle* referred to a light and creamy dish with the alternative name of *fool*. The following is a basic trifle recipe. Fruit was commonly added, and a raspberry trifle can be made by substituting the fruit for the "good jam" mentioned in this recipe.

### Trifle

The whipped cream which is laid over the top of a trifle should be made the day before it is wanted, as then it will be much firmer. Rub the rind of a large fresh lemon with two or three lumps of sugar till all the yellow part is taken off, then add a little more sugar to make up the quantity to three ounces, and crush it to

powder. Warm a pint of cream, and stir the sugar in this till it is dissolved. Add a glassful of sherry, a tea-spoonful of brandy, and the whites of two eggs which have been whipped separately to a firm froth. Mill or whip the mixture in a cool place, and as the froth rises take it off, and place it on an inverted sieve to drain. Continue whisking until the whole of the cream is frothed, and set the sieve in a cool place or upon ice, with a dish under it. The next day put four sponge biscuits, a quarter of a pound of macaroons, and a quarter of a pound of ratafias at the bottom of a trifle-dish, and pour over them a large wine-glassful of sherry, and another of brandy, or if preferred use two parts wine and one part spirit, and let the biscuits soak till they have absorbed all the liquor. Grate a little lemon-rind upon the cakes, and spread over them a layer of good jam, then cover them with a pint of nicely-flavoured, rich, cold custard. Pile the whipped cream lightly over the top as high as possible, and then garnish the dish with pink comfits, bright-coloured jelly, or flowers.
*Cassell's New Dictionary of Cookery* (1910).

Apple Tart: see May 12.
Mock Turtle Soup: see July 4.
Pressed Beef: see February 22.

## November 19

Annual Game Dinner
Grand Pacific Hotel, Chicago, Illinois, 1892

On the Saturday night before Thanksgiving in 1855, John B. Drake, the proprietor of the Tremont House in Chicago, gave a game dinner. He repeated the hospitality for the next 38 consecutive years, and it became *the* social event of the city. In 1874 Drake leased the Grand Pacific Hotel, and the game dinners took place there until the final one in 1893. It was very rare for an invitation to be turned down, and at the penultimate dinner in 1892 there were 600 guests. The bill of fare, as usual, included every beast of the wilderness, mountain, prairie, river, and stream that could possibly be procured.

MENU
Blue Points.

SOUP.
Venison Broth.      Hunter.

FISH.
Baked Whitefish.      Boiled Salmon Trout.
Boiled Leg of Mountain Sheep.

ROAST.
Mountain Sheep.      Loin of Venison.
Blacktail Deer.      Loin of Elk.      Saddle of Antelope.

Black Bear.     Cinnamon Bear.     Wild Goose.

Oppossum.     Racoon.

Pin-tail Duck.     Mallard Duck.     Ruffled Grouse.

Spoonbill Duck.     Partridge.     Redhead Duck.

Wood Duck.     Brant.     Sage Hen.

Fox Squirrel.     Buttertail Duck.     Jack Rabbit.

Green Winged Teal.     Pigeon.     Blue Winged Teal.

Jack Snipe.     Praire Chicken.     Wild Turkey.

Plover.     Pheasant.     Quail.

## BROILED.

Gray squirrel.     Blue winged teal.     Venison steak.

Butterball Duck.     Partridge.     Red winged sterling.

Sand snipe.     Quail.     Black birds.

Reed birds.     Pheasant.     Plover.     Rice birds.

## ENTRÉES.

Breast of partridge with truffles.     Venison cutlets, mushroom sauce.

Bear steak, jelly sauce.

Ragout of squirrel, à la Financière.

American hare, à la Chasseur.

## VEGETABLES.

Green peas.     Boiled and mashed potatoes.     Sweet corn.

Stewed tomatoes.     Sweet potatoes.

## ORNAMENTAL DISHES.

Boned wild turkey in jelly.

Aspic of lobster à la royale.

Pyramid of wild goose livers.     Mallard duck à la Bellevue.

Prairie chicken en plumage.

Partridge au naturel.

Boned wild turkey.     Prairie chicken.

Quail.     Ducks.     Partridge.     Snipe.

Prairie Chicken Salad.     Celery.     Celery Mayonnaise.

## DESSERT.

French kisses.     Assorted fancy pyramids.

Assorted cake.

Confectionary Angel Cake.     Macaroons.

Lady Fingers.     Vanilla Ice Cream.     Siberian Punch.

Oranges.     Grapes.     Nuts.     Raisins.

Coffee.     Crackers.     Cheese.

Many of these species of game are not easily available today (unless one does the hunting), and many are now protected due to their scarcity, humans having eaten them almost to extinction. Descriptions from earlier, more abundant, or less ethical times—such as the nineteenth century—give some clue as to how they tasted.

Cinnamon bear meat is certainly edible, but many frontier "recipes" consist of the old joke-description, "Take two pounds of meat from the rump, boil three days in a deep kettle with the head of an axe, then throw away the meat and eat the axe." The flesh of the fox squirrel "is esteemed very delicate" and that of the prairie chicken (see October 16) "in color and flavor resembles the pigeon." The American hare—whose flesh "though of a dark colour, is much esteemed as an article of food" could provide an unexpected bonus: "The Indians eat the contents of their stomachs, notwithstanding that food is such as we have mentioned." Reed birds—tiny songbirds also called rice birds or "butter birds"—were so popular amongst discerning big-city diners that the demand was often conveniently met by substitution with the ubiquitous English sparrow. Sophisticated restaurant patrons, unaware of the counterfeit, happily paid reed bird prices for a plateful of the introduced pest.

Recipes

~~~

### Roasted Reed Birds

Pick your birds, and with a pair of scissors cut and draw them as chickens. Wash them clean and wipe them dry; make a dressing of bread crumbs, pepper, salt and butter enough to make the crumbs adhere together; chopped onion may be added, with a small quantity of any kind of sweet herb, finely powdered. Fill the birds with this dressing, sew them up, put them on a spit, and baste them with butter whilst they are roasting.

Hannah Mary Bouvier Peterson, *The National Cook Book* (Philadelphia, ca. 1866).

### How to Cook a Squirrel

Late in the afternoon, near dark, you come home from hunt, tired and hungry but all the better for your tramp and the ozone of the splendid autumn. Dress a young squirrel with belly as white as wool and kidney as fat as Welsh mutton; put him in a stewpan with not much water, and give him for company a rasher of rich and sweet bacon. Stew the varmint till as tender as butter, that is innocent of ice in June. Then lift him out, put a cord about his neck, and suspend him from the mantel before the kitchen open fire, with the liquor in which he had been boiled in the pan beneath him, to which has been added a generous quantity of rich Jersey butter. Baste him frequently and roast him till he is thoroughly done, adorably brown and poetically crisp. Then take him down, immerse him in the gravy, serve him hot with grand old hoecake, or, better, pumpkin bread; take a drink of red licker, open your vest, halter your tongue,

> and fall to. That is what a squirrel was made for. The man who does not love that season and such a feast is fit for treasons, stratagems, and spoils.
> *The Washington Post*, November 3, 1910.

Praire Chicken: see October 16.

## November 20

### Dining with Queen Elizabeth I
### England, 1576

When Queen Elizabeth I (1533–1603) came to the throne in 1558, new and interesting food plants (and the turkey) from the New World (see October 12) were gradually becoming known in England. Many of the foods had to overcome the natural suspicion of anything new, and it was a long time before the prejudice was overcome against the potato (accused of being an aphrodisiac and of causing leprosy) and tomato (also accused of having aphrodisiac qualities, hence its alternative name of love apple.)

In the meantime, the Queen continued to eat the same foods more or less that her predecessors had done for centuries. A surviving expense account gives several bills of fare for her table.

---

"Mondaye Dynner the 20th of November, anno ut supra."

"The Queenes Majesty's daylie service."

Cheate and mancheate
Bere and ale
Wine

1st Course
Capon gr. boylde
Cocks boylde
Larks b.
Chickins b.
Mutton b.
Salt brewes
Beafe
Beafe surloyne
Veale rost
Capon gr.
Cocks
Plover
Snites
Connye pies
Custerde

2nd Course
Pullets gr.
Teales
Partridges

---

Fesants
Chickins
Connys
Larks bake
Tarte
Butter
Eggs
Pannado.
Capon gr.

The only *relatively* new item at the queen's dinner was the beer. Ale had been the day to day beverage for centuries—it was low alcohol, and safer than water to drink, and it was the beverage of choice for children too. The terms "beer" and "ale" are often used interchangeably now, but historically there is a difference. The problem with English ale at this time was that it did not keep well and had to be brewed and drunk within a few days. The introduction of hops in the early-fifteenth century meant that the drink (beer) kept longer because as well as adding a bitter edge to the flavor, the hops acted as a preserving agent.

The menu also indicates the different sorts of bread—which was still the staple, even for royalty. The Queen had *cheate* and *mancheate* (manchet) offered to her.

Manchet was the finest white bread—expensive and suitable for aristocratic palates. Cheat was the second quality wheat bread—the flour not quite so white. Further down the scale there was bread made from a mixture of wheat and other flours—called *Maslin* (*mescelin*, meaning mixed—the same root of the word *mesclun* for a mixed salad) or Ravel bread. Then there were breads without wheat at all—hard breads that did not rise well because only wheat has sufficient gluten. These were made from rye or oats, pea or bean flour, and even acorns.

The sixteenth-century chronicler Raphael Hollinshead wrote:

the brede through the land is made of such grains as the soil yeeldeth; nevertheless the gentilitie commonlie provide themselves sufficientlie of wheat for their own tables, whilst their household and poore neighbours, in some shires, are inforced to content themselves with rie or barlie, yea and in time of dearth, manie with bread made of benes, pessen, or oats, or of altogether and some acorns among.

## Recipes

~~~

### Lady of *Arundels Manchet*

Take a bushel of fine wheat-flower, twenty eggs, three pound of fresh butter, then take as much salt and barm as to the ordinary *manchet*, temper it together with new milk pretty hot, then let it lie the space of half an hour to rise, so you may work it up into bread, and bake it, let not your oven be too hot.
*True Gentlewoman's Delight* (1676).

---

### To Bake Chickins (larkes, sparowes etc)

Season them with cloves, mace, sinamon ginger, and some pepper, so put them into your coffin, and put therto corance dates Prunes, and sweet Butter, or els Marow, and when they be halfe baked, put in some sirup of vergious, and some sugar, shake them togither and set them into the oven again. Bake Sparowes, Larkes, or any kinde of small birds, calves feet or sheepes tunges after the same manner.

A. W. *A Book of Cookrye* (1591).

---

### How to Bake Custards

Take to every pinte of Cream five Egs, and put in no whites, and straine your Cream and Egges together, season it with Cloves & mace and sugar, and when your paste is well hardened in the Oven, having small raisins & dates put in your stuffe, and let it not bake too much, for much baking will make your Custard to quaile, or els to fail. Doucets after the same sort.

A W.*A Book of Cookrye* (1591).

---

## November 21

### Lunch with the King of Romania
### Château Rambouillet, France, 1938

The king (and dictator) of Romania, King Carol II (1893–1953), paid a very brief visit to France in November 1938, where he was hosted by the president of France Albert Lebrun (1871–1950). The visit clearly had a diplomatic agenda in the wake of the recent Munich Agreement. Germany had annexed Austria in March of that year, and the dictator Adolf Hitler (1889–1945) was believed to be planning to move into Sudetenland (bordering on Czechoslovakia and inhabited mostly by Czechs). The major European powers (Britain, France, Italy, and Gemany), without the presence of Czechoslovakia, met in Munich and signed an agreement on September 29 in which they agreed to the cession of Sudetenland to Germany.

Carol arrived in Paris on November 20 and had lunch at the Elysée Palace. He met with the president and French officials to discuss how the economic and trade agreements between their two countries might be maintained in the face of German expansion without unnecessarily upsetting Germany. The following day, he was taken to the beautiful Château Rambouillet in the traditional hunting preserve of French leaders since the eighth century.

---

Truites de Rivière Meunière
Poularde de Bresse Bouquetière
Pàté de Canard sauvage à la Gelée
Salade de Chicorée
Glace Plombiéres
Dessert

The morning's pheasant shooting had been hampered by rain, but even if it had been sufficiently successful, the kill would not have appeared on the luncheon menu for the same day as it is traditionally "hung" for some time before preparing for the table. Nevertheless, this was a simple, elegant luncheon. The trout was prepared in one of its most classic ways, with Sauce Meunière, the chicken was from the famous variety reared in Bresse, and the French are accepted masters of the preparation of both duck and pâté in all their forms. A simple salad and a glorious ice cream finished the meal, which was no doubt accompanied by excellent French wine.

*Plomb* is French for lead, and a *plombier* is a plumber. It seems strange to give ice cream a name indicating a dull metal, and as expected there are a number of theories about the name of the dish. The most-repeated says that a chef of Napoleon III (1808–1873) was preparing a "cream" (a custard-type dish) for an important reception in 1858, but the recipe went wrong somehow, and to rescue it he added *kirsch* (cherry liqueur) and candied fruit and Voila! a newly invented semi-frozen dish was presented to guests. A royal origin is always of particularly good value, but in this case it is not correct because there are records of an ice cream by that name being served in Paris in 1798—because it was made in a lead mould. There happens to be a town in *Plombières-le-Bain* in the Vosges region of France, and the coincidence of names was too good to miss, so by the 1880's the town had claimed the ice cream as its own.

After the luncheon the king was seen off on the train to visit his cousin the prince of Hohenzollern on his way back to Romania.

## Recipes

~~~

### Plombières Cream Ice

1 1/2 pint of milk or cream,
6 oz. of cleaned Jordan almonds,
and 15 bitter almonds, thoroughly pounded
with two tablespoonfuls of orange-flower water,
14 oz. of sugar,
6 oz. of apricot jam,
8 yolks of eggs,
2 whites of Italian meringue,
and 1/2 pint of cream whipped.

Mix the milk, sugar, pounded almonds, diluted apricot jam, and the yolks of eggs, and stir this on the fire until the composition begins to thicken; it must then be removed from the fire, stirred a few minutes longer, and rubbed through a hair sieve into a basin. When about to freeze the Plombieres, put the composition into the freezer, twirl it about with quick motion, and occasionally work the ice with the spatula; as soon as it has become set or has frozen pretty stiff, work in the meringue, and when thoroughly incorporated, mix in the whipped cream, and set up or mould the Plombieres. Plombieres cream ice is not always set up in a mould; it is sometimes piled up in rock-like fashion, with apricot jam between the layers, and garnished round the base with some kind of almond cakes. A lace pattern dessert paper, placed upon a folded napkin on a dish or ice stand, is generally used for this purpose.

Charles Elmé Francatelli, *The Royal English and Foreign Confectioner* (1862).

Sauce Meunière: see July 23.

## November 22

### German Society 150th Anniversary Dinner
### Hotel Astor, New York, 1934

The German Society was founded in New York in 1784 by 13 men of German origin and modeled after the similar Philadelphia society. Its aim was to encourage German migration and provide information, practical assistance, and legal advice to those who did make the move. In 1837 John Jacob Astor (1763–1848), the richest man in the country, was elected as president of the society, and in addition to running it for four years he was generous with financial donations. Astor's great grandson, John Jacob IV (1864–1912) who died aboard the *Titanic* (see April 2) was the man who built the Astoria Hotel in 1897 right next to his cousin's Waldorf Hotel.

One hundred fifty years after its founding, the now large society held an anniversary dinner at the Hotel Astor. Eight hundred guests attended, and each received a copy of a commemorative book entitled "Historical Sketches of the German Society of the City of New York, 1784–1934," written by Rudolph Cronau. During the dinner a congratulatory message from President Franklin D. Roosevelt was read aloud to the guests. The president expressed a "sincere hope that the society will continue its fine work and flourish for many years to come."

Schwedische Vorspein
Kraft Suppe auf Hamburger Art
Tafelsellerie      Nuesse      Oliven

Bartsh nach Prinz Ruprecht
Mit Krabben und Austern

Paprika Schnitzel
Mit Hausmacher Nudeln
Neue gruene Bolmen

Junges Huhn am Rost
Kartofflen in Oliven Form      Virginia Speck
Frishe Pilze

Gemischer Salat

Pfirsitch nach Melba Art
Feintes Gebaeck

Mokka
Cocktail
Rhein Wein
Zigatten und Zigaretten

The dinner menu may have been written in German, but the food was fine American hotel-style. The soup "Hamburger-style"—referring to the city, not the meat patty—perhaps had some token German connection, but no less tenuous than dishes styled *"a l'Anglaise"* or *"a l'Italienne"* have with England or Italy. The *schnitzel* may have originated in Germany or Austria, but like spaghetti from Italy and the roast beef of England it had already become part of the world's repertoire and would have been familiar to all of the guests no matter how distant their own German heritage. The dessert dish of peach Melba was an international dish from its conception. It was invented by the famous French Chef Auguste Escoffier (1846–1935) in an English hotel (the Ritz in London) for an Australian opera singer, Dame Nellie Melba (1861–1931) for whom he also invented Melba toast (see November 15).

## Recipes

~~~

A Schnitzel is a veal cutlet, coated with egg and breadcrumbs and fried. It is often called Vienna or Viennese style and is usually served garnished with lemon, with a side of noodles.

---

### Vienna Schnitzels

After providing a two-pound piece from a white, tender leg of veal, cut it into six equal slices and flatten nicely with a cleaver. Season both sides with a teaspoon salt and half teaspoon paprika; lightly roll in flour, next in beaten egg and lastly in bread crumbs. Heat one tablespoon butter in a large frying pan, place the pieces of veal in the pan, one beside another, and fry for eight minutes on each side. Dress on a hot dish. Arrange a thin slice of lemon, with a twisted anchovy in oil placed over each slice of lemon, on top of each schnitzel. Serve with one and a half gills hot tomato sauce in a separate bowl.

Alexander Filippini, *The International Cook Book* (1906).

---

Peach Melba: see April 8.

## November 23

Thanksgiving Day Dinner
aboard *YRBM 16*, Ben Tre, Vietnam, 1967

The U.S. Naval men aboard the "Repair, Berthing & Messing Barge" *YRBM 16* in the Ham Luong River, Ben Tre in 1967, no doubt enjoyed their

Thanksgiving dinner on the evening of November 23. For seven of them, it was to be their last.

---

Shrimp Cocktail
Cream of Tomato Soup
Oysterettes

Roast Young Tom Turkey      Virginia Baked Ham
Giblet Gravy      Pineapple Sauce
Mashed Potatoes      Candied Sweet Potatoes

Cornbread Oyster Dressing
Green Peas w/Mushrooms
O'Brien Corn
Tossed Salad      French Dressing

Hot Dinner Rolls

Pumpkin Pie w/Topping Mincemeat Pie
Fruit Cake
Ass't Candy
Mixed Nuts

---

In the early hours of the next morning, an explosion tore a hole in the hull. Flood and fire followed. Seven men died and fourteen were injured. The damage had been wreaked by a Viet Cong diver who had managed to avoid the nets and plant a bomb against the shell of the vessel.

Whenever people are far from home—especially in dangerous situations such as war—they make a great effort to celebrate national days with even greater fervor. The Thanksgiving dinner enjoyed by the men aboard this vessel had all of the modern classics—from the turkey with cornbread dressing and the pumpkin pie. There was no hint of Asian food or ration packs.

## Recipes

~~~

The following recipes are from the official U.S. Navy recipe manual. The yield for each recipe is 100 servings; the portion size for each of the following recipes is 3/4 cup.

---

Corn O''Brien

Method.
1 Cook bacon until crisp. Drain. Set aside for use in Step 3.
2 Saute chopped onions and green pepppers in oil or shortening.
3 Drain corn, mix with pepper and pimientos and sauted onions and peppers. Add crumbled bacon.
4 Heat at medium heat until hot, stirring constantly. CCP: Heat to 145 F or higher for 15 seconds. Hold at 140 F or higher for service.

| Calories | Carbohydrates | Protein | Fat | Cholesterol | Sodium | Calcium |
|---|---|---|---|---|---|---|
| 136 cal | 26 g | 4 g | 4 g | 1 mg | 302 mg | 10 mg |

| Ingredient. Issue | Weight | Measure |
|---|---|---|
| Bacon, Raw | 1 lbs | |
| Peppers, Green, Fresh, Chopped | 3 lbs | 2 qts 1 cup 3 5/8 lbs |
| Onions, Fresh, Chopped | 2 3/8 lbs | 1 qt 2 3/4 cup 2 2/3 lbs |
| Oil, Salad | 5 3/4 oz | 3/4 cup |
| Corn, Canned, Whole Kernel, Drained | 28 7/8 lb | 5 gal |
| Pepper, Black, Ground | 1/8 lb | 3/8 tsp |
| Pimiento, Canned, Drained, Chopped | 7 5/8 oz | 1 1/8 cup |

---

### Peas with Mushrooms

Method.
1 Add peas to boiling salted water.
2 Bring to a boil; cover; cook gently 6 to 8 minutes until tender. Drain.
3 Saute mushrooms in margarine or butter.
4 Combine hot peas and mushrooms, mix gently. CCP: Internal temperature must reach 145 F or higher for 15 seconds. Hold at 140 F or higher for service.

---

| Calories | Carbohydrates | Protein | Fat | Cholesterol | Sodium | Calcium |
|---|---|---|---|---|---|---|
| 126 cal | 21 g | 7 g | 2 g | 0 mg | 216 mg | 38 mg |

| Ingredient. Issue | Weight | Measure |
|---|---|---|
| Peas, Green, Frozen | 27 lbs | 5 gal 1 1/4 qts |
| Salt | 5/8 oz | 1 tbsp |
| Water, Boiling | 16 3/4 lbs | 1 gall 1/2 qt |
| Mushrooms, Canned, Drained | 6 1/4 lbs | 1 gal 1/2 qt |
| Margarine | 8 oz | 1 cup |

Candied Sweet Potatoes: see December 20.
Pumpkin Pie: see August 25, October 1.

# November 24

## Dining aboard a West India Steamer
### SS *Clyde*, Barbados, 1847

The great steamship races were in full swing in the 1840s (see August 29). On November 2, 1847, the SS *Clyde* was lying in Southampton Water, being provisioned for a voyage to the West Indies. One of the enthusiastic passengers preparing to board was Sir Robert Schomburgk (1804–1865), a German born British explorer, naturalist, cartographer, and diplomat. Schomburgk had recently been knighted by Queen Victoria and was on his way to fill a diplomatic post in the British colony of Barbados.

Schomburgk (or Schomburgh) later wrote an account of his voyage, and he began by describing the ship.

> The Clyde is one of the finest vessels which the company possesses. Her length is two hundred and thirteen feet and her breadty thirty-four feet and a half; her engines are four hundred and twenty horse-power, and she is a vessel of eighteen hundred and fort-one tons. I understand the number of passengers on board exceeds eighty.

Schomburgk also described the dining arrangements aboard the ship.

> According to the regulations established on board, breakfast was served at half-past eight o'clock, luncheon followed at twelve o'clock, and dinner at four o'clock: tea and coffee at seven o'clock. It may be fairly calculated, that a person blessed with a good appetite dedicated at least four hours every day to the enjoyment of the table.

The "floating hotel" set off on November 3 and reached Barbados on November 24. Schomburgk included the bills of fare for the first and last meals aboard—the last one showing that "despite of disasters, we could not say that we suffered from starvation."

---

Soup of bouilli
Mutton broth

—

Roast mutton.    Boiled mutton.
Roast turkey.
Harricoed mutton.    Minced mutton.
Stewed geese.
Ragout of chickens.    Boiled fowls.    Chicken pie.
Stewed fowls.
Tongues.

—

Grilled pudding.    Rice pudding.
Fruit tarts.
Puffs.    Tartlets.    Yam sandwiches.
Dessert.

The bill of fare is not much poorer than that of the first day, and it is clear that the livestock—or at least the sheep and fowl—were still in good supply at the end of the journey. There were no vegetables mentioned on the first day, but it is likely that there were potatoes and turnips and other long-storing produce included in the dishes if not served alongside.

Most of these menu items are recognizable today. "Harricoed mutton" is simply a mutton stew. The name is somewhat of a mystery. Haricots are beans, suggesting they were an integral part of the dish, but they do not feature in "English" recipes, which almost always contain turnips. It is yet another example of a one-pot peasant-type dish such as a *pot-au-feu* (see April 7) or Irish stew (seeDecember 1). The "grilled pudding" was probably a cornmeal (polenta) type like fried hominy (see February 14). The yam sandwiches are a genuine puzzle. They would hardly have been taken aboard in England at the beginning of the journey, but perhaps were ferried out from Barbados ahead of the ships' arrival. To judge from its position in the menu the dish was a sweet "dessert" of some sort.

## Recipes

~~~

---

### To Harrico Mutton

Take the nicest part of the rack, divide it into chops, with one bone in each, beat them flat, sprinkle salt and pepper on them, and broil them nicely; make a rich gravy out of the inferior parts, season it well with pepper, a little spice, and any kind of catsup you choose; when sufficiently done, strain it, and thicken it with butter and brown flour, have some carrots and turnips cut into small dice and boiled till tender, put them in the gravy, lay the chops in and stew them fifteen minutes; serve them up garnished with green pickle.

Mary Randolph, *The Virginia Housewife: Or Methodical Cook* (1838).

---

Rice Pudding: see January 12.

## November 25

### Menu for the Indisposed
### aboard the SS *Fort Victoria*, 1928

Bermuda was a popular destination for Americans trying to escape the restrictions of Prohibition in the 1920s, and at least one shipping line saw and seized the opportunity. The Furness Bermuda Line bought the ship *Willochra* in late December 1919, had her refitted with 373 first-class and 56 second-class cabins, and renamed her the *Fort Victoria* after one of the many historic military outposts of Bermuda. Her first voyage to Bermuda from New York was on February 28, 1920, and from then until she collided with another vessel in the fog and sank in the Ambrose Channel of New York Harbor in December 1929, this was her regular route.

---

DECK MENU

DINNER

Consommé Jardinière
Boiled Kennebeck River Salmon, Sauce Persil
Selection of Cold Meats
Salade
Apple Charlotte      Jelly Macedoine
Dessert
Tea      Coffee
Sandwiches any Style Desired.

This Deck Menu is Provided for passengers who are
indisposed and unable to use the Dining Saloon.

---

Passengers on the *Fort Victoria* and her sister ship the *Bermuda* enjoyed "48 Hours of Transatlantic Luxury" in each direction, for a round-trip fare that started at $70. "Luxury" for first- (and second-) class passengers aboard fine ships includes being fed fine food frequently and with a degree of indulgence. The *Fort Victoria* was midway home to New York on November 25, 1928, when those passengers who felt so inclined could take advantage of the following menu.

The food offered on this menu is certainly light and delicate, although it is unclear whether "indisposed" means unwell or simply disinclined. Perhaps the shipping line was being discreet and making allowances for the passengers who had made the most of their sojourn away from the constraints of Prohibition (see December 6).

---

### Sandwiches for the Sick and Convalescent

The first requisite in the preparation of sandwiches is bread of close, even texture from twenty-four to thirty-six hours old. White, entire wheat, Graham, or brown bread may be used; also Zwieback and some varieties of thin unsweetened crackers. Patients are tempted often to eat bread and butter when served in the form of a sandwich, when they would refuse the slice of bread accompanied by the butter ball. The shape, too, often makes a difference. A heart-shaped sandwich often pleases an adult as well as a child. Men and women are certainly but children of an older growth, which fact is especially emphasized during times of sickness and suffering.

Bread for sandwiches should be cut as thin as possible, and all crusts should be removed. In order to accomplish this a sharp, thin-bladed knife is an essential. If butter is used it should be creamed (using a wooden spoon or silver fork) and spread on the loaf before the slices are cut, unless the sandwiches are to be formed in round or fancy shapes, when there would be a loss of butter. After bread is sliced spread one-half the pieces with filling, cover with remaining pieces, and cut in shapes. If bread is first cut in shapes, then one-half the pieces spread with mixture, the mixture either does not come to edges or extends over them, thus detracting from the appearance of the finished sandwich.

---

If sandwiches are prepared before serving time they may be kept fresh and moist by wrapping in paraffine paper or a napkin wrung as dry as possible out of hot water.

Sandwiches should be served on a plate covered with a doily.

Fannie Merritt Farmer, *Food and Cookery for the Sick and Convalescent* (Boston, 1904).

## Recipes

~~~

### Lettuce Sandwiches

Put fresh, crisp lettuce leaves, washed and thoroughly dried, between thin slices of bread prepared as for Bread and Butter Sandwiches, having a teaspoon of Cream or Mayonnaise Dressing on each leaf. The slices of bread must be put together in pairs, cut in shapes, and then separated to insert the lettuce leaf, which should extend over the edge of bread.

### Fig Sandwiches

Remove stems from figs and chop finely, or force through a meat chopper. Put in double boiler, add a small quantity of water, and cook one hour. Season with lemon juice, cool, and spread between slices of buttered bread.

### Raw Beef Sandwiches

Scrape beef, cut from round. . . . Prepare bread as for Bread and Butter Sandwiches. Spread one-half the pieces with scraped beef seasoned with salt; if pepper is desired, use sparingly. Cover with remaining pieces, then cut in finger-shaped pieces or triangles.

Fannie Merritt Farmer, *Food and Cookery for the Sick and Convalescent* (Boston, 1904).

The club sandwich is an American invention of the 1890s, although the inventor and location are disputed. An early recipe for a club sandwich appeared in the *Good Housekeeping Everyday Cookbook* by Isabel Gordon Curtis in 1903.

### Club Sandwich

Toast a slice of bread evenly and lightly butter it. On one half put, first, a thin slice of bacon which has been broiled till dry and tender, next a slice of the white meat of either turkey or chicken. Over one half of this place a circle cut from a ripe tomato and over the other half a tender leaf of lettuce. Cover these with a

> generous layer of mayonnaise, and complete this delicious "whole meal" sand-
> wich with the remaining piece of toast.

Jelly Macedoine: see May 13.
Persil (Parsley) Sauce: see May 29.
Apple Charlotte: see November 17.

## November 26

### Thanksgiving on the Plains
### Camp Supply, Oklahoma, 1868

Major-General Philip Sheridan (1831–1888) was a famous Union general
during the Civil War. In 1867 he was given a new brief—to subdue "the
refractory savages" of the Great Plains and force them onto reservations.
One of the techniques used by the authorities during the Indian Wars was
to deprive the Indians of access to their traditional and staple food—the
bison (or, as it is incorrectly called, the buffalo). Sheridan was a keen hunter
(see his expedition with Buffalo Bill, September 26), and he made the most of
the incidental fruits of the Indian campaigns. The journalist De B Randolph
Keim accompanied the Sheridan party, and wrote of his experiences in his
book *Sheridan's Troopers on the Border: A Winter Campaign on the Plains*
(1870). In it he described their Thanksgiving dinner.

> The twenty-sixth of November, being the day set apart for a National
> Thanksgiving, the occasion was appropriately celebrated at headquarters in a
> dinner made up entirely of the productions of the country. We were favored with
> a good cook, a burley Teuton, rather slow, but possessed a compensating amount
> of good nature, which enabled him to overlook a few impetuous observations at
> times, particularly when his pans and kettles were not ready to be put in the
> wagon in the morning, or perhaps, the camp stove was too "heavy" to be
> handled just at that moment. However the dinner was not only a novelty, but
> was worthy of all praise as an exhibition of the culinary art. I will give the bill
> of fare as I took it down at the time:
>
> > Soup—Wild Turkey.
> > Boiled—Wild Turkey, Buffalo Tongue.
> > Roast—Buffalo Hump, Wild Turkey, Saddle of Venison.
> > Red Deer, Common Deer, Antelope. Rabbit.
> > Entrees—Rabbit Pies, Wings of Grouse, breaded, Turkey Giblets.
> > Broiled—Quails, Pinnated Grouse.
> > Vegetables (imported)—Canned Tomatoes, Lima Beans, Dessicated Potatoes.
> > Bread—"Hard Tack," plain and toasted, Army Biscuits.
> > Desert (imported)—Rice Pudding, Pies and Tarts.
> > Wines and Liquors—Champagne, "Pinetop Whiskey," Ale.
>
> The flavor of the game of the country was remarkably fine. The turkey
> particularly had a richness about it from the hackberry on which it feeds.

The "thanksgiving turkey" which we were so fortunate as to possess, weighed thirty pounds dressed. With its plumage it was truly a magnificent bird. Indeed the camp was overstocked with game. Turkeys, buffalo meat, deer, and all the other varieties during the first three days after our arrival went begging. In fact everyone soon became surfeited, and returned to salt meat with an evident relish.

The presence of buffalo tongue on this menu is a particularly poignant reminder of the wholesale wasteful destruction of the buffalo herds that occurred in the 1870s. White men would kill a buffalo for its tongue (considered a delicacy) and leave the rest of the carcass to rot. Professional hunters—or more accurately, poachers—turned blind eyes to protected tribal land and killed over four million bison in the decade after Sheridan's Winter Campaign.

Sheridan pleaded the extermination of the buffalo to the Texas Legislature in 1870, as it considered a bill to protect bison herds. He said,

These men [the buffalo hunters] have done more in the last two years and will do more in the next year, to settle the vexed Indian question, than the entire regular army has done in the last thirty years. They are destroying the Indians' commissary. Send them [the hunters] powder and lead if you will, but for the sake of a lasting peace, let them skin and sell until the buffaloes are exterminated. Then your prairies can be covered with speckled cattle and the festive cowboy, who follows the hunter as a second forerunner of an advanced civilization.

### How to Skin Rabbits, Hares, and Squirrels

Cut the skin of all the legs in a circle around the joint nearest the feet, and cut off the fore-feet; then cut the skin off the hind-legs, inside the legs, from the feet to the tail; loosen the skin, and turn it back until it is quite removed from the hind-legs; next, tie the hind-legs together, and hang the carcass up by them; now pull the skin downward toward the head, slipping out the fore-legs when they are reached; when the neck is reached, either cut off the head with the skin attached to it, or leave it on the body, and continue to pull the skin downward until the nose is reached; cut off the end of the nose. As the head is considered a delicacy by some persons, it is generally cooked with the rest of the carcass. After the skin has been removed, the carcass should be carefully wiped with a wet cloth to remove any hairs which may adhere to it; the entrails should then be removed, the blood, and the liver, heart, and kidneys being saved; the inside of the carcass should be washed with a cupful of vinegar, which is to be used with the blood for making whatever sauce or gravy is to be served with the game. The liver, heart, and kidneys are either cooked whole, or chopped very fine and mixed with the gravy.

Juliet Corson, *Miss Corson's Practical American Cookery* (1886).

Recipes

~~~

---

### Wild Turkey

If the turkey is old, or tough, it must be boiled one hour before being stuffed for baking. Then stuff it with oysters, bread and butter, and season with pepper and salt; baste with butter, and the juice of the turkey. Make the gravy by putting in the pan a pint of oysters, or button mushrooms, throw in a cup of cream, or milk, salt and pepper, and send to table hot, with the turkey.

Lafcadio Hearn, *La Cuisine Creole* (ca. 1885).

---

### Broiled Quail

Split the quail down the back. Wipe with a damp towel. Season with salt and pepper, rub thickly with soft butter, and dredge with flour. Broil ten minutes over clear coals. Serve on hot buttered toast, garnishing with parsley.

*Miss Parloa's New Cookbook* (ca. 1880).

---

### Turkey Giblets A La Bourgeoise

The giblets of turkey consist of the pinions, feet, neck and gizzard. After having scalded pick them well and put in a saucepan with a piece of butter, some parsley, green onions, clove of garlic, sprig of thyme, bay-leaf, a spoonful of flour moistened with stock, salt and pepper. Brown to a good color.

Rufus Estes, *Good Things to Eat, As Suggested by Rufus* (Chicago, ca. 1911).

---

Pinetop Whiskey was a homemade beverage brewed from pine cones, twigs, or needles and said to have been traded with the Indians for buffalo robes.

Buffalo Hump: see September 26.
Rice Pudding: see January 12.

## November 27

### Dinner at the Court of Napoleon III
### Paris, France, 1866

The American-born singer Lillie Moulton (1844–1912) was married at the age of 17 to Charles Moulton, an American who moved in diplomatic circles and was frequently a guest at the court of Napoleon III (1801–1873). She kept up a lively correspondence with friends, and these are a witty insight into life at the top.

On November 27, 1866, she was taken to breakfast by Baron Haussmann (1809–1891), the man commissioned by Napoleon III to rebuild and modernize Paris and whose legacy is still seen in the wide boulevards and regular facades of the city. The remodeling necessitated the resumption of some lands and houses, and the Moulton's croquet pitch was one of the sacrifices (a great loss as croquet was enormously popular). When the topic came up for discussion during their post-breakfast stroll, the Baron gallantly offered to put "a piece of the Bois" (the *Bois de Boulogne*, a park on the edge of Paris) at her disposal "in souvenir of our breakfast today."

Lillie was so delighted she "almost screamed with joy," and the subject was discussed that same afternoon at tea with the Empress Eugenie (1826–1920) —to which she, and several others including the Austrian diplomat Prince Metternich (1771–1859) were summoned. Dinner was also at the royal court, where the conversation was equally worth recording in a letter to a friend. Lillie was seated beside the French military hero, the Marquis de Gallifet (1830–1909) who entertained her with a ghoulish but amusing recounting of the story of his war wound which left him with his *entrails* spilled out, necessitating them being covered with a silver plate (which he had engraved) while he languished in hospital for twelve months. The story did not put Lillie off her food, however, and her letter continued:

> The dinner to-night was very good. I give you the menu:
>
> Potage tortue clair, Crême de volaille, Brisotins de foie gras, Saumon Napolitain, Filet de boeuf à la moderne, Suprême de perdreaux, Homards à la Parisienne, Gelinottes rôties, Salade, Petits pois à l'Anglaise, Ananas Montmorency, Glacés assorties, Café—Liqueur (both served at the table).
>
> It was earlier than usual when we began to dance; but we were (at least I was) interrupted by receiving a message from their Majesties, asking me if I would kindly sing something for them. Of course I did not refuse, and we adjourned to the music-room, where the Erard piano was.

## Recipes

~~~

---

### Petits Pois à l'Anglais

Put a pint of young peas, boiled very green, into a stewpan with three tablespoonfuls of bechamel sauce [see January 18], a quarter of an ounce of sugar, a little salt, and two button onions, with parsley, tied together; boil them ten minutes, add two tablespoonfuls of *liaison*, stir it in quickly, and serve.

Liason: Break the yolks of three eggs in a basin, with which mix eight tablespoonfuls of cream or six of milk, pass it through a tammie, and use where directed.

Alexis Soyer, *The Gastronomic Regenerator* (1847).

---

Ananas (Pineapple) Montmorency: "à la Montmorency" means in the style of Montmorency, which is the name of a suburb of Paris and a variety of sour cherry. It refers to dishes made, or garnished, with sour cherries.

# November 28

## Gourmet's Dinner
### *Rocher de Cancale*, Rue Montorgeuil, Paris, France, 1809

Alexandre Balthazar Laurent Grimod de la Reyniere (1758–1837) was born
into a wealthy French family that was distantly aristocratic on his mother's
side. Grimod had a deformity of his hands, which was a shameful disability
at the time and perhaps contributed to him developing (as a coping mecha-
nism) an odd sense of humor and an eccentric pattern of behavior. He trained
as a lawyer, but earning a living became unnecessary when he inherited the
family fortune in his early thirties. He was able to concentrate on his great
love—food.

Grimod became famous—or infamous—for his dinner parties. At one of his
earliest efforts, while his parents were alive but out of town, he held a dinner
presided over by a dressed-up pig. The event got him officially disinherited
and sent out of town in shame. A much later occasion gained him enduring
fame—his famous (or infamous) "Mortuary Dinner." There was a great deal
of secrecy about the plans. Only 17 guests were invited to participate, but
many more to be observers. The dinner took place in a room draped in black,
with incense burning, and a coffin behind each chair.

Grimod became not just an indulgent *bon-vivant* and gourmet, but one of
the first food and restaurant critics and writers. His eight-volume *L'Alma-
nach des Gourmands* is still a classic. In it he described a number of meals
of special import, including one, for 24 guests, at his favorite restaurant,
the *Rocher de Cancale*.

---

Menu de 24 couverts, pour le jeudi 28 novembre 1809

*4 Potages*
Une bisque d'écrevisses.
Un potage à la Reine, au lait d'amandes, avec biscotes.
Une Julienne, aux pointes d'asperges.
Un consommé de volaille.

*4 Relevés de Potages.*
Un brochet à la Chambord.
Une dinde aux truffes.
Un turbot.
Une culotte de bœuf au vin de Madère, garnie de légumes.

*12 Entrées.*
Un aspic de filets mignons de perdreaux.
Une jardinière.
Des filets de poularde piqués aux truffes.
Des perdreaux rouges, au fumet.
Des filets de mauviette sautés.
Des scaloppes de poularde au velouté.
Des filets de lapereaux, en turban.

Un vol-au-vent à la financière.
Des ailerons piqués à la chicorée.
Deux poulets de grains, au beurre d'écrevisse.
Des scaloppes de saumon à l'espagnole.
Des filets mignons, piqués de truffes.

SECOND SERVICE.

*4 grosses Pièces.*
Une truite.
Un pâté de foies gras.
Des écrevisses.
Un jambon glacé.

*4 plats de Rôt.*
Un faisan.
Des éperlans.
Des bécassines.
Des soles.

*8 Entremets.*
Une jatte de blanc-manger.
Un miroton de pommes.
Des asperges, en branche.
Des truffes à la serviette.
Une jatte de gelée d'orange.
Un soufflé, à la vanille.
Des cardons, à la moelle.
Des truffes, à la serviette.

## Recipes

~~~

The cardoon (*Cynara cardunculus*) is related to the artichoke, although it is the stalk that is usually eaten, not the flower bud. The stalks look like hairy celery stalks and are commonly braised and served with a sauce.

### Spanish Cardoons—Cardons d'Espagne, à la Moëlle et à l'Espagnole

Take two or three heads, cut them near the bottoms; only use the solid part; cut those that are full and entire equally about five or six inches long; pare the edges and *blanch* them till they are in a state to be peeled; refresh, peel, and throw them again into fresh water; put them in a *blanc* with two lemons in slices, from which the peel and seeds have been taken: see *Blanc* in the article *Sauce*: make them boil; cover them with a round of buttered paper; put them to simmer upon a *paillasse* three or four hours; when done, drain and put them into a stewpan with a little stock; make them simmer, and nearly fall into jelly; dress and sauce them with a good reduced *espagnole*, to which has been added a pat of butter and a small bit of portable soup; garnish with small sippets fried in butter, covered with marrow, and serve. With respect to the tops of the *cardoons*, take off the

> skin, and pare them as a great carrot; *blanch* and cook them with the *cardoons*, and use them with them; or to garnish *entrées*, as well as in eggs *brouilées*.
> Antoine Beauvilliers, *The Art of French Cookery* (London, 1827).

Blancmanger: see January 7.
Pate de Foie Gras: see May 26.
Vanilla Souffle: see May 18.

## November 29

### Double Thanksgiving
### Maison Tortoni, Seattle, Washington, 1897

It was a double Thanksgiving for Joseph Whiteside Boyle (1867–1923) and his four companions when they dined at a restaurant in Seattle on Monday, November 29, 1897. They were belatedly celebrating the national Thanksgiving that they had missed as they were en route home from the Yukon gold fields, and they no doubt gave even greater thanks that they had survived the journey.

Boyle was a prize fighter and promoter who was in San Francisco when news of the discovery of gold in the Yukon broke in July 1897. He and his sparring partner took off immediately to seek their fortune. They arrived in late August, and Boyle quickly saw an opportunity for greater exploitation of the fields. He realized that only 25 percent of the gold was recoverable by hand, and over the next few years he made his fortune by importing machinery and mechanizing the process, and earning himself the nickname "King of the Klondike." There were other problems to be overcome first in those early days, however.

The cost of living was excruciatingly expensive at the gold fields. Steaks were retailing at $2.50 apiece, and flour was $2 a pound, with a minimum purchase of 50 pounds. As winter approached it became clear that there were not going to be enough supplies at any price, and the diggers faced starvation. There was a mass exodus from the gold-mining town of Dawson by any means possible, and Boyle and his small party were amongst the first to get out. They left Dawson on September 24 and arrived in Seattle, after a perilous journey, on November 27.

---

### MENU

Chicken Salad Boned Turkey
Eastern Oysters on Half-shell
Queen Olives      Celery
Green Turtle Soup a la Maryland
Mountain Trout au Gratin
Pommes Parisienne
Frogs a la Poulette
Spring Chicken saute a la Marengo

Sweetbread Braize with Mushrooms
French Green Peas      Asparagus au Branch
Roast Young Turkey with Cranberry Sauce
Omelette Souffle au Maraschino
Vanilla Ice Cream
Assorted Fruit
Roquefort Cheese      Camembert Cheese
Café Noir with Cognac

It must have been a grand meal indeed for men who had been suffering so many weeks of cold and hunger. The obligatory Thanksgiving turkey and cranberry sauce were there, and the menu on the whole was as typical as it could be for a fine restaurant dinner. The menu card itself was written in no-nonsense English, not French as was common, the only exceptions being the asparagus au branch and a couple of dishes styled "*à la*" something or other—appellations that functioned as shorthand, as everyone knew what they indicated.

## Recipes

~~~

### Sweetbreads with Mushrooms

Lay half a dozen sweetbreads in cold water for twelve hours, changing the water several times. Then boil them five minutes, drop into cold water, remove the skin and lard with fat bacon. Put them in a saucepan with a pint of stock, two small onions and one carrot chopped, a teaspoonful of minced parsley, salt, pepper, cayenne, and a little mace. Stew until tender.

Serve with a mushroom sauce, made as follows: Take a small bottle of mushrooms or one dozen fresh mushrooms sliced and boil them five minutes in water and lime juice. Drain and place in a stew pan with two ounces of butter, one ounce of flour and a pint of well seasoned stock or gravy. Cook until the sauce is reduced one-half. Pour over the hot sweetbreads.

Joe Tilden, *Joe Tilden's Recipes for Epicures* (1907).

### Frogs a la Poulette

Joint the hind legs and backs of twelve frogs; put in a closely covered saucepan with some truffles, a small can of mushrooms sliced, a glass of white wine, salt, white pepper, cayenne, mace and four ounces of butter. Stew gently fifteen minutes, stirring once or twice. If then tender, add one teaspoonful cornstarch rubbed into one ounce of butter. Let it cook two minutes, take from the fire and stir in the yolks of six eggs beaten well with one-half cup of cream. Place this mixture where it will keep hot without cooking. Cut the crust from a loaf of bread, scoop out the center, brush with butter and brown in the oven. Pour the frogs legs and sauce into the bread cup, garnish with mushrooms and truffles.

Joe Tilden, *Joe Tilden's Recipes for Epicures* (1907).

---

### Cranberry Sauce

Pick over and wash four cups cranberries. Put in a stewpan with two cups boiling water, and boil twenty minutes. Rub through a sieve, add two cups sugar, and cook five minutes. Turn into a mould or glasses.

Fannie Merritt Farmer, *The Boston Cooking School Cook Book* (1896).

---

Chicken Marengo: see July 14.
Pommes Parisienne: see June 23.

## November 30

### Patriotic Dinner
### The Freemasons' Tavern, London, England, 1871

The Scottish Corporation and Hospital (commonly called simply the Scottish Hospital) was founded in 1665 to assist Scottish residents of England. It was not a hospital in the modern sense of a place for the treatment of the sick, but a charitable institution to help "decayed natives" (i.e. distressed natives) of Scotland, who were not eligible for relief under English Poor Law (see August 12). The corporation held its annual dinner on November 30, the feast day of the Patron Saint of Scotland.

On its 207th anniversary, the corporation's annual dinner was held at the Freemason's tavern, and tables were laid for 455 guests. The president was the future governor general of Canada, the Marquis of Lorne (1845–1914), who had recently married Queen Victoria's daughter, Princess Louise (1848–1939). *The Times* commented "The menu, it will be seen, was very patriotic."

---

#### SOUPS.
Cocky Leeky.      Scotch Broth.
Mock Turtle.     Julienne.     Game Soup.

#### FISH.
Codfish, Oyster Sauce.      Turbots, Lobster Sauce.
Stewed Eels.      Fillets of Soles.      Lobster Cutlets.

#### SIDE DISHES.
Fricandeaux with Peas.      Mutton Cutlets Provençale.
Larks in Cases *au gratin*.      Salmis of Partridges.

#### SCOTTISH COURSE.
Collops.      Haggis.      Sheeps' Heads.
Shepherds' Pies.      Black Puddings.

REMOVES.

Roast Turkey.      Boiled Fowls.

Hams.      Tongues.

Round of Beef.      Roast Sirloins.      Haunches of Mutton.


SECOND COURSE.

Pheasants.      Black Game.      Wild Ducks.

French Beans.      Fried Potatoes.


SWEETS.

Fruit Jellies.      Raspberry Creams.      Blancmanges.

Russian Charlottes.      Cabinet Puddings.

Compôtes of Oranges.

Maids of Honour.      Goranflot Cakes.

Meringues.      Nesselrode Puddings.

Dessert.

---

The cocky leekie soup, scotch broth, haggis, and sheeps' heads are indisputably associated with Scotland, but there are also some indisputably English and French touches in the meal. *Gorenflot* cake was traditional in France on Twelfth Night (see January 6) and is made from the same sort of sweet, eggy, yeast dough (sometimes with dried fruit) as is brioche (see February 24), savarin, kugelhopf, baba, and panettone. The only significant difference between each of these is in the shaping. A gorenflot is traditionally made in a hexagonal or octagonal mould. A decidedly English contribution are the "maids of honor"—small almond cheesecakes also called Richmond cakes. The "Maid of Honour" concerned is sometimes said to have been Anne Boleyn (1511 or 1507—1536), before she married King Henry VIII (1491–1547), but charming though the story is, the cakes do not seem to have appeared for at least 200 years after her death.

## Recipes

~~~

The following recipe for the famous cocky leeky soup is taken from *The Cook and Housewife's Manual* by Christian Isobel Johnstone or "Mistress Margaret Dods." See January 25 for more on this particular book. The authenticity of prunes as an ingredient of cock-a-leekie soup is a point of contention amongst food historians. Mistress Dods did not include them.

### Cock-a-Leekie

Boil from four to six pounds of good shin-beef, well broken, till the liquor is very good. Strain it, and put to it a capon, or large old fowl, and, when it boils, half the quantity of blanched leeks intended to be used, well cleaned, and cut in inch-lengths, or longer. Skim this carefully. In a half-hour add the remaining part of the leeks, and a seasoning of pepper and salt. The soup must be very thick of leeks, and the first part of them must be boiled down into the soup till it becomes a green lubricious compound. Sometimes the capon is served in the tureen with the cock-a-leekie. This is good leek-soup without a fowl.

Obs.—Some people thicken cock-a-leekie with the fine part of oatmeal. Those who dislike so much of the leeks may substitute shred greens, or spinage and parsley, for one half of them. Reject the coarse part of the leeks. Prunes wont to be put to this.

Scotch Broth: see October 31.
Haggis: see January 25.

# December

## December 1

Australian Meat Banquet
Lambeth Baths, London, England, 1869

There was a great deal of interest in the "cheap food question" in mid-nineteenth-century Britain. The population was expanding but there were serious problems in the beef industry, and the poor had even less chance than usual of finding affordable animal protein. The campaign to increase the consumption of horsemeat (see December 19) faced significant cultural obstacles —the British being far too fond of their horses to seriously consider eating them. A second possibility came along in the form of meat from Australia— one of Britain's colonies that was producing a surplus. Refrigeration technology was in its infancy, and it would not be until February 1880 that the first successful consignment of frozen meat from Australia arrived in England. Imports before this time were of canned meat, and the meat was therefore already cooked.

Invitations were issued through the Working Men's Club and Institute Union to a dinner of Australian meat to be provided by a committee of colonists on December 1, 1869. Fifteen hundred working men attended the dinner, which was cooked not by professionals but "entirely by the wives of artisans," although "the dishes were supervised and prepared under the direction of persons who are engaged in the importation of meat into this country, who also took care that the articles used in the composition of the bill of fare were the best of their kind."

In the end, although a few declared the meat "extremely good," some of the leading speakers agreed that

> the meat which had been served to the company could not be compared with what came from the butchers' shops in London. . . . The best that can be said for it is that it was wholesome; for, whether in mince or a stew, it was certainly not particularly palatable. The sausages served with hot potatoes were something like the German sausage, though scarcely so eatable . . . the stew, on the whole, was not bad . . . but "the minced meat and rice" was an execrable dish.

The dinner was described in the *Penny Illustrated* newspaper as follows:

> There were six courses: the first an Irish stew, the average contents of dish sufficient for four persons, being 1lb. of meat and 4 lb. of vegetables, costing 8d. The second, meat-and-potato pies, the average contents for a dish sufficient for five

persons, being 1 1/2 lb. of meat, 8 lb. of potatoes, and two onions, costing 8d. The third, minced meat and rice, the average contents of a dish for three persons being 1 lb.of meat and 1 lb. of rice, costing 5d. The fourth, sausages and potatoes; the fifth, meat rolls; and the sixth, tea, dessert, biscuits, &c. There were no intoxicating liquors, and in lieu of soup, each visitor was presented with a cake of solid essence of meat to take home with him.

## Recipes

~~~

There were many pamphlets and recipes circulated on the use of Australian meat.

*Cassells Dictionary of Cookery*, published in the 1870s, included a special section on the use of Australian meat which contained 100 recipes. It noted that there was "considerable prejudice" against the tinned meat "owing to a great extent, to the fact that few know how to cook them properly. If the recipes, here given, however, are followed, it will be found easy, even for a cook of moderate abilities, to prepare from Australian meats a succession of tasty as well as digestible and nourishing dishes."

---

### Irish Stew

Boil six onions sliced in a quart of water with six large potatoes peeled and cut in half; pepper and salt pretty freely. When boiled tender, but not broken, thicken the gravy with flour and brown it; then take small pieces about three inches square and one inch thick of Australian mutton, pepper and salt them, an turn them over and over until well covered in flour; fry in a little fat, place in the centre of the dish, put the potatoes round and a few over the meat, pour over the gravy, and serve. A few light dumplings, made with one teaspoonful of baking powder to a pound of flour, may be served with the stew.

---

### Meat with Potato Cover

Mince some Australian mutton, season with pepper and salt, mix with it a teacupful of broth, and put in a shallow dish. Boil up some mealy potatoes, mash them, beat them up with an egg, a bit of butter, and a little milk; spread this mixture smoothly over the meat, and bake till of a golden brown.

---

## December 2

### Scottish Mountaineering Club 10th Annual Dinner
### Central Hotel, Edinburgh, Scotland, 1898

The Scottish Mountaineering Club was founded by a group of enthusiastic and experienced mountaineers, some of whom had experience in the European Alps, who wished to explore and promote the hills and mountains of their own country. From the beginning the club produced a regular journal as well as guidebooks to the hills and mountains of Scotland. In 1990 the club finally decided to admit women, an idea that would have been inconceivable to the 54 men who sat down to the dinner that followed the 10th annual meeting in 1898.

---

MENU

Les Huîtres au Naturel

POTAGES
Consommé Vermicelli
Crême de Celeri

POISSON
Cabillaud bouilli—Sauce Oeufs
Blanchielles Diable

ENTRÉES
Kromeskies a la Russe     Tournedos de Boeuf pique.
—
Haggis

RELEVÉS
Selle de Mouton rôti
Capon bouilli—Sauce Persil

RÔTIS
Perdreaux Rôtis—Sauce Pain

ENTREMETS
Pouding Soufflé a la Vanille
—
Gelée au Vin.     Crême au Café
—
Harengs fumées sur Croûte
—
Dessert et Café Noir

---

It is a testament to a strong national feeling that this formal, elegant dinner of classic dishes had, right in the middle,—a cheap peasant meal made from offal, the iconic Scots dish of haggis. Whether or not it was "piped in" in traditional manner (see January 25) and enjoyed by all, or whether it had a small but symbolic presence at this dinner is unknown, but either way, it was a clear nationalistic statement. The president, in his proposing of the toast to "The Club" reinforced the message in his own way when he "dwelt with satisfaction upon the increased membership of the Club, but remarked that Scotland would require to see to it that the proper proportion of Scots and Sassenachs was maintained, and that the balance of power was not turned in favour of the bold scramblers from south of the Solway, who had been coming into the Club (and they were very welcome) in increased numbers during recent years.'' He then "concluded with a panegyric on the Scottish hills, which he was inclined to think would have been more generally appreciated in Scotland if they had been placed anywhere else—fashionable Switzerland, for instance.''

Recipes

~~~

---

### Bread Sauce (Very Fine)

1/2 pint breadcrumbs,
1/2 pint milk,
1 oz. butter,
2 tablespoonfuls cream,
seasoning pepper and salt,
a very little cayenne.

   Make the milk boiling hot in a lined saucepan. Put the breadcrumbs in a basin, and pour the milk on to them. Cover the basin with a plate and let the crumbs remain to soak for 15 minutes, then turn the sauce back into the saucepan, add the butter, pepper, and salt, and let it simmer for 5 minutes. Stir in the cream, and a very slight sprinkling of cayenne; boil again for 2 minutes, and serve immediately.
   Ethel S. Meyer, *A Practical Dictionary of Cookery* (1898).

---

Cod with Egg Sauce: see March 11.
Parsley Sauce: see May 29.
Blanchielles (blanchailles) Diable (deviled whitebait) see: August 14.
Haggis: see January 25.
Coffee Cream: see April 13.

## December 3

Tithe-Audit Dinner
Weston Longville, Norfolk, England, 1782

James Woodforde (see April 20) was a village parson in Norfolk, England. His curacy provided him with a comfortable livelihood, and he had numerous farmer tenants. Once a year, in the first week of December, it was Tithe Audit Day—the day that the annual rental obligation was calculated and paid. The word "tithe" comes from an old word meaning "a tenth" as this was the traditional part (of produce or money) given to support the clergy or religious house. Parson Woodforde collected 265 pounds on this occasion, and as usual made it into a fine social event. He always gave his tenants a generous dinner.

> Dec. 3. This being the Day for my Tithe Audit, the following Farmers paid me
> their Tithes . . . [he lists 25 names] They all dined here . . . but Jn. Pegg and Mr.
> Mann stayed till near 11 at night. I gave them for Dinner, some Salt Fish, a
> Leg of Mutton boiled and Capers, a Knuckle of Veal, a Piggs Face, a fine Surloin
> of Beef rosted, and plenty of plumb Puddings . . . Wine drank 6 Bottles. Rum
> drank 5 Bottles, besides Quantities of strong Beer and Ale.

Woodforde always enjoyed these occasions, usually referring to them as his
"frolicks." Two small incidents marred this day, when ""Forster behaved so
insolent towards me that I don't intend to have him ever again at my Frolick
. . . Poor Jn. Buck broke one of my decanters."

The tithe-audit dinners always had plenty of meat and plenty of plum pudding. There was often salt fish too, as it kept well and was therefore particularly useful for large gatherings. In the days before refrigeration, catering for
larger parties was particularly problematic, so food that could be preserved
ahead for the occasion, such as the plum pudding, was particularly useful.
Salt fish, which kept for very long periods, was often on the table at Woodforde's tithe audit, and was no doubt a favorite of some of his guests. The
"pigg's face" too was a cheap (but very popular) alternative to ham or bacon,
and could be prepared ahead in a number of ways. A pig's face or "head" consisted of the cheek, lower jaw, and half the tongue and snout. It was boned,
pickled (and sometimes cured) and used to make a type of brawn (see April
28) called "head cheese" or it could be "collared" (see September 15). Sometimes the boned meat was compressed in a mold, then when it was "set," it
was coated in breadcrumbs and sliced and cooked like bacon or eaten cold
like ham.

## Recipes

~~~

### To Roll a Pig's Head

Clean it, rub it with common salt, then strew an ounce of salt petre on it, turn it
every day for seven days, then boil it in soft water till the bones and gristles slip
out, take four cow hells, dress them, boil them till the lantern will come off, lay
the lantern on a cloth, beat the pig's head a little in a bowl, spread it upon the
lantern, roll it up round and tight in a cloth, then put it in a pot or frame the size
you wish it, it must be put in hot, set a lead weight upon it, and in a few days it
will be fit to turn out. It is very good put into a frame or pot without the lantern,
this will be good in a week or ten days, when you find the outside turns soft,
make a pickle as thus, take a gallon of spring water, two handfuls of common
salt, and a large handful of wheat bran, a quarter of an ounce of salt petre, boil
these half an hour, strain it through a hair sieve, and when cold put the roll in.

Sarah Martin.Doncaster, *The New Experienced English-Housekeeper* (1800).

Salt Cod: see March 11.
Boiled Leg of Mutton: see September 21.
Plum Pudding: see June 28.

# December 4

### Funeral Feast of the Bishop of Bath and Wells
### Bishop's Palace, Wells, Somerset, England, 1424

Nicholas Bubwith held the traditional secular offices of Lord Privy Seal and Lord High Treasurer as well as the bishoprics of London and Salisbury before he became bishop of Bath and Wells in October 1407. When he died in 1424, a great funeral feast was held with two different bills of fare—one of fish (*de Piscibus*) for the clergy, and one of meat (*de carnibus*) for the laity.

During the middle ages, the clergy were expected to adhere to a fish diet on more (or all) days in the year than the lay public, because it was considered to

| DE CARNIBUS. | DE PISCIBUS. |
|---|---|
| LE .J. COURS. | LE .J. COURS. |
| Nomblys de Roo. | Elys in sorry. |
| Blamangere. | Blamanger. |
| Braun, cum Mustard. | Bakoun heryng. |
| Chynes de porke. | Mulwyl taylys. |
| Capoun Roste de haut grece. | Lenge taylys. |
| Swan Roste. | Jollys of Samoun. |
| Heroun Rostyd. | Merlyng so[th]e. |
| Aloes de Roo. | Pyke. |
| Puddyng de Swan necke. | Grete Plays. |
| Un Lechemete. | Leche barry. |
| Un bake, viz. Crustade. | Crustade Ryal. |
| | |
| LE .IJ. COURS. | LE .IJ. COURS. |
| Ro Styuyd. | Mammenye. |
| Mammenye. | Crem of Almaundys. |
| Connyng Rostyd. | Codelyng. |
| Curlew. | Haddok. |
| Fesaunt Rostyd. | Freysse hake. |
| Wodecokke Roste. | Solys y-so[th]e |
| Pertryche Roste. | Gurnyd broylid with a syryppe. |
| Plouer Roste. | Brem de Mere. |
| Snytys Roste. | Roche. |
| Grete byrdes Rosted. | Perche. |
| Larkys Rostyd. | Menus fryid. |
| Vennysoun de Ro Rostyd. | Yrchouns. |
| Yrchouns. | Elys y-rostyd. |
| Un leche. | Leche lumbard. |
| Payn puffe. | Grete Crabbys. |
| Colde bakemete. | A cold bakemete. |

be a diet more conducive to higher thought and contemplation (see February 23). This particular meal took place on the first day of Advent, when devout members of the Church began their pre-Nativity "fast."

The master cooks and advisers who planned the food for this event clearly went to some trouble to ensure that there were similarly styled dishes for each set of guests. Standard dishes that appear on many medieval feast menus (spelled in a confusing variety of ways) such as *mammenye* (a dish of ground spiced meat), *yrchouns* (meatballs stuck with almonds or spikes of pastry to resemble urchins or hedgehogs—see September 16), *blamanger* (a white dish of rice and chicken, the ancestor of sweet dessert dishes), *leches* (see October 13) and *crustades* and *bake-metes* (food cooked in pastry "coffins," ancestors of the modern pie; see December 4) all had their non-meat variations.

Recipes

~~~

---

### Blamanger of Fyshe

Take Rys, an sethe hem tylle they brekyn, & late hem kele; þan caste þer-to mylke of Almaundys; nym Perche or Lopstere, & do þer-to, & melle it; þan nym Sugre with pouder Gyngere, & caste þer-to, & make it chargeaunt, and þan serue it forth.

Thomas Austin, *Two Fifteenth-Century Cookery-Books* (1430).

Interpretation: Take rice, and boil it till soft ("breaking up") and let it cool. Then add almond milk, perch or lobster, and mix it. then add sugar and powdered ginger and make it thick, and serve it forth.

---

### Crustardes of Flessh

Take peiouns, chykens, and smale briddes smyte hem in gobettes. & seeþ hem alle ifere in god broþ wiþ veriaws do þerto safroun, make a crust in a trape. and pynche it. & cowche þe flessh þerinne. & cast þerinne Raisouns coraunce. powdour douce and salt. breke ayrenn and wryng hem thurgh a cloth & swyng þe sewe of þe stewe þerwith and helde it uppon the flessh. couere it & bake it wel. and serue it forth.

*The Form of Cury* (1390).

Interpretation: Take pigeons, chickens, and small birds and chop them in pieces and simmer them in good broth with verjuice and add saffron. Make a crust in a trap [a wooden hoop] and pinch it [presumably to decorate the edges of the pastry] and add raisins, currants, sweet powder (a standard spice mix, the ingredients are uncertain) and salt. Break eggs and strain them through a cloth and mix with the meat and put it in the pastry shell and put a pastry lid on it and bake it well and serve it forth.

---

Blamanger: see January 7.
Braun (brawn): see September 22.
Connyng Rostyd: see August 15.
Yrchouns: see September 16.

## December 5

British MPs' Dinner
Hotel Cosmopolitan, Nice, France, 1903

A group of 100 British Parliamentary delegates (accompanied by 80 ladies) visited France in 1903 to "reinforce the improvement in Anglo-French relations." It was noted that the period of estrangement that had existed between the countries for a considerable time had been not just mutually prejudicial, but "there can be no doubt that third parties have understood how to turn it to advantage" and that "The cultivation of direct and friendly intercourse between the peoples themselves is beginning to be recognised as the safest means of avoiding acute international conflicts." It was a reciprocal visit, as a number of French senators and deputies had visited Westminster the previous July.

Although a point had been made that the visit was being made "in the national interest," the delegates clearly had a fine time too. Once the formal few days in Paris were over, about 80 in total ("ladies as well as gentlemen") went on a tour of the French provinces and were entertained at a variety of receptions, dinners, and fêtes.

On December 5, it was the turn of Nice, in the South of France, and a fine dinner was given to the visitors at the Hotel Cosmopolitan.

---

|  |  |
|---|---|
| Oxtail Soup | |
| Crème de Volaille Princesse | |
| Truite de Rivière au Chablis | |
| Pommes Vapeur | |
| Pièce de Boeuf Carrignan aux Primeurs du Littoral | Xérès Montillade |
| Mignonnette de Pauillac Clamart | |
| Parfait de Foie gras Royale | Graves 1898 |
| Sorbets Dame Blanche | |
| Faisans d'Ecosse en Grande Chasse | Moët et Chandon 1893, Cuvée 20 |
| Salade Niçoise | |
| Asperges en branches Sauce Vierge | Saint-Emilion |
| Bombe Edouard VII | Mont-Bousquet 1893 |
| Gâteau Historié | |
| Pièce Montée | Chambertin 1897 |
| Corbeille de Fruits panachés | |
| Fromages | Louis Roederer |
| Desserts | Extra Dry, Reserve for Great Britain |
| Café et Liqueurs | |
| Grande Fine Champagne Bisquit Dubouché | |

---

The usual compliments to the visitors were given via the naming of some of the menu items. It was ox-tail soup (an English favorite), not *soupe* (or potage) *de queue de bœuf*, the ice cream bombe was named for the King of England, and the grouse was from Scotland. There is the quintessentially French *foie gras*, and a local specialty was featured too—the still-popular *Salade Niçoise*. As with most if not all regional and other speciality dishes, there is an ongoing debate about authenticity of recipes. There are arguments about whether greens, potatoes, or beans should be included in a salade Niçoise. Most "authorities" agree that good quality canned tuna is to be preferred to fresh. Reasonably consistent inclusions are tomatoes, olives, anchovies, and a garlicky dressing. There is also reasonably consistent agreement that it should *not* contain cheese. As for the originator, there are many claimants, but the most popular is that it was the choreographer George Balanchine, and the place was Monte Carlo, not Nice.

Recipes

~~~

To show how widely the recipes for salade Niçoise vary, here are two quite different versions, both from authoritative French sources. The first one does not contain any tuna, the second one no potatoes or beans, and neither has olives.

---

Salade Niçoise

1. Mix equal parts of potatoes and French (string) beans, both cut in dice. Season with oil, vinegar, salt and pepper. Arrange in a dome in a salad dish. Decorate with fillets of anchovies, olives, and capers. Garnish with quartered tomatoes. Sprinkle with chopped chervil and tarragon.
   Prosper Montagne, *Larousse Gastronomique* (1961 English edition).

2. Tunny fish in oil, tomato, anchovy fillets cut into cubes, mixed with vinaigrette sauce with chopped tarragon, chervil, chives. A little mustard may be added.
   Auguste Escoffier, *Ma Cuisine* (1965).

---

Sauce Vierge (virgin sauce) is virgin olive oil.
Oxtail Soup: see March 21.

## December 6

Repeal Dinner
Waldorf-Astoria Hotel, New York, 1933

The "Noble Experiment" of Prohibition finally ended just before nightfall on December 5, 1933, in the Unites States. For 13 years, 10 months, 19 days, 17 hours, 32 1/2 minutes, since the ratification of the National Prohibition Act (the "Volstead Act"), the country had been officially "dry." Customers had been glued to radios across the country, waiting eagerly for the moment

Repeal rush to buy liquor. (AP Photo)

to be announced, and they expected to be able to celebrate immediately. There was a scramble for sufficient stocks of alcohol to fuel the expected rush amongst restaurant and hotel owners who were just as eager for prohibition to end. Some were in readiness for special dinners on the night of the fifth, but many others, uncertain of repeal actually going ahead, unsure of supplies, and wanting time to plan a sufficiently magnificent event, held off until the following day.

The Waldorf-Astoria in New York held its Repeal Dinner on the night of the sixth of December. The dinner was arranged by the hotel's famous *maître d'hotel*, Oscar Tschirky ("Oscar of the Waldorf"). Guests paid $10 each for which they received one pint of champagne in addition to the following menu.

Delices Escoffier
Oxtail Parisienne
Almonds, Celery, Olives
Filet of Pompano, Saute Meunière
Pommes Persillees
Tournedo Saute Aux Fines Herbes
Petits Pois a la Francaise
Sorbet au Kirsch
Supreme de Pintade Lavalliere
Hearts of Endive and Beet Salad
Peche de France des Gourmets
Friandises      Demi Tasse

Sherry, Sauterne, Claret, Champagne, or Still
Or Sparkling Burgundy, Cognac

Prohibition did not reduce alcohol consumption, and many historians believe that in fact it actually increased, and the number of drinking establishments may have doubled. It is ironic that the 1920s are also referred to as the Cocktail Age. Cocktails perhaps flourished because being brightly colored and garnished they were not immediately identifiable as alcoholic drinks. One large downside to the Noble Experiment was that organized crime and corruption flourished to meet the demand for the illegal substance. There were also loopholes in the law which encouraged creative solutions. Alcohol could be prescribed for medicinal reasons, and wine could be brewed at home, for example. Restaurants confident of the discretion of regular customers would supply it in their private dining rooms, and the Biltmore listed its offerings via a little note called an *Entre Nous* (Between Ourselves) slipped into the spine of its menu.

## Recipes

~~~

Oscar Tshirky was not a chef, but he was a magnificent *maître d'hotel* or organizer of events, and he supervised the activities of the kitchen minutely. He wrote his own cookbook, called simply *The Cook Book*, in 1896. The artichoke and potatoes recipes are from this book.

*Delices Escoffier* are hearts of artichoke stuffed with crab meat. The following recipe from Tschirky's book shows how the artichoke itself must be prepared.

---

### Artichokes Boiled Plain

Cut off the tips of the leaves and round off the bottoms, removing the stalk and trimming the under leaves away. Soak in salt and water, washing well. Boil them in salt and water until they are quite tender; the leaves come away readily when they are done. Use a large quantity of water for the boiling, as it helps to rid them of a slight bitterness prevalent, especially in the autumn. When cooked drain on a cloth, and then remove with a spoon the soft fibrous substance found inside, and which is sometimes termed the ''choke.'' Then place once more in boiling water to heat up and take out again, drain and serve in a vegetable dish with a strainer, or upon a neatly-folded napkin. Serve with melted butter.

---

### Pommes Persillees (Potatoes and Parsley)

Place in a saucepan of boiling water some well washed and peeled small potatoes, boil for five minutes and then strain off the water, and pour in enough fresh boiling water to height of potatoes, add a lump of butter and a little salt and boil them until they become quite tender; then remove them carefully and put them in a deep dish, keeping them near the fire. Place in the liquor in which the potatoes were boiled a moderate quantity of finely-chopped parsley, boil for a few minutes and until somewhat thickly reduced; then pour the sauce over the potatoes, and serve.

---

Petits Pois à la Française: see December 6.
Sauce Meuniere: see July 23.

## December 7

### Dinner with Sir Arthur Conan Doyle
### Aldine Club, 75 Fifth Avenue, New York, 1894

The Aldine Club was started in 1889, its membership being ''composed chiefly of editors, artists, and men generally of artistic and literary tastes.'' In 1894, the writer Arthur Conan Doyle (1859–1930) made it his head-quarters while he was visiting the United States. Conan Doyle was a Scot (his gravestone declares him to be Patriot, Physician & Man Of Letters), and he is best known as the creator of the enormously popular detective Sherlock Holmes.

On the eve of Doyle's departure home aboard the Cunard ship *Etruria*, the members of the Aldine Club gave a dinner in his honor, at which there were 60 guests.

---

BILL OF FARE

Oysters
Olives      Radishes

Mock Turtle      Consommé

Bluefish
Potato Croquettes

Saddle of Mutton
Brussels Sprouts

Chicken Cutlets
French Peas

Orange Sherbert

Squab on Toast

Lettuce Salad

Roquefort and Camembert Cheese
Toasted Crackers

Ice Cream

Cake

Coffee

Crème De Menthe

---

The specific inclusion on this menu of the sweet mint liqueur *crème de menthe* is a little unusual. If any after-dinner spirit or liqueur was mentioned at all on a menu such as this, it was usually port or brandy. It is doubly strange because crème de menthe has a long-standing reputation of being a ladies' drink, and this was certainly an all male dinner.

It is not unusual to end a meal with mint—although nowadays it is in chocolate-coated form. The roots of the tradition are very old indeed. Mint has an ancient reputation as a remedy, particularly as a digestive. It was first mentioned in this capacity in a ninth-century leechbook (a *leech* was an ancient name for someone who practiced the healing art), and it was still in the British Pharmacopoeia in 1833. There are many species of mint, as the plant is notorious for interbreeding, but all contain the volatile oil that give it its characteristic smell and its supposed medicinal quality.

## Recipes

~~~

---

### Potato Croquettes

2 cups hot riced potatoes.
2 tablespoons butter.
1/2 teaspoon salt.
1/8 teaspoon pepper.
1/4 teaspoon celery salt.
Few drops onion juice.
Yolk 1 egg.
1 teaspoon finely chopped parsley.

Mix ingredients in order given, and beat thoroughly. Shape, dip in crumbs, egg, and crumbs again, fry one minute in deep fat, and drain on brown paper. Croquettes are shaped in a variety of forms. The most common way is to first form a smooth ball by rolling one rounding tablespoon mixture between hands. Then roll on a board until of desired length, and flatten ends.

Fannie Merritt Farmer, *The Boston Cooking-School Cookbook* (Boston, 1896).

---

### Bluefish Baked Whole

Choose a medium-sized bluefish; have it drawn from the gills to avoid splitting it; wash it in cold salted water, and stuff it with the following forcemeat: Soak a pint of stale bread in cold water, and squeeze out the water when the bread is soft; meanwhile chop fine a small onion, two tablespoonfuls of parsley, and a teaspoonful of fresh thyme, savory, or sweet marjoram; put these ingredients into a frying-pan with a tablespoonful of butter and the soaked bread, and stir them over the fire until they are smoking-hot. Use this forcemeat for stuffing the fish. On the bottom of a dripping-pan put half a pound of salt pork, cut in slices; lay the fish on the pork, season it highly with salt and pepper, and put it into a hot oven to bake. Let it cook until it is nicely browned, and the skin begins to crack; a medium-sized fish will cook in about an hour. Change the fish from the pan to a hot platter, lay the pork on it, and serve it as soon as it is done. Bluefish is excellent either fried or broiled.

*Miss Corson's Practical American Cookery and Household Management* (New York, 1886).

---

Mock Turtle Soup: see July 4.

## December 8

Fashionable Hotel Dinner
Fifth Avenue Hotel, New York, 1860

In August 1859 a new hotel opened in New York. The location was a bit further "uptown" than other prominent hotels in the city, but not, it was hoped, too far to render it an inconvenient location for travellers. It was on Fifth Avenue, on the west side of Madison Square between 23rd and 24th streets. The disadvantage of distance was compensated for by all modern conveniences being provided. There were separate entrances and reception rooms for ladies, and "vertical railways to each and every corner of the house." That it was both massive and beautiful were certain. Eight hundred guests could be accommodated, the exterior was clad in white marble in the Italian style, and a superb view of the city could be obtained from the observatory at the top.

The kitchens and dining rooms were equally impressive. The chimneys reached 25 above the roof to ensure smoke and cooking smells did not annoy any of the guests. The main dining hall (or "grand ordinary") was 90 feet long by 60 feet wide and 21 feet high and had adjacent to it wine closets, pantries, and a carving room with steam tables. There was another small dining room for those wishing to have early dinners and breakfasts, and a ladies' tea room. And finally, there was a separately managed restaurant. Diners could choose to dine *à la carte* (from the menu) or *table d'hôte* (see October 10).

A few months before the outbreak of the Civil War, on December 8, 1860, the hotel guests were offered the following dinner menu.

---

SOUP.
Pea Soup.
Vegetable.

FISH.
Boiled Haddock, Oyster Sauce.      Baked Bass, Claret Sauce.

BOILED.
Leg of Mutton, Caper Sauce.      Corned Beef and Cabbage.
Turkey, Oyster Sauce.      Capons, Celery Sauce.
Beef Tongue.      Calf's Head, Brain Sauce.      Ham.

COLD DISHES.
Roast Beef.      Tongue.
Chicken Salad.      Pressed Corned Beef.      Boned Turkey.
Ham.      Lamb.

ENTREES.
Mutton Cutlets, Breaded, Tomato Sauce.
Broiled Squabs, à la Maitre d'Hôtel.

Fillet of Fish, à la Chambrois.

Fillet of Pork, with Apples.

Escalloped Oysters, à la Crême.

Venison Steaks, Jelly Sauce.

Calf's Liver, à l'Italienne.

Poulettes à la Toulouse.

Macaroni, with Cheese.

Kidneys, in Cases.

### ROAST.

Beef.    Turkey.

Tame Ducks.    Spring Chickens.

Lamb.    Ham, Champagne Sauce.

### GAME.

Mallard Ducks.    Widgeons.

### VEGETABLES.

Mashed Potatoes.    Spinach.    Boiled Rice.

Boiled Potatoes.    Turnips.    Cabbage.

Cauliflowers.    Squash.    Boiled Hominy.

Onions.    Boiled Beets.    Stewed Tomatoes.

Baked Potatoes.    Corn. Baked.    Sweet Potatoes.

Parsnips.

### PASTRY.

Sago Pudding.

Jelly Puffs.    Apple Pies.

Lafayette Cake.    Peach Pies.

Charlotte Russe.    Gooseberry Pies.

Wine Jelly.    Confectionery.

### DESSERT.

Raisins.    Almonds.    Pecan Nuts.

English Walnuts.    Filberts.    Apples.

Oranges.    Hickory Nuts.

Vanilla and Orange Ice Cream.

Coffee.

---

The menu was typical of its time for a large hotel and so comprehensive that every guest could not have failed to find something desirable for dinner.

Recipes

~~~

## Lafayette Cakes

Make a Savoy biscuit [see below] and bake it in a tin pan, with straight sides; when cold, cut it in thin slices (a quarter of an inch in thickness), spread each with jelly, or jam, and put it together again, three or four slices for each, or put them all together; ice the cake on the top and sides, and serve cut in quarters.

## Savoy Biscuit

12 eggs,
weight of 12 eggs in sugar,
weight of 7 eggs in flour,
1 lemon.

Beat whites and yellows separately; grate the rind of the lemon, and add the yellows to the sifted sugar, and the juice of the lemon or peach water, after being in the oven a few minutes, grate sugar over.

*The Housekeeper's Assistant, Composed Upon Temperance Principles,* By An Old Housekeeper. (Boston, 1845).

## Celery Sauce

Strip the outer parts of the stem, and, after carefully washing the remaining portion, cut it into small pieces; put to it a blade of mace without any other spice, and stew it in good veal broth until very tender; it will take a good deal of time, more particularly the thick hard end of the root. After this thicken it with melted butter, and flavor it with a small quantity of white wine; or it may be thickened with boiled cream without wine. It is usually served with boiled turkey, but is very delicate with any kind of white poultry or veal.

Elizabeth Fries Ellet, *The Practical Housekeeper; A Cyclopedia of Domestic Economy* (New York, 1867).

## Caper Sauce

Put whole capers into melted butter, adding a little of the vinegar they are pickled in, a pinch of salt, and sufficient cream to make it white. This is used principally for boiled mutton.

Elizabeth Fries Ellet, *The Practical Housekeeper; A Cyclopedia of Domestic Economy* (New York, 1867).

Champagne Sauce for Ham: see May 27.
Oyster Sauce: see August 7.
Charlotte Russe: see September 4.
Calf's Head: see January 30.

## December 9

Firefighters Banquet
Hôtel de la Madeleine, Barberaz, France, 1928

The firefighters of France usually held their annual dinner on, or very close to, December 4, the feast day of their Patron Saint, Saint Barbara. The men of Barberaz in the Savoie region celebrated a few days late in 1928. The menu for the dinner was very much in theme with their occupation.

---

BANQUET DES SAPEURS-POMPIERS
DE BARBERAZ

Dimanche 9 December

*Hôtel de la Madeleine*

Hors d'Œuvre incendie.

—

Boyaux de Polailles au terrine.

—

Jambon, graisses de clapets
Lavarets de l'Alba . . . Meunière

—

Quenelles aux Champi-gnons

—

Cordons à la Moëlle

—

Closses de la Madeleine, rôties

—

Pissenlits Salade

—

Dessert Teculoth

—

Crême Tropeu

—

Fromages avarié

—

Fruits

—

Café—Gnôle de la Suisse

—

On bôsson de rouge petêta

---

The theme becomes clear when the menu names are translated. *Incendie* means a fire or conflagration; a *boyau(x)* is a winding trench leading to an explosive magazine and *polailles* are casings for explosives; *clapets* are valves and *graisse* is fat or grease; *cordons* presumably refers to a line of firefighters handing buckets man to man; and the cheeses are *avariés* or damaged. Some of the menu items are not so clear and may be proper names of individuals in the company, such as *Closses* and *Teculoth*. With the coffee was *gnôle* (booze) from Switzerland.

A green salad was served after the meat dishes and before the dessert, in the common pattern. In this case it was of dandelion leaves which are a popular salad vegetable in France, where it is cultivated—unlike many other countries where is it is considered a weed. The French name *pissenlit* translates as *piss-the-bed*, an acknowledgement of the diuretic qualities of the plant. It is often served as a warm salad with bacon, or, as in the following recipe, with pickled pork.

## Recipes
~~~

---

### Dandelion Salad

A dandelion salad is one of the healthiest of spring salads. Take two quarts of freshly gathered dandelions; wash them well; pick them over carefully; let stand in water over night, as this improves them. Drain, and dry in a napkin; place them in a salad-bowl; add two young spring onions, minced. Serve with a plain dressing.

Thomas Murrey, *The Murrey Collection of Cookery Books* (1895)

---

### Mushroom Quenelles

| | |
|---|---|
| 12 mushrooms | 1/2 oz. butter |
| 1/4 lb. Veal or Chicken | 1 egg |
| 1 oz. flour | 1/2 teacupful Milk |

The mushrooms should be a good size, and cupped a little for this dish. Cut the end only off the stalk, and pare them very carefully.

Now put the butter and flour into a pan and mix; add the milk, and let it boil, stirring very vigorously till a thick, smooth paste is obtained. Add a little salt and pepper, and turn out to cool.

Have the veal chopped, pounded, and rubbed through a wire sieve. Put it back in the mortar, and add to it the paste, and pound till it is thoroughly mixed; then break the egg in amongst it and mix. Again add 1/2 tea-spoonful salt, and a little pepper. Mix very thoroughly.

Have a knife wetted in boiling water. Put some of this mixture into the cup of the mushrooms, smoothing it like a cone round the stalks with the knife.

When all are finished, butter a stewpan and place the quenelles carefully in it; cover with a buttered paper. Add 1/2 teacupful of stock; cover it with the lid, and cook for 20 minutes.

Sauce: boil the trimmings of the mushrooms in a little stock; strain and mix with this 1 teaspoonful of corn-flour; pour all this in the pan the quenelles were cooked in; pour the sauce round. See that it is not too thick.

Mrs. Black, *Choice Cookery "La Bonne Cuisine"* (1890).

## December 10

First Nobel Prize Banquet
Hall of Mirrors, Grand Hotel, Stockholm, Sweden, 1901

Alfred Nobel (1833–1896) was a Swedish chemist and engineer who invented dynamite and owned a large armaments company. On his death he directed that some of his enormous wealth go toward the endowment of several prizes in important areas of human endeavour. The prizes for chemistry and physics were to be awarded by the Swedish Academy of Sciences, and those for physiology or medicine and literature by the Karolinska Institute in Stockholm. There was another prize—for an outstanding contribution to world peace, and Nobel directed that this be awarded by the Norwegian Parliament and delivered in Oslo. The conditions of the Peace Prize are interesting and intriguing because Nobel was a Swede, and at the time of his bequest, Norway was still ruled by Sweden as it had been since the end of the Napoleonic wars in 1814.

The Nobel prizes (except for the Peace Prize) are awarded in a ceremony in Stockholm on December 10, the anniversary of Nobel's death. A grand banquet follows, which has become a great event in its own right. At the first banquet in 1901, there were 113 guests, all of whom were male. The first woman to attend was Marie Curie (1867–1934) who was a joint winner of the physics prize in 1903, with her husband Pierre Curie (1859–1906) and Henri Bequerel (1852–1908).

---

MENU

Hors d´œuvre
Suprême de barbue à la Normande
Filet de bœuf à l'Impériale
Gelinottes rôties, Salade d´Estrée
Succès Grand Hôtel, Pâtisserie

VINS
Niersteiner 1897
Château Abbé Gorsse 1881
Champagne Crème de Bouzy
Doux et Extra Dry
Xerez

---

The number of guests attending the banquet has of course climbed since 1901, and over recent years has been of the order of 1,300. Planning starts months before, as the preparation required is enormous. In the days immediately before the banquet the tables are set up, a job which takes 25 people eight hours, and uses 470 meters of tablecloth. Then another 30 white-gloved workers lay out over 6,000 pieces of porcelain, over 5,000 crystal glasses, and over 9,000 pieces of cutlery.

On the night everything is carried out with military precision and great spectacle. Guests are required to adhere to a stringent dress code. For men, it is white tie, black tails, and no color apart from any medals or state decoration, and women must be in formal evening dress. Guests must also learn the complex rules of protocol and etiquette that apply throughout the evening.

The menu for the event is a tightly kept secret. Over the decades the food has changed with fashion and circumstances. Turtle soup was often on the menu in the early years, but it is now unethical. There is always some concession to the host country, and the obvious frosty climate means that ice cream has been on the menu at virtually every banquet—at the first one it was the *Succès Grand Hôtel*.

## Recipes
~~~

---

### Gelinottes Rôties
### (Roast Guinea Fowl)

Pluck, singe, and truss the guinea fowls carefully, lard with fine fillets of bacon, roast before a good fire and baste frequently, served garnished with watercress.
   *366 Menus and 1200 Recipes of the Baron Brisse* (1869; from the 1905 English translation).

---

## December 11

### Encyclopædia Britannica Dinner
### Hall of Christ's College, Cambridge, England, 1888

The *Encyclopædia Britannica* was the brainchild of two Scots, Colin Macfarquhar (1744/5–1793) and Andrew Bell (1726–1809). With the assistance of William Smellie (1740–1795) they produced the *Encyclopædia* in 100 weekly installments between 1768 and 1771. It is still in print more than 220 years later and has accrued a reputation for being a reliable and comprehensive reference and research tool.

The ninth edition was completed in 1888, thanks to the efforts of about a thousand scholars from around the world, and a banquet was held in Cambridge to celebrate. Nearly a hundred of those involved were able to attend, although there was a disappointingly large number of "letters of declinature," including those from Mr. Phelps, "Minister of the United States" and the French and German ambassadors.

---

Consomme à la Tortue.
Potage à la Reine.

Rougets à l'Italienne.
Filets de Sole à la Tartare.
Attereaux à l'Encylopédie.
Turban de Sarcelles aux olives.

Dinde aux Huitres.
Jambon de York.
Dindon à la Milanaise.
Selle de Mouton.

Faisans        Bécasses.

Poudins à la Victoria.
Gelées de Dantzie aux Fruits.
Charlottes à la Vénitienne.

Biscuits Glacées au Maraquin.
Canapés d'Anchois—Croûtes

Many of the guests this night had traveled up from London by rail, and a tight control of the proceedings was essential as a special train had been arranged for 10:45 to take them back to King's Cross. The end of the dinner was signaled by the passing around of the loving cup (see September 30), and those guests who did not have to meet the train continued on to a reception at the Master's Lodge.

There was one specially named dish on this menu—the *Attereaux à l'Encylopédie*. *Attereaux* (*atelets* or *hatelets*) are pieces of food on skewers. They differ from *brochettes* in that the food is precooked, before being coated in *Atelet* sauce and breadcrumbs before being deep fried and served either on or off the skewers. They can be made from almost anything from lambs' brains and ox palates to pieces of cheese to fried custard.

Recipes

~~~

### Anchovy Croûtes

6 Anchovies.         Bread.
2 Hard-boiled Eggs.  Cayenne, Carmine.
2 oz. Butter.        Parsley.

Wash the anchovies, and bone them; and pound them with the butter, the yolks of the hard-boiled eggs, the seasoning, and a little cayenne. Have eight pieces of fried bread neatly cut; put the mixture in a forcing bag with tube; decorate the rounds prettily with the anchovy paste. Have the whites of the eggs rubbed through a wire sieve; decorate the rounds with this, and a morsel of chopped parsley.

A dish named *Dantzig* or *Danzig* contains flakes of gold leaf. It comes from the liqueur *Danziger Goldwasser* which has been made since the sixteenth century in the city of Danzig (Gdańsk) in Poland. The liqueur has flakes of real gold suspended in it, which were believed to have medicinal value. Note: the purpose of the egg whites and shells is the same as in making a very clear consommé (see May 27). Particles of debris that would spoilt the appearance by making the consommé or jelly cloudy adhere to the protein in the egg white forming larger clumps that can easily be strained out.

---

### Dantzig Jelly

| | |
|---:|:---|
| 6 oz. Sugar. | 6 Cloves. |
| 1 ½ oz. Gelatine. | 2 Lemons. |
| 3 large breakfast-cupfuls of Water. | 2 Small Leaves of Gold Leaf. |
| 1 Blade of Mace. | 1 Small Stick of Cinnamon. |
| 2 Whites and Shells of Eggs. | |

Put the water in a saucepan, and all the other things—except the gold leaf—the rind of the lemons very thinly pared off and the juice pressed out, the cinnamon broken up, and the eggs. Whisk over the fire till it boils; let it boil for five minutes without whisking; let it settle for 5 minutes; pour twice through a jelly bag; put into a mould.

Put the gold leaf in the mould, and with a knife bread it up among the jelly. When firm, turn out. This jelly may be coloured pink and silver leaf put among it.

Mrs. Black, *Choice Cuisine* (1890s).

---

Victoria Pudding: a huge range of dishes go by this name, including frozen bombes, bread and butter puddings, suet puddings, and puddings made with sago and fresh fruit. For one version, see September 9.

Tartar Sauce: see July 20.
Potage a la Reine: see February 17.

## December 12

### Dinner for the Duke of Windsor
aboard the Zurich Express, 1936

When King Edward VIII (1894–1972) announced his wish to marry American socialite Wallis Simpson (1895–1986), her nationality alone would probably have been sufficient to cause a diplomatic crisis in Britain. Added to the horror was the knowledge that she had already been divorced twice—a shameful history according to the social mores of the time. In the end, King Edward gave up his throne rather than the woman he loved. Once he had made his decision events unfolded very rapidly. He informed the government on December 9 and signed the Instrument of Abdication on December 10; it was endorsed by Parliament and announced to the public on December 11; and on December 12 his brother was proclaimed King as George VI. By the end of the same day Edward had been created Duke of Windsor by the new King and was on his way out of the country and into exile, not to return until 1965.

On the evening of December 12, the Duke was aboard an ordinary Pullman train bound initially for Vienna, via Switzerland, with the final destination and exact route a secret. His Pullman car had eight compartments, the middle two occupied by himself, his personal attendants, and his dog, the others by detectives and other necessary staff. His first meal was specially ordered but prepared in the regular dining car, and served in a most unregal way on a makeshift table of stacks of suitcases.

---

Consommé
Filet of Sole
Chicken Salad
Ice Cream
Cheese
Coffee

---

This was a very light and simple meal, although considerable preparation goes into an apparently simple clear soup or consommé. The broth (of meat or fish) must be laboriously "clarified" with egg whites and careful straining. Tiny unwanted particles that would make the broth cloudy attach to the protein in the egg whites, which are then strained off. A good consommé though clear is expected to have a good flavor, so the clear broth must also be concentrated, a process which also results in the slightly gelatinous "mouth feel" that is desirable and is due to the dissolved collagen from the bones. Consommés are classified according to their major ingredient (chicken, beef, game, etc.) and the garnish (Madrilène—tomato, etc.).

## Recipes

~~~

René Roussin was *chef de cuisine* to the royal household in the 1930s. In 1960 he published a book called *Royal Menus* in which menus and recipes are interspersed with anecdotes and observations. The following recipes are from this book.

Filet de Sole Bonne Femme is a classic way of cooking sole.

---

### Filet de Sole Bonne Femme

| | |
|---|---|
| 1 1/2 lb fillets of sole | 2 oz. mushrooms |
| 1 medium shallot | 1 very small sprig parsley |
| 1/2 glass dry, white wine | 1 gill hollandaise sauce |
| pepper | salt |

Peel the mushrooms and cut them into fine strips. Take a shallow heat-proof dish, grease the inside with clarified butter and line the bottom with the mushrooms. Chop the shallot and parsley. Lightly season the fillets with pepper and salt and lay them on top of the mushrooms. Sprinkle the parsley and shallot on top. Add the wine, cover the dish securely with buttered paper, and put in a medium oven till cooked. Allow about 18 minutes.

Now drain off the liquor from the dish, put the dish aside to keep warm, and reduce the liquor in a saucepan on top of the stove, stirring it till it begins to become thick and sticky. Remove from the heat, stir in the hollandaise and coat the fillets in the dish with this sauce. Slip the dish, uncovered, under a hot salamander or grill just long enough for the surface to become golden brown without the hollandaise being brought to boiling point and spoiled. This means it must be browned quickly under a very sharp heat.

Serve at once in the dish in which it has been cooked.

---

### Chicken Salad

This hors d'oeuvre is made with the white meat of cold roast or boiled chicken. The flesh must come from young, tender birds but there is no reason why it should not consist of leftovers from a previous meal.

11/2½ tablespoons olive oil
1 dessertspoon wine vinegar
1 tablespoonful finely chopped chervil, parsley, tarragon (equal quantities of each)
freshly ground black pepper
pinch or two of fine salt, to taste.

Serve in a bowl in the centre of a circle of lettuce hearts.

---

Hollandaise Sauce: see April 14.

## December 13

### Catering Menu
### Calcutta, India, 1943

Life for some in wartime India had its compensations, it would appear from the menu offered by a catering company in Calcutta in 1943.

This is a menu of indisputably British food and A. Firpo's customers were presumably British officials and ex-patriats. There is absolutely nothing on this menu that hints at the "Great Famine of 1943" that was underway in Bengal, nor of the severe rationing restrictions that were in place in Britain at the same time.

The famine was devastating, perhaps as bad a human calamity as the Irish potato famine of 1845. It was due to a multiplicity of factors—the fall of Burma to the Japanese cut off supplies of rice from that country, and the 1942 domestic rice crop had been devastated by disease, and bad weather. Both producers and consumers (those who could afford to) were trying to stockpile food because of the fear of imminent Japanese invasion, and this contributed to price rises. There is no rice on this menu, but it is "British," and in the 1940s the most common use for rice in Britain was to make rice pudding.

Meat was rationed in Britain at this time, and the range of meat dishes on this menu would have been the stuff of forgotten dreams to the ordinary

HAMBURG STEAK AND ONIONS, Rs. 2/-
LUNCHEON, Rs. 3/-
—

1 Consomme Frappe      2 Cream Cauliflower
3 Nouilles Chicken Liver Sauce

4 Fried Becty Tartare Sauce
5 Langoustine Mayonnaise
6 Rognons Saute Turbigo
7 Grilled Ham Steak
8 Sausages & Mashed Potatoes

COLD MEATS: 9 Roast Fowl & Ham
10 Roast Saddle of Mutton or Roast Lamb      11 Roast Pork
12 Roast Sirloin of Beef      13 Roast Duck
14 Roast Teal or Roast Snipe      15 Spiced Hump      16 Tongue
17 Melton Mowbray Pie      18 Steak & Kidney Pie
19 Chicken & Ham Pie      20 Snipe Pie or Game Pie

21 Bread & Butter Pudding

22 Vanilla Icecream      23 Strawberry Icecream

24 Fruits      25 Coffee

---

| OLD ANGUS SCOTCH WHISKY | MONOPOL WHISKY | MONOPOLE WHISKY GIMLET | RUM COLLIN & GIMLET |
|---|---|---|---|
| Available Every Sunday & Wednesday Only | Available Every Day with Soda | Orange or Lime | Rs. 1/6 |
| Rs. 1/8 Half peg. | Rs. 1/12 Full Peg | Rs. 1/4 per Glass | |
| From 7 p.m. | –/14 Half Peg | | |
| Haywards Fine & Dry Gin available daily . | | | |

---

| | Half | Full | | Half | Full |
|---|---|---|---|---|---|
| Gin with Water or Soda | –14 | 1–12 | Gin & Gingerale | 1– | |
| Keo Dry Gin | 13 | 3– | Gin Lime & Soda | 1/4 | |
| Rum & Soda | 1–2 | 2–4 | Keo Gin Gimlet Or John Collins | 2– | 3–3 |

person. Bread was also rationed and the British housewife was exhorted not to waste a single crumb, but to save them to bulk up dishes such as meatloaf. With all fats, milk, and eggs rationed too, the idea of bread and butter pudding (a favorite British pudding) was a rare or nonexistent treat by this stage of the war.

The menu shows the numbering system of ordering common to Asian and Indian menus for English speakers (see March 31, April 25, and July 20). The only dish that is not strictly British and perhaps needs comment is the "spiced hump." This was buffalo hump, and it appeared regularly on A. Firpo's menus as well as those of other companies. Buffalo hump was prepared like corned meat (see April 30) or ham, and a journal article of 1807 comments that "Humps have long been a favorite dish at the splendid entertainments of the great Lords in India" (George and Robert Cruikshank, *Journal is Spirit of the Public Journals for 1807*).

Recipes

~~~

---

Bread and Butter Pudding

for 25 people
Use 1 1/4 quatern loaf,
3–4 eggs,
1 lb. fruit, mixed (this may be reduced),
2 quarts milk,
1/2 lb margarine,
and 1/2 lb. sugar.

Butter dishes well, cut bread thinly, butter it, place in layers in dish, sprinkled with fruit, little peel if possible. Heat milk, pour on to beaten eggs and sugar; mix well, then pour onto the bread. Leave for an hour or so to allow the bread to swell. Place dishes in a tin of water and cook in a slow oven till set and brown on top. Serve sprinkled with sugar.

This ordinary pudding can be so badly made that full instructions are given here. Naturally it can be made much richer if more eggs are used.

"Cookery for Canteens," *The Times*, January 17, 1940.

---

Melton Mowbray Pie: see November 3.
Consommé Frappé is a clear chilled soup.

## December 14

Hospital Fare
St. Luke's Hospital, Chicago, Illinois, 1920

The patients resident in St. Luke's Hospital in Chicago in 1920 had little to complain about in so far as the choice of food was concerned. The menu for the day could have come from a small restaurant or hotel.

BREAKFAST.
Fruit.
Cream of Wheat     Post Toasties
Little Pork Sausages
Apple Pancake
Plain Rolls     Jelly
Toast
Tea     Coffee     Chocolate

DINNER
Consomme Clear
Roast Domestic Duck—Dressing
Baked Apples
Mashed Potatoes
Wax Beans in Cream
Sliced Tomatoes—Dressing
Vanilla Ice Cream     Wafers
Tea     Coffee     Chocolate

SUPPER
Bouillon in Cups
Broiled Lamb Chops
Escalloped Potatoes
Green Peas
Pear Sauce     Sugar Cookies
Toast
Tea     Coffee     Chocolate

The idea of food as medicine is not new. The ancient Greek Hippocrates of Cos (ca. 460 BCE–ca.370 BCE) who is often referred to as the Father of Medicine, said "Let food by thy medicine and medicine be thy food." The basic concept has never gone away, but the specific details of dietary advice have changed over the centuries. It is easy to scoff at the idea of humoral medicine (see February 23) nowadays, but modern insistence on evidence-based medicine has not stopped the regular emergence of new gurus with magical food medicine theories.

A modern dietitian looking at the above menu would probably approve of the clear soup but balk at the idea of roast duck (very fatty) and cream sauce on the beans for any of us, let alone those confined to bed—particularly since many are there because of "over-nutrition" in the first place.

At the time of this hospital menu, dietary ideas were quite different. The author of *Food and Health: A Book for the Lay Reader Who Believes that*

*Health Is What We Make It* in 1924 wrote that "The most nutritious food is that which is (1) laxative in character; (2) the most easily digested; and (3) gives the greatest amount of food substances." Fat was not the enemy it is today. The "Instructor in Dietetics" at the University of Minnesota who wrote the baked apple recipe below wrote this about cream soups:

> Cream soups are combinations of thin white sauce and strained vegetable pulp. They form a light and easily digested form of food for the sick. The vegetables most suitable for use in cream soups are potatoes, peas, celery, tomatoes, beans, asparagus, corn and spinach. Onions are used for flavoring if desired. Food Values. Cream soups are high in food value. The milk or cream furnishes protein and fat in a digestible form, while the vegetables furnish starch and mineral salts. These soups are not suitable for use at a heavy meal, but for luncheon or extra nourishment between meals.

## Recipes

~~~

---

### Baked Apples

Select as many good apples of uniform size as may be needed. Wash, pare, and core them. Place them in a granite baking dish, fill the center of each apple with sugar, add a piece of butter on the top of each. Add enough water to cover the bottom of the pan. Bake in a hot oven until soft, basting often with the juice in the pan. Chill and serve plain, with whipped cream or soft custard.

    Gertrude I. Thomas, *The Dietary of Health and Disease: For the Use of Dietitians, Nurses and Instructors in the Sciences that Pertain to Nutrition* (1923).

---

### Cream of Wheat

Cream of wheat, farina, germea, wheatine: Five cups water to one cup meal. Cook one-half hour.

1. Measure water and put in upper part of double boiler. Put on stove to boil.
2. Add salt, and when boiling, sprinkle in the required amount of meal, stirring all the time to prevent lumps.
3. When thickened, put into the double boiler and cook the required length of time. Do not let the water in the lower part of boiler boil away.
4. Serve with milk or cream.

    The author advises: "Use one teaspoon salt to one quart water. In using prepared cereals, cook them at least twice as long as the time given on the package."

    *The Neighborhood Cook Book/Comp. Under the Auspices of the Portland Section in 1912, Council Of Jewish Women* (Portland, Oregon, 1914).

---

### Pear Sauce

Pare and then cover with just enough water to cook. Cook until tender and then mash and put through a fine sieve or colander. Sweeten to taste, adding juice of

one lemon, one tablespoon of either cinnamon or nutmeg to each quart of the
pear sauce. This may be used and served with roast duck, chicken, or as a side
dish, and in pear shortcake and as a spread for bread and hot cakes.
    Mrs. Mary A. Wilson, *Mrs. Wilson's Cook Book* (1920).

## December 15

Piemontese Society Banquet
All Hotel Campidoglio, Italy, 1897

It is not clear from the Piemontese Society menu for December 15, 1897, in
which city it was held, as there are hotels called *Campidoglio* (the name
means capitol) throughout Italy. It is most likely that this was an expatriate
group, living somewhere other than the Piedmont region, wishing to remain
in touch with their local heritage.

---

ANTIPASTO
Salame, Olive, Proscuitto, Sardine, Grissini.
*Sauterne*

ZUPPA
Consomme con Crostini
*Mezo Chianti*

PESCE
Vol au Vent di Ostriche alla Pozzo

UMIDI
Animelle al Madera
Ravioli alla SAN MARZANO
Filetto de bue con Piselli
ARROSTI
Tacchino novello allo JONA—Insalata indivia

*Frutta assortita—Formaggi assorti*

*Gelato Pezzi alla Napoletana—Caffe*

---

The banquet menu provides a good summary of Italy's contributions to the
world's culinary heritage, and especially its culinary language. The word
"banquet" itself comes from Italian. A "banquet" was originally a separate
course of sweetmeats and the like, served after the meal proper, and often
in a separate room. The word is derived from *banchetto* meaning a board, or
little table, referring presumably to the sideboard or bench where the treats
were spread.
    The word "antipasto" is now used fairly widely and loosely to mean appe-
tizers or *hors d'oeuvre* (see January 20). It means, literally, "before the

pasta"—the pasta being historically the staple food and therefore the reference point of the meal.

The great flowering of ideas in the Renaissance extended to the culinary sphere, and there was wealth enough amongst the elite families for them to indulge their every whim. The competition was intense to put on the most spectacular banquet, or offer an amazing new dish, and to obtain the services of the finest cooks. One of the amazing dishes of the Italian Renaissance was the flavored ice—the forerunner of modern ice cream, such as the *gelato* on this menu. It is not for nothing that the Italians have the best reputation in the world for ice cream—they have been making it a long time, and it was no mean feat in the days before refrigeration (see sherbet, April 29).

## Recipes
~~~

This *gelato* does not have any milk or cream and is more like a granita or sorbet—showing that the words are used quite randomly at times (see box).

---

### Lemon Ice (Gelato di Limone)

Granulated sugar, 3/4 lb.
Water, a pint.
Lemons, three (good sized).

Boil the sugar in the water, with some little pieces of lemon peel, for about ten minutes, in an uncovered kettle. When this syrup is cold, squeeze the lemons one at the time, tasting the mixture to regulate the degree of acidity. Then strain and put in the freezer packed with salt and ice.

Maria Gentile, *The Italian Cook Book: The Art of Eating Well, Practical Recipes of the Italian Cuisine, Pastries, Sweets, Frozen Delicacies, and Syrups* (New York, 1919).

---

Ravioli: see August 20

---

### The Naming of Ices

The differences between the various frozen confections depend on the ingredients (with or without dairy, with or without egg whites or whole eggs) and the texture, which is affected by the ingredients, particularly the concentration of sugar (which determines the freezing point of the mixture) and the method of churning during freezing. The words, however, are not used absolutely consistently between regions or cooks. For manufacturing purposes, there are also legal definitions as to the content of the various ices. In general the various types are as follows:

*Ice cream*: Contains dairy—either milk or cream or both. Very rich ice creams also contain eggs, which are used to make a custard base. The most rich custard-based ice creams are called "French."

*Gelato*: Italian ice cream, also with a custard base but with less cream than "French" ice cream. The result is a less rich but more intensely flavored ice cream.

*Granita*: Italian ice made from a simple syrup mixed with a flavoring (fruit purees, chocolate, coffee, etc.). A lower viscosity (lower sugar) syrup is used than in a sorbet, and less mixing or churning is done during the freezing process. The result is coarse, flaky ice crystals and a gritty but more liquid texture (closer to a drink.) A less elegant version is the brilliantly colored 'slushy" drink sold at movie theaters.

*Semi-freddo*: A"semi-frozen" Italian ice. The composition (high sugar or other ingredients) means that it never becomes completely solid.

*Sorbet/sherbet*: A smooth-textured non-dairy ice that may contains egg whites and is churned while freezing. (See June 10, April 29.)

# December 16

## Chicago Press Club's First Annual Banquet
## Briggs House, Chicago, Illinois, 1870

The first annual banquet of the Chicago Press club was naturally reported with great pride in the Chicago *Tribune*, whose editor, Elias Colbert, was president of the club. About 70 members attended the "most admirable affair." They were "glad of a chance to rest from their labors, on neutral ground, where they might mingle with each other as they mingled their wine around the social board, and where the rivalry of their profession, and the differences of thought and opinion, were left outside the door."

As was expected of the fine venue, the tables were laid with excellent taste, but without elaborate ornamentation, "as it was not desired." The menu was truly an extraordinary one for only 70 guests.

---

BILL OF FARE.

SOUP: Tomato, Oyster.

OYSTERS: Stewed, fried, escaloped, raw, oyster patties.

ORNAMENTAL DISHES: Boned turkey, with truffles on sockle; fortress of venison, ornamented en Bellevue; Pan de Volaille, decorated a la Fontainbleau; chartreuse of wild duck a la Pompadour; bastion of fat livers in jelly on sockle; breast of partridge decorated on a pedestal; Fillets de Dinde, ornamented in jelly; Westphalian ham, decorated a la Rothschild; chaud froid of pheasant a la Gen d'Arme; nests of quail, stuffed au natural on a pedestal; buffalo tongues decorated a la Parisian; aspic of oysters in a border of jelly; breast of prairie chicken a la Macedonie; mayonnaise of lobster in a border of jelly; chicken salads a la ancient.

BOILED: Leg of English mutton, caper sauce; turkey, oyster sauce; capon, egg sauce.

ROAST: Baron of beef; saddle of English mutton, with jelly; turkey, cranberry sauce; chicken, stuffed; mongrel goose, apple sauce; ham champagne sauce.

ENTREES: Fillets of beef larded, garnished with mushrooms; salmi of ducks, sautee, with olives; breast of partridge, larded, with Perigeux sauce; macaroni en timbale a l'Italienne; breast of prairie chicken, larded a la chevaliere; fricandeau of veal larded, tomato sauce; supreme fillets of chicken, sautee a la financier; shoulder of lamb, stuffed a l'Ketaffette; charlotte of apples a la Francaise; mutton cutlets, broiled, garnished with green peas.

GAME: Saddle of venison, with jelly; mallard duck; wild turkey; goose, apple sauce; teal duck; antelope; blue-bill widgeon; wood duck; broiled squirrel; broiled rabbit; buffalo steak broiled, game sauce.

VEGETABLES: Mashed potatoes, stewed tomatoes, squash, boiled potatoes, green corn, green peas, rice with cream, cabbage, beets.

RELISHES: Worcestershire sauce, chow-chow, celery, Boston pickles, horse-radish, French mustard; walnut catsup; India Soy; tomato catsup; sardines, olives.

ORNAMENTAL CONFECTIONARY: Fancy pyramids, Nugat pyramid; horns of plenty.

PASTRY: Mince pie, whortleberry pie, cocoanut pie, golden cake, macaroons, lady fingers, delicate cake, French glacees, fancy kisses, champagne jelly, rum jelly, blancmange, Charlotte de Russ, in fancy baskets; vanilla ice cream.

DESSERTS: Apples, almonds, raisins, English walnuts, filberts, oranges.

FRENCH COFFEE.

Apart from the sheer quantity of food, there was a spectacular range of dishes. There was everything from frontier food such as squirrel and buffalo tongue to the most elegant *chaud-froid* (see July 25), *chartreuse* (see November 9), and *timbales* (see June 12). There were dishes truffled, larded, and jellied and dishes presented in nests, on pedestals, and *sur socle*. The provenance of some dishes is proudly stated: the mutton was English and the coffee French. The list of game alone would not have shamed the Chicago Grand Pacific Hotel's famous annual dinner (see November 19). Finally, in case the multiplicity of sauces and flavors was insufficient, there was an impressive list of relishes.

## Recipes

~~~

### Walnut Catsup

Take three half sieves of walnut shells put them into a tub, mix them up well with common salt, about a pound and a half. Let them stand six days, frequently beating and washing them; by this time the shells become soft and pulpy; then by banking them up on one side of the tub, raising the tub on the same side, the liquor will run clear off to the other; then take that liquor out. The mashing and banking may be repeated as long as any liquor runs. The quantity will be about three quarts. Simmer it in an iron pot as long as any scum rises; then add two ounces of allspice, two ounces of ginger, bruised, one ounce of long pepper, one ounce of cloves, with the above articles; let it boil slowly for half an hour; when bottled, take care that an equal quantity of spice goes into each bottle; let the bottles be quite filled up, cork them tight, and seal them over. Put them into a cool and dry place, for one year before they are used.

J. M. Sanderson, *The Complete Confectioner, Pastry-Cook, and Baker* (1864).

Chaud-Froid: see July 25.
Prairie Chicken: see October 16.
Chow-Chow: see July 27.
Lobster Mayonnaise: see March 31.
Charlotte Russe: see September 4.

## December 17

### Whittier Banquet
#### Hotel Brunswick, Boston, Massachusetts, 1877

One of the most famous banquets in American history took place on December 17, 1877. It was the greatest gathering of literary minds ever to have taken place in the country before or (probably) since, and it attracted a huge amount of attention—and controversy. The banquet was given by the publishers of *The Atlantic Monthly* to celebrate the seventieth birthday of John Greenleaf Whittier (1807–1892), a famous and enormously respected Quaker poet. It was also the twentieth anniversary year of *The Atlantic*, and the publishers clearly intended to cement its reputation as the prominent voice of American literature. There were 60 present at the dinner. At the main table with the guest of honor sat Charles Dudley Warner, William D. Howells, Oliver Wendell Holmes, H. O. Houghton, Ralph Waldo Emerson, and Henry Wadsworth Longfellow, and a host of other "literary fellers" sat at other tables in the beautiful dining hall of the new wing of the hotel.

It was not the food that made the event famous, or controversial. There was the usual vast amount of very fine but predictable hotel banquet fare, starting with the obligatory oysters and continuing through a range of the usual classic dishes to the fancy sweet items and "dessert" (which referred to the dried fruit and nuts at the very end of the meal).

---

MENU.

OYSTERS ON SHELL.     *Sauterne*

SOUPS.
Puree of Tomatoes au Croutons.
Consomme Printanier Royal.     *Sherry*

---

FISH.
Boiled Chicken, Halibut a la Navarine.
Potatoes a la Hollandaise.
Smelts Panne, Sauce Tartar.    *Chablis*

REMOVES.
Capon a l'Anglaise.
Rice.      Cauliflower.
Saddle of English Mutton a la Pontoise.
String Beans.      Turnips.

CHAMPAGNE.
*Mumm's Dry Verzenay,*
*Roederer Imperial.*

ENTREES.
Filet of Beef, larded, Sauce Financiere.
Epinards Veloutes.
Vol au Vent of Oysters a l'Americaine.
Squabs en Compote a la Francaise, Tomatoes.
Sautees.
Terrapin Stewed, Maryland Style.
Sorbet au Kirsh.    *Claret*

GAME.
Broiled Partridges on Toast.    Canvasback Ducks.
Water Cresses, Sweet Potatoes, Dressed Lettuce.    *Burgundy*

PASTRY.
Charlotte Russe. Gelee au Champagne.
Gateaux Varies.
Confectionery.
Fruit.      Dessert.

COFFEE.

The banquet provoked two controversies. One was a result of the "droll speech" by Mark Twain (1835–1910) in which he told a story about his "first and only attempt to travel on his *nom de plume*," which parodied Emerson, Longfellow, and Holmes. The speech was comical, certainly, and appeared to be well received at the time, according to the press reports the next day. Yet paradoxically it was also immediately obvious that Twain had crossed some sort of line, that his speech was at the least in bad taste, but perhaps a monumental insult to some of America's finest literary minds and by extension its whole literary culture. Twain remained deeply embarrassed by his words for the rest of his life.

The other controversy was that women were not invited. This was the usual practice of the time, it not being deemed proper for "ladies" to dine in public. There were, however, a small number of women who belonged to the press, and the exclusion did not go unnoticed. Women journalists were not strangers to the experience. In 1868 they were refused admittance to a banquet being held by the New York Press Club in honor of Charles Dickens —an incident that led to the formation of women-only clubs.

## Recipes

~~~

Twain listed "Canvas-back-duck, from Baltimore" on his wish list in *A Tramp Abroad* (see box).

---

### Broiled Canvas-Back Duck

Pluck, singe, and wipe the duck; split it down the back, and remove the intestines; put it between the bars of a buttered double gridiron, and broil it over a hot fire, leaving the inside turned to the fire for twelve minutes; then turn the skin to the fire just long enough to brown it; season the duck with salt and pepper, and serve it at once. The assertion that canvas-back ducks owe their delicious flavor to the wild celery upon which they feed, is open to question. The writer has eaten ducks killed in the marshes of the great Western lakes, and in the far North-western territories, in localities where there are no beds of wild celery growing; and the flavor of the birds quite equalled that of those bagged at Havre de Grace. The flavor of the birds is best preserved by cooking them quickly by an intense fire, and serving them on very hot plates. The usual garnishes are currant-jelly, fried hominy, or celery. Sometimes a mayonnaise dressing is served with the celery. . . . The ducks should never be overdone.
*Miss Corson's Practical American Cookery and Household Management* (New York, 1886).

---

### Mark Twain's Favorite Foods

From *A Tramp Abroad*, 1880.

It has now been many months, at the present writing, since I have had a nourishing meal, but I shall soon have one—a modest, private affair, all to myself. I have selected a few dishes, and made out a little bill of fare, which will go home in the steamer that precedes me, and be hot when I arrive—as follows:

Radishes. Baked apples, with cream.
Fried oysters; stewed oysters. Frogs.
American coffee, with real cream.
American butter.
Fried chicken, Southern style.
Porter-house steak.
Saratoga potatoes.
Broiled chicken, American style.
Hot biscuits, Southern style.
Hot wheat-bread, Southern style.
Hot buckwheat cakes.
American toast.
Clear maple syrup.
Virginia bacon, broiled.

Blue points, on the half shell.
Cherry-stone clams.
San Francisco mussels, steamed.
Oyster soup. Clam Soup.
Philadelphia Terapin soup.
Oysters roasted in shell-Northern style.
Soft-shell crabs. Connecticut shad.
Baltimore perch.
Brook trout, from Sierra Nevadas.
Lake trout, from Tahoe.
Sheep-head and croakers, from New Orleans.
Black bass from the Mississippi.
American roast beef.
Roast turkey, Thanksgiving style.
Cranberry sauce. Celery.
Roast wild turkey. Woodcock.
Canvas-back-duck, from Baltimore.
Prairie liens, from Illinois.
Missouri partridges, broiled.
'Possum. Coon.
Boston bacon and beans.
Bacon and greens, Southern style.
Hominy. Boiled onions. Turnips.
Pumpkin. Squash. Asparagus.
Butter beans. Sweet potatoes.
Lettuce. Succotash. String beans.
Mashed potatoes. Catsup.
Boiled potatoes, in their skins.
New potatoes, minus the skins.
Early rose potatoes, roasted in the ashes, Southern style, served hot.
Sliced tomatoes, with sugar or vinegar.
Stewed tomatoes.
Green corn, cut from the ear and served with butter and pepper.
Green corn, on the ear.
Hot corn-pone, with chitlings, Southern style.
Hot hoe-cake, Southern style.
Hot egg-bread, Southern style.
Hot light-bread, Southern style.
Buttermilk. Iced sweet milk.
Apple dumplings, with real cream.
Apple pie. Apple fritters.
Apple puffs, Southern style.
Peach cobbler, Southern style
Peach pie. American mince pie.
Pumpkin pie. Squash pie.
All sorts of American pastry.

Fresh American fruits of all sorts, including strawberries which are not to be doled out as if they were jewelry, but in a more liberal way. Ice-water—not prepared in the ineffectual goblet, but in the sincere and capable refrigerator.

---

### Vol-au-Vent of Oysters

Prepare the *vol-au-vent* as directed. Put one quart of oysters on to boil in their own liquor. As soon as a scum rises, skim it off, and drain the oysters. Return half a pint of the oyster liquor to the sauce-pan. Mix two heaping table-spoonfuls of butter with a scant one of flour, and when light and creamy, gradually turn on it the boiling oyster liquor. Season well with salt, pepper and, if you like, a little nutmeg or mace (it must be only a "shadow"). Boil up once, and add three table-spoonfuls of cream and the oysters. Stir over the fire for half a minute. Fill the case, cover, and serve immediately.

*Miss Parloa's New Cookbook: A Guide to Marketing and Cooking* (New York, ca. 1880).

---

Charlotte Russe: see September 4.
Potatoes Hollandaise: see April 16.
Puff paste for vol-au-vents: see September 17.
Terrapin Maryland: see June 5.

## December 18

### Dinner to Honor President Juan Perón
### Alvear Palace Hotel, Buenos Aires, Argentina, 1948

Members of Congress held a dinner in honor of President General D. Juan Perón (1895–1974) and Doña Maria Eva Duarte de Perón (1919–1952) on December 18, 1948, at the exclusive Alvear Palace Hotel.

This was a simple meal featuring a number of foods that originated in South America as well as some regional specialties. Sweet potatoes (batatas) are native to South America and were noted by Christopher Columbus

---

MENU

Pejerrey del Paraná a la Tártara

—

Crema de Tomate

JEREZ TIO PACO                                    —

CALVET RESERVA BLANCO          Jamón al Vino Madera con Espinacas

VIEJA ABADIA TINTO                            —

CHAMPAÑA DUC DE ST. REMY            Pavo asado
EXTRA SECO

VILLAVICENCIO                              Batatas doradas
                                         Ensalada Primaveral

—

Higos Alvear Palace

—

Café

---

during his fourth voyage (see October 12). They were "golden" or "gilded" at this dinner—perhaps by being roasted to that color, or maybe candied.

*Pejerrey* is a fish similar to whiting, from the Paraná river, served with the very old traditional accompaniment of tartar sauce. One slightly odd thing is that this fish is served before the cream of tomato soup, against the usual order of formal dinners. The dish of figs is named for the hotel, and was presumably a signature dish.

The beverages list looks French, but is also in fact Argentinian. The *Champaña Duc De St. Remy Extra Seco* in spite of its name is local, and the *Villavalencio* is a mineral water from the Andes.

## Recipes

~~~

---

### Cream Tomato Soup

Put on to stew, one can or six ripe tomatoes, with one medium-sized onion and one small stalk of celery. When all are cooked very soft, rub through a sieve and season to taste with salt and pepper. Heat in a double boiler one pint of sweet milk thickened with two teaspoonfuls of flour, rubbed smooth in a very little cold milk. Cook moderately for ten minutes and add two heaping teaspoons of butter. Add to the tomato one-half teaspoonful of soda (if canned tomatoes are used, they will require a little more soda than fresh tomatoes). Stir well and add the boiling milk. Strain and serve immediately with salted crackers. Be careful to prevent curdling by ceasing to cook as soon as the milk is added.

*The Times Cook Book, No. 2* (Los Angeles: Times-Mirror Co., 1905).

---

Tartar Sauce: see December 18.

## December 19

### Horsemeat Banquet
### London, England, 1867

Britain's population explosion in the mid-nineteenth century in combination with the absolute beef shortage precipitated by a Europe-wide cattle plague meant that meat was increasingly unaffordable by the poorer classes (who had never been able to afford much anyway). A move to popularize horsemeat as a nutritious and cheap food for the poor had been gathering force in France over the previous few decades and had been sufficiently successful that by the end of 1867 there were 23 licensed horsemeat butchers in Paris. English enthusiasts took up the French idea of a series of *Banquets Hippophagiques* to publicize the cause.

The dinner was described in a letter to *The Times* signed by a correspondent who signed himself Savarini Discipulus. It was the writer's first "unprejudiced hippophagic experience," and the "subject of the experiment" was an 18-year-old pony "entirely past work" who had been "fattened with care." The cook was no less than the great Charles Elmé Francatelli (1805–1876) who had briefly been chef to Queen Victoria.

---

Consommé de Cheval aux Quenelles.
Saucisses de Cheval aux Pistaches.
Escallopes de Cheval aux Fines Herbes.
Emincée de Cheval à la Polonaise.
Culotte de Cheval braisée aux Choux.
Filet de Cheval Piqué, Sauce Poivrade.
Mayonnaise d'Homard à l'Huile de Cheval.

---

*The Times* correspondent gave his opinion of each dish:

The *consommé* presented a clear amber colour to the eye, to the nose it offered a peculiar odour, recalling a faint, far-away echo of game.... The sausage so entirely resembled the common run of continental sausages as to leave a strong mental conviction behind its taste that horseflesh is the normal component of these edible cylinders.... Of the escaloppes and emincée it need merely be said that they gratified the palate and bore testimony to the metamorphous skill which a chef can display in his entrées.... The crucial test was at hand, and the culotte de cheval and filet piqué, exhibiting horseflesh under the simplest culinary conditions, were tasted with that conscientious and analytical care which the first trial of a gastronomic problem so momentously demanded. The meat was extremely tender, somewhat loose in texture, wanting finenes in the grain, and it was a shade darker than beef similarly dressed. It had the same odour which characterised the soup and the same special flavour ... It is an intervening [flavour] between butcher's meat [beef] and game.

The knotty philosophical issues that the worthy men at this banquet "who, by their high social position, could exert a salutary influence on public opinion" hoped to address were summed up in a letter to *The Times* in 1867:

the real question is not whether horseflesh is as good as beef, but first, whether, when many are too poor to procure animal food, we are justified in wasting millions of pounds of meat, which, whatever it may resemble, is certainly excellent; next, whether horses would not be more humanely treated if they represented some value in their old age; and lastly, whether it is not the duty of every one to assist in rooting out a national prejudice.

At another *Banquet Hippophagique* at Langhams Hotel a few months later, on February 6, 1868, there were 29 dishes served. One of the guests was Frank Buckland—a naturalist famous for his willingness to consider anything as food, including on one occasion a recently deceased leopard from the zoo, which he had had disinterred. His comments on the horsemeat dinner are most revealing:

I devoutly wished I had the talent of a Hogarth to be able to record the various expressions ... there seemed to be a dubious and inquisitive cast spread over the features of most who were present ... A very pleasant party at our end of the table, but the meat simply horrible.

## Recipes
~~~

Francatelli simply substituted horsemeat for beef in some of his classic recipes. *Piqué* means larded, which is a technique of threading thin strips of fat bacon through the meat to tenderize and flavor it. The following recipes are taken from Francatelli's book *The Cook's Guide*, published in 1867.

---

### Filet of Beef Larded

Procure a piece of fillet of beef, such as might be removed for the purpose from a piece of sirloin which would serve very well the next day for roasting, and with a sharp knife pare off the sinewy covering of the fillet, and lard the smooth surface with small shreds of fat bacon an inch and a quarter long, and about the sixteenth part of an inch square; these are to be inserted in straight rows, across the fillet, and arranged so that each row dovetails into the other, thus forming a correct series of rows representing raised basket-work. The fillet should now be placed in the braizing-pan upon its drainer, garnished with the trimmings, carrot, celery, garnished bouquet, two onions with three cloves in each, a blade of mace, and a good spoonful of salt, moistened with sufficient stock or water to just barely reach up to the commencement of the larding, and set to braize, either in a brisk oven or over a slow fire with live embers on the lid of the pan; it will take about two hours' very gentle stewing to cook it quite mellow and tender. When the fillet is done, remove it on to a dish, and set it in the oven to dry the larding; glaze it over and dish it up. Strain the liquor, free it from grease, clarify and reduce it to half-glaze, to be served as a sauce; or else incorporate it with any sauce fitted for braized meats; garnish the fillet round the base with potatoes cut in the form of walnuts or large olives, and fried in butter, alternately placed with groups of green peas, cauliflower, French beans, or else with a Jardiniere, or Macedoine of vegetables; pour the sauce round, and serve.

---

### Poivrade Sauce

Cut up into very small square pieces an ounce of lean ham or bacon, the same quantities of carrot, celery, and onion, a bay-leaf and thyme, twenty peppercorns, and a bit of mace; Fry these ingredients in a small stewpan, with a piece of butter the size of a walnut, until the whole becomes well browned; add a wine-glass of vinegar and half that quantity of mushroom catsup, and a teaspoonful of anchovy; and when this has boiled down to half its original quantity, then add about half a pint of brown sauce, a few spoonfuls of good stock, and a wineglass-ful of sherry; Let the sauce boil gently by the side of the fire, to throw up the grease, &c, which having been removed, strain through a sieve or strainer into a small stewpan for use.

## December 20

Heinz Company 50th Anniversary Dinner
Pittsburgh, Pennsylvania, 1919

In 1919, the board of directors of the H. J. Heinz Company gave a banquet for their employees to celebrate the 50th anniversary of the founding of the company. The founder of the company, Henry J. Heinz (1844–1919), had died earlier in the year, and his son Howard Heinz was the host for the evening.

In addition to listing the food, the menu gave a brief summary of the progress achieved in the first 50 years of the company, and the employee count was given as 6,523 (plus 100,000 "Harvesters of the Crops we use"), so presumably only a select number of these were invited to the celebration. Not surprisingly, a number of Heinz products was featured at the dinner.

---

Heinz Cream of Tomato Soup
Sweet Pickles      Olives      Pascal Celery
Salted Pecans      Salted Almonds
Roast Spring Chicken
Green Peas      Candied Sweet Potatoes
Hearts of Lettuce
Cheese Straws      Heinz Salad Dressing
Neapolitan Ice Cream
Coffee      Cakes
Dinner Mints
Assorted Fruits

---

The success of the Heinz Company brand has been phenomenal. The first product in 1869 was simply horseradish bottled in clear glass jars, and the company went on to produce many iconic brands—far more than the "57 Varieties" of its famous slogan. The tomato soup (introduced in the 1870s) which is featured on this menu is perhaps its most famous product. It was promoted as an upmarket soup so good that it could be served at a dinner party and the hostess could be confident that "her guests couldn't believe it." It was good enough even for the famous and luxurious Raffles Hotel in Singapore to specifically list it on a menu in 1910. In 2003, the BBC television show *The Nation's Favorite Food* listed it at number 7 in the list of Britain's all time favorites.

---

Origin of the "57 Varieties" Slogan

Mr. Heinz, while in an elevated railroad train in New York, saw among the car-advertising cards one about shoes with the expression "21 Styles." It set him to thinking, and as he told it, "I said to myself, 'we do not have styles of products, but we do have varieties of products.' Counting up how many we had, I counted well beyond 57, but '57' kept coming back into my mind. 'Seven, seven'—there are so many illustrations of the psychological influence of that figure and of its alluring significance to people of all ages and races that '58 Varieties' or '59 Varieties' did not appeal at all to me as being equally strong."

E. D. McCafferty, *Henry J. Heinz: A Biography* (1923).

## Recipes
~~~

### Candied Sweet Potatoes

Boil medium potatoes of even size, till a fork will pierce—steaming is better though a bit more trouble—throw in cold water for a minute, peel, and brush over with soft butter, then lay separately in a wide skillet, with an inch of very rich syrup over the bottom and set over slow fire. Turn the potatoes often in the syrup, letting it coat all sides. Keep turning them until candied and a little brown. If wanted very rich put butter and lemon juice in the syrup when making it. Blade mace also flavors it very well.

Martha McCulloch-Williams, *Dishes & Beverages of the Old South* (New York, 1913).

"A rich syrup" is made from three cups sugar, one cup water.

### Neapolitan Ice Cream

Neapolitan or harlequin ice cream is made by packing the mould with layers of various colored creams after they are frozen; usually vanilla, pistache, and strawberry creams are used.

### Vanilla Ice-Cream

A good vanilla ice-cream is made from cream over-sweetened, and flavoured with powdered vanilla bean; when it is half frozen, the white of an egg, beaten to a stiff froth, is stirred thoroughly into it, and the freezing is completed.

### Pistache ice-cream

Pistache ice-cream is made by adding about two ounces of blanched pistache nuts to a quart of good ice-cream; the nuts are shelled, boiling water is poured over the kernels, and the skins rubbed off with a wet towel; the nuts are then pounded to a smooth paste in a mortar, a few drops of rosewater being added to prevent oiling, and colored with spinach green, a harmless vegetable coloring sold by dealers in confectioners' supplies.

*Miss Corson's Practical American Cookery* (1886).

Salted Almonds: see April 3.

## December 21

``Pease and Pork Dinner''
Livery House, Bristol,
England, 1911

St. Thomas's Day (December 21) is a traditional day to be particularly charitable to the poor, as the saint himself was, according to the standard story. St. Thomas was supposedly give money to build a palace in India, but he gave it to the poor instead and went to jail for his generosity. In many parts of England it was a variously called "doleing day," "corning day," or "mumping" (begging) day, because the less fortunate could "go a gooding" (ask for charity) and not be expected to be refused.

In 1551, St. Thomas's Day was the birthday of Thomas White in Bristol, England. He took the responsibilities implicit in his name seriously, it seems, and went to Oxford University, entered the Church, and eventually founded Temple Hospital in 1613. A "hospital" in the early-seventeenth century was not a place of medical assistance as it is today, it had a more general brief to assist the poor. White's original Almshouse had ten dwellings and was for "the finding, sustenation and relief of poor and needy people." He ordered that every St. Thomas's Day, according to the *Bristol Times*, the governors should assemble, listen to any complaints, and "read the rules to the assembled poor, so that they may understand what to do in their places." After the poor were reminded of their obligations, the governors, mayor, and guests attended a pease and pork dinner, for which White allowed 40 shillings. The poor were to receive the leftovers from the dinner. Almost 300 years later the tradition was still alive, and the dinner virtually unchanged.

Two boiled legs of pork, two bellies of pork, 106lb of Baron beef, a loin of veal weighing 30lb, two pease puddings, sea-kale and brussels sprouts, baked and boiled potatoes and an apple tart made from 99 apples and one quince.

### Recipes

~~~

Pease pudding was a traditional accompaniment to pork in many parts of England. It was not necessary to specify "pickled" (brined) pork—this was understood, as the following observations show.

Obs.: In this country, boiled pork is never presented without its satellite, pease pudding; and as much of its goodness depends upon the nature of the pease, care should be taken that they be of the melting sort, and whole in preference to being split. It is a good practice to steep the pease in cold water for an hour, before the boiling.

---

## Pease Pudding

Take any quantity of yellow split pease, and after washing them put them in a cloth so loose as to allow the pease to swell, and after boiling about four hours, beat them quite smooth, adding to them a lump of butter and some salt. Put the pease when quite smooth into a cloth tied so tight as to prevent the entrance of any water, and after boiling about half an hour, the pudding may be turned out and sent to table.

Obs.: If the pease be of the melting sort this will prove a most excellent pudding. After beating quite smooth, the pease will swell no more, so care must be taken to tie the cloth very tight.

Alexander Hunter, *Culina Famulatrix Medicinæ: Or, Receipts in Modern Cookery* (1810).

---

## To Boil a Leg of Pork

Lay a leg which has been ten days in salt, half an hour in cold water; then put it on the fire; allow fifteen minutes for every pound, and thirty over from the time that it boils up: take the scum off frequently. Observe, to have your meat look well, it should be boiled in a cloth; when enough, serve with pease pudding.

Elizabeth Hammond, *Modern Domestic Cookery, and Useful Receipt Book* (1819).

---

## December 22

### First Celebration of Forefathers' Day Dinner
### Old Colony Club of Plymouth, Massachusetts, 1769

The founding members of the Old Colony Club got the date wrong when they decided to celebrate the anniversary of the colony, but they made no error with their dinner. It was unequivocally symbolic of the natural bounty of their homeland, its native people, and—the food being dressed "in the plainest manner"—of their own Puritan ancestors.

---

A large baked Indian Whortleberry Pudding
A dish of Souquetash
A dish of Clamms
A dish of Oysters and a dish of Codfish
A haunch of venison roasted by the first jack bro't to the Colony
A dish of seafowl
A ditto of frost fish and Eeels
An apple Pye
A course of Cranberry Tarts and Cheese made in the Old Colony

---

The Old Colony Club was formed in Plymouth in January 1769 by seven gentlemen who wished to avoid "the many disadvantages and inconveniences that arise from intermixing with the company at the taverns in this town at Plymouth.'' On December 22 of the same year, they celebrated the anniversary of the foundation of the colony in 1620—the same event that is now accepted to have occurred on December 21, but that the original settlers knew with the certainty afforded by their own calendars was December 11.

The error was not discovered until 1850, long after this first incarnation of the club was defunct. That it took so long reflects the long and complex evolution of the calendar—the tool by which humans attempt to synchronize their civil life with celestial and seasonal events. The problem arose because the human calendar year was slightly shorter than the solar year, and over time they became increasingly out of sync. Revisions of the calendar were instigated by Julius Caesar in 45 BCE and again in 1581 by Pope Gregory XIII. The Gregorian changes were taken up at various times by different countries, the staunchly anti-Popish Britain hanging out until 1752, by which time the discrepancy was eleven days. The Forefathers' Club failed to realize that in 1620 the discrepancy only amounted to ten days—and no body noticed the error for almost a century.

The new colonists of 1620 initially attempted to farm the familiar foods of their homeland, but the country was not ideal for wheat—the staple "corn" of their own native land—and they would have starved but for the assistance of the local Indians who gave them maize and taught them how to grow it. Maize does not make good bread because it does not contain gluten, the protein that gives bread its structure. It does, however, make a fine version of the other staple of peasants—the thick porridge called hasty pudding which can be varied or enriched in an almost infinite number of ways. Made with the "Indian corn" this was the Indian pudding of the menu, embellished in this case with local whortleberries.

The remainder of the menu is an ode to the food of New England—plenty of seafood and apples, and another Indian staple called succotash. Again, it is an infinitely variable recipe, but the obligatory ingredients are corn and beans. The name comes from the Algonquian (Narragansett) word *msickquatash*, which refers to boiled whole-kernel corn.

### Recipes
~~~

The following recipe is from the first American cookbook: the author gives three variations.

---

#### A Tasty Indian Pudding

3 pints scalded milk,
7 spoons fine Indian Meal,

stir well together while hot,
let stand till cooled;

add 4 eggs,
half pound raisins,

4 ounces butter,
spice and sugar,

bake four hours.

Amelia Simmons, *American Cookery* (1796).

---

### Cranberry Tart

Stewed, strained and sweetened, put into paste No. 9, add spices till grateful, and baked gently.
  Frank Hamilton Cushing, *Zuni Breadstuff* (1920).

---

### Royal Paste

Rub half a pound of butter into one pound of flour, four whites beaten to a foam, two ounces fine sugar; roll often, rubbing one third and rolling two thirds of butter is best; excellent for tarts.
  Frank Hamilton Cushing, *Zuni Breadstuff* (1920).

Succotash: see August 28.
Codfish, to dress: see March 11.

## December 23

### Noble Family's Dinner
### Aldersgate Street, London, England, 1626

Sir Edward Dering (1598–1644) was an antiquarian, politician, and peer of the realm. He owed his baronetcy to his new mother-in-law, the well-connected widow, Elizabeth Ashburton. Elizabeth married her second husband, Sir Thomas Richardson, chief justice of the Court of Common Pleas, on December 14, 1626, and a little over a week later Sir Edward entertained the family at his home. He noted details of the dinner and the bill of fare in his account book.

"A Dinner att London, made when my Lady Richardson, my sister Elizabeth Ashbornham, and Kate Ashbornham,—my brother John Ashbornham, my cosen Walldron and her sister, and S'r John Skeffington, were with me att Aldersgate streete, December 23, 1626. My sister Frances Ashbornham and cosen Mary Hill did fayle of coming.

---

The dinner was at y'e first course—

  A peece of Brawne.
  a boiled ducke in white broathe.
  a boiled haunch of powdered venison.
  2 minct pyes.

a boyled legge of mutton.
a venison pasty.
a roast ducke.
a powdered goose roasted.
a breast of veale.
a cold Capon py.

Second course—
a couple of rabbitts.
3 plovers.
12 larks.
4 snikes. pickled oysters—2 dishes.
a cold warden py.
a joull of Sturgeon.

Complement—
Apples and Carrawayes.
wardens bakt and cold.
A Cake and Cheese.
A banquett ready in y'e next room.

This was a typical seventeenth-century dinner: two courses with a mixture of dishes, tending to be lighter and finer dishes such as small game birds in the second course, but with sweet and savory dishes in both. The "banquett" at this time was the name for the final course of the meal, the course which developed into our modern dessert course (see March 9). The banquet was usually taken in another room, while the servants cleared the main dining table, and it consisted of a variety of sweetmeats, fruits, comfits, and wafers (see table).

"Wardens" were a type of cooking pear and were very popular in pies because they could be preserved that way for considerable periods of time.

## The Names of All Thinges Necessary for a Banquet.

| | | |
|---|---|---|
| Suger | Sinamon | Liquorice |
| Pepper | Nutmegs | All kindes of |
| Saffron | Saunders | Comfets |
| Anniseeds | Coliander | Orenges |
| Pomegranet | Lemmons | Damaske water |
| Tornesell | Rosewater | Dates |
| Prunes | Raysins | Cherryes conserved |
| Currans | Rye flower | Sweet Orenges |
| Barberries conserved | Ginger | Wafers |
| Pepper white and brown. | Cloves and Mace | |

Thomas Dawson, *A Booke of Cookerie* (1620).

Recipes

~~~

---

### To Bake a Quince or a Warden Pie so as the Fruit May Be Redde, and the Crust Pale and Tender

Pare faire Quinces or Wardens and set them into an earthen pane with the crownes upward, put to them a little Claret-wine and a graine of Muske or more, according to the quantity of the fruit, put in a little Sugar, cover them close with a sheete of Paste, set them into a Bakers Oven with wheaten bread, but not household bread: when they have stood three of foure houres in the Oven they will be very red and tender, then you may keep them a weeke or more for use: when you have occasion to make your Pie, take of butter and the yolkes of Egges, and make short Paste, and raise a Coffin fit for your stuffe, one by another, put in whole Cloves, and a little whole Sinamon, poure in some sirrup from their former baking, or if you want it, then put in Claret-wine, and some more Sugar, set them in an Oven as hot as for Pies, and in one houre they will be bakte, and your fruit orient red: Remember before your first baking, that you coare your Quinces.
   John Murrell, *Murrels Two Books of Cookerie and Carving* (1638).

---

Brawn: see April 28.
Mince Pies: see January 9.
Ducke in White Broathe (broth): this would have been prepared in the same manner as the Capon in White Broth in the recipe given on September 13.

## December 24

### Englishmen's Dinner
### Queen's Hotel, Dundee, Scotland, 1885

The Queen's Hotel in the center of the town of Dundee was built in 1878 in the best Victorian style and was a prestigious establishment from the first day. It is likely that many of its guests were English folk on tours of Scotland, or perhaps English businessmen, and undoubtedly, as fine hotels do, the Queen's Hotel staff worked hard to make their guests feel at home. Nevertheless, it seems a little above and beyond the call of hospitality duty to provide an "Englishmen's Dinner," as the hotel did on Christmas Eve, 1885.

---

SOUPS.

. . .

Brunoise

FISH.
Codfish, Hollandaise Sauce.
Fillets of Whiting.

JOINTS.
Sirloin of Beef.
Roast Goose and Apple Sauce.

Veal and Ham Pie.
Boiled Turkey, Oyster Sauce.
Tongue.
Spiced Round of Beef.
Yorkshire Pudding.
Spinach.        Brussels Sprouts.
Duchesse Potatoes.

SWEETS.
Plum Pudding.        Mince Pies.
Apple Tarts.        Custard
Jellies.        Creams.
Chartreuse of Fruit.

DESSERT.

This was certainly a very English dinner. Any late-nineteenth century Englishman worthy of his birthright would have been very happy to sit down to this groaning table. There is a great deal of meat, as an Englishman would have expected at any decent dinner, not just at Christmas. The "Roast Beef of Old England" is represented in the form of a sirloin, the cut of beef that legend says got its name when the King (variously said to be Henry VIII, James I, or Charles I), being delighted with a particularly fine example, taking his sword and knighting it on the spot. The sirloin, however, was never "Sir Loin" but got its name from its position on the beast—*sur longe*, that is "above the loin."

The traditional accompaniment to roast beef in England is Yorkshire Pudding—a dish that is baffling to many without personal connections to England. It is simply one variation of the old theme of a starchy "filler" to make the meat go further. In this case it is a batter, which in the old days was cooked in a dish placed under the roasting meat as it turned on the spit in front of the fire. Today it is usually baked in a hot roasting pan containing some of the fat from the already roasted (actually, baked) meat. In other areas the starchy filler might be polenta, or hominy, or dumplings. In the case of boiled meat, an old English saying was "no broth, no ball, no ball, no meat," meaning that if one did not have some of the broth, one was not allowed the "ball" (dumpling), and if one did not have the ball, one was not allowed any meat. If one did have broth and ball of course then one would eat less meat, which was the whole idea.

## Recipes

~~~

Recipe books always lag behind actual culinary practice, and everyday items that every cook would be expected to know how to make were often not thought necessary to include. The first known written recipe for Yorkshire pudding dates from 1747, but it was certainly made for a very long time before this. It appeared in *The Art of Cookery, Made Plain and Easy; Which Far Exceeds Any Thing of the Kind Ever Yet Published*, by Hannah Glasse.

The same batter baked in small individual tins makes what are sometimes now called "popovers."

---

### A Yorkshire Pudding

Take a Quart of Milk, four Eggs, and a little Salt. Make it up into a thick Batter with Flour, like a Pancake Batter. You must have a good Piece of Meat at the Fire, take a Stew-Pan and put some Dripping in, set it on the Fire, when it boils, pour in your Pudding, let it bake on the Fire till you think it is nigh enough, then turn a Plate upside-down in the Dripping-pan that the Dripping may not be blackened; set your Stew-pan on it under your Meat, and let the Dripping drip on the Pudding and the Heat of the Fire come to it, to make it of a fine brown. When your Meat is done and set to Table, drain all the Fat from your Pudding, and set it on the Fire again to dry a little; then slide it as dry as you can into a Dish, melt some butter, and pour into a Cup, and set it into the Middle of the Pudding. It is an exceedingly good Pudding, the Gravy of the Meat eats well with it.

---

Duchesse Potatoes: see July 11.
Hollandaise Sauce: see April 14.

## December 25

### Queen Victoria's Christmas Dinner
### Windsor Castle, London, England, 1899

Queen Victoria usually spent Christmas at what she considered her family home at Osborne on the Isle of Wight. In 1899, a year before her death, she was at Windsor. The Christmas dinner menu was virtually indistinguishable from every other one that had preceded it.

---

POTAGES.
Cousommé à la Monaco.     Du Berry

POISSONS.
Filet de Sole à la Vassant.
Eperlans frits, sauce Verneuil.

ENTREÉ
Côtelettes de Volaille à la York.

RELEVÉS
Dinde à la Chipolata.
Roast Beef.     Chine of Pork.

ENTREMÊTS.
Asperges, sauce Hollandaise.
Mince Pies.     Plum Pudding.
Gelée d'Orange à l'Anglaise.

BUFFET.

Baron of Beef.    Boar's Head.     Game Pie.

Woodcock Pie.     Brawn.

Roast Fowl.    Tongue.

Many of the elements of today's traditional Christmas customs are nineteenth-century inventions. Many are specifically attributable to Queen Victoria and Prince Albert (with their German heritage), and author Charles Dickens, on account of his *Christmas Carol*. Although the tree was a focus of all sorts of pagan celebrations—particularly the evergreen tree in association with the northern winter solstice, the idea of bringing a tree into the house and decorating it at Christmas

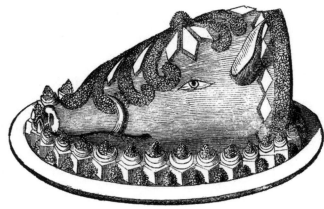

Boar's head on platter.

has its roots in German tradition. Prince Albert established the custom in the royal household, the rest of the population followed, and a tradition was born almost instantly.

As far as the traditional foods are concerned, plum puddings and mince pies (and their precursor, the enriched form of the everyday staple called frumenty, see February 23) were a medieval staple at sorts of special occasions. Over time they became less important, and eventually they remained only at Christmas. No Christmas table would be considered complete today without a turkey, but it only became a "traditional" Christmas essential during the nineteenth century; before that it was far more likely for diners to eat goose.

There are almost two menus here. The first part, set out in French, as British royal menus still are, and the second part, under the heading of "buffet." This buffet—the dishes listed in English—is a mini-medieval feast all on its own. Many of the elements of a medieval dinner are here, including the boar's head (see January 4), brawn (see April 23), the raised pies, and the massive baron of beef from the Queen's own estates

## Recipes

~~~

The Woodcock Pie that always graced the buffet table at Queen Victoria's Christmas dinner was a traditional gift from the Lord Lieutenant of Ireland. It contained a hundred birds. Here is a chatty description of the pie from *Cakes and Ale; A Dissertation of Banquets, Interspersed with Various*

*Recipes, More or Less Original, and Anecdotes, Mainly Veracious* (1913), by
Edward Spencer.

---

### A Woodcock Pie

[This] will be found extremely palatable at any shooting luncheon, although
more frequently to be met with on the sideboards of the great and wealthy. In
fact, at Christmas time, 'tis a pie which is specially concocted in the royal
kitchen at Windsor Castle, to adorn Her Most Gracious Majesty's board at
Osborne, together with the time-honoured baron of specially fed beef. This last
named joint hardly meets my views as part of a breakfast menu; but here is
the recipe for the woodcock pie.

Bone four woodcocks I don't mean take them off the hooks when the gentleman is not in his shop, but tell your cook to take the bones out of one you've shot
yourself put bones and trimmings into a saucepan with one shallot, one small
onion, and a sprig of thyme, cover them with some good stock, and let this gravy
simmer awhile. Take the gizzards away from the heart and liver, pound, and
mix these with some good veal forcemeat. Place the woodcocks, skin downwards,
on a board ; spread over each two layers of forcemeat, with a layer of sliced truffles in between the two. Make your crust, either in a mould, or with the hands,
put a layer of forcemeat at the bottom, then two woodcocks, then a layer of truffles, then the other two woodcocks, another layer of truffles, and a top layer of
forcemeat, and some thin slices of fat bacon. Cover the pie, leaving a hole for
the gravy, and bake in a moderate oven. After taking out pour in the gravy, then
close the orifice and let the pie get cold before serving.

N.B. It will stimulate the digging industry if one or two whole truffles have
been hidden away in the recesses of the pie.

---

Hollandaise Sauce: see April 14.
Brawn: see April 28.


## December 26

### Elegant Dinner
### Empire Hotel, Bath, England, 1907

The town of Bath in Somerset, England, is the site of the most famous geo-
thermal (hot water) springs in the country. Visitors have flocked to the area
for millennia to enjoy the natural hot water, but its popularity and fortune
have fluctuated over time. The first to exploit the site were the Romans, who
built a temple and baths there in about 60–70 AD. Bath had its heyday in the
Georgian era, as readers of Jane Austen's novels know. The town then slipped
into a slight decline, but its fortunes were revived again in the late-nineteenth
century when the remains of the old Roman baths were excavated.

The Empire Hotel was built in 1901 to take advantage of the new wave of
interest, and it was a fine venue indeed. There are no details of the event
for which this dinner was held on Boxing Day, the day after Christmas,
1907; it appears to be a regular hotel dinner.

Bortsh à la Russe.

—

Filet de Sole au Fines Herbes.

—

Roast Turkey with Bacon and Sausages.

—

Roast Beef and Yorkshire Pudding.
Spinach and Brussels Sprouts.
Mashed, Baked, and Boiled Potatoes.

—

Apple Tart.      Plum Pudding.      Mince Pies.
Stewed Fruits.

—

*Buffet.*

Petits Aspic de Crevettes.
Mousse de Foie Gras en Mosaic.
Caneton à la Rouenaise.
Paté de Veau et Jambon.
Paté de Pigeon.
Hare de Sanglier Truffée.
Paté de Bécasse Modèrne.
Poulet, Faisan et Dindonneaux au Cresson.
Filets de Bœuf Bouquetière en Gelée.
Langue de Bœuf à l'Ecarlatte.
Jambon d'York en Gelée.
Bœuf Pressé.
Quartier d'Agneaux, Sauce Menthe.
Côtes de Bœuf au Raiforts.

—

*Salades.*

Tomates.      Celeries.      Pommes de Terre.
Concombres

—

*Entremets*:

Gelée à la Dantzig.      Gateaux Richelieu.
Suedoise de Fruits.      Piece Montée.

Caterers and hotel managers did not seem to appreciate the incongruities that seem to stand out today on this menu. There is no consistency in the language (French or English) in which specific dishes are named or in their place on the menu. The arrangement of the dishes at the Empire Hotel seems to be reversed in comparison with Queen Victoria's Christmas dinner (see

December 25) in 1899. The buffet consists of a mix of French "made" dishes and plain English roasts with their traditional sauces (beef with horseradish, lamb with mint). These very English-style roasts have French names when they appear in the "buffet" section but are in plain English at the top of the menu. It seems particularly incongruous that the unequivocally English York ham should be called *Jambon de York*.

The hotel obviously attempted to keep up with food fashions—and there have always been fashions in food. The "borsht" or "Russian" beetroot soup became quite the latest thing at this time. There are many, many variations of this simple peasant soup, some hot, some chilled. The original borsht may not necessarily have included beetroot—the Russian vegetable called *borshch* is a plant of the carrot family, similar to a parsnip. One traveler in Russia, according to Pierce Balthasar Campenhausen in his *Travels through Several Provinces of the Russian Empire* (1808) said, "They have a kind of soup, however, which is made of groats and vegetables, of which they are very fond: this soup is rather sour, and is called borsch, from the name of the carrot which is boiled in it."

At the other end of the scale from a peasant-inspired soup is the *suédoise*—an elaborate mode of preparing dishes of fruit "fruit according to the highest arts of confectionery." As with many culinary terms, it was not used consistently, but generally it referred to a highly decorative pyramid of fruit, as the recipe here shows.

## Recipes

~~~

---

### Borsht

Take some red beetroots, wash thoroughly and peel, and then boil in a moderate quantity of water from two to three hours over a slow fire, by which time a strong red liquor should have been obtained. Strain off the liquor, adding lemon juice, sugar, and salt to taste, and when it has cooled a little, stir in sufficient yolks of eggs to slightly thicken it. May be used either cold or hot. In the latter case a little home-made beef stock may be added to the beet soup.

If after straining off the soup the remaining beetroot is not too much boiled away, it may be chopped fine with a little onion, vinegar and dripping, flavored with pepper and salt, and used as a vegetable.

Florence Greenbaum, *International Jewish Cook Book* (1919).

---

### Suédoise of Apples

Make a marmalade of apples as compact as possible. Then take small pieces of apples cut into corks, and of different colours. To dye them you need only dilute with syrup a little carmine or saffron, and boil them once. Next let the apples cool in the syrup, that the colour may spread equally over them. When you dish the suédoise, first spread some marmalade over the middle of the dish, and arrange the apple corks symmetrically, viz.. one white, one red, one yellow, and so on. As the ros ascend, make the next always narrowere, and decorate the top with cherries of a pink hue, greengages, angelica, &c. Have some apple jelly, with which cover the suédoise, and put it into ice to cool. When the suédoise is decorated in an agreeable form, use some jelly for garnishing, and place it gently over and round the suédoise. The jelly must be of a sufficient substance not to run down the fruit.

Louis Eustache Ude, *The French Cook* (1829).

Dantzig Jelly: see December 12.
Yorkshire Pudding: see December 24.

## December 27

### Blackhawk Restaurant
### Chicago, 1920

Prohibition became law on January 16, 1920, and it proved to be the death-knell for many restaurants and clubs. It was a brave act on the part of the entrepreneur Don Roth to open a new venue the same year. Roth had many contacts in the music and theatre business, and he decided that music would be the main attraction. The Blackhawk Restaurant on 139 N. Wabash became famous for its jazz and big band music.

As big band music became less of a drawcard, Roth determined that "Food's the Show." His stars were a rolling beef cart, a 15-shrimp cocktail, and the famous "spinning salad bowl" in which a patron's salad (with its secret-recipe dressing) was prepared table-side, with great theatricality. That was all a long time away when the restaurant opened its doors on December 27, 1920, with the following menu.

---

TID BITS
—
Celery     Olives     Almonds
—
Green Turtle, Blackhawk
—
Lobster, Thermidor
Julienne Potatoes
—
Supreme of Chicken, Florida
—
Romaine and Chicory
Roquefort Cheese Dressing
—
Chocolate Parfait
Assorted Cakes
—
Demi Tasse

The Blackhawk's list of beverages was reasonably long. There were a number of brand-name bottled waters, fruit cups, and lemonades as well as what appeared to be several beers, such as Budweiser. These were the allowable "near beers," containing one half of one percent or less by volume of alcohol, sold as "cereal beverages." Like other establishments that found creative ways to flout Prohibition or at least avoid getting caught (see December 6), the Blackhawk managed to serve alcohol. There were a number of "high-balls," and "cocktails." It is ironic that the 1920s, the age of Prohibition, was also the Cocktail era. Many classic alcoholic cocktails were invented during this time, and it is said that one of the motivating factors was that their bright colors and fruity garnishes made them look like soft drinks and fruit cups. For nostalgia reasons, or perhaps to enhance the illusion, the Blackhawk's cock-tails certainly sounded authentic. There was a Blackhawk Rickey for example, and a horse's neck. The Horse's Neck began as a nonalcoholic drink. Origi-nally it was just ginger ale with the long, curly peel of an entire lemon hanging over the edge of the glass, giving the drink its name. Later, bourbon was added, in which case it was sometimes called a "Horse's Neck, with a kick."

## Recipes

~~~

---

### Roquefort Dressing

One-half teaspoon of salt,
One-half teaspoon of paprika,
One tablespoon of Roquefort cheese,
One tablespoon of lemon juice,
Two tablespoons of salad oil.

Mix smooth and serve.
*Mrs. Wilson's Cook Book* (Philadelphia, 1920).

---

### Chocolate Parafait

Place in a mixing bowl
White of one egg,
One-half glass of apple jelly.

Beat until the mixture holds its shape and then fold in one cup of whipped cream and then prepared chocolate. Pour into a mould and pack with ice and salt for two and one-half hours.

To prepare the chocolate: Place one cup of sugar in a saucepan and add five tablespoons of water. Heat slowly to the boiling point, and then boil for one minute, then add two ounces of chocolate, cut in tine pieces. Stir until the choco-late is melted, taking care that the mixture does not boil, then add

One-quarter teaspoon of cinnamon,
One teaspoon of vanilla.

Beat to mix. Cool, and add to the prepared cream.
*Mrs. Wilson's Cook Book* (Philadelphia, 1920).

---

## December 28

Queen Victoria Diamond Jubilee Ball
Toronto City Armouries, Toronto, Canada, 1897

There was an opportunity—an obligation perhaps—for Queen Victoria's subjects in the Dominion of Canada to celebrate her Diamond Jubilee in 1897. The governor general of Canada at the time was Lord Aberdeen (1847–1934), and the role of social director fell, as was traditional, to his wife, Lady Aberdeen (1857–1939). She clearly enjoyed this part of her responsibilities and organized a magnificent ball at which Her Majesty's citizens in Toronto (the well-to-do ones, that is) were thoroughly entertained while simultaneously being reminded of the bonds of Empire.

Two and a half thousand guests attended the ball—no insignificant number for the caterers of the ball supper which was served close to midnight. According to *The Globe* newspaper report, they did a creditable job with the following menu.

---

BILL OF FARE

CHAUD
Bouillon
Petits salpicons de venaison

FROID
Galantine a l'Imperatrice
Dindonneau roti
Aspic de langue      Jambon
Mayonnaise de volaille

Cailles roties aux tomates

ENTREMETS DE DOUCEUR
Baba a la Parisienne
Charlotte Russe      Gelee en bellevue
Gateaux varies

Glace Neapolitaine      Petits fours
Bonbons      Fruits glaces
Café

---

There was nothing special or fancy about this ball supper menu—it was standard for the time—and the sophisticated guests would all have understood the culinary terms, and would have been familiar with the dishes. The novelty at the ball was in the costuming of the guests, for Lady Aberdeen had devised a fancy dress theme.

There were various "sets" within the overall theme of the ball, all celebrating some aspect of "The Victorian Era" in an extravaganza of mutual admiration between the two countries, and the benefits to both of their Imperial connections. There was a North American set, with the guests dressed to represent Canada's resources such as forests, mines, fishing, and fur and their various workers such as the lumberman, miners, and so on. There was also a European set indicating that part of the world dominated by Britain, and many others including a Victorian costume set and sports and amusements set. Lady Aberdeen herself was in the Empire colors of red, white, and blue, her gown decorated with Irish lace and embroidery based on Celtic designs.

## Recipes

~~~

*Salpicon*, like *petits fours* (see November 14) and *hors d'oeuvre* (see January 20) is one of the French culinary words which has no real equivalent in English—unless it be "hash," which hardly sounds elegant. A *salpicon* is a dish made of minced or diced ingredients (savory or sweet) bound with a sauce and used as a garnish or filling (for example, for tartlets or *vol-au-vents*, see September 17). The description in *Cassell's Dictionary of Cookery* (circa 1870s) describes a *salpicon* used to fill "patties," which are the same as *vol-au-vents*.

---

### Salpicons

Salpicons are elegant little trifles composed of a mixture of poultry, game, fish, forcemeat, sweetbreads, ham, tongue, or foie gras, together with mushrooms, truffles, artichokes &c. The various materials should be cooked separately, cut into dice, and heated in a thick brown or white sauce, whichever is most suitable for them. The remains of meat and vegetables are often served in this way. Salpicons may either be served in a dish with the different ingredients divided by small sippets into compartments, then covered over with bread-crumbs, and browned; or they may be put into little patties, and served on a napkin garnished with parsley. The latter is the more usual method. To prepare these patties, make some good puff paste [see September 17]—stamp it into small rounds with a cutter, two inches in diameter, put these on ice for a few minutes, then brush them over with beaten egg to glaze them. Dip a smaller cutter into hot water, and stamp the rounds through one-third of the thickness of the pastry. Bake the patties in a quick oven. When they are done, lift off the cover which was formed by the smaller cutter, and smooth the pastry. Have ready whatever is to form the contents of the patties. Heat it in a sauce, but on no account allow it to boil, or the meat will be hard; fill the patties, put on the covers again, and serve.

---

Baba à la Parisienne: A *baba* is a sweet butter and egg-enriched bread made from brioche dough (see February 24). For the variation called *Baba à la Parisienne* the dough is placed into a mold (or small individual molds) which have been buttered thickly and strewn with blanched slivered almonds.

Charlotte Russe: see September 4.
Petits Fours: see November 14.
Glace Neapolitaine (Neapolitan ice cream): see December 20.


## December 29

Sunday Lunch in Paris
Le Grand Hôtel, Paris, France, 1878

The Grand Hôtel (originally the *Grand Hôtel de la Paix*) on the Boulevard des Capucines in Paris is indeed one of the city's grandest and most famous hotels. Its construction was part of the huge scale reconstruction and modernization of Paris instigated by the Emperor Napoleon III (1808–1873) and supervised by Baron Haussmann (1809–1891) (see November 27). The hotel was staggeringly beautiful. The Empress Eugenie (1826–1920) who opened it in 1862 apparently said that it equalled every royal apartment she had lived in.

The hotel had 800 rooms, several state apartments, and 65 lounges, the main banquet room was three stories high, and there was a prestigious restaurant called the Café de la Paix. Being the luxurious hotel that it was, there were many different dining alternatives at the Grand Hotel, and one of them was from the fixed-price menu, such as the one here. Dinner could be had from a similar menu for 6 francs.

---

DEJEUNER A 4 FRANCS

2 Hors d' Œvres—2 Plats au Choix
2 Desserts—½ Bouteille Médoc—Café au Cognac.

Huitres Armoricaines Victoria
Merlans frits
Soles à la Normande
Côtelette de veau en papillotes
Entrecôte grillèe purée de pommes
Rognons en brochette
Eminé de chevreau / sauce poivrade
Gigot de Présalé au cresson
Viande Froide
Flageolets au beurre
Œufs sure le Plat—a la Coque
Brouillès—en Omelette
Desserts.

---

*Oysters Armoricaine* are oysters from Brittany. Amorica was the old name for the northwest region of Gaul, and the oysters from there are considered very choice. It is possible that the name of the well-known dish *lobster Americaine* is a corruption of *Armoricaine*. *Sole à la Normande* is a classic method of serving sole. The dish consists of the fish poached in white wine, with a garnish of oysters, mussels, smelts, mushrooms, and sometimes gudgeon and crayfish. Classic dishes such as this are labor intensive and rarely cooked in the traditional manner, especially in the home where there is no army of kitchen hands to help.

The veal cutlets were cooked *en papillote*—meaning in paper. Sometimes the cutlets are pre-fried before being cooled and coated in sauce or a garnish before being wrapped in the paper, which serves to stop the dish from drying out. The cutlets are served in their folded paper packets.

## Recipes
~~~

---

### Veal Cutlets in Paper— Cotelettes de Veau en Papillotes

Prepare the cutlets and put them with butter, as above [i.e., dip them in melted butter and place them in a single layer in the pan], to grow firm upon the fire: let minced parsley, mushrooms, and small onions be added in equal quantities, a little rasped bacon, with salt, pepper, and fine spices; let them simmer; when enough, take out the fine herbs and add to them a large spoonful or two of Espagnel, or veloute, and reduce; taste if it is good, and thicken with a sufficient quantity of yolks of eggs; let it cool: cut the paper covers in the form of kites, and oil the middles where the cutlets will be placed; put a very thin slice of bacon upon the paper, then half a spoonful of fine herbs upon the bacon, and lay over it a cutlet, then more herbs, covering them with another slice of bacon; wrap up the cutlet, tie the joint with a thread, oil the paper or papillotes all over, grill them, taking care that the paper does not burn; let the paper take a fine colour, untie, and serve.

Antoine B. Beauvilliers, *The Art of French Cookery* (1827).

---

### Sole à la Normande

The following receipt, with the alteration of a word or two, is borrowed from Gouffé, who says that he had it direct from Langlais, the chef of the Rocher de Cancale [see November 28], who invented it. Butter a silver dish; strew it with onions chopped fine and previously blanched; season the sole with pepper and salt; put it on the dish; cover it with white French wine and cook it in the oven. In the meantime prepare some mussels, oysters, mushrooms, fried smelts, and crusts [croutons] for garnish. Add the liquor of the sole and that of the mussels to some mock Velvet-down, reduce it, and thicken it with yolk of egg. Place the mussels, oysters, and mushrooms on the sole; pour over all some sauce, return the dish to the oven for five minutes, being careful not to brown the sauce, which should be of a rich cream colour; garnish the top with the fried smelts and the crusts; and serve the remaining sauce in a boat.

Eneas Sweetland, *Kettner's Book of the Table* (Dallas, 1877).

## December 30

Coronation Banquet for the Last Ruler of the Austro-Hungarian Empire
Budapest, Hungary, 1916

Károly I (1887–1925) was the last ruler of the Austro-Hungarian Empire. The assassination of his uncle, Franz Ferdinand, in Sarajevo in 1914, was the precipitating event of World War I. Karoly (his name is frequently Anglicized to Carl or Charles) inherited the throne only two years later on the death of his grand uncle Francis Joseph I.

The rather unusual aspect of the coronation was shaped by two situations —the war itself and the long-standing internal conflict in the Balkans. The coronation was almost entirely a Hungarian event. The only foreign royal invited was King Ferdinand of Bulgaria, who was a Magyar by birth. The American ambassador and his wife were treated with "conspicuous honor" because of America's neutral status at the time—in fact they were treated as *de facto* royals, and the ambassador's wife even wore a diamond tiara.

Several diplomats from Southern Slav parties boycotted the event on the grounds that Hungary oppressed her Slav citizens.

After the coronation in the Matthias Kirche, the king performed the traditional symbolic sword ceremony on the Coronation Mound and then rode to the Palace where the coronation banquet was to take place. It turned out to be the most unusual coronation banquet in history.

---

"Roast of homage"
Roast pheasant, in its plumage
Goose liver pâté with truffles
Chicken à la reine
Salad of assorted poultry
Venison pâté with truffles
Roast ham
Quails in jelly
Stuffed roast sirloin of venison
Roast pork
Spit-roasted duck
Turkey roasted in the medieval manner
Young roasted rooster
Mountain trout
Fruit jelly from Tokay
Assortment of pastries
Bonbons
Assortment of fruit
"Homage basket for the Crown Prince"

---

Each dish was ceremonially paraded into the hall and presented to the king. The king waved every dish aside, and ate nothing—which meant, according to the rules of protocol, that no one could eat. There were serious food shortages in Hungary at this point in the war, and Karoly insisted that the food be taken away and distributed to the wounded soldiers. It is unknown whether the four-year-old crown prince got his basket of sweetmeats.

## Recipes
~~~

---

### Chicken à la Reine

Truss two small spring chickens for boiling, rub them over with lemon juice, and wrap them up separately in a sheet of thickly buttered paper; then place the chickens in a stewpan, with a garnished faggot of parsley, a carrot and an onion stuck with two cloves; moisten with some of the surface of the boiling stockpot, in sufficient quantity to nearly cover the chickens; set them to boil gently for about forty minutes, when they will be done. When about to send to table, drain the chickens upon a napkin, and after having removed the paper and string, dish them up side by side, and cover them with supreme sauce, garnish the dish with four groups of very small quenelles of fowl, and serve.

Charles Elmé Francatelli, *The Modern Cook* (1846).

---

## December 31

### Final Dinner Party Given by François Mitterand
### Souston, Landes, France, 1995

François Mitterand (1916–1996) served as the president of France between 1981–1995. He died on January 8, 1996, of prostate cancer, a little over a week after holding a very exclusive dinner party for a couple of dozen friends and relatives. Rumors about the menu began circulating immediately, and the meal became one of the most controversial "last meals" in history. The menu appears modest enough at first glance.

---

Marennes oysters
Foie gras
Roast Capon
Ortolans

---

The controversy was due to the inclusion of the ortolan (*Emberiza hortulana*), a tiny European songbird weighing barely an ounce. The bird is found in southwest France, the home of the president, and was already on the protected species list. Conservationists were outraged when the news leaked out —as were, for a different reason, the jealous epicures who had not been invited. At the time, guests maintained silence or hotly denied the claims that the little birds had been eaten, but they were forced to admit the truth when it was revealed a couple of years later in a book written by Mitterand's confidante, Georges-Marc Benamou, who had been present at the dinner.

The ortolan had long been a very expensive, extreme delicacy for European gourmets. These "delicate Fowl of an exquisite taste, about the bigness of a Lark," said seventeenth-century French chef François Massialot, were "lumps of celestial fatness," "the epicure's prime morçeau," and according to the famous chef Alexis Soyer (1810–1858) provided the *"transendentalism of gastronomy."* The English Prime Minister Benjamin Disraeli famously wrote, "All paradise opens! Let me die eating ortolans to the sound of soft music." The birds were caught alive and fattened—traditionally on figs—until wanted for the table. When required they were killed by suffocation (to avoid damaging the fragile flesh), or drowned in armagnac, and simply roasted.

There is a certain ritual attached to eating the ortolan. A huge napkin is placed over the head of the diner and the plate while the bird is eaten. The diner takes the entire little bird, blisteringly hot from the spit, into his mouth, and eats it, bones and all (it is permissible to leave the beak). There are several theories about this ritual of the napkin—that it captures the exquisite aroma of the flesh, that it hides the messy process from other guests, or that it hides the act of greediness from God.

The story is that the dying Mitterand consumed thirty oysters and two of the ortolans before returning to his bed. Three years after his death, France officially banned the hunting or sale of the ortolan, although rumors still surface from time to time of their secret availability to those in the know.

## Recipes

~~~

---

### Of Ortolans
### From Mr. Renaud

The Ortolan is a Bird brought from France, and is fed in large Cages with Canary-Seeds till they become a Lump of Fat ... When you kill them, take them by the Beak, and holding it close between your Finger and Thumb, the Bird will be stifled in about a Minute. Roast them quick, with the Heads on (without drawing) setting small Toasts under them to drip upon. Serve them with strong Gravy, and as much White-wine hot, and garnish with Slices of Lemon, and raspings of Bread, sifted and toasted before the Fire.

You may lard them, if you think proper, and put a Vine-leaf betwixt them: when they are spitted, some Crumbs of Bread may be used as for Larks: the best way is to spit them sideways.

Richard Bradley, *The Country Housewife, and Lady's Director* (London, 1762).

---

Foie Gras: see May 26.

# Glossary

alouette.
A lark.

aspic.
A savory jelly of meat, fish, eggs, etc.

assiette.
A dish or plate.

baba.
A sweet butter and egg-enriched bread made from brioche dough.

bakemete, bakemeat.
Something cooked in dough or pastry; essentially an early sort of pie; "meat" used in its old sense of a general word for food.

bavarois.
A custard made with cream, sometimes eggs, and various flavorings, set with gelatin.

blanch monge, blank maunger, blamange, blancmange.
A dish made in medieval times from chicken, rice, and cream or almond milk, now a sweet dessert made from cornflour and milk, flavored, and set with gelatin.

bouchée.
A bite-sized piece of food (from the French for "mouth").

bouilli.
A boiled dish.

brawn, brawne, braun.
Originally referred to the muscle or fleshy parts of an animal when used as food. It later came to refer particularly to meat from the pig (or boar) boiled, then pressed or potted and served sliced when cold.

caille.
Quail.

canapé.
Small savories based on small pieces of toast or bread.

caneton.
French for duckling.

Charlotte.
A dessert dish that has several interpretations but usually refers to a trifle-like dish made in a mold lined with sponge cake and filled with custard.

chartreuse.
A highly ornamental dish of meat or vegetables made in a mold.

chaud.
Warm or hot.

chine.
A joint of meat consisting of part of the spine of the animal and the adjoining flesh; the same as a "saddle."

compote, compost.
Now most commonly refers to fruit in syrup.

conies, conneis, conyng, connye.
Rabbit.

consommé.
A clear soup.

coupe.
A dish of ice cream with fruit or sauce and sometimes wafers, served in a shallow bowl.

croquette, croquet.
A small cake of finely minced or mashed food (rice, poultry, fish, etc.) coated with egg and breadcrumbs and fried until crisp.

croustade.
A dish in a crust of some sort, usually pastry but sometimes rice.

demi-tasse.
A small cup of coffee.

devil, diable.
A highly seasoned dish, generally "hot" with spices such as cayenne or curry powder.

dinde (dindonneau).
Turkey (young turkey).

endored.
Made golden-colored with yellow spices such as saffron, or egg yolk, or real gold leaf.

entremets.
Originally referred to side dishes, later came to refer especially to sweet (i.e. dessert-type) dishes.

*eyroun.*
Egg.

*farce* (noun and verb).
A forcemeat or stuffing. To stuff or fill.

*flampayne, flampeyne.*
From *flan pointé*—a type of tart decorated with pointed pieces of pastry.

*floringtyne, florindine, florentine.*
A type of pie or tart, varied in style, but usually with a top crust, and containing minced meat, dried fruit, etc., so similar to a modern mince pie.

*friand, friandise.*
A small delicacy, a dainty dish. Now usually refers to a small cake.

*fricandeau, fricadeau.*
A dish of sliced meat (usually veal) stewed and served in a sauce, so essentially the same as a fricassee.

*froid.*
Cold.

*frumentie, ffurmente, furmenty.*
A very ancient dish made from wheat hulled, soaked, then boiled to a thick porridge-like consistency. It was the staple food of peasants and a traditional accompaniment to venison for the rich. It was enriched for special occasions with cream, eggs, ale or wine, fruit, spices, and sugar.

*galantine.*
Originally referred to a sauce for fish but later became a dish made of bread sopped in any remaining sauce, later still a dish of white meat or fish served cold in its jellied juice (so similar to an aspic, or a modern brawn).

*gibier.*
Game.

*gigot.*
A leg of lamb, mutton, or veal.

*gill.*
An old measure for liquids; the exact volume varies depending on the location, but most usually refers to five fluid ounces, or approximately 120 mls.

*grosse pièce.*
Literally "a large piece" of anything; as a menu heading usually refers to large ornamental dishes, not necessarily meant to be eaten, that were similar in intent to medieval "subtelties' and often remained on the table throughout the meal, to be admired.

**haricot, harricot.**
Beans. Haricots verts are green beans, and haricots blans are white beans.
Also applies to a type of stew (especially of lamb or mutton) that contained
these beans.

**homard.**
Lobster.

**huitres.**
Oysters.

**jambon.**
Ham

**jigget, jiggite.**
A leg or haunch of mutton.

**jole, jowl, jowle.**
The head and shoulders of certain types of fish, notably salmon and sturgeon.

**langue.**
Tongue.

**lapereaux.**
Young rabbit.

**lard, larded.**
To lard is to insert small strips of fat such as bacon into the fish or meat
before cooking it, to enrich and tenderize it.

**leche, lesshe.**
A dish that can be served sliced, such as a meatloaf-type dish.

**macedoine.**
A mixture, usually of fruit, cut in small pieces.

**mauviette.**
A skylark.

**mess.**
This has several meanings in the context of food. It refers to a portion of food
(usually enough for four people), a company of people eating together (such
as soldiers or monks), and sharing from the same serving bowl, or the com-
munal meal itself.

**neat.**
A calf.

**noisette.**
A hazelnut, also a "nut-shaped" (round) piece of meat, usually lamb or
mutton.

pièce montée.
Literally "mounted pieces"; similar to medieval subtelties; highly decorative sculpted pieces—made of food, made for display and not necessarily to be eaten. They were made in the form of buildings, forests, vases, armorial devices, etc., and mounted on pedestals

poisson.
Fish.

pommes de terre.
Potatoes.

pottage, potage.
A soup, although at one time it could mean a dish such as a whole chicken served in its broth.

Poulet à la Godard (Francatelli's version).
Chicken served with a classic Godard garniture. Francatelli also adds a crayfish to each end of the dish. The garnish is of lambs' sweetbreads, cock's combs, quenelles of fowl, mushrooms, and truffles.

relevé.
The same as remove.

ris de veau.
Veal sweetbreads.

rôti.
Roast.

sack.
Dry white wine, sherry.

salmi.
A dish of meat, usually game, cut small or minced, in a highly seasoned sauce.

socle, sur.
On a plank or plinth raised on a pedestal.

soltelte, soltetie, soltiltie, sotyltie, subtelty.
A highly ornamental dish or device (not necessarily edible), presented between the courses of a medieval feast for entertainment, or to provide a symbolic message.

sucré.
Sweet.

suprême.
A type of sauce, or the breast of a chicken or other bird served with the sauce.

timbale.
A dish of minced or finely chopped ingredients, cooked in a crust of pastry (or rice) in a drum-shaped mold.

turban.
A dish in which the ingredients are rolled up, or cooked in a ring mold, to resemble the style of the turban (headdress).

viand, vyand.
A general word for an article of food.

volaille.
Fowl, poultry.

vol-au-vent.
A type of pie made with very light puff pastry and a variety of fillings.

# Selected Bibliography

## General
## Books

Albala, Ken. *Food in Early Modern Europe.* Westport, CT: Greenwood Press, 2003.

Davidson, Alan. *The Oxford Companion to Food.* New York: Oxford University Press, 1999.

Drummond, J. J., and Anne Wilbraham. *The Englishman's Food.* London: Jonathan Cape, 1958.

Fernandez-Armesto, Felipe. *Food: A History.* New York: Macmillan, 2001.

Flandrin, Jean-Louis, and Massimo Montanari. *Food: A Culinary History,* trans. Albert Sonnenfeld. New York: Columbia University Press, 1999.

Heiatt, Constance B. *An Ordinance of Pottage.* London: Prospect Books, 1988.

Hess, L. John, and Karen Hess. *The Taste of America.* New York: Grossman Publishers, 1977.

Kiple, Kenneth F., and Kremhild Coneè Ornelas. *The Cambridge World History of Food,* Vol. I and II. New York: Cambridge University Press, 2001.

*Larousse Gastronomique.* New York: Random House, 2001.

Toussaint-Samat, Maguelonne. *History of Food,* trans. Anthea Bell. Oxford: Blackwell, 2000.

Trager, James. *The Food Chronology.* New York: Henry Holt, 1995.

## Web Sites

*The Forme of Cury*
   www.pbm.com/~lindahl/foc.

*Gode Cookery*
   www.godecookery.com/godeboke/godeboke.htm.

*Historic Food* by food historian and professional cook Ivan Day.
   www.historicfood.com/portal.htm.

*The Food Timeline*
   www.foodtimeline.org/.

## Menus

There is a dearth of books devoted to menus, and those that have been published tend to focus on menu design from a graphics perspective.

## Books

Alejandro, Reynaldo. *Classic Menu Design, from the Collection of the New York Public Library.* New York: Rizzoli, 1988.

Fellows, Charles. *Fellows' Menu Maker.* Chicago, 1910.

Greenstein, Lou. *A la Carte: A Tour of Dining History*. New York: PBC International, 1992.

Heimann, Jim. *May I Take Your Order? American Menu Design, 1920–1960*. San Francisco: Chronicle Books, 1998.

Lane, John. *A Taste of the Past*. Newton Abbot, Devon: David and Charles Publishers, 2004.

Patten, Marguerite. *The Coronation Cookbook*. London: Hamlyn, 2002.

## Web Sites

The Buttolph Collection at the New York Public Library Digital Gallery contains images of thousand of menus from 1851 to 1914.
http:/digitalgallery.nypl.org/nypldigital/

The Los Angeles Public Library has a large database of menu images, predominantly from the Los Angeles area, dating from the 1860s.
http:/www.lapl.org/resources/en/menu_collection.html

Australian Menus.
Predominantly from South Australia.
http:/www.winelit.slsa.sa.gov.au/sipsup.htm

French Menus.
From Menustory.
http:/www.menustory.com/site3/pages/accueil.php

## Historic Cook Books

There is a large and increasing number of historic recipe books freely available over the Internet. Following are good sources.

*Thomas Gloning's Culinary & Dietetic Texts of Europe from the Middle Ages to 1800*
www.uni-giessen.de/gloning/kobu.htm

*Feeding America: The Historic American Cook Book Project*
This is a marvelous resource offered by the Michigan State University Library and the MSU Museum. It comprises a fully searchable online collection of some of the most important American cookbooks published between 1798 and 1922.
http:/digital.lib.msu.edu/projects/cookbooks/index.html

*HEARTH: The Home Economics Archive—Research—Tradition—History*
This is an electronic collection of books and journals in home economics and related disciplines, published between 1850 and 1950 and made available by Mann Library at Cornell University.
http:/hearth.library.cornell.edu/

Google Books:
There are hundreds of cook books in this database, dating from the early-eighteenth century up to today, including many classic historic cookery and food texts.
http:/books.google.com/

Internet Archive:
This is another rapidly increasing database. There are many historic cookery books in the text archive.
http:/www.archive.org/index.php

I have a large and regularly updated spreadsheet of historic cookbooks from the fourteenth to twentieth centuries sourced from the above and other databases which I am happy to send on request to my email address at jclarkso@ bigpond.net.au.

Two invaluable databases that jointly contain thousands of books, but require a subscription, are

Early English Books Online.
   http:/eebo.chadwyck.com/home

The Thomson-Gale Group's Eighteenth Century Collections Online.
   www.gale.cengage.com/DigitalCollections/products/ecco/index.htm

## Glossaries

Medieval and Renaissance Culinary Terms. Compiled by Cindy Renfrow.
   http:/www.thousandeggs.com/glossary.html

Prospect Books glossaries compiled from six English cookery texts of the seventeenth and eighteenth centuries.
   www.kal69.dial.pipex.com/shop/system/index.html

French to English Food Glossary. Compiled by Patricia Wells.
   www.patriciawells.com/glossary/french_english_food_glossary.pdf

Food Glossary from Oregan State University.
   http:/food.oregonstate.edu/glossary/

# General Index

# Recipe Index

## About the Author

**Janet Clarkson** is a culinary historian and food writer in Australia. Her lively blog is *The Old Foodie*.